CONTEMPORARY BLACK HISTORY

Manning Marable, Founding Series Editor

Peniel Joseph (Tufts University) and
Yohuru Williams (Fairfield University),
Series Editors

This series features cutting-edge scholarship in Contemporary Black History, underlining the importance of the study of history as a form of public advocacy and political activism. It focuses on postwar African-American history, from 1945 to the early 1990s, but it also includes international black history, bringing in high-quality interdisciplinary scholarship from around the globe. It is the series editors' firm belief that outstanding critical research can also be accessible and well written. To this end, books in the series incorporate different methodologies that lend themselves to narrative richness, such as oral history and ethnography, and combine disciplines such as African American Studies, Political Science, Sociology, Ethnic and Women's Studies, Cultural Studies, Anthropology, and Criminal Justice.

Published by Palgrave Macmillan:

Biko Lives!: The Contested Legacies of Steve Biko
    Edited by Andile Mngxitama, Amanda Alexander, and Nigel C. Gibson

Anticommunism and the African American Freedom Movement: "Another Side of the Story"
    Edited by Robbie Lieberman and Clarence Lang

Africana Cultures and Policy Studies: Scholarship and the Transformation of Public Policy
    Edited by Zachery Williams

Black Feminist Politics from Kennedy to Obama
    By Duchess Harris

Mau Mau in Harlem?: The U.S. and the Liberation of Kenya
    By Gerald Horne

Black Power in Bermuda: The Struggle for Decolonization
    By Quito Swan

Neighborhood Rebels: Black Power at the Local Level
    Edited by Peniel E. Joseph

Living Fanon: Global Perspectives
    Edited by Nigel C. Gibson

From Black Power to Prison Power: The Making of Jones v. North Carolina Prisoners' Labor Union
    By Donald F. Tibbs

The Black Campus Movement: Black Students and the Racial Reconstitution of Higher Education, 1965–1972
    By Ibram H. Rogers

Black Power beyond Borders: The Global Dimensions of the Black Power Movement
    Edited by Nico Slate

Soul Thieves

The Appropriation and Misrepresentation of African American Popular Culture

Edited by

Tamara Lizette Brown and Baruti N. Kopano

First published in 2014 by
PALGRAVE MACMILLAN®
in the United States—a division of St. Martin's Press LLC,
175 Fifth Avenue, New York, NY 10010.

Where this book is distributed in the UK, Europe and the rest of the world,
this is by Palgrave Macmillan, a division of Macmillan Publishers Limited,
registered in England, company number 785998, of Houndmills,
Basingstoke, Hampshire RG21 6XS.

Palgrave Macmillan is the global academic imprint of the above companies
and has companies and representatives throughout the world.

Palgrave® and Macmillan® are registered trademarks in the United States,
the United Kingdom, Europe and other countries.

ISBN: 978–0–230–10891–2 (hc)
ISBN: 978–0–230–10897–4 (pbk)

Library of Congress Cataloging-in-Publication Data is available from the
Library of Congress.

A catalogue record of the book is available from the British Library.

Design by Newgen Knowledge Works (P) Ltd., Chennai, India.

First edition: December 2014

10 9 8 7 6 5 4 3 2 1

Contents

Preface

Culture is the beliefs, values, norms, traditions, and artifacts shared among the inhabitants of a common society. Harold Cruse in *The Crisis of the Negro Intellectual* validates culture in the African American tradition by directly linking and interlinking it with politics and economics.[1] Popular culture is that culture literally of the people. It is distinguished from high culture or that which is of, or reflective of, the elite. Its value for mass consumption and entertainment purposes distinguishes it from the more "legitimate" artistic pursuits. Music, movies, television, fashion fads, slang, magazines, and the like are examples of popular culture. Today's popular culture will be tomorrow's cultural history and a means by which to analyze society at a given moment. Popular culture as a general term is "used to distinguish the mass of the people—not 'people' in general—from the titled, wealthy or educated classes of people."[2] It can include both folk and mass objects, as well as traditions and beliefs. Such material culture manifests itself as readable objects—open for evaluation and interpretation.[3]

Soul Thieves: The Appropriation and Misrepresentation of African American Popular Culture is an analysis of the misuse and, in some cases, outright abuse of African American popular culture through various genres. Hip hop is, and has been, one of the most dominant African American popular culture creations and is denoted in many of the offerings in this volume; however, *Soul Thieves* is a historically inclusive documentation of the misappropriation of black popular culture, thus spanning other areas and genres besides the contemporary and current craze. This book documents that historically African Americans have been in the forefront in the creation of American popular culture. As scholar Harry Shaw demonstrated in *Perspectives of Black Popular Culture*, black popular culture traditionally has been synonymous with American popular culture, but not credited with the innovation. "To look at Black popular culture...through any medium is to get a glimpse of the essential Blackness. It is the DNA that affects all Black—and, to a great extent American—artistic achievements." Such shared experiences and artistic pursuits form the foundation of African American culture and identify, explain, and retain Africanisms (cultural traits that can be traced to an African foundation) and the intrinsic essence of that blackness that emanates from the everyday lives of African American people. Moreover, emerging from this base, "[o]nly Black culture has retained identifiable Africanisms and Black culture traits in a culturally competitive environment while making innumerable significant contributions to American and Western Culture [*sic*]."[4] In the use of the term African American, the editors acknowledge the African diaspora and its inherent cultural implications, but pay particular attention to the African American impact on American popular culture.

Nearing the end of the twentieth century, historians Robin D. G. Kelley and Lawrence Levine debated the interpretations of popular culture in the pages of the *American Historical Review*. Levine lamented that in its current state scholars were not adequately assessing this mass medium that he pitted as a battle, at times, between consumers and producers over the construed meaning and intent, and suggested a varied approach to studying the field, since scholars tended to focus on the intent of the producers rather than that of the consumers.[5] Kelley, in responding to Levine's article, stated that in the latter's analysis over production and consumption historians should view "popular culture as contested terrain."[6] Kelley emphasized that scholars should consider race, class, and gender in rendering the relationship of power and popular culture. This cultural form for public consumption can suppress as well as fight oppression. He proposed that such studies should take into account the "defeats, constraints, and, more generally, the reproduction of hegemony [which] ought to be just as important as the power of audiences to invest mass-produced cultural forms with oppositional meanings."[7] Kelley called for research that considered the product, the producers, and the intended audience. Moreover, as one grapples with the ever-changing nature of popular culture, the influence of the impetus of the production—the tapped source of the creativity—must be a factor as well.

While black popular culture often defines American popular culture and has global implications, a need for a separate category for black popular culture remains. To a large extent American popular culture has been driven or influenced by black popular culture without the reverse necessarily being true. "Black popular culture is a hotbed of America's popular culture, especially in the music, dance, and language."[8] This particular form of popular culture cannot be separated from African American culture in general. In her research, sociologist Joyce Ladner addresses the issue of the dominant "norm" and the "deviant" Other. Traditionally a *termed* minority has knowledge of the dominant culture, but the dominant culture does not have an accurate view of the minority. Therefore, defining that minority as implicated by the terms of the majority is problematic. The group in power will cast an interpretive light through a clouded lens to analyze the behavior of all others. This analysis and the appropriation of the culture in question as a reinterpreted facet of their own helps to solidify their hierarchical standing while diluting the meaning and initiatives of the original. "For, the presence of viable cultural alternatives among those they label as inferior provides evidence which threatens to shatter their carefully but precariously constructed social definition of reality, a definition which justifies their domination and self-interested rule."[9]

As the title of this book suggests, appropriation denotes taking possession of something that one has no right to, and misrepresentation refers to the deliberate, typically negative, depiction of a false ideal. Both can relate to commodification or turning something of inherent value into an instrument for monetary gain.

Such characterizations often form a dialectic with regard to African Americans and popular culture that pit white against black. As culture separates from its formative grounding, its meaning, emphasis, and focus change. Take, for example, the work of dance anthropologist and ethnographer Katherine Dunham. Through performing research in the Caribbean on African survivals in dance in the 1930s, Dunham documented the machinations of the beguine, the national dance of Martinique—where it is danced, why it is danced, and how it is danced. This dance form involved various classes of people. Blacks (upper class men) basically came to dance with the lower class women. A middle-class or upper-class female would be shamed if she entered the dancehall—even just to dance. This is because while it was a place for people to dance for the pleasure, it was also a "working girl's" place to do business. Therefore, blacks came to dance and whites came for other pleasures where dance served as a prelude to other physical activities. "The real beguine...is a work of muscular art...The sailor [white man] who watches drools at the mouth and calls for more rum. For him this is a paradise of debauchery...[T]he young man of color, he is merely seeking entertainment in the dance. Finding [his] pleasure in this sole form of amusement."[10] In this instance, the dance was removed from its traditional cultural context, altering the intended meaning and morphing the message and movement into another existence.

Many recent publications dealing with black popular culture center on music and the influence of rap and hip hop in particular. *Soul Thieves*, as stated, does not solely concentrate on hip hop's or music's proliferation as popular culture phenomena, nor is it the first to bemoan specifically white America's appropriation, misrepresentation, and commodification of black cultural expression. Several mediums of popular culture such as film, television, fashion, comic books, and dance are thematically treated in this work. In many instances this volume outlines specific instances where blacks have contributed to their own demise or have misappropriated culture to or for others' benefit. There is "capital" (and capital gain) in culture, cultural capital, and though African Americans continue to create, many in white America exploit these creations. "The fact remains that Black popular communication is an integral part of (American and global) culture." However, some communicative forms "that purport to represent Blackness have, at times, bastardized Black culture."[11]

Some critics may decry that the premise of this volume promotes racism, or more precisely reverse racism. It does not, and an entire work could be dedicated as to why this is not possible. However, even prior to the erroneous belief of a postracial America because of the election of President Barack Obama, any dialogue on race (a human-made construct rather than a biological classification) could incur the accusation of racism. Talk of race makes people uncomfortable and oftentimes prompts those with a living memory of the past to remember the ugly sphere of a separate and unequal America. Suppressing such knowledge helps to alleviate feelings of guilt and the uneasiness that a complete picture of history conjures. When black people proclaim pride in their heritage and history as well as the rights and privileges of American citizenship, bringing the ugliness of the past together with the hard-fought gains of the present and continued hope for the future, some become upset and wonder why color need be stressed. As political scientist Andrew Hacker points out in *Two Nations: Black and White, Separate, Hostile, Unequal*, an analysis depicting the viewpoints of white Americans toward African Americans, it is easier to forget. "To be black in America means reigning in your opinions and emotions as no whites ever have to do. Not to mention the forced and false smiles you are expected to contrive, to assure white Americans that you harbor nor grievances against them."[12] Attempting to bury the history of the United States of America into an abyss of falsified, good-feeling rhetoric goes against history and does a disservice. The category of African American popular culture exists because of the exclusive rather than inclusive historical narrative of the country, and the history of black expressive culture mirrors that of its citizenry. Culture, as a reflection of a people, cannot be separated from those people. With African Americans, that is a confluence of the African, with parts of the European, into the melding of the African American.

Although American popular culture is intrinsically tied to its African American impetus, the emphasis on blackness has not always found support from either group. In reassessing the merits of the New Negro Renaissance in the decade following its inception and proliferation, Alain Locke, lamented the categorization of black creative impulse as Negro art since this would stigmatize the art. "Consistently applied it [categorizing] would shut the minority art up in a spiritual ghetto and deny vital and unrestricted creative participation in the general culture."[13] This analysis pertaining to the creation of art for art's sake without overemphasis on the cultural foundation that drives such endeavors surfaces over and over—typically in times when blacks themselves trumpet heritage as a catalyst. Langston Hughes advocated for artistic freedom but also did not deny or downplay his race since it fueled his art. For instance, writing after the historic *Brown v. Board of Education* decision and during the early years of the modern Civil Rights Movement cultural critics Harold Cruse and Saunders Redding raised similar, yet opposing, concerns expressed in the earlier era. Cruse, like Hughes, supported the idea of a separate identity born out of an exclusionist history while lamenting those artists who readily attempted to mimic mainstream art and aesthetics. Saunders, on the other hand, could not comprehend a black American culture distinct from its American counterpart and any interpretation to the contrary invited division and impeded progress.[14]

Contemporaneous with the promotion of Afrocentricity as a philosophical construct that moved out of the academy to permeate the broader masses and placed Africa at the center of thought and action, *Time* magazine proclaimed 1994 to be another resurgence of black cultural renaissance. This was not because of the prolific creativity of African Americans, but because the art was now acceptable to and, supposedly, geared toward mainstream audiences. "Exploiting the new freedom created by the drive for civil rights during the past generation, black artists have escaped from the aesthetic ghetto to which they were once confined, where the patronizing assumption was that they would find inspiration only in their own milieu." The new racial climate allowed for the integration rather than desegregation of the art world. In this instance, integration becomes synonymous with assimilation whereas desegregation has the connotation of access. "As they move from the periphery to the mainstream, they are free at last to follow their various muses." The entrée into the institutions of mainstream America could now dilute any strain of possible black resentment eradiating from the historical past. "Largely reared in integrated suburbs and educated at prestigious [white] colleges and universities, they lay claim to both blacks and whites."[15] In reality, many of the highlighted artists did not consider themselves black artists or that their race played a factor in the creation of their art. Most relayed that funding (tied to the white establishment) was the most important factor in the relevance of their art. So, what made this a black renaissance?

Looking at the proliferation and more ready access to the popular manifestation of African American expressive culture, the definition of such, as well as who gets to define it must be taken into account through analyzing the "intersections between consumer culture and the making, remaking, and the distribution of Blackness in its symbolic forms." When moving out of the realm of the folk and into the mainstream, can what was African American popular cultural expression still be considered as such? The tie to blackness is only as strong as it is expedient. Though in its original form the popular can be political, in its altered state economics loom large. If race makes something more popular and thus profitable, then the connection exists. However, if a diluted whiteness reaps benefits, any link to the original will be severed. As black popular continues to be commodified and globally distributed, some may ponder the true expense historically and contemporarily paid for this mass production of black culture.[16] Much of the research in *Soul Thieves* addresses this issue.

Throughout waves of immigration, various ethnic groups have come to the American shores with distinct aspects of cultural traditions—some of which were absorbed into the larger American culture as successive generations intermarried and shed the distinguishable traits that characterized their uniqueness. Though a good amount of African American culture and popular culture has been amalgamated into the more ubiquitous whole, the same is not true for the people, African Americans, who historically as a group have been shut out of the mainstream through discriminating laws and associative behaviors. Despite tangible gains in the years following the Civil Rights and Black Power movements, historical memory should not suffer an engrammic lapse. Many erroneously surmise that the fight for black liberation was one of assimilation; it was for opportunity and inclusion—not to ignore history or heritage. "White Americans often respond that it rests with blacks to put aside their own culture so they can be absorbed into the dominant stream."[17] Thus, the popular historically has been political as black culture often represents hegemonic contestation. *Soul Thieves* delineates this "contested terrain" in documenting various representations of popular culture. The book does not have a hidden agenda other than bringing to light otherwise neglected aspects of this emerging and underrepresented scholarship. The offerings reflect the particular interest and bent of the included scholars and may not be reflexive of the analysis or viewpoints of the whole or others.

This first section of *Soul Thieves* examines the appropriation of black music as part of a long-standing tradition in white America. This usurpation can be found in black musical genres including jazz, blues, and rock 'n' roll. White clarinetist Benjamin David "Benny" Goodman becomes the King of Swing and Elvis A. Presley the King of Rock 'n' Roll, both in popularizing black forms of music. Harry Shaw notes this irony of this extension of African American musical forms since "when whites emulate whites in popular music, they often emulate whites who first emulated Blacks."[18]

Out of the basements of the Bronx, rapping, a cultural continuation of spoken word artists like The Last Poets, boomed over a back beat that would be produced with turntables, vinyl records, and a deejay scratching by pioneers such as Kool Herc and Afrika Baambata. The Sugar Hill Gang found commercial success with their top twenty hit in 1979 known as "Rapper's Delight."[19] Music critics thought that this music with spoken, sing-songy, rhyming lyrics was a fleeting moment in musical history: a flash in the pan by urban, black, Caribbean and Latino youth who drove and popularized it. It certainly would not last, but it did and does endure (in various forms). Although rap in its initial state existed as part of hip hop culture, white corporate executives, once they began to understand the amount of money that the music could generate, worked to redefine hip hop to exploit it for the monetary gain.[20] Baruti Kopano dissects the dynamics of this cultural theft with regard to the proliferation of hip hop music in "Soul Thieves: White America and the Appropriation of Hip Hop and Black Culture." Carlos Morrison and Ronald Jackson, II merge the music and reality television by dissecting the hidden meanings, significance and cultural usurpation in "The Appropriation of Blackness in Ego Trip's *The (White) Rapper Show.*" This take on the reality show competition format becomes an oppositional trope of the music and lifestyle that it purports to support. Diarra Osei Robertson explores cultural theory and the possibility of political agency thorough the genre of hip hop in "Cash Rules Everything around Me! Appropriation, Commodification, and the Politics of Hip Hop and Contemporary Protest Music." A central part of Robertson's study looks at how corporate entities have shaped and influenced the creative impulse and production of the musical form. In "I'm Hip: An Exploration of Rap Music's Creative Guise," Kawachi Clemmons fuses the personal and professional by challenging the naysayers through mapping hip hop's significance as a valuable musical and artistic form.

When *Ice Loves Coco* premiered on the E! Entertainment Television network following *Keeping Up with the Kardashians* in the summer of 2011, many billed the popular reality hour on the cable station as a battle of ample derrieres. Puerto Rican entertainer, Jennifer Lopez, also known for her backside, was edged out by these two who celebrated their physical assets and received unprecedented attention because of this anomalous body part that departed from the Caucasian norm. Perhaps not since fans raved over blond actress Bo Derek who debuted her cornrows in the movie *10*, has such a fuss been made over white women's embrace of black women's physical attributes. Typically, women of African descent have been ogled or maligned for their physical characteristics and sense of style even if the trend or fashion was then copied or appropriated.[21] White women permed their hair in an attempt to achieve the 1970s afro, got lip injections to make their mouths fuller while ridiculing African Americans for naturally full lips, tanned to the point of premature aging or the possibility of melanoma to achieve a darker color while black women might internalize skin color as the antithesis to the beauty standard. In 2011, social scientist Satoshi Kanazawa's questionable data for "Why Are Black Women Less Physically Attractive than Other Women?" in the online journal *Psychology Today* caused the website to crash and forced the removal of the offensive posting. The study cited an increased percentage of the male hormone testosterone as the main reason why black women were the least attractive female racial demographic. Such a study typifies the norm of celebrating European standards of beauty, which have in turn defined women of African descent as less than beautiful if they did not have these physical characteristics. "Euro American women see their body image and beauty reified and accepted by mainstream society, as opposed to African American women whose body image has traditionally been defiled."[22]

Historically often shut out of the mainstream fashion industry and forced to exist in an alternative environment with regard to designing, modeling and promotion, the black presence in the fashion industry dates back to enslaved seamstresses who possessed a valuable skill that could earn freedom and, of course, Elizabeth Keckley, Mary Todd Lincoln's dressmaker. Abena Lewis-Mhoon gives a voice to the voiceless in documenting the innovation and trendsetting rarely acknowledged to black women in "Foraging Fashion: African American Influences on Cultural Aesthetics" by tracing the historical roots of this creative expression from slavery to current street fashion epitomized by hip hop culture. Kimberly Brown has another take on the beauty and fashion industry. "In the Eye of the Beholder: Definitions of Beauty in Popular Black Magazines" she discusses the intersection of European versus black standards of beauty as promoted by African American periodicals that often embodied class and color in their glossy pages: at times reinforcing the dominant, hegemonic view of the beauty aesthetic and, as the times dictated, also asserting more culturally sensitive amplifications of pulchritude.

The advent of film in the late nineteenth century coincided with the migration of African Americans from rural to urban areas, but prior to the numbers in the waves of the Great Migration. In their infancy, movies were popular with the working class, especially in northeastern cities where the industry initially was located, because they offered a means of mass communication for news and current events. At times, blacks appeared in the early film shorts as simple subjects, not necessarily the caricatured stereotypical images prevalent in minstrelsy and in the burgeoning advertising industry. As the industry progressed into the twentieth century and began to produce a narrative story for entertainment, racial stereotypical fodder surfaced. Black film creators produced early forays in cinematography through limited black-cast films or movies made specifically for black audiences—the initial race movie. These short-lived attempts at filmmaking could not compete with the ever-increasing licensing fees associated with the movie-making industry. The Motion Pictures Patent Company, which regulated the patents held by several companies, including Thomas Edison's, owned cameras and other film production machinery and attempted to extract money for any production, distribution, or presentation of movies. This striation would lead the industry to relocate to California and the formation of major movie houses.[23]

Upon its release in 1915, David Llewelyn Wark Griffith's *The Birth of a Nation* was hailed as a marvel of modern filmmaking because of the techniques used in its creation. These techniques like the closeup and fade-in and -out allowed the viewer to experience the action in new and exciting ways. The movie based on Thomas Dixon's novel, *The Clansman*, recounted the idea of the happy, docile slave, the valor of southern whites during the Civil War and the corruptness, criminality, and lasciviousness of blacks during their newfound freedom into the Reconstruction period. The possibility of the attainment of civil rights and African Americans entering into the political arena called for the establishment of the Ku Klux Klan to reinforce white supremacy and protect white womanhood. "Thus a combination of political, psychic, and material motives shaped the new stereotype deployed by the Klan's racist thugs to justify their terror, murder, and repression against black people in the South and unite white supremacists, North and South at the demise of Reconstruction."[24] It inspired President Woodrow Wilson to profess its, in his estimation, true depiction of history, and the National Association for the Advancement of Colored People (NAACP) to mount a futile campaign against the film. [25] "More than any other early film, *The Birth of a Nation* gave birth to the shocking and degrading stereotypes that were to plague African American movie images throughout the twentieth century."[26] Black-faced white actors played any major role in the film, though Griffith used actual black extras for a plantation scene that required numbers of enslaved blacks. The director hired black actress Madame Sul-Te-Wan to play some minor roles.

The racist depictions in *Birth of a Nation* influenced Booker T. Washington's former secretary Emmett J. Scott to produce *The Birth of a Race* (1918) and other short-lived movie production companies to form. George and Noble Johnson founded the Lincoln Motion Picture Company, which produced films from 1916 to 1927. Oscar Micheaux, a novelist, brought stories to the screen and his race movies dominated the decade of the 1920s. The most prolific and enduring of the early black cinematographers, Micheaux made movies into the 1940s, and attempted to counteract the images of African Americans as portrayed in mainstream films by broadening the characterization of and storyline for blacks on the big screen. As money could be made from targeting a specific audience, white firms also produced race movies with black casts. In many instances these films spoke to African Americans' sense of striving to attain a certain level in life and the moral undertone of good against evil permeated a sense of racial uplift. Mainstream movies for the most part continued the portrayal of black characters in exaggerated stereotypical roles. Oftentimes, scenes featuring black cast numbers that could be construed as offensive to southern sensibilities were routinely edited out when showed throughout the South.

After World War II, more sympathetic roles for African American actors appeared but did not approximate the true complexities of black life in the United States. Pressure from the NAACP and other progressives forced Hollywood to expand its perspective and presentation of black images though it still restricted available roles for performers of color. The emergence of the Civil Rights Movement and challenge of television would force Hollywood to be more inclusive in its limited offerings. In 1969, famed photographer Gordon Parks became the first black director of a major studio-backed feature film, *The Learning Tree*, based on his autobiography. Ossie Davis followed in 1970 with *Cotton Comes to Harlem*, adapted from the Chester Himes novel. These films provided a lens into the possibilities of black filmmaking, as backed by large studios, to depict a more dimensional black reality. In 1971 Melvin Van Peebles attained commercial but controversial success with his independent movie *Sweet Sweetback's Baadassss Song*, and Parks would follow his earlier directorial debut with the crossover hit *Shaft* (1971). Hollywood took notice. As studios lost revenue, they searched for a way to rejuvenate the industry. Capitalizing on the possibility of catering to black moviegoers starved for black images on the screen, and coinciding with the Black Power Movement and its cultural and artistic offshoots, Hollywood would rediscover the race movie replete with stock but, at times, negative portrayals of antiheroes and action figures while taking place in a typical ghetto setting. In the attempt to replicate the remunerative gain of *Sweetback* and *Shaft*, black exploitation (blaxploitation) films would help save the Hollywood movie industry. Again, civil rights groups would react and mount protests against these movies. Moreover, black film professionals formed the Coalition against Blaxploitation though fighting against the establishment could further curtail already constricted employment opportunities.

Sophisticated audiences eventually grew tired of the formulaic productions; therefore, the black moviegoing public replaced blaxploitation films with martial arts action movies by the mid-1970s. By the 1980s the NAACP addressed the dearth of black movie professionals behind the scenes and urged the public to boycott theaters. Aside from *The Color Purple*, black actors appeared in buddy and comedy movies rather than in any with specific black thematic or dramatic content. Moreover, actors fought to win roles in movies with characters not specifically written for black performers. Work in television and attendance at films schools helped usher in a new generation of black filmmakers in the late 1980s and into the 1990s. At times critics castigated black directors for focusing on gritty urban dramas, often involving violence and death, that did not address various facets of black life, or presenting stories so unique to the African American experience that they were genre specific and not universal.

Like film, blacks were part of the infancy of television. The *Ethel Waters Show* as a one-time special debuted in 1939 on the National Broadcasting Network (NBC), a subsidiary of the Radio Corporation of America (RCA). Though television as an entertainment medium would not come into its own until after World War II, the companies that owned the radio airwaves would rule those of the small screen as well. The Columbia Broadcasting System (CBS), American Broadcasting Company (ABC), DuMont, and NBC transferred much of their dramatic fare from the radio to their television audiences. At times, African Americans performed as guest stars on variety shows. *The Bob Howard Show* and *Sugar Hill Times* were early attempts at black performance shows in the late 1940s and paved the way for musical prodigy and former wife of Adam Clayton Powell, Jr., Hazel Scott, to premiere *The Hazel Scott Show* in 1950. Scott got caught in the crosshairs of the House Un-American Activities Committee and her show, which promoted a positive portrayal of the black woman, went off the air after three months. Instead, the staple of the movies, the black domestic, appeared on television as well. Amanda Randolph first played this stigmatized character in *The Laytons*, which ran for two months in 1948 on the DuMont network. *Beulah*, played to the stereotypical hilt on radio by white men, Marlin Hurt and Bob Corley, before actress Hattie McDaniel took over, starred Ethel Waters when transplanted to television in 1950.[27] The televised mammy as portrayed in *Beulah* remained a problematic characterization taken to represent the televised African American female.

Television stations on the whole tried to avoid controversial situations, and NBC adopted a policy of abrogating the outright debasing of racial or cultural affiliations. On radio humor had to be experienced through the auditory senses, so exaggerated dialects, and affected speech specifically of African Americans was used for comedic effect and entrench racial stereotypes solidified during the antebellum period and further manifested during minstrelsy. *Amos 'n' Andy* exemplified this trend of paternalistic and patronizing portrayals of black characters specifically and ethnic programming generally. Popular on radio where whites portrayed the lead black characters, once it transitioned to television with a black cast, whites could readily picture and transfer the stereotypes into a perceived reality of black existence and circumstance. Although a certain segment of the black population found the humor amusing—laughing with the characters rather than at them—the NAACP protested the release of the show, which ran on CBS from 1951 to 1953. *Amos 'n' Andy* garnered more popularity when released in syndication (1954–1966) than during its original run.[28]

The Civil Rights Movement and discovery of African Americans as marketable advertising demographic helped to colorize the television landscape into the 1960s. *I Spy* (1965–1968), starring the interracial secret agent duo of Bill Cosby and Robert Culp, reversed previous stereotypes by de-racing Cosby's character, Alexander Scott, so that his skin color was the only essence of blackness visible; Scott could just as easily have been white. Along similar lines, Diahann Carroll brought the widowed, single mother Julia Baker into American homes. *Julia* (1968–1971), a situation drama, as Carroll described it, about a middle-class African American nurse, broke the mammy mold but showed a version of a black family that many found unbelievable—mainly because it did not buy into prevailing race and class stereotypes as well as the near erasure except for skin color of most inklings of black cultural attributes.

By the 1970s, blacks typically were underrepresented, if at all, in network television news programming, but an ever-increasing presence in situation comedies like *Sanford and Son*, *Good Times*, and *The Jeffersons*. Black television personnel attempted to press for greater representation and opportunity on the small screen. The dramatic interpretation of Alex Haley's *Roots*, the January 1977 miniseries, forced the industry to acknowledge the critically acclaimed family history, spanning generations of Haley's enslaved black family from capture in Africa prior to the American Revolution until after the Civil War and into Reconstruction, and garnered nearly 130 million viewers nightly for the eight nights it played. *Roots* offered the hope for the prospect of a shift in black-oriented programming. While other limited black dramatic offerings did well with audiences, African American actors had few possibilities outside of the comedic sitcom. Protests against NBC's *Beulah Land*, a miniseries about the South from the antebellum period through Reconstruction because of the portrayal of enslaved blacks as docile and complacent, demonstrated that blacks could affect change but fighting for change also jeopardized the limited opportunities for African American television actors.

The late 1970s into the 1980s saw African American actors and actresses take their primetime star turns in series such as *Fame, The A-Team, Miami Vice,* and as well as comedies like *Diff'rent Strokes, Benson, Facts of Life,* and *Gimme a Break!*[29] However, simply having a black headliner or featured character did not ensure that it was a black television show. Moreover, ratings success meant that whites had to tune in as well as black audiences. Bill Cosby's *Cosby Show* and its spin-off *A Different World* proved that a black-themed show with black creative input could win over audiences without pretense, pretext, or stereotype. In fact, a criticism of *Cosby* was, like *Julia* decades prior, that it was unrealistic though many in the black community saw themselves in the Huxtable family capers or longed to be part of that family unit. "*The Cosby Show* demonstrated the unique perspective that could be brought to the primetime series when an African American artist was in control of the material."[30]

Other situation comedies, *The Fresh Prince of Bel-Air, Martin, Living Single, The Steve Harvey Show, Moesha, The Parkers, Half & Half,* and *Girlfriends* offered comic relief on some level throughout the nineties and into the twenty-first century, but few dramatic shows with a predominately black cast or creative input graced the air waves. The crime drama, *New York Undercover* (1994–1998), sported an interracial cast with the two main characters of African American and Puerto Rican descent, J. C. Williams (Malik Yoba) and Eddie Torres (Michael DeLorenzo).[31] Black and Latino viewers watched the show enhanced by the musical montages and celebrity guests in the first three seasons. After Torres's character was murdered in the third season, the show to its demise took a different creative path to expand viewership and, in turn, alienated its loyal viewers.[32] Cable television with Showtime's *Soul Food* (2000–2004) and Home Box Office's (HBO) *The Wire* (2002–2008), though not a specifically black show through writing, producing, or casting, portrayed very different aspects of black life and received critical praise and a loyal fan following.

"Neutering the Black Power Movement: The Hijacking of Protest Symbolism" is historian James Stewart's cogent work on blaxploitation movies from the 1970s and their effect on subsequent fare. Through plots, characters, and soundtracks this essay analyzes the co-opting of black cultural symbols from the struggle for black liberation as manifested through the Civil Rights and Black Power movements to inoculate the public against political action and resistance and lull them into a false sense of pride and progress by viewing their own through the medium of exploitative popular film. As this film medium loses popularity, television in the form of the situation comedy fills the void.

In *Forty Million Dollar Slaves*, sportswriter William C. Rhoden compares African American professional athletes and the whites who finance and control the sports world to a modern-day plantation system. "The power relationship that had been established on the plantation has not changed, even if the circumstances around it have."[33] He points to current athletes' lack of knowledge of the history of blacks in sports as a reason for helping to perpetuate the unbalanced economic situation. In the past, athletes such as Jack Johnson, Joe Louis, Jesse Owens, Jackie Robinson, Cassius Clay/Muhammad Ali, and Jim Brown represented certain political ideals as well as athletic prowess through their respective sport. In an industry that resisted desegregation, black achievement was a double-edged sword, which spoke both toward team victory (or in the case of Louis and Owens country pride at a time that they were not guaranteed full citizenship rights) and the potential of African American achievement in the larger society through the symbolism of sport.[34] The style and swagger of the black sports figure often court fan favor and dictate the popularity of the franchise. However, measures to check such adoration and adulation and reinforce the power structure. In 1984, the National Football League (NFL) limited end zone celebrations, ostensibly because of the Washington Football Team's Fun Bunch's (a group of wide receivers) celebrations when they scored a touchdown, but black players in general have become synonymous with end zone antics (resulting in stricter regulations against such celebrations in the twenty-first century).[35]

Michael Jordan became the epitome of the separation of the black athlete from political undertakings and sport's segregated past. At the height of his fame and marketing power ability, Jordan refused to support black candidate for the US Senate Harvey Gantt against Jesse Helms in the 1990 North Carolina race. The latter's campaign had no qualms in running a controversial commercial where white hands destroy a letter informing the recipient that because of affirmative action he will not get the job. Jordan responded that "Republicans buy sneakers too," when Gantt's campaign asked for his endorsement. This nonchalance accompanied by near silence when predominately black, inner-city youth often fought and died over his namesake shoe, the Air Jordan, demonstrated how African American athletes could reap the benefits that black style brought and limit the liability of race. Other black athletes who wanted to be like Mike and land endorsement deals also found that race neutrality made them more palatable to corporate concerns and mainstream America. By taking "black style and showmanship, but somehow leav[ing] behind all of the more 'inconvenient' features of blackness in America" can "make race visible and invisible simultaneously," and in turn garner monetary gain.[36] In a reversal of attempting to separate race and sport, Jamal Ratchford, looks at the political awakening of sprinters Tommie Smith and John Carlos that led to the black-gloved salute before the world during the 1968 Mexico City Olympics in support of the human rights–denied African Americans in the United States. In the wake of an aborted Olympic boycott, Smith and Carlos in a demonstrative display of solidarity with their fellow black citizens raised their fists on the medal stand and suffered greatly for it. "A Silent Protest: The 1968 Olympics and the Appropriation of Black Athletic Power" situates the medal-stand protest in the larger struggle for black liberation by delineating the oppositional white and black definitions of black athletic power.

Faster than a speeding bullet! Able to leap tall buildings in a single bound! Even the comic book novice knows that these phrases describe Superman, the first superhero introduced to the world of comic books in 1938—just five years after the nascent industry produced its first book *Funnies on Parade*. Other luminaries such as Archie and Wonder Woman followed in the next decade and the burgeoning business saw the printing of 125 various titles that sold 25 million copies per month and grossed $30 million annually. During World War II, soldiers escaped the drudgery of battle by reading comics, a "cheap and exchangeable" form of entertainment. The offerings proliferated in the postwar era with a variety of more adult-centered themes including romance, crime dramas, horror thrillers, and science fiction. The superhero category suffered a decline from which it would not recover until it was again the predominant genre in the 1960s. Though romance comics garnered the largest segment of adult readership, the growth of the crime and horror market alarmed the public and ushered in an "anti-comic book crusade." Self-sanctioning by the industry in 1954 decimated the adult audience and allowed for the trade to refocus on men and some women with superhuman strength and abilities.[37] It is in this era coinciding with the Civil Rights and Black Power movements and the gains won and lost entering into the conservative eighties that David Taft Terry centers "Imagining a Strange New World: Racial Integration and Social Justice Advocacy in Marvel Comics, 1966–1980." He does a masterful job in demonstrating how Marvel Comics attempted to react to the changing times by introducing black characters in several of its series. Terry chronicles the comic giant in its attempts at integrationist advocacy, reform of the black ghetto, embrace of blaxploitation, and eventual move to deemphasize race and thus de-race superheroes as the industry becomes more specialized. Such themes treated with a dearth of black writers and artists are problematic in that whites typically presented their take on racial issues by embodying characters with a manufactured blackness. At the same time such race-based situations and attitudes were emblematic of the double-consciousness and isolation that African Americans experienced in the real world as civil rights gains opened previously off-limit employment opportunities where many found themselves as the solitary, or one of few, blacks in the workplace attempting to prove their merit and ability against a perceived affirmative action quota.

From plantation dances to popular dance crazes such as the cakewalk, Lindy hop, twist, disco, and b-boying/breakdancing, popular African American dance has been appropriated by mainstream America and has permeated popular culture. In the new appropriated form, the meaning, context, and image have been compromised as it migrates from its cultural origins. "So You Think You Can Dance: Black Dance and American Popular Culture" traces the trajectory of popular cultural history through the medium of dance. From the vestiges of slavery to the present day, this section documents this migration and appropriation of black social dance in the wider, mainstream popular arena by providing numerous examples of the morphing of the intended meaning of the dance as it is usurped and then absorbed into the American vernacular.

"Soul" in the African American vernacular, similar to spiritual references, is the essence of being and essential to being.[38] It is one cultural factor that links the black community. The appropriation and/or misrepresentation of such are types of theft that leaves one empty or a vacuous cultural form. *Soul Thieves: The Appropriation and Misrepresentation of African American Popular Culture* exposes this plundering in the hope that such disclosure helps to strengthen and proliferate this black popular creative aesthetic as a soulful, instead of soulless, expression of the people.

TAMARA LIZETTE BROWN

Notes

1. Harold Cruse, *The Crisis of the Negro Intellectual: A Historical Analysis of the Failure of Black Leadership* (1967, New York: Quill, 1984), 42, 71.
2. Katrina E. Bell, "Language, Allusion, and Performance: A Critical-Cultural Study of Black American Popular Culture as Minor Discourse" (PhD diss., Ohio University, 1997), 9. "This term was synonymous with what was considered 'gross, vile, riff-raff, common, low, vulgar [plebian], [and] cheap,' because most writers on the subject were members of the titled, wealthy or educated classes. The "popular" has slowly lost such pejorative connotations, however, as its importance to and impact on society gradually have been recognized."
3. Chandra Mukerji and Michael Schudson, "Popular Culture," *Annual Review of Sociology* 12 (1986): 48. In defining the popular in popular culture, Raymond Williams categorized it as something liked by a wide range of people, something seen as "unworthy or inferior," something produced to be absorbed in large numbers by the populace, and that culture produced by the people for their own consumption. See Laura Grindstaff, "Culture and Popular Culture: A Case for Sociology," *Annals of the American Academy of Political and Social Science* 619 (September 2008): 207.
4. Harry B. Shaw, ed., *Perspectives of Black Popular Culture* (Bowling Green, OH: Bowling Green State University Popular Press, 1990), 6.
5. Lawrence Levine, "The Folklore of Industrial Society: Popular Culture and Its Audiences," *American Historical Review* 97, no.5 (December 1992): 1370. In the article Levine reports that "I have learned...that popular culture is seen as the antithesis of folk culture: not as emanating from within the community but created—often artificially by people with pecuniary of ideological motives—*for* the community, or rather for the masses who no longer had an organic community of producing culture."
6. Robin D. G. Kelley, "Notes on Deconstructing 'The Folk,' " *American Historical Review* 97, no. 5 (December 1992): 1400–01.
7. Ibid., 1408. Kelley highlighted that the "battles with cultural producers were not just over tastes and the preservation of the "folk"; they were ultimately about power—victories and losses in the struggle for hegemony."
8. Shaw, 3.
9. Joyce Ladner, "Introduction to Tomorrow's Tomorrow," in *Feminism and Methodology,* ed. Sandra Harding (Bloomington: Indiana University Press, 1987), 75; Brooke Baldwin, The Cakewalk: A Study in Stereotype and Reality," *Journal of Social History* 15, no. 2 (Winter 1981): 211.

10. Katherine Dunham, "La Boule Blanche," in *Kaiso! Katherine Dunham: An Anthology of Writings*, ed. VéVé Clark and Margaret Wilkerson (Berkeley: Institute for the Study of Social Change CCEW Women's Center University of California, 1988), 52.

11. Robin R. Means Coleman, "Elmo Is Black! Black Popular Communication and the Marking and Marketing of Black Identity," Popular Communication 1 no. 1 (2003): 54–55.

12. Andrew Hacker, *Two Nations: Black and White, Separate, Hostile, Unequal* (New York: Charles Scribner's Sons, 1992), 49.

13. Alain Locke, "The Negro's Contribution to American Culture," *The Journal of Negro Education* 9 (July 1939): 522.

14. Tejumola Olaniyan, "African-American Critical Discourse and the Invention of Cultural Identities," *African American Review* 26, no. 4 (Winter 1992): 533–34. Houston A. Baker, Henry Louis Gates, and Joyce A. Joyce will continue the debate in the pages of *New Literary History* (1987).

15. Jack White, "The Beauty of Black Art," *Time*, October 10, 1994, 68.

16. Coleman, 52, 63.

17. Hacker, 23.

18. Shaw, 4.

19. Rapper's Delight is considered the first commercially successful rap record released by Sugar Hill Records; however, Spring Records put out "King Tim III (Personality Jock)" by the Fatback Band prior to "Rapper's Delight."

20. For history and insight into hip hop, see Jeff Chang, *Can't Stop Won't Stop: A History of the Hip-Hop Generation* (New York: Picador, 2005) and William Jelani Cobb, *To the Break of Dawn: A Freestyle on the Hip Hop Aesthetic* (New York: New York University Press, 2007).

21. Saarjite Baartman, a Khosian from Southern Africa, was taken from her homeland and put on display in England and France as the "Hottentot Venus." At a time when Europeans routinely displayed people of color or those with a physical challenge or deformity as natives or oddities, Baartman was exhibited because of her large buttocks and genitalia, or steatopygia. Brought to England in 1810 by a military doctor and her African owner to make a profit, she was put in a cage in Piccadilly and flaunted nearly naked in a type of flesh-toned body stocking with affected African costuming for which she received a nominal fee and a panoply of alcohol to numb the pain of human exposure. Abolitionists took up her cause but she refused the help, believing her life as a human spectacle was preferable to the life she had left as a servant. She later became a living, then deceased, specimen of scientist Georges Cuvier who, once she had died at the age of twenty-six in December 1815, dissected her body for further study—ostensibly to ascertain the reason for her enlarged posterior and genitals. Cuvier and his colleagues further humiliated Baartman, and all women of African descent, in death by proclaiming that her supposed sexual proclivity was the reason for the physical appendage. See Sander L. Gilman, "Black Bodies, White Bodies: Toward an Iconography of Female Sexuality in Late Nineteenth-Century Art, Medicine and Literature," in *Race, Writing and Difference*, ed. Henry Louis Gates, Jr. (Chicago: University of Chicago Press, 1986), and Rachel Holmes, *African Queen: The Real Life of the Hottentot Venus* (New York: Random House, 2007).

22. Tracey Owens Patton, "Hey Girl, Am I More than My Hair? African American Women and Their Struggles with Beauty, Body Image, and Hair," *NWSA Journal* 18, no. 2 (Summer 2006): 34.

23. For information on African Americans and the movies see Donald Bogle, *Bright Boulevards, Bold Dreams: The Story of Black Hollywood* (New York: Ballantine Books,

2005); Thomas Cripps, *Making Movies Black: The Hollywood Message Movie from World War II to the Civil Rights Era* (Oxford, New York: Oxford University Press, 1993); Thomas Cripps, *Slow Fade to Black: The Negro in American Film, 1900–1942* (1977; Oxford, New York: Oxford University Press, 1993) ; and Ed Guerrero, *Framing Blackness: The African American Image in Film* (Philadelphia: Temple University Press, 1993).

24. Guerrero, 12.

25. Wilson's documentation of Reconstruction in his *History of the American People* helped to inform Griffith's screen adaptation of this historical interpretation. The NAACP succeeded in getting some scenes cut and the continued protest forced Wilson to forfeit his endorsement of the movie. Ibid., 11–14.

26. Bogle, *Bright Boulevards*, 13.

27. McDaniel reprised her role for a short time on Beulah after Waters quit and the show relocated to Los Angeles. Finally, ABC cast Louise Beavers in the role of the mammified maid. Donald Bogle, *Primetime Blues: African Americans on Network Television* (New York: Farrar, Strauss and Giroux, 2001), chap. 1.

28. *Amos 'n' Andy* was the longest running radio show. Kenya and Nigeria reportedly purchased the series from CBS in 1963, whereupon Kenya prohibited the airing of the show.

29. For more information on African Americans and television see Christine Acham, *Revolution Televised: Prime Time and the Struggle for Black Power* (Minneapolis: University of Minnesota Press, 2005).

30. Bogle, *Primetime*, 5.

31. Andre Harrell of Uptown Entertainment was a creative force behind the original guise of the show then known as *Uptown Undercover* and served as executive producer or co-executive producer for many of the first three-year episodes.

32. C. Sean Currie, "New York Undercover," http://www.imdb.com/title/tt0108876/reviews

33. William C. Rhoden, *Forty Million Dollar Slaves: The Rise, Fall, and Redemption of the Black Athlete* (New York: Crown Publishers, 2006), x.

34. Ibid., 3.

35. The Washington Football Team is professionally known by the derogatory term Redskins. Dallas Cowboy coach Tom Landry vociferously complained about the celebratory Fun Bunch which helped lead to the curtailment of end zone displays.

36. Ibid., 204–5. Jordan later endorsed former basketball player Bill Bradley during his bid for the presidency and Barack Obama in his senatorial and presidential campaigns.

37. Paul Lopes, "Culture and Stigma: Popular Culture and the Case of Comic Books," *Sociological Forum* 21, no. 3 (September 2006): 400.

38. Soul is defined as "essentially the essence of blackness; the sensitivity and emotional essence that derives from the blues;... a sense of racial history or of the suffering of the thousands of black people killed or tortured or worked to death since the 1620s." Clarence Major, ed. *Juba to Jive: A Dictionary of African-American Slang* (1970; New York: Penguin Books, 1994), 434.

my black and white influences though my educational focus on the African diaspora, in general, and African American culture, specifically, helped me to view my popular culture obsession in a new light. I guess this work was always on the backburner even before I was aware that it existed.

Fast forward again to an innocent work conversation about the movie *Undercover Brother*. As I talked about the satirical stereotypes prevalent in this flick with my then Smithsonian coworker and friend, librarian extraordinaire Shauna Collier, I could finally envision *Soul Thieves*: a work about how American popular culture has historically derived from African American culture and moreover in the process been reinvented and commodified to serve a certain purpose or function. Throughout this process, Shauna has acted as a sounding board and research associate locating some of the most obscure sources. She further cyber introduced me to Baasil Wilder of the Smithsonian Institution Library System who also found needles in haystacks for me. Though initially this was a solo project, one of my theme song- singing and rhyme-busting partners from the party long ago and a great friend, Yohuru Williams, introduced me to his colleague, Baruti Kopano, who shared a similar vision and *Soul Thieves* was born.

An undertaking of this magnitude is never a solitary effort. I want to thank my family who could have starred in its own sitcom for being supportive and encouraging in all of my professional endeavors. My mother can be satisfied that my multitasking was not in vain, and my father can rest assured that all of those years watching dance and music acts with me has finally paid off. My sister, Joyce Boykin, has read my papers for years and this work was no different. I hope that some of the submissions given to her to proof brought back fun memories from our childhood. Ron Bailey has bared the brunt of *Soul Thieves*, having to deal with the various situations and frustrations, good and bad, that come with completing a book. For the most part, he would take a deep breath and let me vent, and I am forever grateful for his love and support. The contributing scholars were eager to lend their expertise to this work and rarely complained about deadlines, edits, or other tasks asked of them. I can probably never repay my good friend Carolyn Shuttlesworth, a professional editor, who generously offered her services by reading, editing, and commenting on most of the submissions: an immense appreciation goes out to her! Celia Daniel of Howard University's Founders Library made the Pollock-Channing Theatre Collection available to me and Ishmael Childs of the Moorland-Spingarn Reading Room assisted me with sources that only could be found there. Dance historian Melanye White Dixon read a draft of my work in this volume and gave me suggestions for clarity and improvement.

I must extend my gratitude to my colleagues from Bowie State University's Department of History & Government, especially Dr. M. Sammye Miller, former department assistant Michelle Thurston, and current department assistant Betty Carrico. My former chair at Delaware State University, Akwasi Osei, helped me obtain a travel grant so that I could present portions of my research for this work at a conference of the National Council for Black Studies. The feedback was invaluable. I would be remiss if I did not recognize my former boss and friend Steven C. Newsome, who always supported my research endeavors and was one of my biggest fans while he was alive. My soul-steppin', Pan-Hellenic relatives and friends (Rinaldi, Karla, Joe, Darlena, Eric, and Shauna) assisted me with the specifics of their fraternity and sorority-stepping history when I needed to refresh my memory of undergraduate years.

Finally, it is an honor that this work is part of the series on black contemporary life first edited by Manning Marable and Peniel Joseph and now (since Dr. Marable's passing) Peniel and Yohuru. Thank you for sharing the vision. The staff at Palgrave Macmillan has been helpful and understanding as this process has progressed from idea to manuscript. Thank you all.

TAMARA LIZETTE BROWN, PhD

* * *

At the end of the spring semester in 1991, I was a young instructor in the Department of English at what was then Delaware State College. I eagerly accepted the challenge from the department chair, Dr. James Scott King, to teach a section of African American Literature for the fall 1991 semester. In preparation for the class I read Henry Highland Garnet's 1843 speech, "An Address to the Slaves of the United States in America," delivered to his fellow abolitionists at the National Negro Convention in upstate New York in hopes of convincing his peers to take up arms to end the enslavement of Africans. I was struck by Garnet's use of the term *soul-thief* to describe the perpetrators of the greatest forced movement of people in world history.

Perhaps this term resonated with me because I am told that as a two-year-old I would go through stacks of the dozens of records that my father owned to find Sam and Dave's "Soul Man" and insist that my parents play the song ad nauseam. I guess the pursuit of understanding and expressing soul was my destiny. To that regard, I thank my late father Wyatt Watson for surrounding me with music in the house and with the rich sounds of black Baltimore radio as a child growing up in the 1960s and 1970s. The jive-talking smooth deliveries of black radio disc jockeys awed me as a child and fuel my research interests today. Thanks Dad.

Reading Garnet's speech in 1991 inspired me to reread Alfred Pasteur's and Ivory Toldson's 1982 *Roots of Soul: Black Expressiveness—An Unprecedented and Intensive Examination of Black Folk Expressions in the Enrichment of Life*. My undergraduate professor and mentor Gary Ware gave this book to me as a gift for my graduation from Morgan State University in 1988. Professor Ware paved the way for a penchant for asking difficult questions and seeking their answers as well as cultivating an appetite for understanding the multilayered nuances of black life and culture. Professor Ware purchased for me and donated to me hundreds of albums and CDs and books from his multitudinous libraries. *Roots of Souls* is among the most influential books that inform the work that this volume seeks to address. I am eternally grateful to Gary Ware for his mentorship and friendship over the years.

I certainly could not have predicted that Professor Ware's purchase of Nelson George's *The Death of Rhythm and Blues* for me immediately upon its release would serve as a gateway to a lifelong conversation with Dr. Roosevelt "Rick"

Wright of the Newhouse School of Public Communication at Syracuse University. George's book ignited a conversation between Dr. Wright and me when I was a graduate student at Syracuse in 1988. Dr. Wright eventually served on my dissertation committee and shared his knowledge and resources with me as one of the nation's foremost experts on radio in general, and black radio specifically. I thank Dr. Wright for the many conversations we have enjoyed over the years and for his continued guidance of my intellectual pursuits surrounding black radio and popular culture.

It is true for me as it is for many scholars that students are among the most important testing grounds for academic inquiries. My fifteen years at Delaware State University blessed me with the chance to engage students in a broad range of intellectual inquiry. Without a doubt, the two students most important to my work with hip hop and popular culture are Bonsu Thompson and Angie Beatty. Bonsu is currently a self-described "cultural engineer" after serving in various capacities at *XXL* and assuming the editor-in-chief's position at *The Source*. Bonsu offered me the opportunity to write the feature article for the August/September 2011 *Source* edition. It was quite humbling to have the student become the teacher as Bonsu "schooled" me while editing my work. I thank Bonsu.

Angie Beatty was a brilliant student—period. I knew that after reading the first paper she submitted to me at Delaware State University. Fortunately, Angie shared her brilliance with me as she pursued her doctoral studies at the University of Michigan. Her award-winning dissertation on black women's and girls' aggression in hip hop reminded me of the need to expand the questions I ask about hip hop and popular culture. I thank Angie for her reminders.

I presented various manifestations of the work found within this collection at various conferences. However, it was at the Popular Culture Association/Berklee College of Music Conference in Boston on April 6, 2007, as well as at the Ninety-fifth Annual Convention of the National Communication Association in Chicago, Illinois, on November 14, 2009, that I received the strongest encouragement and suggestions for improving my various arguments. I thank my colleagues for their feedback.

I extend my gratitude to my colleagues from Morgan State University's Department of Communication Studies, especially Sean McCollough. Sean helped organize drafts, contacted contributors, and helped me in numerous ways in the early stages of the draft. Carl Hyden lent his careful eye and writing acumen to this project to assure a smoother read than what I proposed. Carl read many drafts, offered constructive criticism, and was prompt to do so. Who could ask for anything more? Todd Burroughs is an expert on black media, particularly the black press. I thank him for sharing his expertise. Jared Ball's knowledge about hip hop and popular culture is matched by few. I am honored to say that I not only know him, I am privileged to work with him. I appreciate the many closed-door office talks and parking lot discussions and debates that Jared and I have shared.

My greatest fan and supporter is my wife, life partner, and friend Monifa Kopano. Thanks for the undying love and support for this project. I hope you never tire of receiving my praises. You still move me. I also thank my two favorite young scholars, my sons Bomani and Olu Kopano. Thank you, *watoto*.

I extend my most sincere thanks to my coeditor, Tamara Brown, who assumed Herculean tasks in this project. Thank you.

I share my coeditor's sentiment on the humility that I experience as a contributor to the series on black contemporary life first edited by our giant scholars Dr. Manning Marable and Dr. Peniel Joseph. How befitting for me it is that Dr. Yohuru Williams picks up the baton from Dr. Marable. Yohuru is not only one of the contemporary scholars I most respect, he is a friend and a brother. Thank you, brother.

Finally, the staff at Palgrave Macmillan has been supportive of this process. I thank you all.

BARUTI N. KOPANO, PHD

Soul Thieves: White America and the Appropriation of Hip Hop and Black Culture

Baruti N. Kopano

You should…use the same manner of resistance as would have been just in our ancestors when the bloody foot-prints of the first remorseless *soul-thief* was placed upon the shores of our fatherland.

Henry Highland Garnet's "An Address to the Slaves of the United States in America" delivered at the National Negro Convention in Buffalo, New York, 1843

Speaking passionately at the National Negro Convention in upstate New York in 1843, Henry Highland Garnet presented a plan to abolish European enslavement of Africans. Much to the chagrin of the moral suasionists and Garrisonians, Garnet sounded the call to arm enslaved Africans to end the peculiar institution. Garnet described the perpetrators of the greatest forced movement of people in world history as "soul thieves." Six decades after Garnet's historic address, one of Africa's brightest children on American soil, W. E. B. Du Bois, released a sociological treatise and literary classic that sought to explain *The Souls of Black Folk*.[1] He offered an examination and explanation into the innermost parts of black women and men—their spirit. The essence of black folk is marked by triumph and pain, and that pain has been channeled into artistic expressions where "we [blacks] transformed our suffering into an opportunity to express spirit."[2] Those spiritual expressions are at the crux of what soul is.

Soul music was an official designation for some of the music African Americans created during the 1950s and 1960s. Similarly, soul radio was the appellation bestowed upon the delivery style of the African American disc jockeys and the music they played on the airwaves during the 1960s and early 1970s. These labels are befitting, for the characteristics of these genres match with the features found within the definition of soul, at least black soul. Improvisation, call, and response, and blending of the spiritual with the secular dominate soul music as well as soul radio. In their pioneering work *Roots of Soul: The Psychology of Black Expressiveness*, Alfred Pasteur and Ivory Toldson identify soul as black expressiveness that is characterized by vital emotionalism, spontaneity, and rhythm.[3] It is this vital emotionalism that overcomes inhibitions about expressing one's feelings. A clear example is the traditional black church experience that allows and encourages participants to embrace and to accept their emotions. Soul encompasses spontaneity that inspires the ability to go off script, to ad lib, to free style. Rhythm is more than synchronized movement of naturally flowing related elements. Rhythm is "the thread that runs through the fabric of black culture; it is therefore at the base of black expressive behavior."[4] The soul of black folk is the essence of their being. It is their thoughts and feelings conveyed in their music, dance, fashion, language, humor, and in other aspects of their lives. These cultural expressions serve as conduits for the regeneration of black folks and for all who would partake.

While no racial or cultural group can claim exclusivity on soul it is hard to dispute the idea that blacks have given "America and the West a cherishable facet of their African heritage—soul—a medium for the attainment of increased happiness."[5] A major objective of the work here in *Soul Thieves* is not only to answer Public Enemy's question "Who Stole the Soul?"[6] but also to posit an explanation for this pilfering.

It is tempting to determine that the continued pattern of white exploitation of black music and culture is simply for white financial rewards. However, that conclusion is too simplistic. Leon Wynter is partly correct in connecting white appropriation of black culture to the "institution of whiteness [that] requires dissociation from much of the essence of the American experience, if not the human experience.... From the beginning this dissociation created a vacuum that people and cultures of color have been conscripted to fill and in which they have voluntarily sought opportunity under conditions of white political hegemony."[7] Wynter's point is that black cultural creations helped the white American need for identity and expression. Much of what America has presented as uniquely American—"music, dance, fashion, humor, spirituality, grassroots politics, slang, literature, and sports—was uniquely African-American in origin, conception, and inspiration."[8] How can this apparent contradiction exist? How can a society with such rigid and punitive policies entrenched to reinforce racial boundaries prioritizing the supremacy of whiteness and the inferiority of blackness establish its mass cultural forms on the culture of the group it so despises?

Jared Ball's discussion of the "hip-hop nation" offers some understanding of white America's general approach to the music and culture of people of color.[9] Couched within internal colonialism theory, Ball proffers that black America exists as an internal colony (or colonies) within the United States. Ball identifies the "hip-hop nation" as an extension of black America, an internal colony in itself. There are "a number of strategies for securing the obedience of the colonized through a manipulation of popular culture including the control of political media, the development of popular stereotypes, and the use of the natural tendency to be creative as a semiotic weapon against a population."[10] The effect of this colonized relationship is that

> popular representations of Black people (African people), First Nations people, Latinos, and certainly women of all backgrounds are incomplete, mythological creations designed to stand in for the more complex realities experienced by these people. Black people are not what is imaged in popular culture. The popular image is determined by the role they are meant to play in society (that of colonized people).[11]

To be clear, colonial masters are committed to preserving a role for colonized people as dominated, controlled, and exploited subjects. Although the culture of black America is the foundation for much of American popular culture, black art forms are offered in the popular imagination to marginalize blacks and other nonwhites and to reaffirm white supremacy. Popular culture and the media that are used to disseminate its messages are arsenals of the hegemonic class.

M. K. Asante uses similar analogies of colonialism in his analysis of the rise of what is often referred to as the post–hip hop nation. Quoting rapper Immortal Technique, Asante observes that corporations sponsor colonialism.[12] Just as England, Portugal, France, and Spain were the four dominant colonial powers that pillaged Africa, Latin America, and Asia, Universal Music Group, Sony BMG, EMI Group, and Warner Music Group "according to Nielsen SoundScan, account for 81.87 percent of the U.S. music market and supply 'retailers with 90 percent of the music' that the public purchases."[13] In continuing his comparisons, Asante reminds us that colonial powers are called "mother" countries while the "Big Four" of the music industry are called "parent companies."[14] Finally, in the colonial system raw materials were extracted from the colonies and sent to the mother country to be "finished and commodified for the marketplaces of the mother country. Additionally, these products were often sold back to the same colonies from which the raw materials were extracted in the first place."[15] In the case of hip hop, citizens of the parent companies are "45 million Hip-Hop consumers between the ages of 13 and 34, 80% of whom are white and has [sic] $1 trillion in spending power."[16]

Asante's argument, then, is that the relationship that most black rappers have—most black entertainers in general—is one where the raw sources (talents) of black performers are pillaged to provide products for the black and particularly for the white masses. Certainly, black dollars matter, too. However, as Ball forcefully argues the greatest objective of this pilfering is not merely for the financial rewards; the booty is but one objective.

There are far greater rewards than "the simple extraction of material wealth and goods from the colony. This process also assured control over the popular form the colonized cultural expression would take."[17] Controlling the messages and the values emanating from the cultural creations is the supreme recompense for the colonial master. Rapper Too Short makes strong claims of the colonial powers' commitment to domination and exploitation. The West Coast rapper in an interview with HipHopDx claims that his record label, Jive Records, prevented him from producing socially conscious songs about poverty, the deleterious effects of drug addiction, and police brutality in favor of sex songs.[18] Too Short maintains that the president of Jive Records, Barry Weiss, refused to honor a verbal agreement they reached to produce a "whole album of positive Too Short songs, just to keep that balance."[19] Instead, the artist asserts that it was the "executive running the company advising me to put out an entire album of just cursing and sex."[20]

Too Short's allegations are consistent with the Ghanian writer Ayi Kwei Armah's supposition on how the "white destroyers from the West" would come to rule the African continent and much of the world for 2,000 years.[21] To conquer Africa two steps would be necessary. First, black folks would have to be reduced in their mental state to focus on triviality. Or in Armah's words, blacks would have to be reduced to beasts:

> To reduce them to beasts the predators starved their minds. The predators lowered in number and in seriousness the matters that could cause these hangers-on to think, till in the end there was nothing at all they cared to exercise their minds on. To reduce them to things the predators fed their bodies, indulging their crassest physical wants promptly, overflowingly. The predators fed them huge meals of meat and drink and added abundant *dagga* for their smoking. The predators supplied them with women and watched their copulation as another kind of sport...From morning til sleep they were either at some sport, eating, drinking, copulating, smoking or defecating.[22]

Controlling mass-mediated images and the major distribution mechanisms of these images fulfills the tripartite objectives of increasing the subjugation of the masses, amplifying black self-degradation, and profiting financially from the media production. Too Short appeased his colonial master's wishes to produce the "raunchiest Too Short album ever"—one replete with photo shoots for the CD cover featuring a porn star. To Too Short's chagrin, "Once I did what they wanted, they would never let me do what I wanted," which was to balance his "raunchy" CD with a socially conscious one.[23] Too Short was like many other hip hop artists and other black cultural creators whose experience in the entertainment industry corroborated Armah's proclamation that "everything filthy among us was now being deliberately supported and helped to multiply by the white destroyers...for their own ends, a deliberate sickening of our people, since only from our disease could the white destroyers hope to get the things they had come looking for."[24] What exactly were the "white destroyers" seeking?

The acquisition of black bodies was at the core of what the "white destroyers" had come looking for during the physical raid of the African continent. These black bodies would be responsible for providing the labor and natural resources that would propel all of the Western powerhouses to their global supremacy. However, as Europeans continued to be dispersed throughout the world many of them found themselves mired in a quagmire of sort in trying to find a social space in the New World. In America in the 1830s and 1840s, as many European

immigrants spurred an acceleration in urban growth, these continental trans-
plants became increasingly aware and insecure about their lowly state in their
new environs in a highly class-conscious society. Their arrival and increased
insecurities dovetailed with the popularity of minstrelsy. Abundant in white
interpretation of black music and culture and awash in caricatures and stereotypes of blacks, minstrels became an American craze. With minstrel shows as
America's popular culture signature piece, the basis for American identity was
formed:

> From the start, pop culture has been constructed on the facts as well as white fan-
> tasies of nonwhites and their cultural forms. American identity within this pop
> culture, history shows, is in large part projected onto the culture at large through
> certain mass-marketed, commodified projections of nonwhite identity. To loosely
> paraphrase President Bill Clinton's 1998 appearance on a prime-time television
> tribute to Motown Records, white America has always depended on nonwhite
> America to know itself....Whiteness, in both American and European identity,
> comes from a careful consideration of what the African or African-American is
> not.[25]

Minstrels fit that bill perfectly. Whites took the music, humor, and dance tradition of black culture and meshed it with harsh stereotypes. As is true with all
verbal art, minstrel shows taught values and norms, sanctioned transgressors,
and served as vehicles for social criticism and fantasy.[26] Minstrels allowed whites
to deflect many of their inhibitions, unfulfilled desires, and insecurities onto
a group with relative powerlessness. James Baldwin's admonishment rang true
here for white Americans, "If I am not what you say I am, then you are not who
you think you are." Whites needed blacks to be inferior so that they could find
humanity among themselves despite their persistent inhumanity toward their
dark-pigmented sisters and brothers.

A closer examination of minstrels reveals that the "white destroyers" were in
search of black bodies for purposes greater than their physicality. Pasteur and
Toldson submit that the real attraction of minstrelsy was that it allowed whites
to experience the soulful expressiveness of black culture. Minstrel star George
Thatcher reflects on the psychic impact of minstrelsy: "I found myself dreaming
of minstrels; I would wake with an imaginary tambourine in my hand, and rub
my face with my hands to see if I was blacked up...The dream of my life was
to see or speak to a performer."[27] After Dave Wambold, later a minstrel tenor,
attended his first minstrel show in Newark, New Jersey, his parents could not
keep him in school because "he was prone to play truant and get up minstrel
performances among his companions."[28] To be clear, Pasteur and Toldson maintain that in minstrel shows in particular and in black cultural expressiveness in
general an African ethos (an African way of feeling and being) exists that offers
folks a certain freedom if they could only feel free to embrace and accept it.

Some critics focus on blackface minstrel strictly as negative stereotyping, and
in some ways it was, but in other ways Pasteur and Toldson are correct in calling minstrelsy "a compliment, in spite of the racist stereotyped acts intended to

denigrate black people, because the performers were demonstrating, for all to see, the vital emotionalism, spontaneity, and rhythm unique to black expression."[29] For many minstrel performers and their white patrons, minstrel shows provided pure emotional escape and release, even if they had to engage in cultural voyeurism to experience this freedom. Pasteur and Toldson detail how minstrelsy became a "major vehicle through which white Americans conceptualized and coped with many of their problems"[30] and offered some of them a "potential for humanness."[31] Other black cultural forms, including hip hop, offer whites that same potential. In the end, along with the rewards of the financial gain and the satisfaction of tightening the grips of hegemonic control of masses the appropriation of black culture allows soul thieves a temporary quenching of the starvation of their souls.

Black culture, particularly as it is imagined by white minds, is the foundation for American popular entertainment:

> Everything about African-Americans—their bodies, dances, songs, dialects, passions, worldview, and so on, real and especially as imagined by whites (and eventually imagined by other blacks, too)—became the base material for the popular entertainments that matured into mass culture. The black condition became a canvas for projecting all that the whiteness ideal sublimated; black cultural output became the paint.[32]

The black body was necessary not only for its material contribution to the colonial power but also for the ephemeral emotional release it provides to its captors. The black body was one that many whites simultaneously admired, feared, and hated. Norman Podhoretz is lucid about his ambivalence in the 1963 essay "My Negro Problem—And Ours":

> Yet just as in childhood I envied Negroes for what seemed to me their superior masculinity, so I envy them today for what seems to be their superior physical grace and beauty. I have come to value physical grace very highly, and I am now capable of aching with all my being when I watch a Negro couple on the dance floor, or a Negro playing baseball or basketball. They are on the kind of terms with their own bodies that I should like to be on with mine, and for that precious quality they seem blessed to me.[33]

Podhoretz's envy as a child stems largely from what he perceived to be the masculinity and toughness of black males as well as an overall courage that he lacked and imagined came naturally to blacks. This toughness freed the "Negro's" spirit, and this freedom of spirit also made its way into the body movements for black folks in Podhoretz's mind. It was that freedom of movement that caused the "aching" that Podhoretz experienced when he saw a "Negro couple on the dance floor" or in sports. He ached with desire to have this grace and wanted to live and move without having to repress natural impulses. "Negroes" acquiesced to these impulses, so Podhoretz's thinking continued. The envy of this freedom was responsible for the fear that Podhoretz admits to having and for "hat[ing] them [blacks] with all my heart"[34] in childhood—a feeling that followed Podhoretz into adulthood. Greg Tate attempts to explain this contradiction as a "peculiarly African-American twist on Marx's and Engel's observations about capitalism's commodity-fetish effect—the transformation of a marketable object into a magical thing of desire."[35] In other words, the black body is a desired taboo, something to be "possessed and something to be erased—an operation that explains not only the ceaseless parade of troublesome Black stereotypes still proffered and preferred by Hollywood . . . but the American music industry's never-ending quest for a white artist who can completely perform a Black musical impersonation."[36]

This paradoxical relationship between African American cultural creators and their white admirers and commercial molders is brilliantly captured in Alice Walker's short story "Nineteen Fifty-five."[37] The two main characters, Traynor and Gracie Mae "Little Mama" Still, represent thinly veiled fictional portraits of Elvis Presley and Willie Mae "Big Mama" Thornton. Traynor is a white singer who becomes rich and famous in the entertainment industry after he buys a blues song from Gracie Mae for $500. In this process, Traynor becomes a "soul thief;" he steals what he does not understand: "I've sung it and sung it, and I'm making forty thousand dollars a day offa it, and you know what, I don't have the faintest notion what that song means."[38] As Gracie Mae notes, Traynor uses "my voice, my tone, my inflection, everything."[39] As the cultural theft process often works, the imitator becomes the halted one while the originator often is lost in obscurity. Indeed, even Gracie Mae's "children didn't call it my song anymore. Nobody did."[40] Traynor eventually would be donned the "Emperor of Rock and Roll,"[41] but he never gains an understanding of the music, but to his credit at least he knows that he does not understand. He concedes that "they want what I got only it ain't mine. . . . They getting the flavor of something but they ain't getting the thing itself."[42]

Over the years, Traynor attempts to assuage his conscious for the wealth he has obtained through Gracie Mae's talent by providing her with material possessions: a car, a farm, a house, and other trinkets. Unfortunately for Traynor, neither his possession of materials nor his bestowing of objects on Gracie Mae allows his soul to connect to the music or to the spirit that created it. It is precisely this disconnect that marks the relationship of "soul thieves" to black cultural creators. Financial remuneration can never compensate for soul theft. Alice Walker's character Traynor continues his interactions with the black blues woman Gracie Mae for over two decades to talk about his life. The majority of that time is about Traynor's attempt to use both the music and Gracie Mae as an interpreter of that music in his eternal pursuit of the fulfillment of his soul—a mission he never accomplishes.

Instead of seeing white musicians' imitation of black musical and cultural styles as flattering, black jazz genius Thelonius Monk charged that white bands had "carried off the healthiest child of Negro music, and starved it of its *spirit* [emphasis added] until its parents no longer recognized it."[43] Along those lines, hip hop assassin Harry Allen offers a critique of Eminem's prominence in hip hop.[44] That critique can apply to Walker's fictional character Traynor or to today's urban music stars Justin Timberlake and Robin Thicke or to some of the "hip" hip hop magazine founders or other white hip hop artistic and corporate pioneers. For Allen, the best way to understand their presence in the black cultural arena is to understand the Tarzan narrative, that is, a white infant being abandoned by his white mother and father and being raised by apes only years later to grow to dominate the nonwhite people and their environment. Allen adds that the Tarzan myth carries with it one of the edicts of racism (white supremacy)—black facilitation of white development. In the case of the subject of Allen's biting critique—Eminem—music producer and rapper Dr. Dre is the black facilitator of Eminem's development so that similar to Walker's character Traynor, Eminem comes to know:

> I am the worst thing since Elvis Presley
> to do black music so selfishly
> and used it to get myself wealthy
> (Hey!!) There's a concept that works.[45]

Traynor's offering of money and other material possession to Gracie Mae does not mitigate the soul thievery. Neither should the individual success of today's black musicians and entertainers distract us from identifying the cultural degradation that marks much of the music and entertainment industries. A key turning point in the music industry that led to some of this degradation—one that has contemporary ramifications—occurred during the 1970s.

A young, ambitious white executive at Columbia Records Group (CRG), Clive Davis, was fresh off of the signing of Sly and the Family Stone to his label. Davis was adamant that CRG was missing out on a ton of money by not increasing its market share of "soul" music. Consequently, he commissioned Harvard University Business School to analyze the black music market. The report was entitled, "A Study of the Soul Music Environment," (also called "The Harvard Report") and was delivered to Davis on May 11, 1972.[46] Yvonne Bynoe signals this study as the beginning of the "systematic colonization of Black music."[47] Some of the implemented recommendations of this study had immediate deleterious effects on the black music industry. For example, Columbia paved the way for what became a floodgate of major record companies buying small independent music labels, including its purchase of Stax and Philadelphia International and Warner Brothers Records's purchase of Atlantic. By the "mid-1970s most of the black independents had been either bought up or edged out, their artists and executive talent lured away to the growing 'Black departments' at the six big record companies—CBS, Warner, RCA, MCA, EMI, and Polygram."[48] In essence, "by the mid-1970s, the lucrative business of Black music was largely out of Black hands."[49]

The Harvard Report also found that soul music "has a broad appeal that extends far beyond black customers."[50] Many white music executives believed that white consumers would purchase soul music, but only if its sound could be made palatable to white tastes. Asante and Ball in their independent works remind us that in the colonial model, the purpose of the raw talent (i.e., black cultural creators) is to produce raw materials[51] (i.e., black music) to be consumed by white masses for the benefit of the colonial parent (i.e., parent record companies). To effectuate this colonial goal, part of the Harvard Report's proposal recommended involving "soul radio."

The Harvard Report showed that "soul radio" was important to record companies for two reasons. First, it gave them access to an increasingly large music-buying audience—the black one. More important for many record companies was that "soul radio" was "perhaps the most effective way of getting a record to a Top 40 playlist."[52] Many white radio stations would not play black songs on their airwaves until they had been made popular on black radio. The involvement of soul radio essentially led to the demise of independent, black-controlled radio and was responsible for what Nelson George called the "death of rhythm and blues." The fading of "soul radio" also was abetted by the radio industry's shift in popularity from AM radio to FM radio. Almost all of the African American–owned radio stations during this time were AM radio stations, so a major link in the music industry power wheel—radio—was essentially out of black hands, too. The transition to FM radio also dovetailed with the decimating of the power of the black radio disc jockey (DJ). Black DJs often determined what music was to be played and what artists were to be to spotlight, and were the real power cogs in the power distribution wheel.[53] That power was largely negated by the work of Bill Drake and other white radio station program directors and consultants who implemented tight playlists that required DJs to generally keep their comments under eight seconds, the by-product of which "reduced the role of the dj to a robot."[54] Increasingly, a strong corporate force dominated the major decisions about what music would be played and how it would be promoted. For sure, most DJs were left with little decision-making power about what music was to be played, a role that many black disc jockeys had during the heyday of "soul radio."

Black-owned radio company Radio One continued the trend of relying on the expertise of white radio programming experts in determining music tastes for a black audience. Mary Catherine Sneed, as a fifty-something-year-old white woman, served as Radio One's chief operating officer in the early 2000s. The Alabama native arrived at Radio One with no prior rap music programming experience. Radio One turned over most of the major decisions as to what music would be played on its stations to "MC," as she preferred to be called, Sneed would obtain so much programming muscle she would come to be labeled "one of the most powerful people in black radio."[55]

The Harvard Report also recommended that Columbia Records, through a "broadened distribution in the black community, which an expanded soul program would bring, could serve as a distribution arm for their proprietary product under a custom label program."[56] This recommendation would serve as the forerunner for the independent label deals that Russell Simmons (Def Jam Records), Sean "Diddy" Combs (Bad Boy Records), Percy "Master P" Miller (No Limit Records), Damon Dash and Shawn "Jay Z" Carter (Roc-a-Fella Records) among others would sign with major record company conglomerates. These companies were blackfaced music labels serving as pied pipers to their corporate parent colonial masters. Images of crass materialism, gross objectification and disrespect of women, and alcohol and drug use consumption were the dominant themes on these labels. All but No Limit Records sold major interests of their independent labels to multinationals. No Limit filed bankruptcy and implemented a few company reorganization strategies, but has faded in significance as a music and entertainment company.

Columbia Records implemented many of the recommendations from the Harvard Report shortly upon its release. From 1971 to 1980 Columbia Records expanded its roster of black artists from two to 125 acts.[57] By the time the first recorded rap song appears in 1979, the colonial map had been drawn as to how to control the black music industry, regardless of the genre. That map drew some distinguishing marks as to how to control the record labels, the means of music distribution, the promotions vehicle (i.e., the radio industry), and how to coopt black promotions and production talent at small independent labels. The cumulative effect of these efforts would be the weakening of independent music companies—white and black owned—and the simultaneous emboldening of the majors. The epitome of how this strategy works was the black wife and husband team of Sylvia and Joe Robinson and the rap label they founded—Sugar Hill Records.

The combination of poor business practices and the omnipotence of the major labels proved too powerful of a force for the small rap label to withstand. The proverbial straw that broke the camel's back was Sugar Hill's distribution deal with MCA. The Robinsons lost the rights to the catalog of Chess/Checkers/Cadet, which included works of Muddy Waters and Etta James, as part of collateral it offered to MCA for its distribution deal.[58] That deal also called for MCA to receive 25 percent of gross sales. Despite filing a multimillion lawsuit against MCA alleging an MCA-led racketeering scheme, Sugar Hill sold its Checker Records and Chess catalogue for a meager $481,000 and settled its lawsuit out of court in 1991 with the Robinsons receiving no money.[59]

Sylvia and Joe Robinson were not only at the front door of the business of rap music; they built the door. Few black music and business people understood the music and financial potential of this "new" music form in its early stages. Many skilled black business people may have eschewed rap music and hip hop cultural forms—at least openly and in the early stages of their creations—presumably because of their noticeably racial identification. In the case of rap, many black radio executives were particularly turned off by the music: "image conscious and bound at the navel to crossover styles, they were generally unwilling to give rap a break."[60] This rejection opened the door for white entrance and domination. Enterprising Whites quickly formed Profile Records, Tommy Boy Records, and Def Jam Records, some of the first and most important independent record labels in the hip hop industry.

Yvonee Bynoe differentiates the "Hip Hop industry" from the "Hip Hop community." The hip hop industry is a moneymaking behemoth that encompasses "record companies, music publishers, radio stations, record stores, music-video show, recording studios, talent booker, performance venues, promoters, managers, disc jockeys, lawyers, accountants, music publication, and music/entertainment websites."[61] The hip hop industry also comprises service sectors that depend on the hip hop industry clientele. Those areas include "restaurants, florists, hotels, travel agents, limousine services, party planners, publicists, rental agents, fashion designers, stylists, barbers, hairstylists, make-up artists, and photographers."[62] On the other hand, the hip hop community is "comprised of adherents to Hip Hop culture and mere consumers of rap music and its accouterments—the fans."[63]

There are many complicated pieces in the appropriation of black music and culture, especially the hip hop industry. Part of this complication involves the duplicity of the exploited class. Ayi Kwei Armah's *The Healers* helps to peel back some of the layers of this duplicity.[64] One of the characters of this book, an elder, confronts the young Densu to inform him that changes are coming. Europeans are set to exert full power to control their land and all of their lives. The elder presents this as an "opportunity" for Densu. Whites will need "Black people they trust.... We shall have to help the whites by finding men to fight for them, here and everywhere.... Once we agree to work for the whites, we put ourselves on the road to power. It is a road without end."[65] Various hip artists are seemingly heeding the advice given to Densu: they have positioned themselves to be on the "road without end."

When Snoop appeared on *Saturday Night Live* in 1994 wearing a grand jersey with a Tommy Hilfiger logo on it, sales for the company jumped $93 million the following year.[66] Intended or not, the question of hip hop's potential to expand commercial exploits had been answered definitively. Acknowledging this success in 1996, Hilfiger employed rapper Spinderalla (of Salt 'N Pepa fame) and Quincy Jones's daughter Kidada to help introduce his new line of women's casual clothes and a floral fragrance, both called Tommy Girl.[67] Although rappers had long rapped about brand names and their personal styles—a la Run-DMC's 1986 "My Adidas"—Snoop's appearance on national television had opened the door for a full-court press of the commercial exploitation of rap music and hip hop. The release of Snoop's "Gin and Juice" may be a case of unintended consequence. In the revolving door of music company ownership and crosspollination, Seagram's eventually bought Death Row Records—the independent label that released "Gin and Juice." This relationship became a triple victory: money from record sales, money from alcohol sales, and the celebration of the degradation of black life and culture with the song's glorification of sex, drugs, and alcohol.

If Snoop's shout out to gin was an unintended financial shot in the arm to Seagram's bottom financial line, the conglomerate was deliberate in its dealings with rapper Petey Pablo. While Snoop rapped about gin in general, years after Snoop's gin tribute Pablo moved from rapping about gin in general to rapping about Seagram's gin specifically after striking a deal with Allied-Domecq's Seagram brand. There was a more than 10 percent increase in gin purchases in urban markets after this deal was struck.[68] Marketers have seized on the power of the shout out or as spoken in marketing vernacular—product placement—in rap music and hip hop culture. Cadillac credits the record setting sales of its Escalade SUV with the popularity and frequent references in rap music.[69]

Rapper 50 Cent epitomizes the exploitation of rappers rhyming to sell trinkets. At one point, 50 Cent had his own line of Reebok shoes and apparel surpassing Reebok's sales for any NBA star. A major part of the "deal called for 50

Cent to help develop products, perform in ads, and wear the clothes and shoes in performances and videos."[70] Reebok, meanwhile, cross-promoted 50 Cent's music. Even established companies like the two hundred-year-old French cognac Courvoisier have found commercial benefit from rap music. Sales took off for the company after rapper Busta Rhymes wrote the hit song "Pass the Courvoisier." According to Agenda, Incorporated, a San Francisco–based brand research firm, brands were mentioned almost a thousand times in the 2004 top twenty singles on the Billboard charts. The top brands were Cadillac (70 mentions), Hennessy (69), Mercedes-Benz (63), Rolls Royce (62), and Gucci (49).[71] The advertising trade magazine *Advertising Age* reported that McDonald's struck a deal to pay rappers between $1 and $5 each time their song was played if they included "Big Mac" in their lyrics.[72]

Contrary to contradicting one of the major arguments of this research, the deals that these rappers are striking with companies do not point to an end of the centuries of white appropriation of black music and culture. Remember the rap assassin's Harry Allen's warning: one of the edicts of racism (white supremacy) is that there must be black facilitation of white development. While at an individual level, one can applaud the financial gains of individual artists, the art was never theirs alone. The individual decision to exploit the art spoils the potential spirit-fulfilling components of the art. While some rap music was about dancing and partying in its infancy, it also was about retrospection and elevation. It certainly was not about writing lyrics to "shout out" specific brand names for pay.

The unadulterated objectification of women, emphasis on crass material-ism, adulation of violence (but only violence perpetuated on nonwhites), and other forms of self-degradation are ubiquitous in the commercial rap and hip hop world. Alice Walker's character Traynor was searching for the spirit that created blues. How could so much pain create so much beauty? That rhetori-cal question has been behind many black expressive creations, including rap and hip hop. Defying odds, blacks have created beauty out of seemingly noth-ing. Although Traynor mastered the technical skills of Gracie Mae's song, he had not lived the experiences that birthed that song, so despite the abundance of money he made from the song it could never be his because the experiences were not his.

The greed of white corporations and their black facilitators are threatening the voice and creativity of the marginalized. Black creativity, particularly that created by the marginalized must be allowed to exist, for in this creativity healing potential exists.

Notes

1. W. E. B. Du Bois, *The Souls of Black Folk*, in *Three Negro Classics* (Chicago: A. C. McClurg & Company, 1903; New York: Avon, 1965), 207–389.
2. Dona Richards, *Let the Circle Be Unbroken* (Trenton, NJ: Red Sea Press, 1989), 25.
3. Alfred Pasteur and Ivory Toldson, *The Roots of Soul: The Psychology of Black Expressiveness* (Garden City, New York: Anchor Press, Doubleday, 1982), 4.
4. Ibid., 4.
5. Ibid., 6.

6. Public Enemy, "Who Stole the Soul?" *Fear of a Black Planet*, Def Jam Recordings/ Columbia Records 1990, CD.

7. Leon Wynter, *American Skin: Pop Culture, Big Business & the End of White America* (New York: Crown Publishers, 2002), 22–23.

8. Greg Tate, "Nigs R Us, or How Blackfolk Became Fetish Objects," in *Everything But the Burden: What White People Are Taking from Black Culture* (New York: Broadway Books, 2003), 3.

9. Jared Ball, *I Mix What I Like* (Oakland, CA: AK Press, 2011).

10. Ibid., 75.

11. Ibid.

12. M. K. Asante, Jr., *It's Bigger than Hip Hop: The Rise of the Post-Hip-Hop Generation* (New York: St. Martin's Griffin, 2008), 111.

13. Asante, 111.

14. Ibid.

15. Asante, 112–113.

16. Ibid., 113.

17. Ball, 78.

18. Paul Arnold, "Too Short Says There Was an Industry-Wide Plot to Shut Down Conscious Hip Hop," *HipHop DX*, February 29, 2012, http://www.hiphopdx.com /index/news/id.18861/title.too-short-says-there-was-an-industry-wide-plot-to-shut -down-conscious-hip-hop

19. Ibid.

20. Ibid.

21. Ayi Kwei Armah, *Two Thousand Seasons* (London: Heinemann, 1973).

22. Ibid., 29–30.

23. Arnold.

24. Armah, *Seasons*, 104–105.

25. Wynter, 20.

26. Pasteur and Toldson, 42.

27. Ibid., 40.

28. Ibid., 40–41.

29. Ibid., 40.

30. Ibid., 41

31. Ibid., 133.

32. Wynter, 22–23.

33. Norman Podhoretz, "My Negro Problem–and Ours," *Commentary* 35 (February 1963): 99.

34. Ibid., 93.

35. Tate, 2.

36. Ibid., 4.

37. Alice Walker, "Nineteen Fifty-five," in *You Can't Keep a Good Woman Down* (New York: Harcourt, 1981), 3–20.

38. Ibid., 8.

39. Ibid., 18.

40. Ibid., 7.

41. Ibid., 9.

42. Ibid., 17.

43. Pasteur and Toldson, 137.

44. Harry Allen, "The Unbearable Whiteness of Emceeing: What the Eminence of Eminem Says about Race," *The Source*, February 2003, http://www.harryallen.info /docs/TheUnbearableWhitenessofEmceeing.pdf.

45. Eminem, "Without Me," *The Eminem Show*, Shady Records/Aftermath Entertainment/ Interscope Records 2002, CD.
46. Dan Charnas, *The Big Payback: The History of the Business of Hip-Hop* (New York: New American Library, 2010), 12.
47. Yvonne Bynoe, "Money, Power, and Respect: A Critique of the Business of Rap Music," in *Rhythm & Business: The Political Economy of Black Music*, ed. Norman Kelley (New York: Akashic, 2002), 223.
48. Charnas, 12.
49. Ibid.
50. Cited in Bynoe, 223.
51. Nelson George, *The Death of Rhythm & Blues* (New York: Pantheon Books, 1988), 136.
52. Ibid.
53. Baruti Kopano, "Rap Music as an Extension of the Black Rhetorical Tradition: 'Keepin' It Real,'" *Western Journal of Black Studies* 26, no. 4 (Winter 2002): 204–214.
54. Reebee Garafolo, "Crossing Over: 1939–1992," in *Split Image: African Americans in the Mass Media*, ed. Jannette Dates and William Barlow (Washington, DC: Howard University Press, 1990), 99; and George, 117–19.
55. Krissah Williams, "Hip-Hop's Unlikely Voice," *Washington Post*, January 12, 2004, A1.
56. Bynoe, 224–25.
57. George, 136.
58. Charnas, 117–118; and Bynoe, 226.
59. Bynoe, 226.
60. George, 191.
61. Bynoe, 221–22.
62. Bynoe, 222.
63. Ibid.
64. Ayi Kwei Armah, *The Healers* (London: Heinemann, 1978), 30.
65. Ibid., 30.
66. Martha Duffy, "H Stands for Hilfiger," *Time*, September 16, 1996, 96.
67. Ibid.
68. David Kiley, "Hip Hop Gets Down with the Deals," *Business Week*, May 16, 2005, http://www.businessweek.com/bwdaily/dnflash/may2005/nf20050516_5797_db016 .htm.
69. Ibid.
70. Ibid.
71. Krissah Williams, "In Hip-Hop, Making Name-Dropping Pay," *Washington Post*, August 29, 2005, D1.
72. Ibid.

2

The Appropriation of Blackness in *Ego Trip's The (White) Rapper Show*

Carlos D. Morrison and Ronald L. Jackson, II

The fixity and fluidity of whiteness in the United States is astounding. It is amazing that a social force can be so stable that it cements the social order, yet so flexible that it eludes the average American. Whether wanting to admit it or not, as scholar McCarthy indicates, whiteness benefits from identity politics associated with the racial Other.[1] It does so, in part, because of how unattractive the stereotype of the racial Other becomes. The more the caricature of the racial Other is drawn, the more ridiculous it looks and the more the public becomes repulsed by the Other. Although the racial Other becomes unappealing it is now safe for whites to casually perform or episodically emulate the Other because it is low-risk; after all it is unlikely any decent person will want to be the embodiment of the caricature. In some cases performing the Other may mean mocking other races as witnessed in the recent past during one of San Diego State University's ghetto-themed fraternity parties known as the "Compton Cookout." Much like the "Compton Cookout," reality shows like *Ego Trip's The (White) Rapper Show* (called *The White Rapper Show* from this point on) show whites in "ghetto," "urban," or hip hop apparel, wearing jewelry, otherwise known as "bling bling," in supposed celebration of rap music.[2] Both performances are sinister, stereotypical, offensive, and race-intensive.

Clearly, there is epistemic danger with whiteness; however, while "race traitors" call for the abolition of whiteness, historian David Roediger's clarion call to first critically assess the libratory potential in such an act of disinvestment is wise.[3] By fooling oneself into entanglements and bound by whiteness time is wasted. Instead, African American intellectuals ought to continue the steady work of pointing out white hegemony wherever it tries to conceal itself, and exposing its material, political, social, and racial intent. This is the purpose of this research.

In order to grasp the rationale for this essay it is critical that one acknowledge how whiteness is deployed throughout everyday American life in the United States. While this research explores popular media, whiteness pervades education, state politics, health care, immigration reform, and numerous other categories. It is easy to recognize because it cannot resist the tendency to exploit Others. It presents itself as elegant, refined, poised, dominant, normal, appropriate, and the most civil order. Its racial signifiers are restrictive and pronounced codes that implicitly suggest an exoticism that accompanies the Other. So, whiteness is always evident when the Other is presented in essentialist terms and distinguished by its oddity, arcaneness, roughness, and tattered simplicity.[4] In popular media, especially in this age of reality television, those manufactured qualities of the Other are what make "good TV." Those qualities are actually stock features of reality television because they not only entice audiences to see more, but they also fuel the appetite for negative competition, negative difference, and ultimate success (however that gets defined contextually).

This study that critically analyzes *The White Rapper Show* hosted by white rapper MC Serch demonstrates that when taken out of cultural context, the sophisticated lyrical genre of rap music appears puerile at best. When extracted from its sociopolitical habitat rap and hip hop music seem to be merely comprised of a motley crew of characters performing energizing sexually suggestive dances, developing neologisms (because they have a limited grasp of standard American English), sporting bling bling, and composing rhythmically interesting verse. When converted into a game show where individuals lyrically compete for monetary gain, it reduces the substance of a musical genre that emerged from the ghettoes and barrios in inner cities out of a struggle to have youth voices heard. The packaging of rap into a reality show simplifies the initial intent of rap music as a youth social protest genre hell bent on being recognized for its creativity as much as an uplifting set of inspirational messages to youth who belong to the underclass. These messages were meant to inform these youth that they too are capable of rising above what appears to be overwhelming materialist conditions and becoming successful. That message, as well as any substantive sociopolitical commentary, is lost as white rapper MC Serch, of the famed rap group 3rd Bass, sometimes angrily tries to school the contestants of *The White Rapper Show* about the seriousness of both the competition and rap music. What is interesting in this reality show is how MC Serch, born Michael Berrin, even as an accepted rap artist among black rappers, performs whiteness, devalues the Other, and hence contravenes even his most valiant attempts to celebrate blackness. Furthermore, *The White Rapper Show* becomes textual evidence of cultural raiding.

The entertainment industry, particularly in the area of music, has provided and promoted a major context for cultural raiding by whites. Cultural raiding is a term used to indicate mimetic cultural representation. Perhaps anthropologist Michael Taussig explains it best when he defines mimesis as the cumulative act of "alterity" in which one's behaviors simultaneously demonstrate both an appreciation for and distancing from cultural modes of expression, and hence the cultural Other.[5] This often occurs when performing cultural rituals so as to appropriate them, but may also happen when individuals emulate other kinds of performances such as popular cultural ones like rap music. This research examines the notion of cultural raiding or appropriation of African American popular culture in the new millennium by analyzing how mimesis takes place in *The White Rapper Show*.

The White Rapper Show was a television reality show released in 2007 that brought together ten white rappers to compete for a chance to win a $100,000 grand prize. Although bona fide rappers and hip hop icons like Grandmaster Flash, Kurtis Blow, Prince Paul, and Juelz Santana made occasional cameo appearances, MC Serch hosted and codirected this televised show, which cable network VH1 aired over eight episodes. Producers intentionally set the show in the South Bronx, New York, the birthplace of rap music in the 1970s, as a way of granting authenticity to this venture. The "boogie down" Bronx also offered a space and place for conflating hip hop audiences with any black resident of the city.

Cultural theorist Molefi Asante's notion of "location,"[6] textual analysis, and the propaganda technique called "transfer" discussed by Larson[7] are applicable as theoretic tools of analysis in order to show how the white rappers on *The White Rapper Show* reinforce and perpetuate whiteness and white supremacy through the strategy of appropriation. This essay first discusses *Ego Trip's The (White) Rappers Show* followed by a discussion of Episode One. Second, it critically analyzes the appropriation of (1) the African naming process and white privilege; (2) contestants Persia and John Brown's co-optation of the African American style of speech called "signification"; (3) Persia's appropriation of black hip hop masculinity; and finally (4) the cultural raiding of black hairstyles, clothing, and other outward appearances of blackness by the white contestants.

Who (or What) is *Ego Trip*: The Beginning

Like both *Vibe* and the *Source, Ego Trip* was a hip hop magazine that took pride in focusing on hip hop culture and was devoted to the rap music faithful. The magazine started in New York City in 1994 under the leadership of Sacha Jenkins, Elliott Wilson, Chairman Mao, Gabriel Alvarez, Brent Rollins, and Henry Chalfant. Yet, unlike both the *Source* and *Vibe, Ego Trip*, while "spreading the gospel of hip-hop," focused on the "underground" rap movement culture along with the alternative music scene and its relationship to hip hop culture.

As a result of supposed cutting edge journalistic work and in-depth analysis of the culture, critics dubbed the magazine the "arrogant voice of musical truth." Moreover, *Ego Trip* brought a bold, defiant, and unapologetic approach to hip hop journalism for thirteen issues before the magazine ceased publication. Some of hip hop culture's most well known artists at the time graced its covers such as KRS-One, Easy-E, Redman, Biggie Smalls, the Wu-Tang Clan, and Nas.

After the demise of the publication, the founders of *Ego Trip* got an idea to develop a series of other media-related projects to further their perception of the cause of hip hop. These projects ranged from developing book projects such as

Ego Trip's Book of Rap Lists and *Ego Trip's Big Book of Racism* to television shows such as *TV's Illest Minority Moments, Race-of-Rama,* and, for the purpose of this focus and analysis, *Ego Trip's The (White) Rappers Show.*

Ego Trip's The (White) Rappers Show

As briefly discussed in the introduction, *Ego Trip's The (White) Rappers Show* was a reality-based television show that brought ten white rappers together to "battle" for the title of "next white emcee of the new millennium."[8] The ten contestants donned the nicknames and personas of "G-Child," "Misfit Dior," "Jus Rhyme," "Persia," "100 Proof", "Shamrock," "John Brown," "Sullee," "Dasit," and "Jon Boy." Ken Mok and his 10×10 Production company produced the show, as well *America's Next Top Model*, which is the reason why *Ego Trip's The (White) Rapper Show* displayed a similar in format to the model competition.

Unlike *America's Next Top Model* often set in New York City (Manhattan, specifically) and Los Angeles, *The (White) Rapper Show* took place in the South Bronx, the birthplace of rap music, "where (ten) contestants hailing from all over America...find a way to make it through challenges that will test their musical cred(ability), knowledge of hip-hop culture and their ideas about race along the way."[9]

Episode One

Episode One embodies many of the cultural-contested zones denoted in this research. This will serve several purposes: (1) specifically, Episode One introduces the contestants to the viewing audience and they discuss their background and nicknames; (2) Persia's controversial use of the n-word took place in Episode One; and (3) Persia and John Brown's verbal battle illustrates a very good example of the appropriation of signification or specifically, playing the (dirty) dozens.

The show opens with the previously mentioned ten white rappers, all of whom made the audition cut for the show. After showing the rappers some love, the show's host MC Serch welcomes the crew to the South Bronx, and to their new home called "Tha White House." Tha White House is anything but luxurious and sophisticated. It is quite the opposite and has a décor that more closely resembles Animal House. MC Serch tells the contestants that their living arrangements represent a way to "keep the true essence of hip hop" and not the "life style of the rich and famous."

As the rappers begin to unwind in Tha White House, tempers begin to flare between two contestants, Persia and John Brown. From the start, Brown constantly brags about his rap crew called Ghetto Revival and that he is the self-styled "King of the 'Burbs." Persia, quite frankly, tires of hearing all of his boasting and bragging and challenges Brown to a freestyle battle. John Brown refuses and Persia goes on a verbal rampage that would make the late comedian Rudy Ray Moore blush. And as if taunting Brown with words was not enough, Persia shakes her dildo in his face for reinforcement and John Brown retreats.

As Persia continues to taunt John Brown hoping he will challenge her to a freestyle duel, she uses the word "nigga." Her use of the forbidden word draws the attention of some of the other crew members such as Jus Rhyme. Jus Rhyme asked Persia to refrain from using the "n-word," citing the word's derogatory past. However, Persia continues to use the contested, racially charged word while stating that she is not using nigga in a racist way. For Persia, the word is a term of endearment that her "niggas" and she say to each other. Nevertheless, though unresolved, the verbal beef between Persia and John Brown soon comes to an end.

As a new day comes to Tha White House, Serch greets the crew. Having heard about Persia and John Brown's beef, the host commends Persia for "putting it down" in her verbal altercation with Brown. Moreover, he tells Persia that he has a special gift for her. For her continued use of the forbidden word, MC Serch surprises Persia with an overly large and extremely bulky "nigga" chain for her to rock (i.e., wear for twenty-four hours), while the crew spends the day at a miniature golf course. Over the course of the day, Persia becomes filled with sadness, embarrassment, and remorse for having used such language. Persia confessed to the crew, while leaving the golf course, that she had learned a valuable lesson and vowed not to use the n-word again.

The next day, the crew, split into two teams, is presented with a unique challenge to get them oriented to their new neighbors in the South Bronx. Each crew goes from door-to-door and introduces themselves by showcasing their rap skills for their neighbors. In the end, Persia's team, which consisted of Jus Rhyme, Sullee, G-Child, and Shamrock, received the best review. John Brown's team, which included Jon Boy, Misfit Dior, Dasit, and 100 Proof, was sent to the elimination round. Each member of John Brown's crew had to write a lyrical verse about his or her experiences earlier that day. Dasit refused to write a verse and thus set himself up for elimination by an angry MC Serch. As Dasit left Tha White House, a giant cockroach sprayed him with a can of Step Off!

White Rappers and the Appropriation of the African Practice of Naming

The above episode of *The White Rapper Show* demonstrates a variety of ways in which the white rappers appropriated their view of blackness on the show. Dines and Humez define appropriation as "the process whereby members of relatively privileged groups 'raid' the culture of marginalized groups, abstracting cultural practices or artifacts from their historically specific contexts."[10] The white rappers raid or co-opt the cultural practices or artifacts of African Americans in three areas: modes of language use (speech), modes of style, and modes of dress.

One of the most noticeable areas of cultural raiding among the white rappers involves the process of naming. From an Afrocentric perspective, nommo serves as the foundation for the creation of reality; it possesses the magical and generative power of the word manifested in the naming process. For example, when African American parents name their new baby girl Imani, she receives (1) an existence in the world and, equally important, (2) meaning—her name means faith. Naming is a powerful phenomenon of self-definition. Linguist Haig Bosmajian claims that "to receive a name is to be elevated to the status of a human being; without a name one's identity is questionable."[11]

Asante asserts that nicknames, for example, make powerful markers of an "African presence in the 'sounding-sense' of black America. Almost all young men and women receive nicknames at an early age and these names typically designate one's physical appearance (e.g., Red...), character (e.g., Bull, Slick...), or relationship (e.g. Buddy, Bro' Boy...)." So, naming is not a casual act in African diaspora cultures. It represents a significant process in which one's name becomes the embodiment of certain characteristics important within a community.[12]

Moreover, the name that one chooses locates the user in a particular ideological position. As Asante states, "my attempt is always to locate a situation, an event, an author. Location tells you where someone is, that is, where they are standing....Thus, the person who uses terms like minority, third world, primitives, natives, and mainstream is definitely in a particular intellectual space."[13]

Upon close examination, the ten white contestants on *The White Rapper Show* all adopted names that functioned to both mask (true) Eurocentric identity and perpetuate whiteness by validating white popular cultural icons or images. For example, within the colonized cultural space of the contrived television show, the white rapper Jon Wetz masks a Eurocentric identity behind his nickname Jon Boy. White privilege makes this phenomenon possible. "White privilege is like an invisible weightless knapsack of special provisions, assurances, tools, maps, guides, codebooks, passports, visas, clothes, compass, emergency gear, and blank checks" that are implicitly granted. [14] Thus, Jon Wetz's Jon Boy, and Lateticia Guzman's Misfit Dior permits them the ability to conceal their real Eurocentric identity, and claim a "special provision," (i.e., "We support hip hop culture *financially*, and have a *right* [author's emphasis] to participate in our investment any way we like.") status of privilege that, in the end, allows them to give the appearance through their use of the strategy of appropriation that they are "true believers" of the hip hop faith. In reality, they are not and their actions of co-optation, which further the cause of maintaining structures of white domination and white supremacy, say so.

The second function that the naming process serves for the white rappers is the perpetuation of whiteness through self-definition. Several of the rapper's names are located in historical and cultural space concerning Eurocentric culture. Greg Kaysen, aka John Brown, has a nickname that connects him to the radical abolitionist and insurrectionist John Brown who led a raid of men, both black and white, on the federal armory at Harper's Ferry in 1859. Laeticia Guzman, aka Misfit Dior, chose a name that cleverly pays homage to Christian Dior, the French fashion designer who during World War II dressed the wives of Nazi officers and French collaborators. Jon Wetz's alias, Jon Boy, links him with John-Boy Walton of the 1970s hit television show, *The Waltons*. On the show, the character, John-Boy Walton, illustrates a thinker, writer, and very humble country boy that lived with his family on Walton's Mountain in Virginia throughout the Great Depression and World War II. Timothy Rasmussen, better known as

Shamrock, has a stage name that locates him within the confines of Irish culture and Irish luck, that is, the dollar sign symbol in his name. In the end Rasmussen proves the victor by winning the contest. And finally, Chuck Baker's, aka 100 Proof, has a name that is a shout out to grain alcohol and moonshine whiskey and locates him in the space occupied by the alternative rockers (he has a rock band) and grunge cultists.

The above nicknames are important for two reasons. The names (1) validate white cultural icons or practices, that is, drinking grain 100 proof alcohol; and (2) the meaning(s) and symbolism associated with the cultural icons or practices are transferred to the white rappers. The propaganda technique called transfer "seeks to 'carry over the authority, sanction and prestige of something we respect and revere [white cultural icons and practices] to something [the white rapper] would have us accept."[15] So, for example, the brave, bold, and rebellious behaviors and attitudes associated with the insurrectionist John Brown are transferred to Greg Kaysen. In so doing, Kaysen claims that, like the historical figure, John Brown, his behavior, and attitude are bold and rebellious; Kaysen finds these attributes necessary if, like John Brown, he is to lead a white "insurrection" against the multiethnic forces that have dominated hip hop culture. Coupled with John Brown's credibility, Kaysen becomes a Lone Ranger for the cause of whiteness bent on keeping the hip hop natives in check.

Another good example of the use of the transfer techniques involves rapper Jon Wertz aka Jon Boy. As the main character in the television series that ran from 1973 to 1981 on the Columbia Broadcast Station (CBS), John-Boy Walton opened and closed each show as narrator. Given the social upheaval of the 1970s, the show grew in popularity because of the emphasis *The Waltons* placed on the importance of family and 1930s/1940s white conservative and Christian values that, in the end, gave older television viewers of the era a sense of normalcy as well as nostalgia. In the end, *The Waltons* represented the embodiment of an American value system that privileged whiteness (*note*: there was only one person of color on the show).

It is precisely this value system that transfers to Jon Wertz. On the show Wertz asserts that, like John-Boy Walton, he is an old fashion country boy (who really hails from rural Reedville, Virginia) with good white American conservative values; these values are important for Wertz to have if he is to survive the "liberal onslaught of multiculturalism" that permeates throughout the recording industry and hip hop culture specifically. Equipped with Jon Boy's credibility, Wertz perpetuates a conservative voice of reason and common sense in a cultural climate run amuck.

A final example of the use of the transfer technique involves rapper Laeticia Guzman, aka Misfit Dior. Guzman chose an interesting tag. While the "Misfit" part of the name speaks to Guzman as a British female trying to make her way in the rap game, dominated by African American males, the "Dior" is the more interesting aspect of her nickname for the purpose of analysis. Clearly, she references Christian Dior, the famed French couturier. Moreover, Dior was one of the twentieth century's most influential designers. He faced many hardships and setbacks, but possessed the determination to follow his dream of becoming a fashion designer regardless of the challenges. Dior symbolized wealth, power, prestige, individualism, sophistication, and elegance: the embodiment of Old World or European success undergirded with white privilege.

Rugged individualism, power, prestige, sophistication, and elegance are the attributes that are transferred to Laeticia Guzman. Now Guzman can insert a level of prestige, sophistication, and elegance into the rap game in general and *The White Rapper Show* specifically. Moreover, these attributes only work to reinforce Guzman's conventional looks (a 27-year-old blond), sex appeal, and Barbie-doll physique. And while Guzman can rap, the credibility garnered from Dior coupled with her good looks and sexiness ensures that she, as a British female, can use the seductive and sexual power of white femininity (as historically has been the case) to advance her music career, which, in the end, furthers the cause of white supremacy.

The above analysis clearly demonstrates that the white contestants on *The White Rapper Show* understand the power associated with the appropriation of the African naming process. For the contestants, the names selected are intentionally racialized. They are tag reminders to the audience and to themselves that they are whites performing and appropriating the Other. The nicknames analyzed become more than merely stage names used while freestyling or deejaying. Names such as John Brown, Misfit Dior, and Jon Boy, represent, in the words of Asante, "markers of identity."[16] The names and locations occupied by the Guzman, Wertz, and Kaysen symbolize, despite their so-called love for hip hop culture, still spaces of whiteness.

In addition to the appropriation of language practices (i.e., the naming process), the contestants on *The White Rapper Show* also co-opted African American styles of speech. Linguist Geneva Smitherman posits, "style refers to the way speakers put sounds and grammatical structure together to communicate meaning in a larger context. Put another way, language is the words, style is what you do with the words."[17] And what do speakers do with words? Scholar Evelyn Dandy states that African American speakers use words for dramatic repetition, call-response, signification, and improvisation. [18]

As mentioned earlier in the synopsis of the episode, Persia and John Brown have a verbal altercation. Persia calls out John Brown challenging him to a freestyle bout because she doubts his rapping skills. John Brown refuses to engage her and the following dialogue takes place:

Persia: "I don't like you!"
JohnBrown: "Get yo weight up, not yo hate up!"
Persia: "You got to have skills for me to hate you!"
Persia: "John Brown is the bitch and the clown of 'da' house. I got a dildo in my draw
and I'm goin' put it in his f—— mouth!"
JohnBrown: "Halleluiah holla back!!"
Persia: "Holla at these nuts, bitch!!"
JohnBrown: "I got too much game!"
Persia: "You got game?!" Baby, spit it!! Spit it!!" "I'll give you saliva to spit it with,
you dry mouth slut!!"[19]

While both Persia and John Brown appropriate the use of signification, Persia effectively uses it the best as a rhetorical knife in the above verbal interaction with Brown. Signification, according to Smitherman, is a mode of discourse that "refers to the verbal art of insult in which a speaker humorously puts down, talks about, needles [or otherwise] signifies on-the listener."[20] The above dialogue clearly shows that Persia's put down of John Brown is beyond being humorous. Persia's discourse comes as an all-out verbal assault on Brown, highlighted by her use of rhythm, slang, and expletives; she, in essence, played not just the dozens, but she played the (dirty) dozens with Brown specifically because of her use of the expletives. Hecht, Jackson, and Ribeau claim that playing the dozens "is an aggressive contest sometimes using obscene language in which the goal is to demonstrate verbal prowess by having the quickest, wittiest comeback insults."[21] In the end, both Persia and John Brown demonstrated, through co-opting signification: (1) verbal dexterity, which is a proficient and skillful use of word play, (2) the ability to maintain a level of coolness under pressure, and (3) lyrical spontaneity—skills needed for rapping and a historic part of black verbal popular culture.

White people tend to avoid confrontation, so the irony of the verbal duel between Persia and John Brown surfaces.[22] Generally, whites believe that words, coupled with hostile and aggressive behavior, can potentially lead to a fight or some type of violent confrontation. In the book, *Black and White Styles in Conflict*, Kochman asserts that "Whites tend to see the public expression of hostility as a point on a words–actions continuum: angry verbal exchanges, if not stopped, will inevitably escalate into violence. Within this conception, hostile words and hostile acts become different forms of the same thing-fighting."[23]

It is clear, both verbally and nonverbally, that John Brown responded to Persia's use of signifying practices in the more preferred conflict style that exists among whites. Throughout the interaction, John Brown never communicated in an aggressive manner nor did he use any expletives in his speech. As Persia got closer and closer to his face, he merely moved away while retorting with a "halleluiah holla back" or ghetto revival shout out. John Brown's use of signification possessed more humor and had less sting. No doubt, Brown, after having a sexual toy shoved in his face believed the possible potential for violence and thus took a nonconfrontational stance with Persia. In the final analysis, "direct confrontation [was] viewed by [John Brown] as a sign of instability, with the possibility that [Persia] might punch [him]."[24]

Persia and the Appropriation of Black (Hip Hop) Masculinity

Not only did Persia demonstrate a strong presence in the verbal interaction with John Brown, but she demonstrated that same presence and more throughout the show and the entire run of the series. Of all the contestants, Persia appears the most vocal and has the more dominant personality, thus taking on the seeming characteristics of masculinity. She likely honed this attitude growing up on the streets of Queens, New York, where life was tough and gritty for the young female rapper. Adopting a hard-core, yet cool image became necessary for her survival on the streets and in the rap game. In order to survive, Persia appropriated various aspects of black masculinity to hold it down in the streets and maintain her credibility as a serious female emcee. Persia has culturally raided black masculine hip hop culture in three ways: (1) adoption of the cool pose; (2) use of the n-word; and (3) adoption of nonverbal styling.

One of the black masculine behaviors that Persia co-opted is the notion of cool pose. According to psychologist Richard Majors and sociologist Janet Billson, "cool pose is a ritualized form of masculinity that entails behaviors, scripts, physical posturing, impression management, and carefully crafted performances that deliver a single, critical message: pride, strength, and control."[25] Persia became the embodiment of cool pose when she engaged John Brown in the verbal interaction previously discussed. Despite being overly agitated by Brown and his king of the burbs behavior, Persia maintained a level of coolness even in the mist of playing the (dirty) dozens with John Brown. Persia's cool pose persona allowed her to hit Brown with her words and not with her fist or vibrator. After all, that is what keeping it real emcees do—they battle each other with words. Therefore, Persia demonstrated her strength as a fierce competitor and that she had the ability to maintain control of the situation whether battling an opponent on the mike or in a verbal interaction.

In addition to the appropriation of the cool pose persona, Persia also uses derogatory, racially charged language in her interaction with John Brown. Specifically, she uses the word nigga to maintain her street credibility in the eyes of the other contestants and to keep it real. Her language, however, offended Jus Rhyme. The argument that African American masculine rappers who liberally use nigga are just keeping it real is still a controversial issue in hip hop culture.[26] Nevertheless, for Persia, this term is strictly one of endearment; she tells Jus Rhyme that "all the people that are close to me at home are niggas." In his book, *Nigger: The Strange Career of a Troublesome Word*, Randall Kennedy provides some clarity about the use of nigger in various manifestations when he suggests that "as a linguistic landmark, "nigger" is being renovated…Whites are increasingly referring to other Whites as niggers, and indeed, the term both as an insult and as a sign of affection is being affixed to people of all sorts."[27] Both spellings of the word, regardless of connotation, present loaded meanings. Although Persia seemed oblivious to this initially, she is made aware of the volatility of the word during the show.

Interesting enough, Persia's awareness of the volatile and harmful nature of the n-word comes about from wearing the bling given to her by Serch. It can be argued that Persia's blatant jewelry is a form of appropriation that serves three important functions. First, the pendant reinforces Persia's verbal use of the term; secondly, the hip hop cultural practice of blinging is co-opted by Persia and finally the appropriation of the n-word, verbally and more importantly, nonverbally, creates a burden for the wearer. As a direct result of her having to carry nigga as an albatross of shame and humiliation around her neck for everyone to see, Persia encounters a newfound awareness. Ultimately, Persia realized that saying as well as blinging the n-word was too great of a burden for a person, whether white or black, to have to bear in society.

Nonverbal styling is the final area of appropriation carried out by Persia. Denoting characteristics of black masculinity, Majors and Billson assert that nonverbal styling involves the use of clothing, gestures, "body stance, hand-shakes, and eyework that communicates in a controlled and purposive fashion" and expresses one's sense of identity.[28] While arguing with John Brown, Persia demonstrates some very strong eyework. Specifically, she cuts her eyes at Brown in order to visually convey her anger and disgust with his refusal to engage her in a freestyle battle.

In addition to cutting her eyes at John Brown, Persia also co-opts a version or derivative of the standing stance. The standing stance is a stationary position whereby usually an "African American male stands with his arms folded some-times diagonally across his chest and intensely stares at the teacher or another authority figure. This stance translates as 'I'm bad and I know I'm bad.' "[29] When Persia taunted John Brown with the dildo, she at times stood literally in his face with her hands shaking the sex toy or with her hands perched down at her side. As she encroached upon John Brown's personal space, he retreated. Therefore Persia's act of defiance, that was communicated in her co-opted stance, signaled that she had won the nonverbal showdown with John Brown—the so-called musical insurrectionist.

In *The White Rapper Show*, Persia represents the major culprit of cultural raid-ing. Not only does she appropriate styles of speech through playing the dozens and signification, in an effort to enhance her stature as a female emcee in a male dominated arena, but she also appropriates black male hip hop masculinity in the previously stated ways. Furthermore, Persia can lay claim to the idea that a white female rapper who masterfully co-opts African American male masculinity is a better or more authentic rapper, by and large, than even the best black male rapper. This sort of thinking is best sized-up as the Eminem phenomenon, that is, white America's quest for the great White hope of rap music who will defend and ultimately usher in an artistic takeover of the music industry from its black inhabitants.

Like rapper/producer Dr. Dre's validation of Eminem, legendary rapper Grandmaster Flash, and other African American males, during the meet the neighbors portion of the episode, validate the white female's rap skills. Hip hop activist Harry Allen has labeled this validation of white rap artists by credible rap artists, entertainers, etc. as black facilitation of white development (BFWD), which is the notion that "Black people, often at great cost to themselves, work to again, improve White people."[30] By black rappers and community members on *The White Rapper Show* telling Persia that she has great rap skills and by assist-ing her in her efforts to be even better, black folks participate in and perpetuate a hegemonic discourse that keeps white performances of blackness firmly intact.

The Appropriation of Hip Hop Dress on *The White Rapper Show*

In addition to language and style, the final area of appropriation involves modes of dress. In the same way that words represent markers of cultural identity, clothes as a sign and language system, can also signify cultural meaning.[31] For example, the afro and the dashiki worn by African Americans during the socially conscious 1960s, was a marker of an identity rooted in self-love and self-determination, and further grounded in black cultural nationalist thought. Moreover, the natural hairstyle was such a powerful symbol of racial pride and antiestablishment, that the young white female radicals during the 1960s and 1970s imitated the ethnic hairdo by sporting their "Jewish Afro."[32] Similarly, by the late 1970s, actress Bo Derek, in the movie, *10* made wearing braids and cornrows popular among white women who could afford the hairstyle.[33]

In *The White Rapper Show*, two of the three female rappers, G-Child and Persia, appropriate black female hairstyles. Misfit Dior does not appropriate any African American hairstyle or any from hip hop culture. This could be because the appropriation of a cultural hairstyle would conflict with her Barbie-doll look and designer fashion taste. At the other end of the spectrum, G-Child co-opts the hairstyle and dress made popular by African American female rapper Da Brat, who reigned as one of the top black female rappers in the late 1990s with her debut album, *Funkdafied*. G-Child's hair is braided; two braids of equal length hang down in the front of her head while two braids of the same length hang down in the back. Her trademark hairstyle, as she calls it, was also worn and popularized by West Coast rappers such as Snoop Doggy Dogg, and Xzibit. In addition to the braids like Da Brat, G-Child also wore oversized gear, baggy jeans, and tennis shoes that deemphasized her gender and reinforced a "butch" look and more of a b-boy swagger.

Persia co-opts the wavy hair look, which gives her a more exotic and ethnic feel. Moreover, the wavy brunette hair, coupled with the sexy facial features, gives her the appearance of a video vixen who could easily make *Smooth* magazine's annual "Smooth Girl 100" list, and thus plays up her ethnic background and looks of the hot-blooded Italian femme. Even her nickname conjures up an image of a female with an exotic persona. The only time Persia does not look like a video vixen is when she appropriates the wearing of the baseball cap. The baseball cap is a major artifact in hip hop culture that, when worn to the side and slightly over the eyes, symbolizes a hardcore image. As a note, Persia wore a baseball cap with a four-leaf clover on it when she played the dozens with John Brown suggesting that she was going to come hard at Brown with her verbal assault because she had both skill and luck on her side.

Most of the male contestants, except for 100 Proof who wore a mohawk, all appropriated the short hair, close cut to the head look popularized by rappers such as the Beastie Boys and Eminem, but which has its roots in black male hair culture. All of the haircuts appear to be a variation of the haircut called the fade where the hair is cut skin-tight (hair is cut low to the skin of the head or all off) on the sides of the head and then cut short on top. In addition to the haircuts, some of the white rappers wore matching camouflage-colored shirts and ban-danas (Jus Rhyme), grills (Shamrock), and baseball caps (John Brown).

Dress, like nicknames, is important to hip hop culture because it helps iden-tify the wearer of the clothing or owner of the name as a participant in the hip hop community. Moreover, these nonverbal artifacts—hair, baseball caps, grills—have persuasive power that communicate to recipients in the rap music community that the wearer is down with the music and, equally important, the culture. Through the strategy of appropriation, the white rappers on *The White Rapper Show* are able to keep it real.

The Appropriation of Blackness

The White Rapper Show clearly demonstrated the appropriation or mimetic representation of African Americans within hip hop culture. As contestants tried to emulate the rhythm, syncopation, energy, and verse of mainstream rap, they also signaled a negotiation of their own identities as urban, suburban, and non-American white youth trying to appear authentic within a hip hop context that a mostly black artistry has popularized. *The White Rapper Show* raises many issues such as whether it is okay for whites to not only listen to and be a fan of hip hop music, but also to perform it? Another question is whether one can be comfortable as a non-black person performing hip hop? Perhaps Eminem has answered that question many times over. While the hip hop community has accepted him as a bona fide rapper he rarely attempts to be black. *The White Rapper Show* leaves audiences with the impression that the only way to portray an authentic rapper is to try to appropriate blackness first. Of course this unravels all sorts of problems related to identity politics and otherness. In order to be black, one has to first define the black essence, package it, and then perform it authentically. This presumes there is only one way to be black and the show suggests there is only one way to be a rapper, and these are synonymous. Furthermore, as the meet the neighbors segment demonstrates the primary way to authenticate good rap skills is to ask any random African American person walking down the street whether "you're doing it right," as if all black people know how to rap and are adequate purveyors of rap competence.

There are two ways in which one may view *Ego Trip's The (White) Rapper Show*—as a bad joke or as a symbolic visual text indicative of the status of rap and hip hop music. On the one hand one may view the show as a bad joke that under no circumstances should be taken seriously, and hence serve as merely comic relief. Some viewers believed that the contestants were not very good rappers and did not deserve to be on the show. These viewers saw the show as a huge farce that was out to make white people look silly. Various Internet posts either lambasted the show and its utter contrivance or found the reality competition believable and enjoyable.

However, there is a second way in which to critically read *The White Rapper Show*. This analysis reveals that while it may appear at first glance that the show is a farce and has no redeeming value, this could not be further from the truth. The truth of the matter is that *The White Rapper Show* is a very serious piece of Eurocentric media propaganda that must be taken serious if for no other reason than its appropriation of the African naming process used to promote white cultural icons and thus whiteness. As suggested, the naming process has meaning and power in the African oral tradition. Naming, via the power of nommo—the magical and generative power of the word, brings a phenomenon into existence and gives that phenomenon meaning. The example given at the beginning of this essay was the name Imani, an African name, which means faith, and gives the baby girl an existence by offering a meaningful name.

This is an important point. Had the white rappers on the show chose African names to appropriate, their true intentions would have been less dubious. Moreover, had the rappers chose to co-opt names such as Faith Evans, African Bambaataa, or Tupac Shakur, the white rappers would have been able to make a better case for truly loving hip hop and being down with the art form. Indeed, it would take a special white person to have an African name and survive the comments, criticisms, and put-downs from his/her fellow whites. For white people to truly bear the burden of appropriating an African name would cause scholars of African American popular culture to rethink the authenticity debate in hip hop culture.

Nevertheless, this is merely wishful thinking because white rappers, such as John Brown and Misfit Dior, chose to appropriate the African naming process in order to pick a Eurocentric name that would promote whiteness and further the cause of white supremacy. Not only are white cultural icons such as insurrectionist John Brown and fashion designer Christian Dior validated, but more importantly, Greg Kaysen and Laeticia Guzman are empowered with the cultural attributes of their white heroes. Kaysen and Guzman are ready to invade the rap industry and take it over; Guzman will woo the black rappers and industry executives with her sex appeal and business savvy until Kaysen can lead the insurrection on the music industry's executives.

Despite existing in the "age of Obama," and the cultural backlash that still exists, the white fascination with African American cultural production will continue. There is a sort of voyeuristic desire related to the black Other. The distancing and desire work to fuel this racial gaze but perhaps also to appropriate African American culture in order to lay claim to one of its most potent popular dimensions—its music. In the book, *Stupid White Men and Other Sorry Excuses for the State of the Nation,* filmmaker Michael Moore says that white people love to appropriate African American culture because they love the way that lack people express themselves and try, for example, their "darndest to 'Be like [Michael Jordan].' Of course the operative word there is *like,* because no matter how many millions he makes, to *be* Mike would mean spending an awful lot of time pulled over on the New Jersey Turnpike."[34] Moore is suggesting here that, in the final analysis for white people, it is about maintaining their whiteness because the burden to be black is too great.

Notes

1. Cameron McCarthy, "Living with Anxiety: Race and the Renarration of Public Life," in *White Reign: Deploying Whiteness in America,* ed. Joe Kincheloe, Shirley Steinberg, Nelson Rodriguez, and Ronald Chenault (New York: St. Martin's Press, 1991), 329–42.

2. About *Ego Trip's (White) Rapper Show,* 2010, accessed March 5, 2010, http://www.vh1.com/shows/white_rapper/series.jhtml#moreinfro.

3. David Roediger, "White without End? The Abolition of Whiteness, or the Rearticulation of Race," in *Race Struggles,* ed. Theodore Koditschek, Sundiata Cha-Jua, and Helen Neville (Urbana, IL: University of Illinois Press, 2009), 98–110.

4. Ronald Jackson, *Scripting the Black Masculine Body in Popular Media* (Albany: SUNY Press, 2006), 36.

5. Michael Taussig, *Mimesis and Alterity: A Particular History of the Senses* (New York: Routledge, 1993), 101.

6. Molefi K. Asante, *Malcolm X as Cultural Hero & Other Afrocentric Essays* (Trenton, NJ: African World Press, Inc., 1993), 100.

7. Charles U. Larson, *Persuasion: Reception and Responsibility* (Belmont, CA: Wadsworth/Thomson Learning, 2001), 323.

8. About *Ego Trip.*

9. Ibid.

10. Gail Dines and Jean McMahon Humez, eds. *Gender, Race and Class in Media: A Text-Reader* (Thousand Oaks, CA: SAGE Publications, 1195), 567.

11. Haig A. Bosmajian, *The Language of Oppression* (Lanham, MD: University Press of America, 1983), 2.

12. Molefi K. Asante, *The Afrocentric Idea* (Philadelphia: Temple University Press, 1987), 72–74.

13. Molefi K. Asante, *Malcolm X as Cultural Hero & Other Afrocentric Essays* (Trenton, NJ: African World Press, Inc., 1993), 100.

14. Peggy McIntosh, "White Privilege and Male Privilege: A Personal Account of Coming to See Correspondences through the Work in Women's Studies," in *Race, Class, and Gender: An Anthology,* ed. Margaret Andersen and Patricia Hill Collins (Belmont, CA: Wadsworth Publishing Company, 1992).

15. Charles U. Larson, *Persuasion: Reception and Responsibility* (Belmont, CA: Wadsworth/Thomson Learning, 2001), 323.

16. Asante, *Malcolm X as Cultural Hero,* 100.

17. Geneva Smitherman, *Talkin and Testifyin: The Language of Black America* (Detroit: Wayne State University Press, 1977), 16.

18. Evelyn B. Dandy, *Black Communication: Breaking Down the Barriers* (Chicago: African American Images, 1991), 12–13.

19. *Ego Trip's (White) Rapper Show,* season 1, episode 1, directed by Mike L. Taylor, aired January 8, 2007, on VH1.

20. Smitherman, 118.

21. Michael L. Hecht, Ronald L. Jackson, and Sidney A. Ribeau, *African American Communication: Exploring Identity and Culture* (Mahwah, NJ: Lawrence Erlbaum Associates, Publishers, 2003), 164.

22. Christian Lander, *Stuff White People Like: The Definitive Guide to the Unique Taste of Millions* (New York: Random House Trade Paperback, 2008), 171.

23. Thomas Kochman, *Black and White Styles in Conflict* (Chicago: University of Chicago Press, 1981), 48.

24. Christian Lander, *Stuff White People Like: The Definitive Guide to the Unique Taste of Millions* (New York: Random House Trade Paperback, 2008), 173.

25. Richard Majors and Janet Mancini Billson, *Cool Pose: The Dilemmas of Black Manhood in America* (New York: Touchstone, 1992), 4.

26. Jabari Asim, *The N Word: Who Can Say It, Who Shouldn't and Why* (New York: Houghton Mifflin, 2007), 222.

27. Randall Kennedy, *Nigger: The Strange Career of a Troublesome Word* (New York: Pantheon Books, 2002), 174.
28. Majors and Billson, 73.
29. Dandy, 64–65.
30. Harry Allen, "The Unbearable Whiteness of Emceeing: What the Eminence of Eminem says about Race," *Source*, February 2003, 92, accessed July 15, 2010, http://www.harryallen.info/docs/TheUnbearableWhitenessofEmceeing.pdf
31. Allison Lurie, *The Language of Clothes* (New York: Vintage Books, 1981), 3–36.
32. Ibid., 100.
33. Ibid.
34. Michael Moore, *Stupid White Men and Other Sorry Excuses for the State of the Nation* (New York: Regan Books, 2001), 66.

3

Cash Rules Everything around Me: Appropriation, Commodification, and the Politics of Contemporary Protest Music and Hip Hop

Diarra Osei Robertson

In 2006 Nas released an album entitled *Hip Hop Is Dead*, sparking widespread debate among music enthusiasts and scholars about the current state of hip hop. Nas, in subsequent interviews, indicated that the title was not to be viewed literally and it was chosen to provoke debate among listeners. The current state of hip hop is one that critics both inside and outside the academy have debated over the past fifteen years. Some observers lament the hypercommericialization of the music in the mainstream, with a consistent focus on negative and stereotypical imagery, while others point to the global appropriation of the genre and a fear that the African American urban roots of the music will be lost. These concerns are a result of a complex mix of factors, including industry factors, appropriation, and moderate political context that have significantly transformed the genre over the past twenty years.

This study explores how cultural appropriation and industrial incorporation have impacted and influenced the growth of hip hop over the past twenty years (from the golden age to the present). The research is divided into three parts. The first section reviews some of the theoretical dynamics that guide this study as it relates to both cultural production and appropriation. The second part examines how the appropriative process combined with industry forces have altered hip hop over the past two decades. One of central concerns of many scholars is hip hop's role as potential subversive voice or mobilization asset within the political process. The final section of this study delineates some recent examples of the genre's activity in contemporary politics.

Cultural Significance

Toward the turn of the last century, more social scientists began investigating the sociopolitical significance of culture.[1] Claims of universal reason or knowledge are now seen in a context dependent on cultural and political factors. As a result, positions advanced by dominant groups are not only seen as culturally dependent, but also politically biased. Regarding this relationship, political scientist Lisa Wedeen suggests that "[p]olitics is not merely about material interests but also about the contest over the symbolic world, over the management and appropriation of meaning. Regimes attempt to control and manipulate the symbolic world, just as they attempt to control material resources or to construct institutions for enforcement and punishment."[2] Responding to these assaults, many oppressed groups have sought to reclaim their stolen past. In this regard, cultural production can serve as counterhegemonic narratives for oppressed people.[3]

From an Africana perspective, Harold Cruse also viewed culture as a system of meaning that needed to be modified for the purpose of African American advancement. He suggested that a critical shortcoming of black leadership has been their inability to integrate political, economic, and cultural elements into one program. Similar to contemporary Afrocentric authors, he viewed culture a critical first step grounding political and economic efforts. It was the lack of a cultural foundation, in his opinion, that undermined the movements of the 1960s. A key factor in Cruse's reasoning is the view that culture serves a key socializing role; it defines identity. He argues that culture should be created for aesthetic and institutional purposes.[4] Like some contemporary identity theorists, Cruse was aware of the role of socialization and identity in group politics. While people do make rationally based decisions, the decisions are often filtered through a cultural matrix of beliefs and historical experiences. Cruse saw culture serving as a key binding mechanism, and a foundation from which critical analyses must be based.

Counter to Cruse, W. E. B. Du Bois focused on the role of cultural production as a component for improving the conditions of African Americans. Du Bois's solution to the "Negro problem" was for those possessing skills—the middle class or black elite—to serve in a leadership role for the black community to elevate themselves as a whole. One of the roles of the "talented tenth" was to cultivate African American culture.[5] Regarding this role, philosopher Ernest Allen suggests that "it was the concern of late 19th-century blacks who, first of all, possessed the reflective capacity as well as the time to reflect; who refused to view the world through imposed categorical blinders; and who, constrained by the absence of possibilities for direct political struggle…, chose as their principle battleground the domain of culture."[6] His view of culture was not simple folk culture, but the elevation of black culture to the tribute status of high culture. Black intellectuals were to embrace this culture, as they should also embrace attempts at autonomous institution building. "It is likely," historian Sterling Stuckey posits, "that he [Du Bois] wanted to work out an autonomous aesthetic, one independent of European values and enabling black writers to contribute to the liberation of their people."[7] A key concern of the early twentieth-century thinkers was the need to demonstrate, in a number of areas, that blacks were not inferior to Europeans. Du Bois felt that cultural production was an essential area where African Americans could demonstrate their humanness. By building and fostering African American cultural production blacks could improve their position in society, and continue the political struggle of demonstrating their humanness to whites.

Du Bois's cultural advocacy focused on art as propaganda in the service of group interest. The propaganda created by artists may not ultimately threaten the system, but their artistic works would contribute to the general atmosphere of dissident culture. Works of poetry or music often contribute to the aggregate cultural system from which ideological or organizational formations emerge. The work of popular artists, moreover, can contribute greatly to the levels of oppositional consciousness in a movement. In terms of interpretative positions, Barbara Harlow offers some important insights into this process. She sets her sights specifically on political forms of poetry and literature. From her vantage point, these authors serve a pivotal role in resistance movements. Poems evoke battle cries and new cultural practices, while narratives connect with the past "in order to open up possibilities of future."[8] This mirrors the positions of historian Robin D. G. Kelley who highlights the importance of these cultural forms. He avers: "progressive social movements do not simply produce statistics and narratives of oppression; rather, the best ones do what great poetry always does: transport us to another place, compel us to relive horrors and, more importantly, enable us to imagine a new society."[9] Thus, cultural production contributes to this matrix of meaning and symbols around which movement activists may mobilize.

Appropriation and Commodification

Counter to the ideals that some cultural theorists advance, musicians are not independent agents in producing their music, as they have to incorporate the goals and objectives of record companies during the creative process. The appropriation of black culture is conducted primarily for financial reasons, whereby art is transformed into a commodity that can be packaged and sold. It is important to locate this process within the structural environment of late capitalism and Western hegemony, where cultural appropriation represents another institutional mechanism that perpetuates inequality between superordinate and subordinate groups. Like all capitalist endeavors, particularly in popular music, the focus on is on profitability, not the authentic or creative elements of the music. Many scholars suggest that the commodification (the mass marketing and production of a commodity) process eliminates or negates the fundamental truth(s) that art is meant to represent. Cultural theorist and activist Amiri Baraka, for example, asserts that "commerce wants art as commodity, not feeling and intelligence."[10] Critical theorist Herbert Marcuse argued that culture loses its "subversive force" and "destructive content" when it is incorporated "into the established order" and reproduced on a mass scale.[11]

The negative effects of commodification that Marcuse and Baraka discuss can be closely linked to the appropriation process. Appropriation is a process of a nongroup member employing the culture of another group in the cultural production. In his discussion of offensive types of cultural appropriation, James Young delineates three forms of cultural appropriation, of which two are pertinent to this study: subject and content appropriation. "Subject appropriation occurs when an outsider represents members or aspects of another culture."[12] Conversely, content appropriation occurs "when an artist uses another culture in the production of his or her own art....Sometimes, the content appropriated is not an entire work of art but rather a style or motif. " Examples of subject appropriation in contemporary music would include white rhythm and blues artists like Joss Stone, Amy Winehouse, or Adele, while an example of content appropriation is Linkin Park, the rock-rap band that uses lyrical techniques of a rapper, or an artist like Kid Rock.

Appropriation within itself may not be offensive to members of the native culture, as it all depends on the context. For example, the architects of early rock 'n' roll such as Little Richard and Chuck Berry were less concerned with the fact that white musicians were playing their music, but rather with an environment in which white rock musicians such as Jerry Lee or Elvis Presley received more recognition or financial gain than black artists. While some may complain about issues of misrepresentation or reifying stereotypes, the most salient factor when it comes to appropriation is financial. On the matter Fung laments that "if there were huge numbers of prospering non-white artists producing culture in their own terms, a white person's appropriation would be insignificant."[13] Power relations are a critical part of the discussion because they often dictate the terms of representation of the Other, particularly through the process of mass commodification. It is important to remember that when one begins examining the arts, the majority of artists when they begin their careers have for a variety of reasons that have nothing to do with sociopolitical issues, and several become entertainers for strictly financial reasons. Sunaina Maira notes, "Hip hop culture may in some instances be oppositional or subversive, but it is always engaged with the realm of commerce, as are other forms of popular culture that are marketed, distributed, and consumed."[14] When one looks at the legacy of iconic black labels from Motown to Def Jam the goal of the record executives was to maximize profit, not produce protest music.

Artist Types

For the purposes of this study, one may distinguish between three types of artists: activist-artist, sociopolitical artists, and contextual/occasional sociopolitical artists. Activist-artists are those artists whose cultural production supports or reinforces their political activism. Several artists operating during the black power period occupied this role, most notably people like Amiri Baraka and Emory Douglas. Although Baraka's (LeRoi Jones) career began as a writer producing "art for art's sake," in the early years of the Black Power Movement he became fully immersed in sociopolitical cultural production. Emory Douglas occupied a similar role with the Black Panther Party. Douglas was the primary visual artist who contributed art to the Black Panther newspaper. In the examples of Baraka and Douglas, both artists used their art for political purposes, and they were also actively involved in groups pursuing political-economic strategies. This first category may be distinguished from sociopolitical artists, who produced culture with political themes, but their careers are not defined by full-time activism. For example, Gil Scott-Heron falls into this category because the bulk his music in the 1970s explored sociopolitical themes, but he was not a political actor in the events of the period. This is not to suggest, however, that such artists may not participate or contribute to an organization or cause, but that these activities serve a secondary function to their careers as entertainers.

The final analytical category—popular/occasional sociopolitical artists—represents the primary focus of this study. People like Stevie Wonder, Marvin Gaye, and Bill Withers occupy this area, as their cultural production is not defined by sociopolitical commentary. Although Stevie Wonder's "You Haven't Done Nothing" and "Happy Birthday" represent classic songs with deep sociopolitical meaning, Stevie Wonder is more popularly known for love songs such as "Ribbon in Sky," "You and I," and "Overjoyed." It is important to differentiate between artists who regularly engage in sociopolitical commentary and artists who occasionally weigh in on political issues. Marvin Gaye's "Mercy, Mercy, Me," Stevie Wonder's "You Haven't Done Nothing," or Bill Withers's "I Can't Write with My Left Hand" are examples of popular artists producing notable sociopolitical music, but none of these musicians careers have been defined by their sociopolitical commentary.

Appropriation, Commodification, and Hip Hop

Hip hop has evolved a great deal since its widespread urban radio beginnings in late 1970s. Hip hop in the new millennium has become a thorough part of popular culture. The current highest selling hip hop artist is Tupac with thirty-seven million units sold, and the top-selling album is *Speakerboxx/The Love Below* by Outkast with ten million albums sold. There was a time when artist like EPMD boasted about "going gold" (selling a half million albums), now hip hop accounts for the third largest amount of market share, behind rock and country, in sales.[15] In 1989 cultural critic and author Nelson George, commemorating hip hop's tenth birthday, noted "to proclaim the death of rap is…premature. But the farther the control of rap gets from its street-corner constituency and the more corporations grasp it—record conglomerates, Burger King and Minute Maid, *Yo! MTV Raps*, etc.—the more vulnerable it becomes to cultural emasculation."[16] While it is questionable whether this dire result has transpired, it is clear today that rap is employed by various corporate entities in marketing their products.

Since the mid-1980s artists have sought endorsement deals in a variety of areas. Run-DMC's contract with the shoe company Adidas was one of the first cases of rappers receiving support from a major corporation. By the 1990s several large corporations began embracing the broad commercial appeal of hip hop. For example, Dan Charnas chronicles how the decision of Sprite in 1994 to sign deals with several artists, under the "Obey Your Thirst" campaign, to market their product was a major development in the alignment of hip hop and corporate America. He notes that the deal was critical for two reasons. One, the company signed artists like Q-Tip and Pete Rock who had "authentic" street credibility, not rappers in the mold of the Fresh Prince (Will Smith). Secondly, the campaign was a huge financial success, making "Sprite the fastest growing soft-drink brand in America for two years straight."[17] It signaled to other corporations that hip hop had vast marketing potential and it mirrored, and eventually surpassed, pop music in its appeal to young consumers.

Like a golf or tennis player, popular hip hop artists have used endorsements to not only supplement their revenue from record sales and concerts, but in some cases significantly dwarf the money they receive from music. A more recent example may be seen in rapper 50 Cent's deal with Vitamin Water, where he owns 10 percent of the company (he initially purchased stock in the company Glaceau, but it was bought out by Coca-Cola) valued at $60–100 million. There are several other examples of the corporate embrace of hip hop and the appropriation of its culture into mainstream society. The question arises, nevertheless, whether this type of appropriation is negative or positive? While the commodification process has altered the nature of the music, these artists cannot be simply classified as passive actors being exploited by corporate interest. In the tradition of Def Jam Records cofounder Russell Simmons, many artists are becoming shrewd entrepreneurs with diverse investment portfolios.

Though the earnings of marquee artists like Jay Z or Little Wayne demonstrate how far hip hop has evolved, some argue that this process has come at a cost. When Sprite launched its "Obey Your Thirst" campaign it signed artists who were known for representing authentic or real hip hop. Today the artists who sign these types of deals—Drake or The Black Eye Peas, for example—are not viewed as representing the same constituency that earlier artists did. The perceived authenticity that artists like Gang Starr or Q-Tip represent has been sacrificed in exchange for certain forms of hip hop that lack the creative authenticity or consciousness that was present before. If one wishes to appeal to corporate America or pop culture, a shallower form of hip hop is necessary. Jay Z on his song "Moment of Clarity" acknowledges this dynamic as he raps: "I dumbed down for my audience to double my dollars/ They criticized me for it yet they all yell 'holla!'/ If skills sold, truth be told, I'd probably be lyrically, Talib Kweli. Truthfully I wanna rhyme like Common Sense/ But I did five mill'[million]—I ain't been rhymin like Common since."[18]

Whether or not Jay Z would be able to match the lyrical depths of artists like Kweli or Common is debatable, but his comments point to the influence of commodification where authenticity and creativity are sacrificed before the alter of capitalism. Some artists, like Mos Def(who has since changed his name to Yasiin Bey), argue that these forces have racial undertones. In response to a interviewer's question regarding the difference between being an artist and being a product, Mos Def suggests, "a lot of it is the manifestation of society and colonialism in the industry. Radiohead can be as avant-garde as they want and still have pop success, but if you're black you have surrender yourself to the flashing lights…There's a problem with those dudes man, they need to be chastised."[19] His comments indicate labels support the creative efforts of white artists but black artists do not receive such support without "dumbing down" the music. Without the presence of sociopolitical forces popular artists are not encouraged or motivated to engage in sociopolitical commentary or critiques of society today.

The sanctioning influence of the music industry is a dynamic that has long frustrated several musicians. Those rappers who seek engage in political commentary are often the ones who face the most obstacles from major labels. Lupe Fiasco is one of the few artists signed to a major label, Atlantic Records, who consistently creates music with sociopolitical content. His debut album *Food and Liquor* featured the song "American Terrorist," which highlights the contradictory history of America versus the modern idea of terrorism that is popularly portrayed. "Now if a Muslim woman strapped with a bomb on a bus/with the seconds running give you the jitters?/Just imagine a American-based Christian organization planning to poison water supplies to bring the second-coming quicker."[20] The conscious rapper also criticized the drive for shallow music by artists and the industry in his song "Dumb It Down." His aesthetic preferences led to tensions with Atlantic Records, as a later release *Lasers* was delayed for a number of years because of creative differences. In an interview from 2010, the artist alludes to these tensions. "The situation with me and my record company has gotten to the point where it's just like…we're really at our final straws."[21] Without acknowledging pressure from his record company, he understands a need to make his music more popular. "I was actually making my own music, in the studio making the songs, and rapping on them. And at the same time, making the music more acceptable. *Not making it more poppy, but making it more popular.* Putting it in the position where more people can understand it but at the same time still satisfy my hardcore fanbase."[22] His narrative is all too familiar in the music industry where artists who seek to be more creative or produce socially conscious music encounter several obstacles. To fully grasp the sanctioning influence of record companies and how they facilitate cultural appropriation it is necessary to examine some of the more salient dynamics of the music industry.

The Industry

The music industry is dominated by the Big Four—Sony, Time Warner, Universal, and Bertelsman—who account for more than 70 percent of market share in the music industry.[23] These companies are run by people who specialize in business and most instances care very little about the quality of music they produce. This leads to tremendous pressure on musicians to sell records with little concern for integrity. Moreover, because these companies are multimedia conglomerates they have a major influence on the distribution of the product via their relationships with radio, TV, and major retail outlets. Because of the size of these media entities the primary concern is not the quality of content but the profit margin of the product. New artists often sign contracts that offer them very little in terms of royalties, and most artists lose money when production costs are passed on to them (studio time, video cost, and touring fees). McLeod notes that "the vast majority of musicians do not make money from album sales, which end up benefitting a very, very small minority of artists like Madonna, Metallica, or Aerosmith."[24] There are several examples of artists going bankrupt, such as TLC, because they failed to keep track of the costs they were charged.

Some observers have suggested that the artist–record company relationship is like sharecropping during Jim Crow due to the questionable accounting that some labels engage in. Because of the significant drop in record sales over the past ten years due to file-sharing, record companies have become even more controlling in the contracts artists now sign. Today musicians sign "360" or "multiple right" deals, which give the labels a percentage of nearly everything the artist is involved with, including concerts and endorsement deals. Some observers view these deals as even worse arrangement for artists, while others suggest that it removes the pressure to sell records and allows for more artistic growth. Part of the logic from the labels perspective is that although record sales have declined over the past ten years revenues from concerts have steadily increased. According to eMarketer, worldwide record sales declined from 36 billion in 2006 to 34.7 billion in 2011, but live music revenues increased from 16.6 billion in 2006 to 23.5 billion in 2011.[25]

The advent of digital technologies over the past twenty years has dramatically altered the landscape of the record industry.[26] The ability of users to make exact duplicates of music CDs and share them with others, either directly or via sharing sites such as Lime Wire, has led to a significant decline in record sales over the past ten years. One industry organization has suggested that over 90 percent of music available online was obtained illegally.[27] Conversely, artists have benefitted from similar technological advances. Cheaper recording equipment and computers have made it much easier for musicians to record their music with respectable audio quality, and the Internet allows them easily advertise and distribute the music to a global audience. This development has created a space for smaller artists, what Talib Kweli refers to as blue collar or working class MC. Responding to an interviewers question on the current state of hip hop, he offers:

> People complain about hip-hop all the time, but in 1999 people like Murs and Little Brother and MF Doom and Danger Mouse would still [have been] struggling to get their 12 inches out in a crowded 12-inch market. In 2006, those same artists can be on MTV2. They can book tours and travel the world. It's the rise of the working-class MC. The blue collar MC..., hip-hop has made a world where you can be a working class artist.[28]

The ability of an artist to make a living and build up a loyal fan base has been significantly enhanced by the Internet, but this direction rarely leads to type of revenues that artists affiliated with major labels make. While it may be easier for an independent artist to create and distribute their music (via the web) today, the music industry still serves as a gatekeeper for who gets access to radio, TV, concert venues, and major retail like Wal-Mart and Best Buy.

Because the industry is driven by profit, companies are often searching for the next big artists in the mold of whatever is popular at the time. For example, the success of Master P's (Percy Miller) No Limit Records in the mid-1990s in New Orleans led the industry to seek out other artists in the area, which paved the way for Cash Money Records to sign a $40 million contract with Universal Records shortly thereafter. By the late 1990s there was a rush by most labels to find the next big southern rapper. Critics maintain this is a very common practice, as record labels are not interested in originality but finding a replica of whomever is popular. Within this environment artists who do not fit the current model may find themselves marginalized, and this may lead to poor record sales because the labels are not employing their vast resources to get the music heard on the radio or the Internet, or seen on TV. Talib Kweli recounts how he was marginalized by Interscope records (part of the Universal group) after his original label Rawkus was acquired by them. He points out that his album *Beautiful Struggle* was largely ignored by the label, but other artists like southern rapper Slim Thug received a lot of assistance from the label. "At the time I was like, damn, why they ain't trying to get involved in my project like that? But I understand he's doing it in Houston and Houston was about to be big. So the Houston thing was about to take off and this label is about to go in a different direction. So I was thinking, let me try to get out of here."[29] Kweli contends that other artists who are known for their sociopolitical commentary were treated similarly by Interscope. "I think they were like this to other artists. On their last album, I don't think they did The Roots properly. I don't think they did Common properly on his last album...But I think that that's what they do. Interscope artists come first. The whole G-Unit/Aftermath/Shady thing, that comes first. Gwen Stefani, will.i.am, that comes first."[30]

The music industry's role in the commodification hip hop is unquestionable, and a key part of this process is appropriating the genre so it can be more palatable to whites. In February 2011 the rapper 50 Cent tweeted that "No black artists is gonna sell like EM [Eminem]." Although entertainers in a variety of areas are actively involved in Twitter, that tweet caught a lot of people's attention because it contained, at minimum, an element of truth. Eminem has sold more records than any other artist during the first decade of the new millennium, with a total of over thirty-two million albums sold, and with his release—*Recovery*—he may surpass Tupac's record. Despite Eminem's success over the past decade, hip hop was appropriated by other groups (most notably whites) as early as the mid-1980s. The Beastie Boys, who were signed on the legendary Def Jam label, broke all of Run-DMC's sales records at the time. Moreover the production behind some of Def Jam's earlier artists—T La Rock, the Beastie Boys, and LL Cool J—were produced by Rick Rubin (a Jewish college student at New York University when the label was formed). For whites who become hip hop artists, the central question is always authenticity. How does a white artist gain the license to engage in an art form created by blacks? In most cases their legitimacy is derived from association and biography.

Eminem represents the most notable examples of cultural appropriation of hip hop by whites, primarily because of his fame and financial standing within the industry. There are several current white MCs (such as Paul Waul, Yellow Boy, and Macklemore), but Eminem often provokes the most debate.[31] With the exception of a few critics, most observers acknowledge his lyrical skills are above average at the minimum. The question of whether he is the "best" rapper today cannot be answered because it is a normative inquiry based on one's subjective views of aesthetic preferences. Enthusiastic supporters of several forms of art have long debated who they consider to be the best, but rarely is there any consensus. For example, jazz enthusiasts may debate whether Miles Davis or Clifford Brown was the best trumpet player advancing a variety of valid points, but that does not resolve the dispute because of its normative nature. The fact that Eminem was selected as the best rapper by *Vibe* magazine readers' online poll is partially a reflection of the global audience of hip hop where listeners represent many racial and ethnic groups, and partially an acknowledgment that he is a gifted artist. The story of Eminem's success, however, is more complicated than him possessing lyrical skills or being a white rapper.

Without the support of legendary producer Dr. Dre, Eminem probably would not be in the position he is today. Although he was known in underground circles, by signing with Dr. Dre, and his Aftermath label (a division of Interscope), Eminem gained immediate street credibility that may not have been possible without Dr. Dre's affiliation. He has acknowledged his influence commentating "He believed in me when not many others did. It would have been a lot easier for Dre to dismiss me like most people did: What's with the white guy from Detroit that raps with a funny voice? But he didn't."[32] In addition to Dre's endorsement, Eminem was part of an all-black group of MCs called D-12, and his biography indicated he came from a life of poverty. Each of these components were key in marketing Eminem as an authentic hip hop artist, and it is a model that white artists have adopted decades. Part of the failure of Vanilla Ice in the late 1980s and early 1990s, and his platinum single "Ice, Ice, Baby," was the rapper claimed to grow up in a tough urban neighborhood but it was soon discovered he was from an all-white suburb.

As noted earlier, subject appropriation by white artists has long created concern among artists and critics. In all American musical genres that blacks have created whites at some point have appropriated the culture, and in some instances they received greater recognition or financial return than black artists. "There is abundant evidence," historian Tricia Rose notes, "that white artists imitating black styles have greater economic opportunity and access to larger audiences than black innovators."[33] This is at the heart of the concerns voiced by some critics. As noted earlier, the financial aspect of appropriation is the most troubling to most observers. In the case of hip hop, it was created by a subordinate group that continues to face a disproportionate number of inequalities as compared to the dominant group. So when forces of appropriation and commodification foster a situation where a white artist is more profitable than a black artist a different type of inequality is manifested, creating a situation where whites may have a better opportunity for record deals and creative freedom than African Americans.

The growth of hip hop as an industry has mirrored the genre's appropriation by white artists and consumers. The goal of many artists and label executives has long been to spread hip hop to the broadest possible audience, and in the United States that has meant marketing to whites. From a financial and demographic perspective, there has been less regard for black consumers than whites. Once hip hop moved into the mainstream it was clear to several agents in the industry that young black kids were only a peripheral concern as consumers. Targeting a global audience has altered the landscape both in terms of content and perceptions. The combination of commercialization and appropriation have given rise to the "wigger" phenomena, in which whites who consume hip hop view themselves as aesthetically black and referring to themselves as the n-word or classifying themselves as wiggers (a white nigger). In 2009, for example, a Minnesota High School held "Wigger Day" in which sixty students dressed in "oversized sports jerseys, low-slung pants, baseball hats cocked to the side and 'doo rags."[34] An African American woman who attended the school sued the school district in federal court, arguing that the event (which also occurred in 2007 and 2008) caused her severe emotional distress and the school failed to stop the activity after the student's parents contacted the school about the incident. This is not an isolated event as there are several websites, blogs, and Facebook pages that endorse the wigger lifestyle.

The appropriation of hip hop culture by white youth is also a by-product of the agency of both black rappers and executives. One of the myths of hip hop is that it went through a period where all rappers were positive and authentic, but the history of hip hop demonstrates various artists and executives packaging and selling the imagery and language that young whites replicate today from the beginning. For example in the mid-1980s, Ice-T glamorized gang culture with his debut album *Rhyme Pays*, Too Short romanticized pimp culture with *Born to Mack*, and 2 Live Crew released some of the most demeaning songs ever when it came to black women on many of their albums. Moreover, as music scholar Bakari Kitwana notes, "African American record executives, from Russell Simmons to P. Diddy to Suge Knight, have unashamedly had a significant hand in peddling stereotypical images of Black Americans as their white counterparts."[35] This reality reminds one of the primary goals of the majority of artists—financial gain and fame. As noted earlier, the bulk of artists are not engaged the arts because of the sociopolitical views and most rarely deviate from this path with the exception of occasional commentary when a major event happens.

Music and Politics

When many observers highlight the shortcomings of hip hop often they are articulating a desire for the genre to represent a broader role in society. As noted at the beginning of this chapter, works of poetry and music can serve many roles in a political movement ranging from a mobilization resource to collective narrative of resistance or subversive acts. A prime example of this relationship was exhibited during the black liberation struggle when several popular artists resisted pressures of conformity and became active in the movement or used their music to reflect the collective sentiment of young blacks in the country. Nina Simone, for example, once asserted that it was "an artist's duty is to reflect the times."[36] It is no coincidence that some of the most politically relevant cultural production often mirrors critical moments in history. The lack of serious sociopolitical tension or crisis since the protest period of the 1960s has impacted contemporary artistic production. Moreover, in the case of hip hop, the appropriation process over the past two decades has led to a mass commodification of the music, which diminishes the presence of sociopolitical commentary among mainstream artists. The political context of any given period has a significant impact on all cultural production. When one compares some of the popular music created during the late 1960s to contemporary hip hop, the lack of socially conscious music is glaring.

Throughout African American history, few periods match the collective political cultural production of the Civil Rights and Black Power movements. Cultural positions were an important factor in the emerging consciousness of the Black Power Movement. The inferior notions of self were interrogated and replaced by more positive reaffirming notions of the black "self." Popular artists such as The Impressions (featuring Curtis Mayfield), Martha and the Vandellas, and James Brown created music that represented the tensions and shifts of the period. A classic example of this process may be seen in the cultural production of James Brown. For all the attention his classic song "Say It Loud (I'm Black and I'm Proud)" receives, the song reflects the mood of the period more so than Brown's cultural or political awareness. His transformation during the 1960s is reflective of the political context, as Brown went from funk-centered "Papa's Got a Brand New Bag" (1965) followed by the integrationist tone "America My Home" (1967). In this song Brown proclaimed: "Now you tell me if I'm wrong America is still the best country...but name me any other country you can start out as a shoeshine boy and shake hand with the president."[37] This song echoes themes of cooperation and integration, devoid of any type of racial consciousness, collective identity, or legitimacy critiques.

A black power political context becomes more evident, when one again considers that Brown released one of the classic tunes of the period—"Say It Loud" released only a year later following Dr. King's death. Gone is the conciliatory message of cooperation between blacks and whites, and now the focus becomes group consciousness and a delegitimizing critique of white behavior. He sings: "And now we demands a chance, to do things for ourselves we tired of beating our heads against the wall and working for someone else." The song would become a theme song for the black power period, and Brown followed it up with other tunes like "Soul Power," and "Saying and Doing It" in the early 1970s. However, it is questionable whether or not he would have composed the song had it not been for the political context of the period. The Temptations also experienced a shift during the period, recording *Psychedelic Soul* in 1969, which included the song "Message from a Black Man." This was a break from their traditional love songs and ballads.

Even within this political context music executives, nevertheless, still sought to sanction this emerging black consciousness by preventing some artists from engaging in protest music. For example, the executives at Motown deemed the antiwar song "War" too controversial to be a part of the album *Psychedelic Soul* by The Temptations, but the song was later recorded by Edwin Starr and then became a hit. For all the classic soul artists who were part of the Motown machine, the label attempted to steer clear of "protest music" for much of the 1960s. Although the label would serve as a model for black-owned record companies, Motown followed a predictable pattern of commodification resisting any activity that could undermine founder Berry Gordy's entrepreneurial goals. Analyzing the legacy of Motown, historian Suzanne Smith asserts that it "teaches important lessons about the limits of black capitalism and black culture to institute significant social, political, and economic change. Motown's economic success illustrates how capitalism operates by rules that cannot be held to a racial or local community agenda."[38]

Consequently, the period when Boogie Down Productions and Public Enemy were considered part of the mainstream of hip hop has long passed. Contemporary hip hop operates in a different space than the late 1980s or early 1990s, a period some people refer to as the "golden age of hip hop." In 1989 a group of East Coast MCs, lead by KRS-One, released "Self-Destruction," a song that commented on the increasing black-on-black violence in America; this was followed a year later by the West Coast All-Stars who released a song titled "We're All in the Same Gang," discussing the same theme with a specific focus on the gang problems of California.[39] In both instances, the list of artists who participated in the projects represented a who's who of popular rappers at the time. Nearly twenty years later, the socioeconomic landscape has been significantly altered, the political context is different, and African American public opinion is more moderate than any other point in history. Few popular artists produce politically orientated material. This trend is a by-product of contextual and capitalist forces. Contextually, the current political-economic conditions in America invoke less concern among the general public than in previous periods such as the 1960s and 1970s. Despite American involvement in two wars and increasing gaps between economic classes, there have been no mass social movements in recent decades.

When one compares the cultural production of the 1960s with hip hop released during Barack Obama's presidential campaign there are striking contrast both in involvement and content. The music released during the campaign largely reflects a contemporary ecology devoid of sociopolitical tension. Among the long list of artists who produced songs about Obama's campaign, relatively few made any other music with politically orientated themes or content. Much like the deracialized context that dominates the political arena, many artists who recorded songs during Obama's campaign did not address racial issues directly. They often subtly invoked cues of the historical significance of the event and instances of racism in the past. To illustrate this current state, three songs released during the campaign are examined: Young Jezzy's "My President Is Black," will.i.am.'s "Yes, We Can," and Nas's "Black President" [mixtape and international examples].

Among the long list of artists who produced songs about Obama's campaign, relatively few made any other music with politically orientated themes or content. One example of this pattern may be found in the Atlanta-based rapper Young Jezzy's song "My President." Jezzy represents the current norm of popular or mainstream hip hop, with songs often evoking the stereotypical virtues of thug life. Evoking the carefree "realist nigga" style that Tupac Shukar popularized in the early 1990s, his refrain (hook) proclaims: "My president is black, my Lambo's blue/and I'll be goddamned if my rims ain't too."[40] Despite the thug/capitalist references, Young Jeezy seeks to appeal to collective joy and memory of sorrow that Obama's campaign signified. He raps: "See I motivate the thugs right you motivate us homie that's what it is/ this a hands on policy yeah first Black President Win, lose or draw nigga haha/...My President is black, I'm important too though!"[41] While no one would confuse this with Amiri Baraka's "Nation Time" or Elaine Brown's "Seize The Time," the artist does draw on collective identity and solidarity frames using his message to appeal to the "thugs." Jay Z added a verse on an underground remix of the song during the latter part of the campaign, but the overall structure and message remained: boasting about the prospects of an Obama presidency. It represented a celebration more so than a call to mobilization or any type of political agency.

Hip hop in its most marketable and global form is seen the song "Yes We Can," which was designated as the official theme song by the Obama campaign. The "Yes We Can" song is significant for two reasons as it relates to this study. One, it would become one of the main songs associated with the campaign. Two, the song was recorded by will.i.am. of the Black Eyed Peas. The group Black Eyed Peas represents a classic example of a group transforming itself to appeal to a mainstream audience and embracing an image that maximizes the appropriative process. When the group first appeared on the national scene they were viewed as a traditional hip hop group, featuring three MCs—will.i.am., apl.de. ap., and Taboo—and they released two albums between 1998 and 2000. They were largely viewed as a classic "backpack" hip hop group, who were widely respected but devoid of large record sales. In 2002, however, they added the vocalist Stacy Ann Ferguson, "Fergie," to the group and converted their traditional hip hop aesthetic into a pop-friendly futuristic image. The result of these changes was a dramatic increase in the group's popularity, which resulted in over fifty-five million records sold, several endorsement deals, and being the featured half-time act for the Super Bowl in 2011.

Unlike other songs "Yes We Can" was not written by the artist, instead the producer will.i.am. sampled an Obama speech (given at the January 8, 2011, New Hampshire primary) for lyrics, and utilized several celebrities reciting the lyrics. The video featured close to forty A-list entertainers, including John Legend, Kate Walsh, Aisha Tyler, Amber Valletta, Taryn Manning, Nicole Scherzinger, Scarlett Johansson, Kareem Abdul-Jabbar, and Nick Cannon. Whereas the song of Young Jeezy, for example, focused the collectivity identity of blacks, the "Yes We Can" song framed a multicultural identity present throughout Obama's campaign. Because the song is based on a campaign speech it represents a deracialized form of cultural production, and the artists who appeared in the video represented a cosmopolitan mix of pop entertainers. When contrasted with the cast of the "We're All in the Same Game" or "Self-Destruction" videos, "Yes We Can" is a prime example of globally appropriated pop music: that is the popular form appropriated by the global culture.

One of the few songs from a US-based artist that contained a heightened level political consciousness was Nas's "Black President." Unlike many of the artists mentioned thus far, Nasir "Nas" Jones has released several songs in his career with sociopolitical commentary, such as "Ghetto Prisoners," "I Can," and "These Are Our Heroes." Although he has never been viewed a purely conscious rapper in the mold of KRS-One, Public Enemy, or Immortal Technique, Nas represents an artist who embraces multiple elements of the black community. His song "Black President," released on a mixtape in April 2008, begins with the Tupac sample "Although it seems heaven sent, we ain't ready to have a black president."[42] The song begins with a delegimitizing frame illustrating the struggles that African Americans face. He raps, "They forgot us on the block, got us in the box/ /Solitary confinement, how violent are these cops?/They need an early retirement /How many rallies will I watch? I ain't got it in me to march."[43] Police brutality and high rates of black incarceration have long been common themes in hip hop, as many artists seek to reveal the challenges that younger blacks face in urban environments.

Several incidents of black males being killed or brutalized by law enforcement officials have been reported, and in many cases the police are either not brought to justice or charged with a minor offence. The protest and rallies of community activists often fall on deaf ears. But in such a depressed environment, Nas asserts, "America surprised us, and let a black man guide us." Nas also ties the pattern of racism at the local level with obstacles that Obama could face from right-wing extremists. He continues:

> What's the black pres' thinkin on election night?/Is it, "How can I protect my life? Protect my wife? Protect my rights?"/KKK is like, "What the f—?!", loading they guns up/Loading up mines too, ready to ride/'Cause I'm riding with my crew—he dies, we die too.

The potential danger that was clear to many observers, both then and now, of a person of African descent occupying the White House is evident in the lyric, "How can I protect my life? Protect my wife" is a concern that no other president faced. Despite these dangers, the prospect of an Obama presidency was too significant to ignore. Nas cautiously embraces the idea of Barack Obama becoming president, while drawing on the racialized notion that he would bring justice to blacks and truly care about them.

Among of the three aforementioned songs, "Black President" is the only one that comes close to capturing the complex mix of anxiety, excitement, and apprehension that surrounded the election of the first African American president of the United States from a black American perspective. Whether it was a direct result of industry forces or simply the current political context, the majority of mainstream artists did not become engaged in the discussion. Young Jezzy's "My President" is a curious song fusing all too common frame of materialism with a celebration of Obama's election. Both the lyrics and video for "Yes We Can" reflect the current state of popular hip hop framed and packaged in non-threatening form. The format, one that is reminiscent of the "We Are the World" video, avoids the type of critical commentary that was once an equal part of the hip hop's mainstream, and to a certain degree represents what the genre has become today.

Limits of Hip Hop and the Future

Some critics bemoan the current state of popular hip hop. Noted hip hop scholar Tricia Rose, adapting Nas's 2006 album title *Hip Hop Is Dead*, argues that "hip hop it is not dead, but gravely ill."[44] Though numerous artists engage in what many view as more authentic, classical, or conscious styles, the fact that they mainly reside in the underground limits the impact on mainstream hip hop as a whole. She suggests that more work needs to be done among progressive forces to combat the capitalist dictates that influence the genre. The problem with this reasoning is that at a certain point one must come to terms with notions of self, biography, and capitalism. One must be careful not to overly romanticize the history of hip hop by overlooking both the legacy of capitalist choices, and the diversity that the genre has always represented. Former music industry mogul Russell Simmons, like Berry Gordy before him, sold his stake in Def Jam Records to move onto other entrepreneurial opportunities. All too often the narrative of the "golden age of hip hop" tells a story of the 1980s and 1990s as if all artists were conscious MCs and it neglects to tell the full story that includes Too Short, the Ghetto Boyz, 2 Live Crew, and other artists whose music or imagery strayed far from these golden ideals. The tragedy of the current state, as Rose and others aver, is that the music industry has appropriated a particular form of hip hop and the groups or artists who produce conscious or more authentic forms are no longer part of mainstream. Any critique of the mainstream, however, is not just a critique of popular music, as the music industry is a capitalist entity that shares the same principles and values of other large industries. The music industry is similar to film industry in that many best films in the eyes of critics are not the top-grossing films, instead they are designated as "art" films shown only at film festivals or released straight to DVD.

When delineating popular culture it is always important to remain cognizant that it is a form of entertainment, and entertainment is a billion dollar industry. Cultural appropriation is often a key part of this industry due to the constant push for what is profitable and a desire to influence the consumer's buying choices. In the case of hip hop, once it was determined to be a potentially profitable form of entertainment, industry forces mobilized their considerable influence in radio, television, and retail outlets to push certain forms of the genre viewed more appealing to the general audience. This form often included the frames of thugs, gangsters, and pimps and hoes (with occasional dance music), and it soon became the default form of mainstream hip hop. In many cases, these were the frames that whites and other nonmember audiences embraced.

To put too much emphasis on notions of popular, however, neglects both the vitality and growth of the hip hop over the past thirty years. While this study demonstrates the salience of industry dynamics in moderating certain forms, the impact of the internet and corresponding digital technologies has created a range of opportunities for artists that did not exist during the classical era of the genre. An artist whose fame or influence was only limited to a local market has the opportunity to be recognized nationally and internationally today. It may lead to greater financial opportunities, such as signing with a major label, or just the ability to tour and work as an artist, but the digital resources of today do provide an invaluable tool that artists lacked in the past. Moreover, the underground has allowed many artists/activists, such as Dead Prez and Immortal Technique, to become active in grass roots movements Africa, Latin America, and Europe. This does not mean, nevertheless, that these artists will alter the global industry of hip hop or serve as the basis for political movement. This research noted that appropriation must be viewed as a component of a hegemonic apparatus that creates and perpetuates for people of color globally, and for those who wish hip hop would serve a greater role in this struggle, it must be remembered that it is just music and the primary goal of most artists is not of a sociopolitical nature.

Notes

1. See Hayden White, "Afterword," in *Beyond the Cultural Turn: New Directions in the Study of Society and Culture*, ed. V. Bonnell and Lynn Hunt (Berkeley: University of California Press, 1999); Joanne Freekman, "The Culture of Politics: The Politics of Culture," *Journal of Policy History* 16 (2004): 137–42; and Kyle Grayson et al., "Pop Goes IR? Researching the Popular Culture—World Politics Continuum," *Politics* 29 (2009):155–63.

2. Lisa Wedeen, *Ambiguities of Domination: Politics, Rhetoric, and Symbols in Contemporary Syria* (Chicago: University of Chicago Press, 1999), 30. Review additionally: Wedeen, "Conceptualizing Culture: Possibilities for Political Science," *American Political Science Review* 96, no. 4 (December 2002): 713–28; and John Bowen and Roger Petersen eds., *Critical Comparisons in Politics and Culture* (Cambridge: Cambridge University Press, 1999).

3. Aldon Morris and Naomi Braine, "Social Movements and Oppositional Consciousness," in *Oppositional Consciousness: The Subjective Roots of Social Protest*, ed. Jane J. Mansbridge and Aldon Morris (Chicago: University of Chicago Press, 2001), 25..

4. Harold Cruse, *The Crisis of the Negro Intellectual: A Historical Analysis of the Failure of Black Leadership* (1967; repr., New York: Quill, 1984), 71.

5. W. E. B. Du Bois, "Of Our Spiritual Strivings," in *The Souls of Black Folk* (Chicago: A.C. McClurg & Company, 1903; New York: Penguin Books, 1989), 5; Adolph Reed, Jr., *W. E. B. Du Bois and American Political Thought: Fabianism and the Color Line* (New York: Oxford University Press, 1997); and W. E. B. Du Bois, "Talented Tenth: Memorial Address," in *W. E. B. Du Bois: A Reader*, ed. David Levering Lewis (New York: Henry Holt, 1995), 348.

6. Ernest Allen Jr., "On the Reading of Riddles: Rethinking Du Boisian 'Double Consciousness," in *Existence in Black: An Anthology of Black Existential Philosophy*, ed. L. Gordon (New York: Routledge, 1997), 64.

7. Sterling Stuckey, "W.E.B. Du Bois: Black Cultural Reality and the Meaning of Freedom," in *Slave Culture: Nationalist Theory and the Foundations of Black America* (New York: Oxford University Press, 1987), 265. One may also consider Bernard Boxill, "Du Bois and Fanon on Culture," *The Philosophical Forum* (Winter/Spring 1977–78): 326–38; and Stanley Brodwin, "The Veil Transcended: Form and Meaning in W.E.B. Du Bois 'The Souls of Black Folk," *Journal of Black Studies* (March 1972): 303–21.

8. Barbara Harlow, *Resistance Literature* (New York: Routledge, 1987), 28.

9. Robin D.G. Kelley, *Freedom Dreams: The Black Radical Imagination* (Boston: Beacon Press, 2002), 9.

10. Amiri Baraka, *Digging: The Afro-American Soul of American Classical Music* (Berkeley: University of California Press, 2009), 108.

11. Herbert Marcuse, *One-Dimensional Man: Studies in the Ideology of Advanced Society* (Boston: Beacon Press, 1964), 61.

12. James Young, "Profound Offense and Cultural Appropriation," *Journal of Aesthetics and Art Criticism* 63 (Spring 2005): 136.

13. Richard Fung, "Working Through Appropriation," *Fuse* (Summer 1993): 20.

14. Sunaina Maira "Henna and Hip Hop: The Politics of Cultural Production and the Work of Cultural Studies," *Journal of Asian American Studies* 3 (October 2000): 11

15. Recording Industry of America (RIIA), "Gold and Platinum Data;" http://www.riaa.com

16. Nelson George, *Buppies, B-Boys, BAPS,& BOHOS* (New York: DA CAPO Press, 2001), 94.

17. Dan Charnas, *The Big Payback: The History of the Business of Hip-Hop* (New York: New American Library, 2010), 494.

18. Jay Z, "Moment of Clarity," *The Black Album* (Roc-A-Fella Records, 2003).

19. Mos Def interview with Spank Rock, "House Music: Mos Def," June 6, 2009, /www.interviewmagazine.com/blogs/music/2009-06-01/mos-def/

20. Lupe Fiasco, "American Terroist," *Food & Liquor*, Atlantic Records, 2006, CD.

21. Interview: Lupe Fiasco Talks "Lasers" Delay, Japanese Cartoon, and "Food & Liquor II," complexmag.com, September 10, 2010.

22. Ibid., my emphasis.

23. See Patrick Burkart, "Loose Integration and the Popular Music Industry," *Popular Music and Society* 28 (Oct. 2005): 289–500; and the documentary *Money for Nothing: Behind the Business of Pop Music* (2001).

24. Kembrew McLeod, "MP3s Are Killing Home Taping: The Rise of Internet Distribution and Its Challenge to the Major Label Music Monopoly," *Popular Music and Society* 28 (October 2005): 523.

25. http://www.emarketer.com/Report.aspx?code=emarketer_2000428.

26. McLeod, 523.

27. The International Federation of the Phonographic Industry, cited in Amanda Andres, "Changes Rock the Music World as '360 Deals' Rise," *Daily Telegraph* (London), February 6, 2009, online edit: www.telegraph.co.uk.

28. Talib Kweli "Let's Get Free" (Part One), www.xxlmag.com, April 17, 2006.

29. Ibid.

30. Ibid.

31. Rap artist Macklemore (born Ben Haggerty) won Grammy awards in 2014 for best rap album, best rap song, and best rap performance over other artists such as Kendrick Lamar, Jay Z, Kanye West, and Drake. Similarly, he won MTV's 2013 Video Music Award (VMA) for best hip hop video.

32. Comments made at the 23rd Annual ASCAP Rhythm & Soul Awards, June 26, 2010.

33. Tricia Rose, *Black Noise: Rap Music and Black Culture in Contemporary America* (Hanover: Wesleyan University Press, 1994), 5.
34. "Minnesota School Faces Lawsuit Over Racist 'Wigger Day,'" Huffingtonpost.com, August 3, 2011.
35. Bakari Kitwana, *Why White Kids Love Hip-Hop: Wankstas, Wiggers, Wannabes, and the New Reality of Race in America* (New York: Basic Books, 2005), 149.
36. Nina Simone, "Definition of an Artist: interview," *Protest Anthology* (Andy Stoud Incorporated, 2008).
37. James Brown, "America Is My Home Pt.1," *James Brown Singles, Vol. 5 1967–1969*, Universal Records, CD.
38. Suzanne Smith, *Dancing in the Streets: Motown and the Cultural Politics of Detroit* (Cambridge: Harvard University Press, 2000), 238.
39. On "Self-Destruction" participants included BDP, MC Lyte, Public Enemy, Just-Ice, Heavy D, Stetsasonic, among others, and on "Were All in the Same Gang" they included NWA, Tone-Loc, Above The Law, Young MC, and Digital Underground.
40. Young Jeezy, "My President," *The Recession* (Island/ Def Jam Group, 2008).
41. Ibid.
42. Nas, "Black President," *Untitled* (Island/Def Jam Group, 2008).
43. Ibid., passim.
44. Tricia Rose, *The Hip Hop Wars: What We Talk about When We Talk about Hip Hop—and Why It Matters* (New York: Basic Books, 2008), i.

4

I'm Hip: An Exploration of Rap Music's Creative Guise

Kawachi Clemmons

We don't like musicians. We don't respect musicians. The reason why is because they look at people who do rap as people who don't have any knowledge.

Hank Shocklee, producer for Public Enemy

I am a musician. In fact, my musical being is rooted in the art of percussion performance. Throughout the course of my life I have been fortunate to study at some of the finest institutions for musical study, including the Interlochen Center for the Arts, which has provided opportunities to perform with some of the world's finest musicians. As a student of music I have been educated in a system that espouses European classical-derived music as the canon for study. In my maturation as a musician and researcher I have found that the canon, which lays the foundation for my musical being, has been exclusive to the extent that it has not involved multicultural and multiethnic musical forms as a source for musical ways of knowing. Although this research begins with a personal statement, its content is not about me; rather it is about the appropriation of a youth artistic movement and culture known today as hip hop. More specifically, this research is about the victimization of hip hop's music and its compositional practice as "less than" in comparison to other musical genres. What proceeds is a personal commentary and theoretical perspective on hip hop's music through the lens of an educator-musician on a quest to develop academic studies with hip hop as a point of departure for expansive musical skill development and knowledge acquisition.

A great deal of black music's creativity can be found in its inventive handling of language. This assertion includes an aesthetic being that is also rooted in its methods of developing new musical sensibilities. Furthermore, the music industry's appropriation of hip hop has come at the expense of it not being recognized as a true aesthetic art form. As a result, hip hop's musical creators have received an unfair and biased trial. The verdict—guilty on three counts: (1) being nonmusical, (2) lacking originality, and (3) absence of an identifiable culture-specific practice.

The Rhetorical Rhythm of Rap

Throughout the course of my travels in lecturing and presenting on hip hop, I have encountered both positive and negative commentary regarding rap music. The positive dialog is usually encountered with general statements like, "I just love what you're doing. Hip hop is so awesome. LL Cool J—he's the man!" Conversely, others have verbally mauled me as if I am doing a disservice to music and higher education by attempting to engage in academic discourse on hip hop. Further discussion of the subject of hip hop and rap music typically is scoffed at and draws the response that rap is not music. In continuing to make a case, my response frequently includes the question, what makes it nonmusical? The usual response is somewhere on the order of, "well they don't sing and just do that boom de bap de boom stuff." Along similar lines however, James Brown, an artist who performed with a limited tessitura, is highly regarded today as a musical master. My hypothesis is that rap music's use of highly percussive vocals becomes the primary element that differentiates it from many of its popular music predecessors. I posit that the fundamental issue surrounding rap music's aesthetic alienation is the listener's lack of familiarity with musical representations that do not employ melodic lines as the lead voice.

The basis for an individual's musical understanding and appreciation comes as a result of one's interactions in the social world. Psychologist Daniel Levitin's research on musical cognition suggests that this knowledge is based on a perceptive response to musical stimuli he calls a schema. The familiarity or schema, as Levitin posits, "leads to clear expectations, as well as a sense of which of those expectations are flexible which are not."[1] This schema, which is the result of a constructed objectivity, presents a musical hegemony that places rap music on the margins of what is considered as acceptable forms of artistic representation. Levitin further explains, "Our musical schema in Western music includes implicit knowledge of the scales that are normally used. This is why Indian or Pakistani music, for example, sounds 'strange' to us the first time we hear it...it sounds strange by virtue of its being inconsistent with what we have learned to call music."[2] At a deeper level, this need to distinguish between what representations fall under the categorization and demarcation of what is called music becomes the seat of the problem of Hank Shocklee's dissatisfaction with musicians. Ethnomusicologist Thomas Turino contends that "*music* is not a unitary art form, but rather that this term refers to fundamentally distinct types of activities that fulfill different needs and ways of being human."[3]

Software engineer and theorist, Philip Dorrell, suggests that the most dominant and yet unjustified assumption in the field of music science is the assumption that it is music that must be explained. He further asserts that many make assumptions about music without taking into account the plausible nature of human tendencies. These humanistic tendencies that "cause people to compose, perform and/or appreciate music can serve some biological purpose...[and] music is just a side-effect of those tendencies."[4] Moreover, in further pursuing intersections of the music and human tendencies, Cornel West's commentary on jazz must be noted.

> Jazz is the middle road between invisibility and anger. It is where self-confident creativity resides. Black music is paradigmatic of how black persons have best dealt with their humanity, their complexity—their good and bad, negative and positive aspects without being excessively preoccupied with whites. Duke Ellington, Louis Armstrong, and Coltrane were just being themselves.[5]

Jettisoning West's assertion on the idiom of jazz and its musicians—in the spirit of biological and evolutionary musical practice—hip hop artists also were and still are just being themselves.

> Culled from the discourse of the postindustrial city, hip-hop reflected the growing visibility of a young, urban, and often angry so-called "underclass." Aesthetically the genre drew on the diverse musical sensibilities like James Brown and the Parliament/Funkadellic collective and on black oral traditions like the prison toasts, "The Dozens," and the Black Arts poets of the 1960s.[6]

The resulting product was an expressive art form that ignited the fuel that would allow a youth culture to shift previously held notions about music and creativity that beforehand had not been explored.

Creativity and the Inventive Practice of Music

The dawning of a new age is often signified by a monumental achievement sparked by enlightenment. Psychologist Mihaly Csikszentmihalyi, in *Creativity: Flow and the Psychology of Discovery and Invention*, calls this a process by which a symbolic domain in the culture is changed. Quite often these novel achievements are considered to be creative in nature. Much of the critique of hip hop as an atypical musical expression is based on its borrowing of previously recorded music. This assumption, as music professor Robert Walser noted, reflects an ideology that "composers who use previously recorded sounds as their raw materials are parasitic."[7]

When a young composer writes a piece of music in a two-part contrapuntal nature it (the composition) borrows stylistic sensibilities of Johann Sebastian Bach. In the field of jazz many of its musicians employed the use of melodies of popular show tunes or other jazz standards to lay the base of its compositional structure. Outside of the realm of hip hop (i.e., jazz, classical, blues, country, etc.) instances of musical borrowing and variations of existing themes and harmonics to produce "new" sounds and styles has served as a foundation of creativity in the field. Samuel A. Floyd, Henry Louis Gates, and Martin T. Williams all note a specific example of pianist Jelly Roll Morton's interpretation of "Maple Leaf Rag" originally composed and recorded by Scott Joplin. "Morton embellishes the piece two-handedly, with a swinging introduction...Morton's composition does not 'surpass' or 'destroy' Joplin's; it completely *extends* and troupes figures present in the original. Morton's signification is a gesture of admiration and respect."[8] In Morton's case, his adaptation of Joplin's rag was seen as an undertaking of admiration but in the case of hip hop's musical creators the act of sampling, in extreme interpretive cases, has been characterized as "the musical equivalent of shoplifting."[9] Moreover, Walser further notes that "not only is the issue of theft at stake, but also the notion that appropriation is not creative."[10]

In defense of the "music" authenticity debate, it is highly plausible that fellow musicians and music critics are so entrenched in maintaining their own legitimacy that they completely missed the mark. As cultural studies theorist Raymond Williams stated, "there are always important works which belong to these early stages of particular forms, and it is easy to miss their formal significance by comparison with preceding or succeeding mature examples....It is then easy to miss one of the key elements in cultural production: innovation as it is happening; innovation in process."[11]

Hip Hop's Musical Process

When listening to a rap record often the beat sticks in the listener's head long after the song has passed from the ears. It is at this place where hip hop is grounded. Artistic appropriation is the historical source of hip hop music and still remains the core of its aesthetic form and message.[12] Within the artistic process of hip hop's vocal music the MC (rapper) recites poetic verses and catchy sayings over what was known as the *break* or *get down* part of the music at a party. The term "break" refers to any segment of music (usually four measures or less) that could be sampled and repeated.[13] Historically, the deejay would find the break and loop it (play continuously) with the use of two turntables. An early example of this concept in practice is the recording of the Sugar Hill Gang's "Rapper's Delight." This song used a break from the 1979 disco song "Good Times" by Chic. As the role of the MC and the music of hip hop developed there was a need to further experiment with multiple ways to manipulate the break. By nature of this process many deejays evolved into producers or what is commonly referred to in the practice of hip hop music production as beat makers.

The process of making beats like all musical compositions requires an extreme amount of skill and dedication to the artistic practice. The concept of "musicing" (the application of doing music) as employed in this work suggests a practice specific musicianship that involves listening as a part of the compositional process. The musicianship required to compose or sample "particular kinds of music develops in relation to the thinking of other composers and performers, past and present, who have immersed themselves in the achievement and the authority (or the standards and traditions) of particular compositional practices."[14]

The role of music creation in hip hop was quite different than that of other genres. In contrast to preceding African American and black musical forms "hip hop did not take mere melodies or musical phrases, that is, abstract musical patterns exemplifiable in different performances…instead it lifted concrete sound-events, prerecorded token performances of such musical patterns."[15] This occurred not because of the lack of musicians to play, but rather a result of the hip hop producer's inner compositional ear. "One of the major challenges of performing hip-hop on live instruments is…that many of hip-hop's musical gestures (such as sixteenth notes played on a bass drum) are virtually impossible to reproduce without electronic editing."[16]

In following Elliott's notion of musicianship there must be a set of criteria that serves as a foundation for the standards and traditions of a compositional domain. Schloss's research on sample-based hip hop production references what he calls, "sampling ethics" as the basis for its philosophical and aesthetic framework. This musicianship espouses Schloss's ethical principle of "no biting!" Biting refers to the use of a sample or work that someone has already used. Sampling becomes a form of artistic expression, but re-sampling or biting is problematic. For example, MC Hammer's "You Can't Touch This" used a loop of Rick James's "Super Freak." Under the stipulated guidelines it would be unethical to use this same loop in the same fashion. However, it is possible to take a previously used loop and alter it as a means of developing a new sound or feel. As DJ Kool Akiem notes, "I'm not gonna just take a loop that somebody else did—if that's all they did, just loop it—I'm not gonna come and do the same thing without doing something to make it better."[17] This is exactly what producer Just Blaze did with the original Rick James composition. Blaze, under a creative guise, took an existing sample and "created" or "brought to light" a break in the music. Blaze took the basic track and "chopped" the original loop to create a new sound. Chopping refers to altering a sampled phrase by dividing it into smaller segments and reconfiguring them in a different order. "Super Freak," in this new compositional form was commonly referred to as the "Super Freak flip." DJ and Grammy-award winning producer, 9th Wonder, remembered the first time he heard Just Blaze's instrumental "flip" of "Super Freak." "I was like, 'What!' He originally had the beat on his MySpace page. Man I called Pete Rock, Jazzy Jeff, and a few of my other producer friends and was like, 'Have you heard the Super Freak flip that Blaze did?' When I heard it I was like good god!"[18]

The "Super Freak flip" is a concrete example of what Elliott terms "arranging in context." An arranger must know how performing, improvising, composing, conducting, and listening relate within the musical contexts represented by both the original work and the "new" work he is arranging.[19] In the preceding example, Blaze exhibits an understanding on a level comparable to what developmental psychologist Howard Gardner calls the disciplinary expert (or skilled person). The disciplinary expert is an individual of any age who has mastered the concepts and skills of a discipline or domain and can apply such knowledge appropriately in new situations.[20] Through experience, the disciplinary expert learns how to creatively manipulate the underlying structures in music thereby creating sounds and nuances that listeners like. These likes or dislikes in music are largely based on listener perceptions and expectations. As listeners "we expect certain pitches, rhythms, timbres, and so on to co-occur based on a statistical analysis our brain has performed of how often they have gone together in the past."[21] In this manner, a relational process of identifying is fashioned based on a set of prescribed beliefs. In turn, those prior beliefs or frames of reference form a being's conscious state of mind that invariably shapes our methods of interpreting and understanding the physical world. According to cultural theorist Stuart Hall, "we understand the world by referring individual objects, people or events in our heads to the general classificatory schemes into which—according to our culture—they fit."[22] So what happens when an idea, musical forms, or culture falls beyond the margins of fitting into a specified schematic or typology? In the course of situating discourse on a hip hop aesthetic, scholars often encounter a number of critiques that question the validity of the research. As previously stated and explored, for some the mere thought of placing the terms hip hop and art together are paradoxical. For others, the musical critique is often extended to nonmusical domains and frequently places hip hop's visual representations at the forefront of the artistic debate.

The Maher Critique

The practice of signifying to create meaning is nothing new in the media. In fact, to a large extent media's hegemony relies on the public's acceptance of the ideologies posited by the educated and so-called enlightened few. In mass communication and cultural studies this concept is commonly referred to as media hegemony. Italian philosopher Antonio Gramsci defined media hegemony as "the dominance of a certain way of life and thought and to the way in which that dominant concept of reality is diffused throughout public as well as private dimensions of social life."[23] This concept of media hegemony influences the meaning-making process.

Comedian Bill Maher, in an episode of his Home Box Office (HBO) cable series *Politically Incorrect*, commented that "a great percentage of hip hop was affirmative action for the ego, and it was about shoot this and pimp that." He also mentioned that other people did not feel the need to let everybody know how much money they had. The context of the joking commentary centered on whites not flaunting their wealth in such a way (a false premise). Living in a capitalist society, money and power are inextricably intertwined. One may not outright profess their mass riches the way some hip hop artists throw large sums of cash in the air or ride around in expensive Bentleys; however, an individual or group may covertly and overtly proclaim wealth through the use or ability to manipulate their power. Power, it seems, has to be understood here, not only in terms of economic exploitation and physical coercion, but also in broader cultural or symbolic terms, including the power to represent someone or something in a certain way—within a certain "regime of representation."[24] Therefore, the power of appropriation lies within these mediated regimes. Maher used hip hop as a hot button—the burning question in the topical segment of his televised show. However, what he failed to illustrate is how the non–hip hop individuals he so eloquently described have a history of boasting their fortune and fame as well.

The problem with Maher's statement is that it is an opinion. And when placed in a forum setting an individual's opinionated sound bite, taken in or out of context, casually repeated (and repeated) or by more technological means using Twitter (and retweeted), becomes reality. As Turino notes:

> *Redundancy* is the central mechanism for creating new social habits of thought and action—making them cultural common sense and a core aspect of individuals. Just as repetition is basic to the practicing of any musical instrument, art, or sport to create the basic habits necessary for successful performance, redundancy is basic to the shaping of collective thinking.[25]

The 1980s represented a time of conspicuous consumption. The nation elected Ronald Reagan to the presidency of the United States, and the country was deeply involved in the arms and space race. While all of this was going on politically, television depicted a certain imagery of success. Television shows like *Dallas* and *Knots Landing* projected classic representations of a wealthy American lifestyle. The biggest exhibition of them all, *Lifestyles of the Rich and Famous*, with host Robin Leach popularized the tag line "champagne wishes and caviar dreams." This mass consumption of material goods and expensive taste was the popular culture topic on *Lifestyles of the Rich and Famous*. It was viewed, as intended, as an illustration of the pinnacle of success—the American Dream, but in the case of Maher's hip hop commentary the same consumption of materialism is seen as negative (wrong).

Conversely, the media has used the hip hop mogul/materialism to its own benefit. In a television commercial for Straight Talk cell phone service, an older white couple is leaving what appears to be a grocery/department store. The woman is talking on her cell phone with gentleman walking behind. The female character walks up to a gold Bentley clicking the keyless remote. She proceeds to ask, "why isn't this working?" (referring to the remote). The gentleman responds, "cause we drive a station wagon." The tag line that "I think I drive the same car as a hip hop music mogul because I'm feeling richer effect" illustrates to the viewer what "happens when you cut your cell phone bill in half." Therefore, one should "switch to Straight Talk...so you can feel richer too." The result is a socially constructed reality (a created meaning) where hip hop and blackness continue to fall victim to the inferiority paradigm established by white norms. The main point here is to acknowledge, as Hall does, "that meaning does not inhere in things, in the world. It is constructed, produced. It is the result of a signifying practice—a practice that "produces" meaning, that makes things mean.[26]

That's a (w)Rap: Implications and Conclusions

For the hip hop critic the issue of rap music as a true artistic form is not purely based on its musical sensibilities. The way the music is presented or represented in context with the images that have become identifiable norms of hip hop further exacerbate its artistic alienation. In a word—it just does not fit. The dress (whether baggy pants or fitted jeans), gold teeth and grills, and über expensive ride references that have become a representation of hip hop culture stand as tall monuments leaving its creative musical guise in the shadows. What becomes problematic is the fact that the music industry's appropriation of contemporary hip hop is predicated on the "typing" (or stereotyping) of this imagery to create and influence meaning. Meaning associated with this kind of thinking is created in what Stuart Hall promotes as a combination of language (what one says) and practice (what one does). It is this typing that lays the base for music critic Stanley Crouch who has openly stated that rap music is "dick and jane with dirty words. It is not a very complex art form or much of anything."[27] With the use of a very strong semantic Crouch presents a dichotomy where the lyric (what is said) in rap music completely disavows its musicing practice (what one does). Crouch's voice forms what film scholar Richard Dyer and Hall suggest is "a characterization in which a few traits are fore grounded."[28]

In discussion of the hip hop's critics and defenders Rose states:

> Understanding and explaining are not the same as justifying and celebrating, and this is the crucial distinction we must make if we stand a fighting chance in this perpetual storm. The former—understanding and explaining—are an integral part of solving the problems with hip hop; the latter—justifying and celebrating—are lazy, reactionary, dangerous, and lacking in political courage.[29]

It is no doubt that this conversation will take many turns as the debate on hip hop's musical authenticity continues. This research serves as a means to illuminate the musical autonomy paradox and present hip hop's creative guise through a lens that draws attention to the artistic musical talents of its creators. This work also serves to address Rose's commentary that "not nearly enough commercial public conversation addresses the nature of creativity in hip hop, what innovations have taken place, or how musical production techniques and rhyme styles have been elaborated and refined."[30]

Recall Shocklee's thoughts on musicians at the onset of this writing. "We don't like musicians. We don't respect musicians. The reason why is because they look at people who do rap as people who don't have any knowledge."[31] I encourage fellow musicians and critics of hip hop with this narrow perspective to open their eyes that they may begin to behold the opportunities to explore the music of hip hop as a means of an appreciation for its culture. To do this, engagement in an intergenerational discourse that incites change is needed—change in thoughts and habits. In essence, I am proposing more than just an appreciation. What is needed is an understanding.

Notes

1. Daniel J. Levitin, *This Is Your Brain on Music: The Science of a Human Obsession* (New York: Plume/Penguin Group, 2006), 116.
2. Ibid., 117.

3. Thomas Turino, *Music as Social Life: The Politics of Participation* (Chicago: University of Chicago Press, 2008), 1.

4. Philip Dorrell, *What Is Music? Solving a Scientific Mystery* (Lulu.com/http://whatis-music.info/download.html, 2005), PDF e-book, 50.

5. John O. Calmore, "Critical Race Theory, Archie Shepp, and Fire Music: Securing an Authentic Intellectual Life in a Multicultural World," in *Critical Race Theory: The Key Writings that Formed the Movement*, ed. Kimberlé Crenshaw, et al. (New York: The New Press, 1995), 317–18, and Cornell West, "Charlie Parker Didn't Give a Damn," *New Perspectives Quarterly* 8, no. 3 (Summer 1991): 60–63.

6. Mark Anthony Neal, *What the Music Said: Black Popular Music and Black Public Culture* (New York: Routledge, 1999), 125.

7. Robert Walser, "Rhythm, Rhyme, and Rhetoric in the Music of Public Enemy," *Ethnomusicology* 39, no. 2 (Spring 1995), 196–97.

8. Samuel A. Floyd, Jr., *The Power of Black Music: Interpreting Its History from Africa to the United States* (New York: Oxford University Press, 1995), 212–13. Also see, Henry Louis Gates, *The Signifying Monkey: A Theory of African-American Literary Criticism* (New York: Oxford University Press, 1988), and Martin T. Williams, "Liner Notes," *The Smithsonian Collection of Classic Jazz*, Smithsonian Institution/Columbia Special Products P6 11891, 1973.

9. Mark Dery, "Public Enemy: Confrontation," *Keyboard*, September 1990, 84, and Walser, 196.

10. Walser, 196.

11. Murray Forman, "Hip-Hop Ya Don't Stop!: Hip-Hop History and Historiography," in *That's the Joint!: The Hip-Hop Studies Reader*, ed. Murray Forman and Mark Anthony Neal (New York: Routledge, 2004), 9; and Raymond Williams, *Culture* (London: Fontana Press, 1981).

12. Richard Shusterman, "The Fine Art of Rap," *New Literary History* 22, no. 3 (Summer 1991): 614.

13. Joseph G. Schloss, *Making Beats: The Art of Sample-Based Hip-Hop* (Middletown, CT: Wesleyan University Press, 2004), 36.

14. David J. Elliott, *Music Matters: A New Philosophy of Music Education* (New York: Oxford University, Press, 1995), 162.

15. Shusterman, 615.

16. Schloss, 42.

17. Ibid., 106.

18. 9th Wonder, personal communication with the author, October 12, 2007.

19. Elliott, 170.

20. Howard Gardner, *The Unschooled Mind: How Children Think and How Schools Should Teach*, 10th-anniversary ed. (1995; New York: Basic Books, 2004), 7.

21. Levitin, 115.

22. Stuart Hall, *Representation: Cultural Representations and Signifying Practices* (London: Sage, 1997), 257.

23. David L. Atheide, "Media Hegemony: A Failure of Perspective," *Public Opinion Quarterly* 48, no. 2 (Summer 1984): 477. See Antonio Gramsci, *Prison Notebooks* (New York: International Publishers, 1971).

24. Hall, 259.

25. Turino, 197.

26. Hall, 24.

27. Tricia Rose, *The Hip-Hop Wars: What We Talk about When We Talk about Hip Hop—and Why It Matters* (New York: Basic Books, 2008), 218. See Geoff Boucher,

"A Politician Who Runs on Hip-Hop," *Los Angeles Times*, May 1, 2003, http://www
.articles.latimes.com/2003/may/11/nation/na-kwame11

28. Hall, 257. Also see Richard Dyer, ed. *Gays and Films* (London: Film Institute, 1977).
29. Rose, 29.
30. Ibid., 218.
31. Dery, 82, and Walser, 192.

5

Foraging Fashion: African American Influences on Cultural Aesthetics

Abena Lewis-Mhoon

My mother took flour and sugar bags and made my dresses. No patterns. We were tops and saw ourselves as designers. Had nothing, with nothing, but designers!...I am a designer.

Mrs. Elsie Wallace, age 91, April 2000

African American design influences were rejected, ignored, marginalized, and segregated into colored, Negro, black, Afro-American, or African American categories—if acknowledged at all. That did not stop African Americans, however, from fighting to make their contributions recognized as not just customs of a stigmatized subset, but consequential contributions of Americans to America. Only when wider audiences began to accept a more diverse, or enlightened, justification of African American culture, did American "authorities" begin to recognize these contributions.

The integration of hip hop with mainstream culture is an essential example of that reality. The ability of the mainstream to actively solicit the often shunned and segregated part of African American culture into the melting pot of American culture is a critical case study. This coalescence, of sorts, revisits the age old question, "What is American?" This question can be answered in part, with everything African American. The emergence of hip hop has thrust African American culture, particularly with fashion and design trends, into the limelight.

Hip hop culture incorporates different expressions of African American life, including many cultural retentions found in all aspects of American culture, such as art, language, literature, music, and religion. African Americans succeeded in retaining many practices of their past. Extensive and elaborate funeral ceremonies were derived from the West African concern for the souls of ancestors.[1] As new arrivals meshed West African and Euro-American culture, African

Americans were gradually able to create and sustain new traditions.[2] While incorporating the new with retained traditions, African Americans became the keepers of the guard while inadvertently thrusting fashion, style, and creativity forward, subtly infusing it with the African American aesthetic.

The African American community has long had the innate ability to create, dictate, and drive the American fashion and design industry. African American high society, although never fully accepted by white high society, could shape what was in and what was out without fear of being challenged. They had the dollars to impose their thinking, and the fashion sense to back it up.

The unprecedented, unspoken power of this minority group's sense-of-style was real with major mass appeal; but, it was never publicly or officially acknowledged in the larger white society. It is significant to also note the most important aspect of this force was that it did not have to be. The creativity of the African American community did not hinge on whether it would be accepted by white society because African American style was completely marginalized, if not totally excluded from white society altogether. Rather, the African American creative spirit had an unwavering desire to be embraced by its own community.

Examining the African cultural retentions pertaining to dress and aesthetics, including notions of beauty, and conscious body imaging on African Americans is necessary and shows how many customs were recalled and translated into their American experience. Historically, the definition of beauty, conscious body imaging, and dress focuses on their integration of form, activity, and meaning. In their widest context they are a vehicle for the display of human behavior.[3]

The cultural aspects of African Americans' beauty, conscious body imaging, and dress cannot be discussed without first examining the African culture. The Africans who were brought to the English colonies in the seventeenth, eighteenth, and nineteenth centuries did not carry with them a network of belief, customs, institutions, and practices constituting what might be called with accuracy a unified "African" culture. With the advent of the slave trade, many different cultures fell under the umbrella of a collective African culture in the Americas. In fact, no such monolithic cultural entity existed. The peoples of Africa created a myriad of languages, religions, customs, social, political, and economic institutions, which differentiated them and gave them separate identities.[4] These cultural features have remained with Africans throughout their exhaustive "American" experience.

The most obvious feature that causes one to be labeled African American is physical appearance. This physical appearance has been shaped by the historical, scientific, and cultural changes that surround the African American being. Time and space are constantly trying to intersect the paralleled constant of perception for African Americans. The impact of change has shaped and defined the African American existence.

Individuality and creativity in spite of constraints has been the mantra of African American culture. For centuries, the African culture of the enslaved and former slaves helped African Americans assertively (and without apology) turn the world right side up throughout history. Their culture assisted each generation in their continuous move from slavery to freedom. This culture-based aesthetic serves as one of the most distinguishing behaviors in the communication of identity, which allowed African Americans to preserve symbolic elements of their heritage.[5] The cultural-based aesthetics of African American women moved forward, often altering prevailing conventions without appearing to change. Most profoundly, as African Americans moved forward, they were not pushed by a rage to explain the cultural aesthetic to anyone. By the end of the Civil War these aesthetics, like freedom, asserted themselves with dignity and a resolute resistance.

Ancient Aesthetics

From the time of the Bible to the present, many essays were written by Europeans about the African's color, facial features, hair, and adornments. The earliest writings about Africans, females were described as "black and beautiful....Women...looked upon by the sun.... A black woman who is beautiful; for in her is the image of God and she has received her beauty from...God."[6] The ancient Greeks and Romans often wrote about the beauty of blackness without really coming to grips with it. The fables and written stories suggested that "blackness and woollye hair were caused by exposure to the hot sun."[7]

Still, the ugly garments and repulsive hair of African women always demanded the attention of Europeans. In the sixteenth and seventeenth century, some observers decided that the "Negro's jet blackness was more handsome than the lighter tawny hues; this appreciation was coupled with expressions of distaste for the...short wool on their heads.... Their color and wool are innate, or seminal from their first beginning."[8]

In the seventeenth century, the cycle of degradation was fully underway because of the increasing desire for slavery in the New World. The justification of the enslavement of Africans shifted rapidly from simply a religious curse of Ham, as noted in the Bible, to a racial curse. With the growth of this institution, the unarticulated concept of the Negro as a different sort of person, a heathen who is perfect for slavery, takes hold firmly because Africans (and their culture) were judged as inferior. [9] Again, in religion, the justification for slavery stressed that the descendants of Canaan, the son of Ham [and grandson of Noah], would be a servant for Noah's other sons. In science, the gradation of the races would also find use in the justification of an anti-black, pro-slavery argument. It is argued that Europeans enslaved Africans for economic reasons; then, having become utterly dependent on African labor, Europeans found it necessary to rationalize that exploitation on racist terms as well. Oppression follows logically from exploitation, so as to guarantee the latter.[10] It must be added that in cultural studies, when the question of dress, hair, or the principle of color are added, the facts about inferiority and anatomy reflect interesting ideas.

In spite of some scientists' findings, the ornately embellished clothing, hair, and the blackness of Africans proved to be negative in the broader cultural context of the United States. The repulsion for blackness (and anything positive associated with blackness) is very critical in a slave society where white men were masters. The inferior status served as an easily grasped symbol of the Negro's baseness, wickedness, and lack of culture. By the nineteenth century white racism had become so institutionalized in the United States that it ranked above the maximization of profit as a motive for oppressing black people.[11]

This status combined with the Africans' inherent self-concept proved to be an unshakable commodity that remained with the Africans in America. This combined understanding of self was emitted in everything African Americans did. Continuity and congruence in the African American community are clearly inspired by its African inspired sense of design. The African inspired sense of design is essential to any understanding of the intersection of African American culture, adornment, and aesthetics. The traditions of African dress—apparel or hair—is crucial to studies in which African American culture is being restructured or recast.

In African culture, as is the case with any culture, an aesthetic is an image imparted by the wearer and absorbed by the onlooker. Beauty and fashion are the visual images that provide an understanding of a culture's ideal aesthetic beauty. Traditional studies emphasize that people at the highest control and income levels set the trends for the lower population to copy. This only holds true, in many cases, if the lower population is totally discounted.

Enslaved: EnStyle

Within the society of the United States, people at the highest control and income levels set the trends; however, newer studies are examining how the African Americans did not simply copy the styles of the majority culture, but significantly enhanced fashion, set trends, and influenced the creative aesthetic of America. In addition, it is essential to understand how African American enslaved persons rejected standard styles and fashion as well as many of the negative beliefs about African culture through their own personal dress and adornment. This began the pattern of rejecting the traditionally "accepted" styles and outlined the individualistic and innovative styles which emanated within the African American community.

It would be too sweeping a statement to say that all areas of enslavement can be studied to show this cultural rejection. However, it can be affirmed in many different cultural studies of enslavement. In an early study of the United States a former slave described the many ways enslaved persons worked to produce garments that "looked nice, we wanted to dress, no matter what."[12]

The exploration into slave clothing, when compared to other costume studies, has received little attention. Few specific references have come down to scholars from the pre–Civil War period.[13] Most writers on the subject used material paintings and illustrations invariably done by white artists who were politically motivated to defend or attack the institution of slavery. Missed are the methods that "slaves, male and female, learned to create cloth and fabricate clothing, investing some portion of themselves in the work; their skill and cunning brought a personal style [to their dress and adornment] even in their bondage.[14] What is also frequently overlooked are cultural investigations that analyze both the draping and tucking of the clothing worn, even if the clothing was ragged. Cultural linkages can be recognized in the way the cloth is tied around the waist or the head.

Using sartorial adornment, enslaved men and women created their own styles from the cloth (or material culture) that they had. They accepted the fabrics given to them; and with great skill enslaved men and women shaped, reshaped, and supplemented the fabrics they received by using products nature provided and skill produced. They were respected because they were artists with the ability to design cloth. As early as the seventeenth century in the United States, enslaved men and women were weaving, creating textile arts, sewing, and tailoring. Advertisements document that many were excellent dressmakers and seamstresses with peerless skills.[15]

Lois Alexander's research, *Blacks in the History of Fashion*, analyzes the long history of African Americans in dressmaking during slavery. She is able to prove that African Americans designed and produced remarkably fashionable clothing that was worn by the elite slave owners of the United States. She also emphasizes how in the pre–Civil War South many, if not all, of the clothes of the male and female aristocracy were made by African Americans. Annually, ink sketches of European fashions reached the plantations and homes in cities like Richmond, Virginia; Charleston, South Carolina; Atlanta, Georgia; and New Orleans, Louisiana. Slave women recreated the European fashions using only the pictures as guides.[16]

Many African American women purchased their own freedom and that of their loved ones with money they earned as dressmakers. However, racial segregation and fierce job competition worked together to guarantee the exclusion of African American women from the national American fashion and textile industry. Many of these women were restricted to domestic work or work as nonskilled laborers. The national American fashion market never recognized the African American design influence. However, the communities where these women lived respected their skill set and knowledge base. This respect allowed these artisans to continue creatively influencing the masses at the community level while simultaneously changing national styles because, according to fashion's trickle-up theory, creative and pioneering new trends emerge from the street level.

Most fashion historians completely ignore the trickle-up effect of African American modistes from emancipation to the Civil Rights/integration era. These fashion scholars feel this era is devoid of African American influence. This period, full of rampant racism and fierce job competition, banned African American designers from the national American fashion and textile industry, but inadvertently allowed them to flourish within their own communities.

These designing women became stabilizing forces in the African American community using the same entrepreneurial spirit of independence, self-sufficiency, modesty, and dignity to uplift the community. The entrepreneurial spirit that they brought out of enslavement remained with them as they entered freedom after the Civil War. They assumed the task of dressing a group of people by equipping them with the outward armor to face an uncertain future.

Fashioning Freedom

In post–Civil War America, African American women were responsible for reuniting families, creating communities, and keeping African Americans focused on the future. Many black women continued to work as manual laborers, but some possessed a talent and skill that allowed them to escape to a different reality. The skill of sewing allowed African American women to create a reality for themselves, their families, and their communities. Seamstresses were said to have had visions that allowed them to see something in bits and scraps.[17] These visions allowed skilled seamstresses to turn nothing into beautiful designs. The insight of the African American seamstress under intense, murky oppression to create clearly defined designs and creations is a testament to the strength and agility of African American women. At a time when African Americans were considered to be unintelligent, the African American seamstress proves to be aesthetically astute and aware of creative beauty.

African American seamstresses were themselves a metaphor for the African American community. They took scraps of old material, pieces of old out-fits, or simply visions of designs pieced them together and came up with something beautiful. As black women attempted to adjust to freedom, they attracted negative attention from the American society that scorned them. They were accused of immorality and insolence, and they were relegated to a subhuman mockery—not fit for inclusion in the larger female society. African American women attempted to refute this thinking one stitch at a time. African American women began to revolutionize widespread thinking by redressing the template for the judg-ment of women of color. African American seamstresses used many of the inherent cultural continuities to recreate the image of the black woman. African American women single-handedly sparked a movement to reject any degrading notions about them and their peers. They implemented change piece by piece and combated racial stereotypes and racially driven social forces to gradually take notice and incorporate African American women into society's strata.

Despite such circumstances, the fashion industry of the post–Civil War era was heavily influenced by African American designers. One of the earliest was Elizabeth Keckley. Born a slave in Virginia, this woman was able to learn needlework as an early age. Her work was so popular that she was able to use her needlework skill as collateral to borrow money to purchase her freedom and the freedom of her son. After repaying the debt, she moved to Washington, D.C., where she established a shop as a designer. Keckley employed over sixty persons and had clients like Mrs. Jefferson Davis, Mrs. Stephen Douglass, and Mrs. Abraham Lincoln. Many other African American designers began fashion design businesses; however, most were forced to accept the "seamstress" designa-tion because "as colored women no one respected us publicly for our authentic designs and our unparalleled work in the fashion industry."[18]

Hair designers born during slavery also became important businesspersons. Annie Turnbo Malone, Madame C. J. Walker, and Sarah Spencer Washington blossomed into entrepreneurs in the hair care and design business. Each of these persons successfully sold hair adornments and design instruments: tonics, oils, and hair creams. During the post-Reconstruction era, their hair care systems created new opportunities in a race- and sex-segregated labor market that forced most African American women to work in domestic service, laundering, and farm labor. After slavery, beauty and culture were not only paths toward social mobility, economic, and social advancement for African American women, but also allowed them to develop new aesthetics.[19]

Beauty shops (or parlors) from the 1880s throughout 1940s were vital enterprises and unique in many ways. Hair designers, like the clothing modistes, maintained shops for exclusive clients. While most African American clothing designers had exclusively white customers, African American hair designers had a racially mixed clientele until the early 1900s. After various salons criticized the work of African American hair design shops, the African American hair designers began to solicit exclusively African American clients.

The hair adornment businesses were owned and staffed almost exclusively by women. These businesses created jobs, offered highly valued services, and functioned as social centers in many communities. The operators worked on an informal schedule, often in their own homes or in rented booths. They kept hours that accommodated their patrons—many of whom worked as domestic servants. The women took pride in fashioning beautifully arranged coiffures of smooth styles and pleasing waves. In many cases the styles created at the various salons in the African American communities were copied by stylists for white customers. By the early 1920s, hairstyles were created in Harlem and copied all over New York—then, all over the United States. Aristocrats, café society, and just about everyone else copied the styles worn by women from Harlem's Negro beauty establishments. The marcel waves started with black people in Harlem.[20] Hair culture continued the tradition of women using hair care and preparation as a time of shared confidences and laughter; it was one of the ways women were continuously bound together in fellowship.[21]

Mrs. Marie Williams, a recent honoree of the National Association of Fashion and Accessory Designers, Incorporated, stated in an oral interview that "fashion and beauty brings women together in fellowship." One author noted that in the late 1930s to late 1940s a beauty shop in his neighborhood was "considered the best shop because the hairdressers gave the best feather curls in all of North Philadelphia and Germantown. Each hour the trolley brought almost a dozen customers... with the last twelve or so arriving [to begin hair care appointments] well after seven every evening."[22]

During the move from the farms to the factories, the importance of clothing and adornment did not wane for African Americans. The role of clothing, especially in the working class culture of African Americans, is perceived most clearly in its institutional role. The uniform of domestics [80 percent of the population before World War II] and the attire of middle class workers is an area of critical study. However, it is essential to explore African Americans when they are "presenting themselves as people other than workers."[23] For instance:

> dressing up was enormously important in terms of constructing a collective iden-
> tity based on something other than wage work, presenting a public challenge to the
> dominant stereotypes of the black body, and reinforcing a sense of dignity that was
> perpetually being assaulted.[24]

The end of slavery did not free women from the cotton fields, but it did allow them the freedom to create a new standard of beauty on their Sundays, holidays, or anytime they were free from their labors.[25] Beautiful hair, proper grooming, stylishness, and adornment were ideals that signified freedom, femininity, refinement, and respectability. "Again I say women do not want half of a kingdom, they want the right to simply be women. Respected, . . . treated like ladies. Allowed to look our best."[26]

For white Americans from 1880 to 1920, dress was used to display social and economic wealth. A lady wore large, restricting dresses that indicated that she did not work and was the spouse or child of a man who could afford excessive amounts of expensive fabric.[27] As African American women sought the respect given to "ladies," their fashion mirrored that image. African American women wore fashionable clothing that sometimes imitated high European and American style, yet this style was immersed in their own culture.

From 1910 to 1940, dressmaking, millinery, and nonfactory seamstress jobs were three of the six major occupations for females over ten years of age. As a result, many parents and educators felt one of the best ways of learning was by doing. Given the levels of racial discrimination in the labor market, practical training in a wide array of garment industry fields made women versatile and able to adjust and make the best of any situation. Their educations were designed to prepare women to pursue careers that provided well-paid employment. These women sacrificed to give their daughters training with the desire to help them become self-sufficient women. Women with "good skills" were trained well in their trade "because this specialized training . . . made it less difficult for women to secure employment, advance in the field, and develop job security."[28]

Modern Modiste

Well-trained African Americans were often specialists who earned distinction as experts who worked with specific types of fabrics and detailed trimming. Their garments were viewed as more complex and at the same time their skill also added texture, color, depth, and contrast to their work. These details enhanced the feminine ideals, values, and behavior of a proper lady and her status emanated from the clothing she wore. However, working people received criticism when they tried to find respect in public spaces by dressing well.

In the church, the most important community-based institution, the garments every person wore displayed creativity and ingenuity at its best, often without the constraints of class. The dresses of auxiliary members provide examples of persons who creatively coordinated distinctive looks. These distinctive looks were created to show the role of the group in the church without the focus on the expense of the clothing. Individual dress for church frequently required sewing because sewing allowed individuality to be imparted to clothing. Often people obtained clothing from employers, relatives, or neighbors. Rudimentary sewing skills allowed the economical production of new clothing, or the altering of hand-me-downs, or the making-over of garments that were restyled from items acquired from others. African Americans have been quite ingenious in creating dress-up clothing that they felt was appropriate to wear to church. In churches, dressing up was enormously important in terms of constructing a collective identity based on something other than wage work, presenting a public challenge to the dominant stereotypes of the black body, and reinforcing a sense of dignity that was perpetually being assaulted.[29]

The elements of artistic design were imbedded in each garment African American designers sewed; however, their creators were not given the proper titles as artists, or fashion designers. Many African American dressmakers were given garments to design and sew. Yet when the garment was finished, the shop owner inserted the store's or his or her private label and took the credit. The African American women were not hailed as the makers of the new piece, they were simply regarded, or disregarded, as "seamstresses or girls that could sew."[30]

In fashion, the designer's position is secondary to the garment. The garment is revered because it is an original work of an artist. The owner of the garment is also given respect because she now owns an original piece from a creditable artist. This, many times, was not the case with African American designers. They were not given the proper artistic credit they deserved.

When fashion goes through the trickle-down cycle, and becomes available to different financial levels, it is not considered high fashion anymore. This means "the fashionable woman is forced to adopt something still newer in order to preserve her advantage."[31] This is precisely what African American designers have been doing since the end of slavery. They have taken a style, embraced it, altered it, and developed a system that permits them to stay fashionably dressed—just like the "lady" of the time.

African American designers did much of their work in dry cleaning establishments doing alteration work, tailoring shops, small boutiques, or for other people that claimed their work. This did not limit the designers. They made clothing for themselves, their families, friends, or for personal clients on their own time. Designers used this clientele base to begin their own businesses. Although designers were not seen as competition for the couturieres working in the larger society, in the African American community these designers were visible entities that were integral to the daily lives of the people that lived in there. These African American designers were determined to do the sewing that they loved for the people they loved, and for some paying customers.

The paying customers were often people that were not black. They thought of these women as their own personal prize possessions. Once one person "found a good girl…one would tell the other, and that is how it would grow."[32]

These women became well-kept secrets only revealed to "other certain worthy women."[33]

Within the African American community, these designers represented an indispensable part of life. At public occasions such as parties, affairs, functions, not to mention church, these women had to look their best. The designers formed a network where they shared techniques and knowledge. Since these designers did not have a place in the larger society, they worked in their own communities to create a niche. Their self-concept was not diminished because white society did not view their work as creditable or worthy to be called couture, even though it was. This only strengthened their pursuit of greatness within their own community.

During the early days of desegregation, as the workforce slowly opened up to African American women, presentation maintained its importance. Many women made clothes in their homes after work or on the weekends while they worked full time jobs.[34] Other women got clothing made by family members, friends, or other local designers. The client base of African Americans and others grew so much that it allowed some designers to quit supplemental jobs to devote their attentions to designing and creating full time.

In the dress of the late 1950s to the 1990s, understanding the adaptation of African models for the expression of contemporary motivations is critical. The influence of African dress did not begin with "young Americans returning from Peace Corps assignments in Africa wearing articles of clothing they adopted while living there"[35] or "a rediscovered" heritage. The recurrence of African-inspired style in dress must be evaluated in light of the cultural continuum of this era. Factors such as the 1955–56 Montgomery Bus Boycott and the early 1960 sit-ins by North Carolina Agricultural and Technical College students (all before the creation of the Peace Corps) illustrate the central contributors to expanded racial identity and pride. This racial identity and pride led to an increased interest in African styles and more extensive interpretations (and modifications) of these styles.[36]

The African American aesthetic achieved a new, more empowering dynamic because it facilitated the answering of an important cultural conundrum. The cultural continuum explains how culture can [and does] expand when people outside of the African American community hold little or no regard for it. It continues to experience significant growth, however, in spite of its exclusion from the cultural mainstream. Culture and the cultural continuum carve out a special place of privilege for dress that is focused on its own merits and beyond the "ascribed prestige" of temporary fads.

It is important to acknowledge the fusion of cultures and examine the effects it had on the development of African American society, individuality, and creativity, in spite of constraints. This is the heart of the African American cultural continuum. For centuries, the African culture of slaves and former slaves helped African Americans assertively and unapologetically turn the world right side up throughout history. Their culture assisted each generation in their continuous move "from slavery to freedom." African American culture, especially the ever-changing adornment of apparel and hair, is most assertive when the

African-centered aesthetic, from the perspective of many persons, directly meets the dominant aesthetic. This assertion of dignity is not dismissed as peripheral; this is also not a conflicting aesthetic but a continuing one.

As the businesses of African American designers expanded in the twentieth century, the enterprises of African American women were dependent on both the social capital and collective forms of cultural capital. These design businesses succeeded because this group of entrepreneurs combined traditional financial capital, or money to pay for raw materials, equipment, and human capital in the form of the skills and expertise of the workers and managers. In this regard, African Americans' social capital took the form of family networks and labor, community and neighborhood groups, social organizations, and voluntary associations. All of these groups served as an important resource for the successful operation of women's business enterprises. African American designers mobilized their resources to establish unseen but powerful community-based businesses that would benefit not just individuals, but the entire group.

Therefore, the African American aesthetic has seamlessly influenced the American fashion industry, but is still unrecognized. This is an essential fact that is often overlooked by cultural historians who show how women were the targets for consumption, during the twentieth century, yet because of race and class African Americans were not included in this target market. Money for advertising was not spent on African Americans, despite the explosion in marketing and advertising during the twentieth century, because shopping was an activity reserved for ladies of leisure and wealth. As consumerism exploited American culture, African American seamstresses had a hand in shaping the style and image of the American consumers with skills that were taught and passed down through generations. They made beautiful and unique pieces, often one-of-a-kind, that for social reasons they were not able to afford or invited to purchase.[37]

For fashion leaders, designers are less significant when compared to their creations. People wearing these original designs garner respect because they own an artist's original piece. There were a few well-known African American designers who were sought after by white high society. Although in many cases African Americans were asked to design and create beautiful fashions, they were, for the most part, relegated to the role of seamstress or dressmaker. To the outside world, these were viewed as menial positions that did not require any level of artistic skill. The title "designer" was reserved for white business owners whose names appeared in the shop window or the garments' label. This facade—or veil as Du Bois put it—enabled the white business owners to further demean African American women, blatantly steal their ideas, unique designs or design details, and take credit for their work in exchange for low pay.

Underscored by the boom in marketing, advertising, and consumption during the twentieth century, when the target market was clearly not African American, more and more advertising dollars were spent to entice women of status and means. At the end of the twentieth century, African American designers increasingly demanded credit for their design skills as well as their influence on international trends. However, American social forces were unrelenting in their attempts to control fashion and design as it impacts on the concept of self.

Fashion is "culturally constructed and always ephemeral, [yet] race is presumed to be given and unchanging."[38] The two are undoubtedly connected and the disassociation of culture and race is impossible. The African American experience expressed through fashion cannot be easily separated because the translation of African American style has been accepted by the mainstream. The deconstruction of African American fashion has given way to the incorporation of this style into mainstream American culture without its African American cultural aspects or purveyors being given credit for this style.

American style and culture sets trends by using popular images to communicate what people should buy, how they should act, and who they should become. This automatically influences a particular group's beliefs. Within the last fifty years, African Americans, as purveyors of style, have undeniably influenced the American way of acting, talking, dressing, and being. Rapper and popular culture icon Nicki Minaj comments that her personal style that influences many is "still evolving." At times, "I am like a big cartoon. Dressing outside the box is important to me."[39] It is now acceptable for mainstream America to mirror African American culture and cultural identity without recognizing the prevailing notions of inferiority layered within its history. For popular culture's efficacy, African American culture cannot be neatly repackaged and resold without a full acknowledgment of the social limitations imposed on African Americans.

The efforts to marginalize African Americans' designs, fashion, and style only reaffirm the power of African Americans designers as couriers of cutting-edge culture. While not respected, African American designers are the people who have always impelled American style. African American innovators of style must challenge the American social practice of stealing their style, altering its identity, adjusting cultural meaning, and then passing it off as American.

In the United States, contemporary fashion designers continue the four hundred-year-old effort to extricate race from style and fashion. However, this disassociation of race and culture is impossible. The African American experience, expressed through fashion, cannot be separated and lost in simply American style. For four hundred years of African American design and style—although stolen, translated, and incorrectly stamped American as it moves into the mainstream—generated the cultural motion and powered the creative engines that simultaneously transformed and moved forward every component of fashion.

Notes

1. Albert J. Raboteau, *Slave Religion: The "Invisible Institution" in the Antebellum South* (New York: Oxford University Press, 1978), 75.
2. Edward D. Smith, *Climbing Jacob's Ladder: The Rise of Black Churches in Eastern American Cities, 1740–1877* (Washington, D.C.: Smithsonian Institution Press, 1988), 23–26.
3. Barbara M. Starke, Lillian O. Holloman, and Barbara K. Nordquist, eds. *African American Dress and Adornment: A Cultural Perspective* (Dubuque, IA: Kendall/Hunt Publishing Company, 1990), 5.

4. Lawrence Levine, *Black Culture and Black Consciousness: Afro-American Folk Thought From Slavery to Freedom* (New York: Oxford University Press, 1977), 3–4.

5. Anna Atkins Simkins, "Function and Symbol in Hair and Headgear among African American Women," in *African American Dress and Adornment*, ed. Barbara M. Starke, Lillian O. Holloman, and Barbara K. Nordquist (Dubuque, IA: Kendall/Hunt Publishing Company, 1990), 166.

6. M. G. Easton, *Commentary on the Song of Songs and Ecclesiastes* (New York: np, 1885), 26–27; Basil Davidson, *The African Past: Chronicles from Antiquity to Modern Times* (Boston: Little & Brown Publishers, 1964); and Basil Davidson, *Old Africa Rediscovered* (London: Gollancz, 1959).

7. Winthrop Jordan, *White Over Black: American Attitudes Toward the Negro, 1550–1812* (Chapel Hill: University of North Carolina, 1968), 11–12; and Melville Herskovits, "On the Provenience of the New World Negroes," *Social Forces* 12 (1933), 247–62.

8. Jordan, 14–17.

9. Ibid., 96; For a discussion on the historiography of how the early English North American colonists viewed and justified the enslavement of Africans see Alden T. Vaughn, "The Origins of Debate: Slavery and Racism in Seventeenth-Century Virginia," *Virginia Magazine of History and Biography* 97, no. 3 (July 1989): 311–54.

10. Walter Rodney, *How Europe Underdeveloped Africa* (Washington, D.C.: Howard University Press, 1974), 88–89.

11. Ibid., 89.

12. Barbara M. Starke, "Slave Narratives: Accounts of What They Wore," in *African American Dress and Adornment*, ed. Barbara M. Starke, Lillian O. Holloman, and Barbara K. Nordquist (Dubuque, IA: Kendall/Hunt Publishing Company, 1990), chapter V.

13. Ibid., 50–92; Sarah Jane Downing, *Fashion in the Time of Jane Austen* (Botley, Oxford, UK: Shire Publications, 2010).

14. Gloria Williams and Carol Centrallo, in "Clothing Acquisition and Use by the Colonial African American," in *African American Dress and Adornment: A Cultural Perspective*, ed. Barbara M. Starke, Lillian O. Holloman, and Barbara K. Nordquist (Dubuque, IA: Kendall/Hunt Publishing Company, 1990), chapter V, 55. Also see Avril Hart and Susan North, *Seventeenth and Eighteenth Century Fashion in Detail* (New York: Rizzoli, 1998; London: V&A Publishing, 2009).

15. Gerilyn Tanberg, "Field Hand Clothing in Louisiana and Mississippi during the Antebellum Era," *Costume* 15 (1981): 40–48; and Patricia Campbell Warner and Debra Parker in *African American Dress and Adornment: A Cultural Perspective*, 88.

16. Sharon Sadako Taykeda, Kaye Durland Spilker, and Kimberly Chrisman-Campbell, *Fashioning Fashion: European Dress in Detail 1700–1950* (2010); Duanne Hoffler, "The Backbone of African American Couture," in *African American Dress and Adornment*, ed. Barbara M. Starke, Lillian O. Holloman, and Barbara K. Nordquist (Dubuque, IA: Kendall/Hunt Publishing Company, 1990), 131–33.

17. Abena Lewis-Mhoon, "Adorning Adversaries, Affecting Avenues: The African American Women's Impact on Adornment and Fashion Design in Washington, DC 1910–1950" (PhD diss., Howard University, 2005).

18. Lucy Johnston, *Nineteenth-Century Fashion in Detail* (London: V&A Publishers, 2005); Smith, March 18, 1999; and Hoffler, 130–37.

19. Pamela Ferrell, *Let's Talk Hair* (Washington, D.C.: Cornrows & Company, 1996), 1–31.

20. Kathleen Morgan Drowne and Patrick Huber, *The 1920s* (Westport, CT: Greenwood Press, 2004), 108; Lionel C. Bascom, *A Renaissance in Harlem: Lost Essays of the WPA by Ralph Ellison, Dorothy West, and Other Voices of a Generation* (New York: Amistad, 2004); and Mrs. Grace Simpson, beautician since the 1930s, in an interview by author, tape recording, September 15, 1998.

21. Jacqueline Jones, *Labor of Love, Labor of Sorrow: Black Women, Work and the Family, from Slavery to the Present* (New York: Random House, 1985), 214–15.

22. Ernest and Helen Butler, *Neighbors of the 2100 Block: A Philadelphia Story* (New Jersey: The Web Press Printers, 1986), 46.

23. Robin D. G. Kelley, *Race Rebels: Culture, Politics, and the Black Working Class* (New York: Free Press, 1994), 49–50.

24. Donald Bogle, *Toms, Coons, Mulattoes, Mammies, and Bucks: An Interpretive History of Blacks in American Films* (New York: Continuum, 1989), 19–94; and Kelley, 50.

25. See Lewis-Mhoon, "Adorning Adversaries," chapters 2–5.

26. See Ellen C. Du Bois, *The Emergence of an Independent Women's Movement in America, 1848–1869* (Ithaca, NY: Cornell University Press, 1978); Bettina Aptheker, *Woman's Legacy: Essays on Race, Sex, and Class in American History* (Amherst, MA: University of Massachusetts Press, 1982); and Roselyn Terborg-Penn, *African American Women and the Struggle for the Vote* (Bloomington, IN: Indiana University Press, 1998), chapter 1.

27. Natalie Rothstein, ed. *400 Years of Fashion* (London: V&A Publications 2010); Emil Reich, *Woman through the Ages,* vol. 2 (London: Metheun & Co, 1908), 253–63.

28. Francois Baudot, *Fashion: The Twentieth Century,* trans. Jane Brenton rev. ed. (New York: Universe Publishing, 2006); and Traki L. Taylor, "Woman Glorified," *Journal of African American History* 87 (Fall 2002): 393–400.

29. Isabel A. Jones and Lillian Holloman, "The Role of Clothing in the African American Church," in *African American Dress and Adornment*, ed. Barbara M. Starke, Lillian O. Holloman, and Barbara K. Nordquist (Dubuque, IA: Kendall/Hunt Publishing Company, 1990), 150–61; Donald Bogle, 19–94; Kelley, 50; and see Stephanie Shaw, *What a Woman Ought to Be and to Do: Black Professional Women Workers during the Jim Crow Era* (Chicago: University of Chicago Press, 1996), 8, 74, 169, 208 for church roles, charity, and community consciousness.

30. Mrs. Barbara Walker, interview by author, Washington, D.C., April 19, 2000, tape recording.

31. James Laver, *Taste and Fashion* (London: G. G. Harrap and Company, 1945), 202; Kate Hahn, *Forgotten Fashion: An Illustrated Faux History of Outrageous Trends and Their Untimely Demise* (Cincinnati: F&W Media, 2008); and Bonnie English, *A Cultural History of Fashion in the Twentieth Century: From the Catwalk to the Sidewalk* (New York: Berg, 2007).

32. Mrs. Elsie Wallace, interview by author, Washington, D.C., April 21, 2000, tape recording.

33. Ibid.

34. Patricia Rieff Anawalt, *The Worldwide History of Dress* (New York: Thames & Hudson, 2007); Cheryl Buckley "On the Margins: Theorizing the History and Significance of Making and Designing Clothes at Home," *Journal of Design History* 11 (1998): 157–71.

35. Otto Thieme and Joanne Eicher, "African Dress: Form, Action, Meaning," in *African American Dress and Adornment*, ed. Barbara M. Starke, Lillian O. Holloman, and Barbara K. Nordquist (Dubuque, IA: Kendall/Hunt Publishing Company, 1990), 4.

36. Designer Juanita Pacheco of Cape Town, interview by author, Cape Town, South Africa, March 21, 1998, tape recording.; Abena Lewis-Mhoon, "Dressing for Freedom," *Black History Bulletin* 67, nos 1–4 (2004), 26–29.

37. Linda Watson, *Vogue Fashion: Over 100 Years of Fashion by Decade and Designer, in Association with Vogue* (Buffalo: Firefly Books, 2008); Alberta Oliva, Norberto Angeletti, Anna Wintour, and Steven Klien, *In Vogue: An Illustrated History of the World's Most Famous Fashion Magazine* (New York: Rizzoli, 2006); and Angela McRobbie, "Bridging the Gap: Feminism, Fashion and Consumption," *Feminist Review* 55 (Spring, 1997): 73–89.

38. Kimberly Arkin, "Rhinestone Aesthetics and Religious Essence: Looking Jewish in Paris," *American Ethnologist* 36 (2009): 722–34; W. E. B. Du Bois, *The Souls of Black Folk: Essay and Sketches* (Chicago: A.C. McClurg & Company, 1903), vii; and Stuart Hall "Cultural Identity and Diaspora" in *Identity: Community, Culture, Difference,* ed. Jonathan Rutherford (Ann Arbor: University of Michigan, 1990), 222–37; Dick Hebidge, *Subculture: The Meaning of Style* (London: Metheun & Co., 1979); John L. Jackson, Jr., *Real Black: Adventures in Racial Sincerity* (Chicago: University of Chicago Press, 2005); and Jean Comaroff, *Body of Power, Spirit of Resistance: The Culture and History of a South African People* (Chicago: University of Chicago Press, 1985).

39. Nicki Minaj, HoneyMag.com, April 2010, https://www.youtube.com/watch?v=4 CNtaNYPFGc

6

In the Eye of the Beholder: Definitions of Beauty in Popular Black Magazines

Kimberly Brown

Mass communication has long functioned as a forceful and effectual device in the African American quest for dominion over themselves, their ideas, and their future existence in the United States. Particularly, blacks associated with the media as writers and journalists of all sorts worked to further these ideals and triggered a great deal of progress in this very respect. David Walker called for the immediate end of slavery and the use of necessary violence in his *Appeal to the Coloured Citizens of the World*. Frederick Douglass openly challenged racist federal and local laws and, as a survivor, exposed the ugly nature of involuntary drudgery in his *North Star* and *Frederick Douglass' Paper*. Ida B. Wells fiercely called attention to the common horrors of lynching throughout the United States and even suggested in her *Memphis Free Speech* and other papers for which she wrote that white women were the instigators in romantic liaisons with black men rather than the victims of such, as was often used erroneously as justification for the brutal murders of countless men of color throughout the nineteenth and twentieth centuries. Surely these and other publications profoundly and positively affected the cause of black liberation.

The need for such was obvious as illustrated by *Time* magazine's announcement of Josephine Baker in a 1936 *Ziegfeld Follies* show as a "Negro wench" with underwhelming talent and performances.[1] It also called her a "slightly bucked tooth" common woman who was essentially lucky to earn attention in Paris.[2] These types of commentaries on black people were not unusual. Just as victims of physical harm resulting from severe racial tensions sought safe havens, black people seeking ideological, artistic, and cultural freedom required outlets of expression devoid of the nasty attacks prevalent in all forms of white media. More than energizing various movements and reshaping perceptions, these written forms aided in the carving out of space for autonomy in defining standards generated by black people for black people. Representing the same continuum, popular black magazines of the mid-1900s reflect this identical purpose. Through the realm of black popular culture, such a specified medium allowed for an expression of beauty that would, at times, both emulate and eschew popular notions of a beauty standard.

Writing in the *Douglass' Paper* in 1853, William J. Wilson bemoaned, "We despise, we almost hate ourselves, and all that favors us." He likened this condition of the absence of a positive self-image to the lack of favorable depictions of people of African descent. "Well may we scoff at black skins and woolly heads, since every model set before us for admiration, has a palled face and flaxen head."[3] The European norm has been the standard in the measure and definition of what constitutes a beauty aesthetic. Women of African descent have both embraced and redefined such classifications of what is beautiful. "Throughout history and to present day, African American women have challenged White definitions of beauty. What or who is considered beautiful varied among cultures. What remains consistent is that many notions of beauty are rooted in hegemonically defined expectations."[4] For American blacks from enslavement forward, hair texture and skin color denoted one's closeness to European or African ancestry. White Americans, at times, were "more accepting of lighter-skinned Blacks" though the one-drop ruled prevailed in the United States.[5] Thus, in the futile attempt to be accepted and acceptable, "Black people...helped perpetuate this truth by maintaining the straight-hair, light-skin hierarchy within their own ranks."[6] Hair politics was more complicated than skin color. After emancipation, and in a departure from white cosmetic firms that denigrated any African-descended features, early black hair care pioneers touted their products as remedies for ailments such as baldness and scalp disease as well as goods for growing and managing the hair. Critics, however, disapproved of the altering of the natural state of black hair.[7]

Still, such barometers grounded in the Eurocentric ideal constantly degrade the woman of color and relegate her to the diametric opposite of beautiful—ugly—or inundate her with stereotypical images that also detract from pulchritudal attainment. Attempting to replicate a norm outside of a cultural milieu often results in the detrimental "internalization" of unobtainable standards, and exemplifies what scholars Charisse Jones and Kumea Shorter-Gooden classify as the lily complex. This alludes to the "altering, disguising, and covering up of your physical self in order to assimilate, to be accepted as attractive....As Black women deal with the constant pressure to meet a beauty standard that is inauthentic and often unattainable, the lily complex can set in."[8]

When not being assaulted, African American females were altogether excluded from the beauty ideal. Maxine Leeds Craig, in *Ain't I A Beauty Queen?*, puts in plainly. Black women were left out and considered "non-beauties."[9] Furthermore, matters concerning Negroes were not regularly covered in the major mainstream magazines. Black-run monthlies addressed these issues. In November 1947, *Our World* ran a scathing critique on race relations in Richmond, Virginia, asserting "Richmond's 'white folks' are still hanging on desperately to the Southern tradition of 'keeping the Negro in his place.'"[10] The article continued, "Every day the Negro finds his three generations of so-called freedom in Richmond no more than a hand me down paternalism which dictates that he accept certain jobs and stay in his separate ghetto."[11] These bold statements could likely find no home but in a black publication.

The same issue of *Our World* tackled another, and possibly more subconscious, form of white supremacy elsewhere in its pages. The lead concept on the cover asked readers, "What is Negro Beauty?" The inquiry itself suggested the aforementioned need for that special carved out space that would allow not only blacks' access to the societal norms, ideals, and acceptance of others, but also an opening to construct their own and have it stand as valid in an America founded in their subjugation. The article corresponding to the question is straightforward in its striving for inclusion and validation. The very first lines read, "Beauty is no monopoly of any race. True beauty is universal. Here are three varieties of beautiful Negro women...and two of the top beauty analysts to prove it."[12] This question of beauty and its varied responses appeared recurrently throughout African American popular culture print media. This research specifically examines both the visuals and their corresponding descriptions concerning beauty within black-owned magazines popular between World War II and the dawn of the Black Power Movement. The examination tracks the trends and changes in defining African American attractiveness through a cultural lens, with substantial consideration of the following: the simultaneous African American desire for normality/inclusion in the mainstream alongside the development of their own beauty ideal; the typology of women selected as features; the overt and subtle meanings of product advertisements; magazine content as a reflection of class values and behaviors; and the impact of current events and historical change on terminology usage and prototypical beauty modification.

Again, ownership, the ability to define as opposed to being defined by outside forces, and acknowledgment of the self-made definition had long been practiced by and remained serious continued objectives for black people. Organs such as *Color, Ebony, Our World, Sepia*, and *Tan*—even in their titles—spoke to this petition for sovereignty, recognition of dissimilarity from the majority, and pride in that uniqueness. Their black proprietors—such as John P. Davis of *Our World* and John H. Johnson of *Negro Digest, Tan*, and *Ebony*—carried this mission as the grandchildren of slaves, survivors of the Great Depression, and visionaries who generated advancement through the command of literature and media. However, in spite of these aspirations to maintain and perpetuate—and a significant amount of success in doing so—their own canonical models for human conduct, cultural tradition, and aesthetic value, the residuals of living under European customs are also apparent. The ethnocentric tug of war found within the pages of African American publications often gave way to "a peculiar sensation, this double-consciousness, this sense of always looking at one's self through the eyes of others, of measuring one's soul by the tape of a world that looks on in amused contempt and pity. One ever feels his two-ness,—an American, a Negro; two souls, two thoughts, two unreconciled strivings; two warring ideals in one dark body."[13] Perhaps in no other area is W. E. B. Du Bois's double-consciousness theory more detectable than in black people's odd, yet triumphant relationship with beauty in America.

The pages of these popular culture magazines allowed women of color who ordinarily would not have received the same level of coverage elsewhere to be heralded as consummate icons of glamour within the national black community. For many black men and women who read them, these beauties represented attainability too, much more than the white-only examples dominant in general outlets. Women on the covers or featured inside could easily look like a family member, friend, or even the reflection in the mirror. This relatability remained less likely in major stage and film productions, television shows, and national advertisements of the time.

Simultaneously, though, Eurocentric ideals noticeably crept into the interpretation of goodness, superiority, and loveliness, even in black-owned ventures. An advertisement in *Our World,* in November 1950, promises Kombo buyers "the secret of soft, smooth, STRAIGHT hair that will stay that way from 3 to 6 months!"[14] A medium brown-skinned young man, A. Herman Smith of Los Angeles, supposedly demonstrates the results in before-and-after shots: one in which he is wearing a naturally tough texture contoured into a scruffy square and another sporting a shiny process (slicked-back) with a part down the middle. For "only $1.69" and a "money-back guarantee," the company assures the product is "From Hollywood!"[15] This was the very Hollywood that, at that time, had refused to green light an all-black cast in the major motion picture production of *Carmen Jones*, which would not be made until 1954—four years later.

Conflict between a black beauty aesthetic and white predominance emerged once more in *Our World*'s "10 Most Beautiful Negro Women" piece within that same issue. It promoted black beauty and sponsored a contest in the same vein. An excerpt read, "*OUR WORLD* is convinced now is the time to glorify the Negro woman and make her proud of her unusual beauty."[16] Unusual compared to what? Already, she is placed outside of the norm as conceived by black people themselves. The statement implies what the writer perceived to be problematic; black women have not been praised and therefore are to some extent made to feel less-than-proud regarding their natural attractiveness. In all likelihood, a lifestyle publication marketed to black people would avoid making such claims, especially in a lengthy cover story, if it had no hint of validity with readers. Essentially, the need for such affirmation must have been a fairly widely accepted notion among African Americans.

Next to the aforementioned appeal to celebrate African American allure, augmented by surrounding photos reflecting its selection of ten women, sits a picture of a twenty-two-year-old singer from Boston, Massachusetts, in strapless eveningwear described as obviously having a "Caucasian background." Below her is an insert of fair-skinned starlet Lena Horne along with kindly remarks about her beauty. The magazine situates New York model Mary Smith's two-piece bathing suit photo next to Horne and defines her as "the fair-to-white sexy type. Stacked in all the right places, Mary is the kind that attracts many wolf calls. She's often mistaken for white, [and] has no difficulty passing."[17] The glorification of curves might represent African-centered idealism, while the prevalent praise of light complexions almost definitely symbolizes European orthodoxy. The endorsement of mixed women as prototypical beauties goes further. "For that matter we know that somewhere in these United States may exist Negro women many more times beautiful than Lena Horne."[18] Here, the screen idol denotes a standard or ceiling the contest sought to surpass. Based upon a thorough search, a black woman more beautiful than she only *may* exist. On the other hand, while the pictures and words did more than hint at what kind of Negro woman would be exalted, the competition extended, at least in written rule (words hold some value), accessibility to such an echelon and subsequent acclaim to any black applicant.

> This issue officially starts the biggest talent hunt ever planned (we are proud to say)—by any Negro publication to find "the most beautiful Negro woman." We want you to send in all the pictures of women you consider beautiful—yourselves, your sisters, your friends. This contest is nation-wide. Every Negro woman is eligible.[19]

Even if the call for submissions was strictly to increase subscribership, planting the idea of black women as figures of splendor functions as a step in the rehabilitation toward the damage done by history's attack on women of color and their image. Furthermore, at a minimum, all the candidates in *Our World*'s contest would have been, to some degree, of color. Then again, the prizes reflected a bend toward Eurocentrism. In addition to shopping sprees, cash prizes, and an invitation to celebrate at a gala on Broadway's Astor rooftop, *Our World* offered a wardrobe fashioned by exceptional Parisian designers and trips to Paris, the Riviera, Rome, and London.[20]

In *Color*'s November 1949 "America's 100 Most Beautiful Negro Women" layout, racially ambiguous, freelance model Candy Bowman's picture led the pack in size, sequence, and arrangement. The large photo emphasized a sensual pose, with the subject leaned in for added effect, no obvious smile, flirty eyes, slender nose, moderately sized painted lips, soft dark curls just past the shoulders leading into a bit of cleavage, and a honey-colored face. Described as a "ravishing beauty," her image introduces the article and literally dwarfs the subsequent wallet and matchbox size images of various skin hues and shades that follow. Her maiden name, Hjerte Morlina, in addition to her parental heritage in the Virgin Islands, further indicates probable evidence of mixed lineage. Partiality for this kind of look was displayed not only in print but also in many articulations of black people themselves. In fact, Bowman "was voted among the most beautiful Negro women in New York City three times."[21] As these sorts of treatments were unapologetically clear concerning preference, black popular culture publications did create room for darker, more purely African looking women. Not necessarily as cover girls or even leading features on the inside, they were at least included. The assorted exhibition of faces in the "America's 100 Most Beautiful Negro Women" presentation worked to this end. Moreover, by sheer numbers alone, black magazines undergirded the establishment of black beauty representation.

This large volume of ladies, one hundred to be precise, received visual admiration along with a glowing written comment on each one in the magazine, whereas no white publication at that time would glorify black women in that way and certainly not that many at once. Although the black beauty ideal may not have been the deepest of browns, she was still within reach, especially with consideration to the systematic sexual abuse of black families during slavery and the regularity of miscegenation during the years thereafter. It was highly possible that as a Negro in the late 1940s and early 1950s, one was related to or knew someone who looked much like Candy Bowman or any of the women labeled as beautiful.

The practice of black print enterprises blending white proclivity into the black ideological framework is no surprise when considering history. Real advantages came with acceptance/obedience of rules and regulations designed by Europeans. Not doing so, in many cases, meant lack of employment, physical harm, or even death. In her book, *The Paper Bag Principle*, Audrey Elisa Kerr notes some of the less severe examples internalized and executed by black people. About light-only access to social events, the witness claimed, "Nobody would stop you at the door and say, 'Let's get the brown paper bag.' But nobody would dance with you either. But if you came they would call that crashing. It was *understood* that it was a brown bag party. In the culture you just knew it."[22]

Here, just as obviously as restrictive laws and malicious instruction were forced upon African people and their descendants, so was white psychology. These two societal elements— codes/laws and perceptions/psychology—often overlapped, which frequently created a desire for inclusion within white parameters and a need to defend existence within them once allowed. Therefore, black magazines in substance and literal appearance constituted a fusion of African American and white ideology.

Shade preferences in Negro society were apparent not only in pictorial selections and societal gatherings, but also in the language used in major black magazines. The titles *Color*, *Sepia*, and *Tan*, each widely circulated in the 1940s and 1950s, could be interpreted as gestures of coexisting pride in Negro distinctivism and reluctance (as a reaction to white supremacy) to fully place the community's proverbial fist in the air. All three, in name alone, denote café au lait pigmentation. The titles are black with just enough white substance to allow for their production and consumption by a people forcibly infused with a white value system. The nomenclature found within African American magazine pages reinforced, once more, a blend of sorts. For instance, Dorthea Towels graced the cover of *Our World* in August of 1952 as "Paris's Fabulous Negro Model." The article called her "a daring, bronze blonde."[23] It continued, "[t]all, lean, and flat chested, she has a stately regal appearance."[24] The section also announced Towels's return home "to crack big-time New York modeling, which, up to now, has been closed to Negroes." It reported, "Dorthea has proved a Negro model can sell a $1500 gown in Europe."[25] What kind of Negro? A photographer captured her at the Golden State Ballroom standing next to the famed pianist Hazel Scott. A quick glance at it might deceive a set of eyes into mistaking Towels for Marilyn Monroe.

In the same issue of *Our World*, bronze again reigned as the word of choice in describing attractive women of color. This time it was to document the Miss

Bronze Los Angeles Pageant sponsored by historically black Greek fraternity Omega Psi Phi. "After 30 copper-toned beauts showed up for the final judging…when it was over, pretty 5 foot [*sic*] 3 Lynette Cobb was the winner."[26] Ironically, this very august edition placed a spread about worldwide opera sensation Marian Anderson, a moderately brown woman, on the inside, but the cover went to Dorthea Towels. Exactly one year later, color conscious terms resurfaced in *Our World*'s article on cover girl Sylvia Blackburn, a Howard University co-ed. It began, "Beauty, not brains sometimes rules campus."[27] The barely tanned, straight-haired Blackburn received glowing remarks from the magazine. "Fresh and effervescent, Sylvia's olive brown prettiness is becoming one of Washington's landmarks."[28] Writers routinely applied bronze, copper-toned, olive brown, warm sun, medium mahogany, sparkling yellow, golden, and countless other middle-of-the-ground terms to their descriptions of the black beauty ideal.[29] However, the publications remained committed to appreciating color, even if somewhat diluted by white psychological influence.

Advertisements further this point. They undoubtedly spoke to potential customers about a perceived considerable Negro desire for certain European features. The ads used both blacks and Caucasians, a mix, to disseminate their messages. Eastern Human Hair Goods Company of New York offered straight "glamorous long hair at once" in their wigs available in smoothly braided, page boy, and chignon (a French word) styles.[30] The Ronald Company asked, rhetorically, "Do you want straight hair that actually stays straight?"[31] The company answered by offering "Straiteen" as a "thrilling new hope."[32] The underlying assumption denotes that without this texture type, hope was not tangible. With a white woman smiling, waves cascading into a cloud of curls down her back, it promised several things. Supposedly, after working three to six months, it left "your hair softer and easier to manage," and "your hair look[ed] longer immediately."[33] Nadinola guaranteed romance to users of their bleaching cream. The advertisement focused on a fair-skinned woman who wore a short crop of loose waves and was draped in a string of pearls in a shoulder-bearing dress contemplating, "He loves me…he loves me not" as she counted the petals on a flower.[34] Sellers warned, "Don't depend on daises! Be sure with a light, clear complexion."[35] If the bold print left room for misinterpretation, a longer admonishment below read, "Whether he loves you…or loves you not…largely depends on whether your complexion is light and lovely…or dark and dull." The posting also claimed product observers reacted with the exclamation, "How lucky she is to have such lovely, light skin!"[36] Apparently enough women of color bought into this warped sense of aesthetics. According to Susannah Walker, in *Style and Status*, black women purchased so many of these kinds of beauty products that white companies "went so far as to represent themselves as black-run in their advertising" to cash in on the growing economy.[37]

As popular culture lifestyle publications, their events coverage reflected the ways in which this cross-cultural fertilization (as a result of psychological oppression or not) evidenced itself not only in beauty perceptions, but also in societal activity. The constructions of the two paralleled one another. For example, *Our World* in September 1953 asserts, "For class and sheer beauty, you can't beat

Philadelphia's Cotillion."[38] The images show Negro men and women dressed in tuxedos and debutante-inspired gowns. The yearly Christmas event hosted guests such as "Eleanor Roosevelt, Ralph Bunch, Mary McLeod Bethune, Branch Rickey, and native daughter Marian Anderson." Groups such as the National Association for the Advancement of Colored People (NAACP) and the Dru Opera House benefitted from the proceeds.[39] Several pages later, the Girl Friends received the "top Negro social group in the country" title in a report on the organization and its recent festivities.[40] The club, rooted in friendship among black college girls from New York, presented a three-day affair culminating in a ball at which members "tried to outdo one another at the mink-dripping formal."[41] Attracting nearly 1,200 persons, the weekend included auxiliary parties, one of which was hosted "by Mrs. Marie Poston, wife of prize-winning journalist Ted Poston."[42] Though some activities took place at the St. George Hotel, Brooklyn school-teacher Mrs. Hazel Thomas welcomed guests to a function at her "big home."[43] Around the same time, in Richmond, the Merry Moles, a similar group, gathered to celebrate. Their agenda, which included a "luncheon at a business session," also consummated in a formal at which lace, gloves, tulle, corsages, and pearls were in abundance.[44] A writer commented that the "Confederate federal capital has seldom seen a social event equal to the glamor and glitter"[45] of the Moles, who drew their name from the amusing practice by members of drawing a "beauty mark" on their faces.[46] Aside from cosmetic fun, the Moles also devoted time to execute an assembly on "serious community projects" as a part of their regular convention schedule.[47] In earlier years, the Moles "presented a Norfolk hospital with a complete supply of linen." Since then, they "have aided some organization or individual," to include the most recent presentation, in 1953, of "cash to the NAACP Defense Fund."[48]

Although the attire at these galas may have lent itself to the practices of high society in the white community, surely those in attendance, those honored, and the beneficiaries of such events, which often doubled as fundraisers, demonstrated both the sociopolitical and institutional values of black people. Even though some engaged in makeup applications likely embedded in Hollywood's aesthetic idealism, their contributions to the black struggle went even further than their financial contributions. The opportunity to visualize people of color living seemingly fantastic, successful, and even extravagant lives meant an observable, and therefore tangible, alternative to the terrible, ghastly, and stereotypical images offered almost everywhere else. Here, black publications functioned as a safe haven, even if white influences were traceable.

Those traces not only surfaced in the cover images and full-page photos of fair- skinned beauties, but also featured prominently in magazine advertisements. The February 1960 issue of *Ebony* magazine trumpeted the wonders of Artra, a skin-tone cream that promised to provide users with "a lovelier, lighter, skin" that would help achieve "that radiant glow." Even *Ebony* magazine, through its not-so-subtle advertising, slyly discouraged readers from being too ebony. The celebration of black beauty seemed to house a contradictory undercurrent of doubt concerning the validity of a true black beauty aesthetic. Skin bleaching was no taboo and black print media outlets had zero qualms about praising the rich brown hues of its readership one moment while advocating for lighter skin the next. In fact, only a few pages after the Artra ad, an in-depth article followed chronicling a successful beauty revue featuring forty to fifty black women. However, none of the women in the article's photos would have any issue passing the brown paper bag test.

Although in many instances darker women who earned covers often had a more specific claim to fame than lighter women who obtained the same position more frequently, the fact remains that black-owned monthlies shed positive light on a variety of women of color. Sarah Vaughn, Marian Anderson, and Josephine Baker covered *Our World* as performance icons and affirmative examples of show business success. The Johnson Publishing Company's *Ebony* (1945) and *Jet* (1951), first introduced to the reading public relatively around the same time but not yet as popular as John P. Davis's *Our World* (1946), alluded to an appreciation for deeper tints. As they dramatically rose in readership during the freedom struggles of the 1960s, fittingly so with consideration to their titles, unapologetically brown women such as Diana Ross, Leslie Uggams, Diahann Carroll, Shirley Chisholm, and Bettie Shabazz graced their front pages. The magazines spotlighted some as political figures, and others as glamour symbols. *Ebony*'s July 1960 cover girl Claudinette Fouchard, light skinned and "a member of one of Haiti's richest and most distinguished families," held the "Miss Sugar Queen" title and in 1960, as "Miss Haiti," served as her country's representative in the Miss World Pageant.[49] The article discussed her elite background and her preference for being a housewife rather than a beauty queen. *Ebony*'s October 1961cover story read, "Ebony Fashion Fair Beauties" and featured captivating women of all shades dressed in glittering high-end apparel. In January the very next year, a toffee-colored woman, famous for no particular reason, modeled the latest in swimwear on the cover.

By August 1962 Madame Felix Houphouet-Boigny shared the cover with Jacqueline Kennedy. The story, "Glamorous First Ladies," exclaimed, "The Ivory Coast's answer to the most glamorous First Lady ever to occupy the U.S. White House is a smooth, cocoa-complexioned charmer...wife of the African Republic's first president."[50] And in May 1963, *Ebony* featured a bright-eyed, honey-brown teen actress front and center on its cover flanked by two other teen actresses: one Asian and the other white. While the cover image clearly emphasized the woman of color, the fact that she shared front-page real estate with two other nonblack women provides a somewhat confusing juxtaposition when considering *Ebony* magazine's target demographic. Even so, *Ebony* and other black monthlies began to slowly trend toward expanding the range of skin tones published in their pages.

As the civil rights struggle progressed into the Black Power Movement and the popular cultural component professing that black is beautiful, as well as continued independence of African and Caribbean nations from colonial powers, embracement of a more inclusive beauty ideal with respect to a more balanced presentation of color and corresponding ideas about beauty and acceptability gained acceptance. In fact, notions of what constituted beauty were often as political as they were personal. Advertisements also began to embrace African heritage by using darker models, emphasizing black hair in its natural state and, through language, directly associating blackness with beauty. That is not to say, all tinges of European influence had been erased. While minimized on some end, it became more sophisticated on another. The May 1965 issue of *Ebony* dedicated to the Selma to Montgomery civil rights march led by Dr. Martin Luther King, Jr. and other activists, and responsible for the support for and passage of the Voting Rights Act, which effectively ended the direct-action phase of the freedom struggle, included a sales pitch from Nadinola—this time calling itself a brightening formula to "fade skin discolorations" as opposed to a lightening bleach.[51] In June the following year, *Ebony* continued its embrace of a more natural black beauty with a striking cover featuring an un-pressed, un-permed, unbleached, and distinctly African-featured woman. The accompanying headline read, "The Natural Look: A New Mode for Negro Women," further signifying the steady but slow shift to embrace black beauty without qualification.

Even though the late 1960s saw the rise of black pride, years of accepting Eurocentric beauty ideals, in all its forms, transitioned into the era as well. The front page of *Ebony*'s March 1968 issue featured the talented singer, actress, and future variety show host, Leslie Uggams, sporting several styles of wigs. The article inside boasted that wearing wigs could allow readers the opportunity to be "brunette in the morning, a redhead at noon, and a blonde at night." This kind of language underscored the fact that many women of color, and the fashion editors who catered to them, had yet to completely embrace the idea that natural features associated with blackness did not always have to stand in comparison to the natural features of whiteness. However, later in the same article are several pictures of women wearing wigs that mimicked the afro, pressed curls, and even a distinctly African braided style, all of which point exclusively to an Afrocentric aesthetic. To say that the black magazines of the day suffered from a beauty identity crisis would be somewhat of an understatement. Many women of color seemed to struggle with accepting their beauty, as it were, and those struggles played out with striking clarity in the pages of nearly every issue of each published periodical. Excited exclamations of achieving a distinctly Euro-aesthetic shared page space with unequivocal celebrations of the Afro-aesthetic, amounting to a strangely consistent but apparently nonconfusing doublespeak. Interestingly, readers never seemed to find such instances odd, rather there was a tacit acceptance that such juxtapositions were normal and perhaps not even juxtapositions at all. The featuring of popular stars like Uggams further solidified the notion that there was nothing unusual or incongruous about having blonde, brunette, or redheaded aspirations while at the same time embracing a braided wig or the ubiquitous afro.

Though print media appeared indecisive in which direction to promote a beauty ideal, young black America often pushed the envelope in its embrace of a black aesthetic and hair as a political and cultural statement rather than simply a style.[52] Howard University exemplified this. A bastion of black middle and upper class aspirations in higher education, Howard had traditionally signified the ideal of an elite education for those historically barred from Ivy League and other prestigious, predominately white institutions, while promoting a nurturing and academically challenging environment for those who attended. In 1966, Robin Gregory vied for the coveted title of homecoming queen. Gregory was not the typical candidate for the laudatory reign, which featured young co-eds sporting the latest fashions and cars while representing a sponsoring fraternity, sorority, or school organization. Along with her natural hair, she had a serious platform and advocated for black rights. Historian and former classmate Paula Giddings recalled, "Of course, Robin Gregory had no car and always looked sharp, but she was certainly not wearing those elaborate dresses. She had an Afro, which of course was the statement that she made physically." Moreover, Gregory campaigned with two gentlemen who resembled members of the Nation of Islam's security force the Fruit of Islam and stood watch as Gregory spoke around campus. "And Robin talked about the movement. Robin talked about black politics."[53]

Gregory's run for the title enthused many on campus as not simply a break from the norm, but as a nod to the struggles of the day—including the burgeoning feminist movement. "But all of us...felt very excited about Robin's campaign and what it symbolized, not just in terms of politics but in terms of what women should be doing as well, the role of women."[54] Gregory, with her natural hair and political agenda, won the crown and helped usher in a new sense of urgency and militancy on campus. As Giddings recalled:

Well, before you saw Robin you saw the way the lights cast a silhouette on the curtains, and you saw the silhouette of her Afro before you saw her. Well, the auditorium exploded. It was a wonderful moment. People started jumping up and screaming and some were raising their fists, then spontaneously a chant began. The chant was "Umgawa, Black Power, Umgawa, Black Power," and a chain was created. People started to march to the rhythm...and there was a line that went all the way around the auditorium, and more and more people joined the line....And finally out the door and into the streets of Washington, D.C., past the campus and still chanting...and that was really the launching of that movement at Howard.[55]

As the decade of the 1960s came to a close, black beauty culture seemed to come to a greater understanding and acceptance of itself. Popular culture magazines began to jettison words like bronze and fair-skinned to describe the beauties in their pages in favor of more direct terminology. The word "black" became more of a mainstay in printed media. Advertisements also made sure to keep up with the slowly changing times. The November 1969 issue of *Ebony* ran a striking, full-color ad by Raveen marketing their "Au Naturelle" line of hair care products specifically "for women who wear it like it is." The deep brown hue of the afroed-Raveen model contrasted sharply with the soft, yellow, and repetitive skin tones of the models from advertisements that had run only months and years before. In fact, the images of black women throughout the *Ebony*'s November 1969 issue illustrate an arguably deliberate effort to showcase a darker range of skin tone; pictures of lighter complexioned women in the issue are nearly nonexistent. The move toward a self-determining and self-defining beauty ideal was becoming increasingly apparent. Not a single one of *Ebony*'s gorgeous Fashion Fair models could pass; the depth of their brown skin left no room for doubt.

For sure, black magazines functioned as critical channels that helped to positively reshape how black women were presented in the national media, expand employment opportunities for women of color in entertainment, but also slightly reiterate some of the narrow enduring beauty constructs instituted by racism and perpetuated by portions of oppression-affected African American culture. John P. Davis and John H. Johnson, much like black writers and publishers before them and prodded by the changing times and popular public perception and image, created and expanded "freedom spaces" in African American life and beauty culture.

Contemporaneous with the Black Power Movement and the feminist movement, *Essence* magazine premiered in May 1970. This monthly, dedicated to African American women and sounding a black feminist voice during many years of its publication, was the brainchild of a black woman, but created through the investment opportunity of black men.[56] Still, throughout its existence, one can find various skin tones and hair textures gracing its glossy pages. In fact, this publication might signal the manifestation of promoting a more inclusive black beauty aesthetic that previous black-oriented magazines did not, and white publications wholeheartedly ignored.

As the country moved away from the urgency of tangible gains from civil rights and black power and headed into the conservative backlash of the 1980s, the progression forward would be stalled. Music videos, directed and/or produced by men, as the visualization of black music and an embodiment of the era, like that of the media outlets preceding them, often bowed to the European beauty construct in hair and skin color while embracing an African-derived physique. Thus the historical vortex that forced the adherence to an unattainable standard while cultivating a nexus where "African American women created their own standard of beauty . . . [with] a wider range of beauty norms among African American women and more acceptance of different body types and weights"[57] continues to define, subjugate, and judge African American beauty. In the twenty-first century, African American women still grapple with the pull of the African and the European in coming to terms with a norm that supports alternative definitions of beauty that consider historical and cultural factors. Black-controlled popular culture media outlets with gendered sensibilities help to broaden, define/redefine, and uphold a beauty aesthetic for African American women. These "freedom spaces" can allow black women, specifically, to determine a beauty ideal created in their own image.

Notes

1. Ean Wood, *The Josephine Baker Story* (London: Sanctuary Publishing Limited, 2000), 249–50.
2. Ibid.
3. Ayana D. Byrd and Lori L. Tharps, *Hair Story: Untangling the Roots of Black Hair in America* (New York: St. Martin's Press, 2001), 19–20.

4. Tracy Owens Patton, "Hey Girl, Am I More than My Hair?: African American Women and Their Struggles with Beauty, Body Image, and Hair," *NWSA Journal* 18, no. 2 (Summer 2006): 24.

5. Byrd and Tharps, 22. The one-drop racial classification denoted that a person with any traceable amount of black blood (from successive ancestral lines) would be deemed a Negro.

6. Ibid.

7. See A'lelia Perry Bundles, *On Her Own Ground: The Life and Times of Madam C. J. Walker* (New York: Washington Square Press, 2001) 67–68, 196, 268–69; Patton, 28–29; and Byrd and Tharps, 30–36, 76–85.

8. Byrd and Tharps, 26.

9. Maxine Leeds Craig, *Ain't I A Beauty Queen Black Women, Beauty, and the Politics of Race* (New York: Oxford University Press, 2002), 5.

10. "Since Grant Took Richmond," *Our World,* November 1947, 11.

11. Ibid.

12. Ed Branford, "What Is Negro Beauty?" *Our World,* November 1947, 33.

13. W. E. B. Du Bois, *The Souls of Black Folk* (New York: Library of America, 1990), 8.

14. "Kombo Advertisement," *Our World,* November 1950, inside cover.

15. Ibid.

16. "10 Most Beautiful Negro Women," *Our World,* November 1950, 16.

17. Ibid.

18. Ibid.

19. Ibid.

20. Ibid.

21. "America's 100 Most Beautiful Negro Women," *Color,* November 1949, 13.

22. Audrey Elisa Kerr, *The Paper Bag Principle: Class, Complexion, and Community in Black Washington, D.C.* (Knoxville: University of Tennessee, 2006), 30. In some African American circles, the "paper bag" test was used to determine entry into social organizations. The color of the bag often represented the darkest of the complexions allowed into such groups.

23. "Dorthea Towels: Paris's Fabulous Negro Model," *Our World,* August 1952, 44.

24. Ibid.

25. Ibid.

26. "Miss Bronze Los Angeles," *Our World,* August 1952, 25.

27. "Howard U Co-ed Silvia Blackburn," *Our World,* August 1953, 9.

28. Ibid.

29. This research has not produced a single written instance in popular black lifestyle magazines of this era, 1940–1955, where black, dark, ebony or similar terminology was used in the same vein.

30. "Eastern Human Hair Advertisement," *Our World,* November 1947, 4.

31. "Straiteen Advertisement," *Our World,* July 1949, 57.

32. Ibid.

33. Ibid.

34. "Nadinola Advertisement," *Our World,* September 1953, 47.

35. Ibid.

36. Ibid.

37. Susannah Walker, *Style and Status: Selling Beauty to African American Women, 1920–1975* (Lexington: University Press of Kentucky, 2007), 24.

38. *Our World,* September 1953, 30.

39. Ibid.

40. "The Girl Friends Have A Ball," *Our World*, September 1953, 42.
41. Ibid., 44.
42. Ibid.
43. Ibid.
44. "The Merry Moles," *Our World*, August 1953, 50.
45. Ibid., 53.
46. Ibid., 50.
47. Ibid., 53.
48. Ibid.
49. "The Beauty Who Doesn't Want to be Queen?" *Ebony*, July 1960, 111.
50. "Glamorous First Ladies," *Ebony*, July 1962, 21.
51. "Nadinola Advertisement," *Ebony*, August 1965, 19.
52. Byrd and Tharps, 51.
53. Clayborne Carson et al, ed. *The Eyes on the Prize Civil Rights Reader: Documents, Speeches and Firsthand Accounts from the Black Freedom Struggle* (New York: Penguin Books, 1991), 460.
54. Ibid., 461.
55. Ibid., 461–62.
56. In 1968 Jonathan Blount, Ed Lewis, Clarence O. Smith, Cecil Hollingsworth, and Phillip Janniere (who left the group early) attended a meeting on promoting black businesses sponsored by Shearson & Hammill & Company, an investment corporation. The company would back a profitable venture. Jonathan Blount remembered that his mother and/or godmother had complained about the lack of a women's lifestyle magazine geared toward black women. Pat Hollingsworth conducted early focus groups to ascertain black women's interests and Bernadette Carey served as an early editor (prior to the first published issue) to plant the seed of what was to become *Essence*. Though a mostly male-sponsored business venture, women typically directed the magazine's content. See Audrey Edwards, "The Essence of Sweet Success," *Black Enterprise* (June 1980): 134–38; Jennifer Bailey Woodard and Teresa Mastin, "Black Womanhood: 'Essence' and Its Treatment of Stereotypical Images of Black Women," *Journal of Black Studies*, 36 no. 2 (November 2005): 264–81; and Susan L. Taylor, "In the Beginning," in *Essence: 25 Years Celebrating Black Women*, ed. Patricia Mignon Hinds (New York: Harry N. Abrams, Incorporated, 1995), 23–55.
57. Patton, 41.

7

Neutering the Black Power Movement: The Hijacking of Protest Symbolism

James B. Stewart

There exists today a chance for the Negroes to organize a co-operative state within their own group. By letting Negro farmers feed Negro artisans, and Negro technicians guide Negro home industries, and Negro thinkers plan this integration of co-operation, while Negro artists dramatize and beautify the struggle, economic independence can be achieved.

W. E. B. Du Bois, *"A Negro Nation within a Nation"*

W. E. B. Du Bois's quotation imagines a self-contained community in which organized cultural production continually affirms and reinforces connections among individuals and institutions. The Black Arts Movement (BAM) was, in many respects, a concrete manifestation of the type of organized cultural production that Du Bois advocated, and the relationship between the BAM and the Black Power Movement (BPM) roughly paralleled the type of synergism envisioned by Du Bois. The principal thesis of this investigation is that external manipulation and co-optation of important cultural symbols effectively neutralized the potential of organized community-based cultural production to promote BPM objectives. The analysis focuses special attention on the role of blaxploitation films in diluting the potential of important cultural symbols to facilitate political mobilization and collective action. This particular mode of cultural counterattack involved systematic imposition of invisibility on the BPM and/or the misrepresentation of the BPM as dysfunctional, disorganized, opportunistic, and impotent. The propagation of this imagery complemented direct physical assaults and disinformation campaigns waged by governmental officials against BPM organizations and their leaders. The systemic disruption of cultural production as a means of neutering the BPM set in motion a continuing pattern of compromised cultural production that continues to constrain contemporary efforts to develop and implement mass-based resistance to racial oppression.

The examination of the treatment of cultural symbols and institutions associated with "black pride" in blaxploitation films also necessitates exploration of two related subthemes. Because soundtracks played a critical role in shaping audience response to these movies, it is important to understand the linkage between audio and visual imagery in the neutering process. Second, it is also critical to appreciate how caricatured gender representations that permeate most blaxploitation films reinforced the neutering of black power symbolism.

The principal thesis and related subthemes guiding this investigation are interrogated through an in-depth discussion of plots, characters, soundtracks, and other aspects of a subset of blaxploitation films. The discussion is organized to allow the comparison of how the BPM is treated in movies with different types of plots.

Popular Culture and Liberation: From Civil Rights to Black Power

As a starting point, it is useful to consider the significance of the Black Arts Movement to the Black Power Movement. The broader contours of this relationship are best understood in the context of the role played by various media in mobilizing support for confronting institutional segregation in the era of the modern Civil Rights Movement (CRM). As noted by Brian Ward, the role of radio was especially critical. Ward argues "the rising tide of southern black protest in the mid-twentieth century coincided with the emergence of black-oriented radio as one of the most vital, popular, and influential institutions within the African American community."[1] James Stewart's analysis of selected rhythm and blues songs produced from the 1960s to the 1980s has uncovered a variety of types of political messages.[2] Specifically, Stewart proposed a typology of eight types of political messages ranging from documentaries to revolutionary manifestos. However, the delivery of such messages to a targeted audience was always problematic. As observed by William Van Deburg, although "more overtly political music often made little impact on national record charts, the message of these songs was spread underground via a modern-day 'grapevine telegraph.' "[3] This "grapevine telegraph" was simply an extension of the traditional role of music and dance at informal black functions, family gatherings, and organization meetings. Exposure to politicized cultural products in these venues facilitated shared interpretations of embedded political messages. The political saliency of songs was further enhanced by the efforts of some African American disc jockeys to use their shows as platforms for political education.

Ward claims that radio actually compensated for dysfunctional tendencies of some black power groups. He asserts that black-oriented radio "helped to maintain a sense of black unity, collective power, and common purpose" at a time when there was a "flagging interest in mass activism" resulting in part from "a series of internecine battles between cultural nationalists, revolutionary nationalists, political nationalists, and other claimants to the black power throne."[4] He maintains further that many southern stations "distance[d] themselves from the most extreme and controversial expressions of black power and protest."[5]

Whether or not one accepts Ward's interpretation, the political impact of black radio on the BPM and the CRM was largely uncoordinated. In contrast, the Black Arts Movement, which roughly spanned the period 1964–1976, became a conscious vehicle for the dissemination of political messages reflecting black power ideologies. The Black Arts Movement catalyzed the creation of a large body of poems, plays, and essays, much of which employed distinctive expressive modes. Hyperbolic language was marshaled in launching attacks on racism and the organic linguistic conventions associated with African American folk and urban lifestyles were celebrated. New forms of discourse were introduced including techniques borrowed from various musical genres, especially jazz. As Melba Boyd noted, "by 1966, cultural conferences became as commonplace as political rallies, as institutions were founded and alternative theaters were organized to garner political and artistic energy."[6] However, Boyd cautions that "Although the black authors energized a course of activist urgency that was viewed as part of the Black Liberation Movement (BLM) sweeping the country, the Black Arts Movement was primarily literary, and more specifically it generated poetry that needed to be printed."[7] Boyd's comments underscore the fact that BAM participants had their own agenda and did not necessarily think of themselves as playing a vanguard role in the BPM of the type described by Du Bois. However, it is important not to overly privilege the role of literature within BAM. W. S. Tkweme has demonstrated convincingly that there were local settings in which jazz artists actively contributed to the movement, and drew on previous cultural productions to produce multigenre products.[8]

The potential of BAM participants to promote black power objectives was partially compromised by external co-optation efforts. James Smethurst relates that urban uprisings "provoked an avalanche of federal and local public money as well as private foundation support for nationalist black art and artistic institutions closely linked to revolutionary political movements...[that] often resulted in a depoliticized arts bureaucracy that undermined or straitjacketed the Black Arts movement..."[9] At the same time, as Smethurst cogently observes, "Dramatically increased public and private financing...allowed African American artists to reach a black audience receptive to their radical art on a scale never seen before—even during the Popular Front and the New Deal."[10]

Fortunately, the overall influence of the Black Power Movement on the Black Arts Movement limited, to some extent, the impact of co-optation efforts. According to Smethurst, the "various sorts of government and foundation support generated by black political activism...made it possible for black theaters, cultural centers, workshops, presses, journals...to flourish while promoting art with a politically radical content and an often avant-garde form."[11] The political pressures emanating from the BPM enabled the BAM to impact the representation of African Americans in the commercial media and "produced a distinct Black Arts strain in various mass culture media, especially radio, television, film, and popular music."[12] African American poets, for example, performed readings for diverse audiences, including students on college campuses across the country, and produced recordings with musicians and choirs. Several of the BAM poets used jazz to frame their cultural production, especially "free jazz," prioritizing this genre's militant dimensions and reinterpreting the music in their poetry.

The Blaxploitation Film Counterattack on Black
Power Symbolism: An Overview

The introduction of the "blaxploitation" film genre in the early 1970s was both a new tool of economic exploitation and a direct attack on the cultural ethos created by the BAM. The powerful combination of audio and visual imagery had a much more pronounced effect on individual and collective sensibilities than traditional auditory stimuli. Auditory imagery occurs when one has a "song on the brain," that is, has the experience of hearing the song without auditory stimulation. A study by David Kraemer with others examining how the brain processes music finds that similar to previous research regarding "visual imagery," auditory imagery is triggered when an individual is familiar with a song. When subjects heard a version of a song with some missing lyrics, the brain involuntarily supplied the missing words. Moreover, the researchers found that this imaging occurred in a specific part of the brain that was not accessed when subjects were not familiar with a song.[13]

In a progressive sense, audio and visual imagery induced by music can enable listeners to access related memories, an idea used by Samuel Floyd to ground his study of black music. Floyd argues "our responses to music are based on our reactions to the artistic embodiment of struggle and fulfillment" as depicted in contrived events, relationships, refinements, and idealizations."[14] According to Floyd, these constructed scenarios "represent analogs to the daily human struggles to achieve balance between what he describes as various manifestations of tension and repose, including opposition and accommodation, aspiration and hope, and failure and achievement."[15] However, in the case of blaxploitation the combination of auditory and visual imagery was used to neutralize political mobilization efforts. In the contemporary era the music video has emerged as an extremely powerful source of auditory and visual stimulation and has much greater potential than audio recordings to impact the listener's conscious through the combination of auditory and visual imagery effects.

The blaxploitation film genre as the brainchild of Hollywood magnates was designed, in part, to bolster sagging Hollywood revenues by bringing African Americans into the movie houses. Moviemakers tapped into the growing frustration in black communities about persisting poverty and lack of public resources and disseminated a perverse political message glorifying conspicuous consumption, gender exploitation, and extralegal activity, including the drug trade, as elements of a viable strategy for "getting over on the man." On the other hand, as suggested previously, the representation of the BPM in these films was designed to neutralize the attractiveness of black power ideology for moviegoers.

The films typically associated with the blaxploitation genre were released primarily between 1971 and 1975. Josiah Howard defines the genre loosely as "1970s black-cast or black-themed films (or mainstream Hollywood pictures featuring at least one prominent African-American player in a modern-minded narrative steeped in and/or influenced by the concurrent Black Pride movement), created, developed, and most importantly, *heavily promoted* to young, inner-city, black audiences."[16] This broad definition allows Howard to include films such as *Cotton Comes to Harlem* within the genre. Many other critics would use a more restrictive definition that focuses specifically on films produced with a highly formulaic structure that involved violence, drugs, sex, prolific use of negative racial epithets, street talk, fancy clothes and cars, and "getting over on the man." Ultimately the African American audiences realized they were being exploited and abandoned the theaters.[17]

For the purposes of this investigation it is important to appreciate the sheer magnitude of this enterprise. At least 200 blaxploitation films were produced during the very short time frame of 1971 to 1975. The titles of some of these productions are well known and include *Superfly* (1972), *Across 110th Street* (1972), and *Cleopatra Jones* (1973).[18] These films are examined in this investigation along with several others, specifically, *Trouble Man* (1972), *Coffy* (1973), *The Mack* (1973), *Black Caesar* (1973); *Five on the Black Hand Side* (1973), *Willie Dynamite* (1974), and *Friday Foster* (1975). In addition, because of its role as a launching pad for the blaxploitation genre also look at *Cotton Comes to Harlem* (1970). As will be noted, this film provides an important benchmark for assessing how subsequent blaxploitation films distorted the original representation of black power symbolism. The selection of films is specifically designed to foreground the black action film heroine. Yvonne Sims has examined this character type in detail.[19] Sims argues that these characters "confirm[ed] that black women were wresting control of their womanhood and femininity from others and no longer allowing others to define what they should look like or how they should act."[20] To the extent that this claim can be sustained, the black action film heroine played an important role in neutralizing the typical dysfunctional representations of most black women found in blaxploitation films.

Selected information about each of these films is summarized in Table 7.1. The first column indicates the movie title and the musician(s) responsible for the soundtrack.

Focusing first on the subtheme of the relationship between audio and video imagery, the role of highly visible rhythm and blues artists is noteworthy, that is, James Brown, Curtis Mayfield, Bobby Womack, and Marvin Gaye. Only one bona fide jazz artist, Roy Ayers, is represented in this sample.

Some conscious black musicians contracted to develop the soundtracks for blaxploitation films attempted to neutralize the thematic content and visual imagery by producing audio commentaries challenging the glorification of the underground economy. In effect, these cultural warriors engaged in a type of guerrilla campaign against external cultural manipulation. Two of the more notable examples are Curtis Mayfield's "Superfly" (1972) and Bobby Womack's "Across 110th Street" (1972) soundtracks.[21]

Curtis Mayfield's "Freddy's Dead" (1972) is a five and one-half-minute tribute to the tragically naïve Freddy, who perishes unceremoniously in the cutthroat world navigated by the "Superfly" character (Priest), played by the late Ron O'Neal.[22] Mayfield asks listeners to think beyond immediate gratification and understand the larger political and economic forces that shape the scenarios producing tragic endings like the death of Freddy.

Table 7.1 Selected characteristics of a sample of blaxploitation films

Title	Plot summary	Anti-BPM representations	Use of BPM symbols
Cotton Comes to Harlem (1970) Music: Galt MacDermot	Detectives "Gravedigger" Jones (Godfrey Cambridge) and "Coffin Ed" Johnson (Raymond St. Jacques) investigate Rev. Deke O'Malley's (Calvin Lockhart) "Back to Africa" scheme, which results in money being stashed in a bale of cotton.	Caricature of "Back to Africa" movement; Caricature of Black Panther–like militant group; Hypocritical use of phrase "Am I black enough for you?" Black capitalism as control of criminal activity.	Extensive presence of African-inspired clothing and afros; Repeated positive references to Malcolm X and Marcus Garvey; Swahili classes; African artifacts and "Sex and Race" by J.A. Rogers; "Putney Swope" featured on theater marquis.
Superfly (1972) Music: Curtis Mayfield	Priest "Super Fly" (Ron O'Neal) is a cocaine dealer who begins to realize that his life will soon end with either prison or his death. He decides to build an escape from the life by making one last big deal.	Community activists portrayed as shakedown artists.	Malcolm X and Angela Davis poster in top black gangster's office.
Across 110th Street (1972) Music: Bobby Womack	A corrupt white cop (Anthony Quinn) and an honest young black cop (Yaphet Kotto) chase three black robber/murderers who stole $300,000 of Italian mob money.	Invisibility of community activists; Triggerman debates strategy in front of a Martin Luther King poster.	
Trouble Man (1972) Music: Marvin Gaye	Mr. T (Robert Hooks) is a Los Angeles private eye hired by a crime family to find out who is stealing from their gambling operation, but actually attempt to exploit him to destroy a competitor crime family.	Invisibility of community activism and black pride in street scenes.	Authentic African masks, other African artifacts, and paintings in residence of both the protagonist and his girlfriend.
Cleopatra Jones (1973) Music: Joe Simon, Millie Jackson	Cleopatra Jones (Tamara Dobson) is a government special agent fighting drug-trafficking. She takes on the notorious drug-lord "Mommy" who causes trouble for Cleopatra's friends who operate a community drug rehab center.	Disorganized armed self-defense; Underdeveloped community empowerment ideology (drug rehab); Government agent as savior.	Afros as hairstyle; Black power salute (including white cop).
Coffy (1973) Music: Roy Ayers	Coffy (Pam Grier) is a nurse who exacts vengeance for her sister's death, killing drug dealers, pimps, and mobsters.	Invisibility of community activists.	Afros as hairstyle.

Film / Music	Plot		
The Mack (1973) Music: Willie Hutch	Goldie (Max Julien) is the king of the pimping game challenged by corrupt white cops and a crime lord. His brother is a community activist trying to clean up the black community.	Multiracial stable of prostitutes; Goldie and his brother collaborate in killing white cops (no difference in values between "the life" and community empowerment).	Afros as hairstyle; Trivialization of black handshake; Black hero posters in crime kingpin's office.
Black Caesar (1973) Music: James Brown	Tommy Gibbs (Fred Williamson) becomes a kingpin criminal/hit man who rises to power in Harlem and subsequently becomes alienated from all close associates as his criminal empire crumbles.	Protagonist relishes symbols of white affluence— residence, clothes, etc.; Protagonist is eventually killed by gang of black youths; Efforts to foster community uplift dismissed by protagonist.	Afros as hairstyles focus on wigs; One minor character wears a dashiki and kufi.
Five on the Black Hand Side (1973) Music: H. B. Barnum	John Henry Brooks (Leonard Jackson) is a barber and domineering head of a middle-class black family. Jackson is forced to rethink his values when his previously docile wife Gladys (Clarice Taylor) rebels inspired by her youngest son, Gideon (Glen Turman).	Brooks eschews BPM ideology and symbols; Barbershop promotes traditional misogynistic views and behaviors; Characterization of wedding plans as "mumbo jumbo."	Romare Bearden artwork "The Block"; Prolific presence of afros and African clothing; African wedding including libation; Use of Malcolm X's teachings to solve familial conflict.
Willie Dynamite (1974) Music: J. J. Johnson & Gilbert Moses	Willie Dynamite (Roscoe Orman) is a kingpin pimp who is outwitted by a black social worker who rescues women caught up in prostitution rings.	Invisibility of community activists; Multiracial stable of prostitutes.	Afros as hairstyle; Willie's sister wears Ankh earrings at Mother's death bed; "Black is Booti-ful" graffiti on wall in prostitutes' jail holding cell.
Friday Foster (1975) Music: Luchi de Jesus	Photographer Friday Foster (Pam Grier) accidentally uncovers a plot to assassinate top black leaders, which she and private investigator Hawkins (Yaphet Kotto) successfully thwart.	Image of blond white woman featured in magazine office run by black editor; Fashion show models/attendees wear no afros nor African centered clothes; Only neighborhood scene is in a black gay bar in D.C. with a bevy of black female impersonators.	Black unity theme restricted to "traditional" black leaders, i.e., elected officials, businessmen, and ministers; Featured "Africonic Beauty" wears "Kalahari Sunrise" outfit with no African characteristics.

"Across 110th Street," written by Womack and Johnson, also focuses on one character in a larger drama.[23] The tempo of the movie version of this song is decidedly faster than on the record. The faster tempo in the movie served to enhance the sense of fast action projected by the visual images. It is in the closing stanza that Womack offers a collective self-help solution in making a plea for black men to cease and desist from engagement with the drug trade and examine the social function of the ghetto within the larger political economy:

> Hey Brother, there's a better way out
> Snorting that coke, shooting that dope
> Man you're copping out
> Take my advice, its either live or die

This injunction is diametrically opposed to the plot resolution where $300,000 of Italian mob money gets transferred to black hands.

Curtis Mayfield also attempted to broaden the dialogue regarding the sources of oppression in the monologue and first chorus or "The Cocaine Song" on the *Superfly* album with the lyrics:

> Now our lives are in the hands of the pusher man
> We break it all down so you might understand
> How to protect yourself
> Don't make no profit for the man.[24]

For present purposes it is important to note that neither Womack's nor Mayfield's suggested resistance strategies invoke notions of community or collective self-help. The same can be said of Marvin Gaye's "Trouble Man," which lacks even the recognition of a broader system of oppression in championing hard-edged individual survival skills. Thus, even in cases where artists attempted to blunt the celebration of dysfunctional behaviors, those countermessages, by and large, did not invoke the language of the Black Power Movement.

The second column provides a brief plot summary for each film. Common features for all of the movies except *Five on the Black Hand Side* include some combination of externally controlled organized crime, that is, drug trafficking and gambling, prostitution, and small-time hustling. Often there is a battle for control of these illicit activities within black neighborhoods between white and black mobsters or between competing black cabals. Pimping operations are typically black-controlled and black pimps are often depicted as controlling multicultural stables.

The third and fourth columns provide the content that is the central focus of this investigation, that is, anti–black power representations and the use of black liberation symbolism. The iconic film, *Cotton Comes to Harlem*, is a useful benchmark for assessing the treatment of the BPM in subsequent blaxploitation films.

Setting the Stage: *Cotton Comes to Harlem*

Howard proffers that *Cotton Comes to Harlem* "was filled with familiar and inoffensive (though 'hip') Hollywood film characters set in a romanticized urban setting."[25] Laced with multiple comedic scenes, the plot revolves around efforts to unmask Deke O'Malley's fraudulent "Back to Africa" scheme, riffing on the saga of Marcus Garvey. This satirical take on an important BPM forerunner is supported by other anti–black power representations, including a slapstick group of black militants, presumably intended as a caricature of the Black Panthers. The construct of "blackness" is itself subliminally linked to local control of criminal activity via Deke's repeated hypocritical use of the phrase, "Am I black enough for you?"

However, these negative BPM representations are counterbalanced by a number of black power–affirming components. The opening street scene includes several persons attired in African-inspired clothing, visual imagery embedded throughout the film along with afro hair styles. There is also affirming black power graffiti painted on the walls of buildings in several scenes. Although Deke O'Malley is disconnected from authentic black liberation ideology, his black power alienation is offset, to some extent, by the highly visible presence of African artifacts and other black liberation symbols in the residence of his right-hand man, including a copy of Joel Rogers's classic, *Sex and Race*. One scene features a Swahili class in which all participants are attired in African-inspired clothing. Various characters speak positively throughout the movie about both Marcus Garvey and Malcolm X, and the film, *Putney Swope*, is featured on a theater marquee in Harlem. The climactic scene takes place in the famous Apollo Theater. All of these aspects of the film work to convey a sense of community vitality and long-standing social institutions in line with the vision of black liberation movement proponents.

To summarize, although there are various anti–black power representations in *Cotton Comes to Harlem*, they are typically presented in a satiric format that lessened the extent to which viewers would be encouraged to dismiss the saliency of black liberation symbolism. BPM-affirming symbols are normalized throughout the movie. As discussed below, anti–black power representations increasingly came to dominate affirming images in subsequent blaxploitation projects.

Pusherman/Hit Man

The films *Superfly* and *Black Caesar* both portray the complexities of lives heavily intertwined with high-risk/high-stakes criminal activity. In *Superfly,* Priest is a cocaine dealer seeking one big score to get out of the game. Tommy Gibbs (Black Caesar) is a hit man who seeks to become the major black criminal figure in Harlem. As suggested in Table 7.1, *Superfly* is almost devoid of black power images, positive or negative. The only substantive content is a group of alleged community activists that attempts, unsuccessfully, to shakedown Priest for money to support their ventures. The incompetence of their initiative projects a negative image of the efficacy of community activism related to the black liberation struggle.

Representations of the BPM in *Black Caesar* are also heavily censored, consisting of one person wearing a kufi and street vendors selling afro wigs. The plot of *Black Caesar* is much more interesting for present purposes than the formulaic and predictable *Superfly*. *Black Caesar* begins with a flashback to Gibbs's adolescent experiences that led to his incarceration as a juvenile, accompanied by James Brown's "Down and Out in New York City." Gibbs's rise in the criminal hierarchy begins with his release from prison in 1965, and Gibbs' life trajectory is counterpoised to that of his long-time college-educated friend, Joe, who despite a very different socialization, becomes Gibbs's closest criminal associate (accountant) in Gibbs's criminal ventures. For a time Joe holds on to the dream of eventually using some portion of the ill-gotten gains from criminal activity for community uplift—an outcome that never materializes due to Gibbs' lack of support. This narrative is a subtle attack on the idealism of the generation of college students who strongly supported the goals of the Black Power Movement. Gibbs's mother is a maid for his white lawyer. In an interesting turn of events Gibbs acquires the lawyer's Upper East Side New York residence and attempts to give it to his mother as a sort of reparations, a gift that she refuses on moral grounds. This misguided effort to rationalize his activities is reflective of Gibbs's uncritical association of success with the acquisition of the symbols of white affluence. As his rise to the top of the criminal pecking order proceeds, Gibbs alienates all of his friends and family, symbolized most directly by the rape of his love interest and a threat to kill his father.

The destruction of Gibbs's criminal empire ends with his murder by a loosely organized group of young black males. This resolution was signaled earlier in the film by James Brown's soulful rendering of the song, "You Got to Pay the Cost to Be the Boss." In contrast, in *Superfly* Priest succeeds in getting over on the "Man" and survives to enjoy his ill-gained profits. In both of these movies the characters' fates are determined exclusively by their individual agency—notions of community central to black power ideology are marginalized and there is no presence of black liberation formations in the communities they frequent.

Big Pimpin'

As indicated in Table 7.1, *The Mack* and *Willie Dynamite* explore the world of "Big Pimpin'." Aside from the obvious disdain of BPM advocates for the sexual exploitation of women that is the hallmark of the pimping game, antiblack liberation representations of this enterprise are magnified in several ways. The stables of pimps Goldie and Willie Dynamite are both multiracial and the clientele is disproportionately comprised of white males. Such interracial liaisons are clearly antithetical to black power values. The violation of BPM norms is attenuated by the denigration of the symbolism associated with afro hairstyles via their use by prostitutes to increase their exotic allure. In *Willie Dynamite* there is a scene in which several ladies of the night are incarcerated in a jail holding cell with "Black is Booti-ful" graffiti on the wall—an obvious satirical reference to the phrase, "Black is Beautiful." In *The Mack* the legacy of iconic figures in the history of the struggle for racial equality is problematized by the presence of celebratory posters on the wall of the top black crime boss whom Goldie seeks to supplant.

Differences in the portrayal of black power community activists in the two films warrant some commentary. In *Willie Dynamite* community activists associated with the BPM are invisible. Still, in the end Willie is outwitted by a black female social worker whose mission is to rescue women caught up in prostitution rings. In *The Mack* Goldie's brother is a community activist trying to resolve problems plaguing his community. However, in a similar vein to the fate of Joe in *Black Caesar,* Goldie and his brother collaborate in killing racist and corrupt white cops. This subplot serves to blur the important distinction made by some black liberation proponents between morally grounded armed self-defense and other uses of violence.

Although both films disproportionately portray black power symbolism in negative terms, there is one affirming feature of *Willie Dynamite* that deserves mention. Willie's mother and sister serve as the antithesis to the women that Willie exploits so indifferently. His sister's loose attachment to the black liberation struggle is symbolized by highly visible ankh earrings that she wears at her mother's deathbed. Both the earrings and the deathbed ritual introduce reaffirmation of values consistent with black power that offset, to a limited extent, the overall dysfunctional treatment of the BPM that pervades the film.

Walkin' the Tightrope

The extent to which black communities can rely on law enforcement officials to support community uplift efforts has always been a complex issue. In *Cotton Comes to Harlem* black detectives "Gravedigger" Jones (Godfrey Cambridge) and "Coffin Ed" Johnson (Raymond St. Jacques) are both admired and feared for their no-nonsense approach to thwarting criminal activity while respecting community values. The films *Across 110th Street* and *Trouble Man* also explore the ambiguous role of black detectives attempting to balance commitments to community and law and order. In *Across 110th Street* Yaphet Kotto portrays an honest black policeman confronting a triad of corrupt white colleagues, black criminals, and the Italian mob. As indicated in Table 7.1, the antiblack liberation representations are similar to those found in other films such as misuse of images of iconic black heroes (in this case Martin Luther King, Jr., Malcolm X, and Angela Davis), and the invisibility of community activists.

In Ivan Dixon's *Trouble Man* greater care is exercised to incorporate positive BPM symbols. The residence of the protagonist, "Mister T," is laced with a variety of African masks and other artifacts. The same is true of his love interest who proudly sports an afro hairstyle (not a wig). Positive BPM associated representations include paintings, fertility figures, and other statues.

In both films the main characters are able to navigate the complex challenges faced by competing loyalties. However, in many ways traditional law enforcement is portrayed as the only option available, with no consideration of the potential of community self-policing—a strategy advocated by some black power activists.

Soul Sisters

As cogently noted by Yvonne Sims, "Pam Grier and Tamara Dobson brought a new character to the screen that was instrumental in reshaping gender roles, particularly those involving action-centered story lines."[26] The accuracy of Sims's observation is obvious from a cursory review of how women are treated in the other films included in Table 7.1 discussed to this point. The intention here is examine the roles played by these actresses in the films *Cleopatra Jones*, *Coffy*, and *Friday Foster* in the context of the overall treatment of black liberation symbolism.

As indicated in Table 7.1, in *Cleopatra Jones* Tamara Dobson is a US special agent fighting drug trafficking. Her arch enemy is a drug-lord named "Mommy," who eventually causes trouble for Cleopatra's friends who operate a community drug rehabilitation center. While the inclusion of a rehab center in the plot can be seen as signaling efforts at community empowerment, the armed self-defense efforts of its supporters against Mommy's minions are ineffective and it is the government's intervention, that is, Cleopatra Jones, that saves the day. In addition, the ideology that guides the work of the rehab center is underdeveloped. In summary, the government agent as savior trope serves to diminish the significance of the type of community empowerment efforts championed by black liberation advocates.

The roles played by Pam Grier in *Coffy* and *Friday Foster* are more realistic than the James Bond style portrayal of Cleopatra Jones. At the outset Coffy is a nurse who becomes a female warrior as a result of her sister's death. She proceeds to exact vengeance on drug dealers, pimps, and mobsters who are implicated in her sister's demise. Her crusade is largely an individual one undertaken against a background of invisibility of community activists.

Friday Foster is a photographer who accidentally uncovers a plot to assassinate top black leaders. She and a private investigator named Hawkins (Yaphet Kotto) are eventually successful in thwarting this plot. This male–female partnership reflects the type of cooperation championed by some BPM formations. However, there are many more aspects of this film that project anti–black power imagery. While the magazine that employs Friday is headed by a black editor, the most prominent image in his office is a poster-size reproduction of the cover of an issue that features the visage of a blond white woman. One of the most memorable scenes in the movie focuses on a fashion show sponsored by Madame Rena (Eartha Kitt). The fashion show is notable for the virtual absence of natural hair styles and African-inspired clothing. The featured model, who is described as an "Africonic Beauty," does not have a natural and the outfit that she models, termed "Kalahari Sunrise," exhibits no discernable African influences.

The action in this film switches back and forth between Los Angeles and Washington, D.C. In D.C. the only community establishment that is featured is a black gay bar frequented by a bevy of black female impersonators headed by "The Black Widow" (Godfrey Cambridge). In Los Angeles there is a regular visit by a comic pimp who repeatedly attempts to lure Friday into his stable.

The effort to foster black unity by black leaders, who are the target of the assassination plot, is restricted to traditional leadership classes, that is, elected officials, business leaders, and clergy. Grassroots community leaders promoting BPM values and objectives are excluded from this gathering. In summary, while *Cleopatra Jones, Coffy,* and *Friday Foster* are to be celebrated for opening new opportunities for black actresses, at the same time these films contributed to the overall marginalization of the Black Power Movement found in the other films discussed previously.

The Black Hand Side or the Road Not Taken

The preceding critique of the treatment of the BPM in blaxploitation films begs the question of whether there are counterexamples that illustrate alternative possibilities. *Five on the Black Hand Side,* produced by Brock Peters and Michael Tolan, provides such an alternative vision. This film is a comedy that chronicles the attempts of a middle-class black family to negotiate conflicting aspirations and values of its members. The foregrounding of the black middle class is a welcome counterweight to the relentless microscopic focus on the underbelly of black society in the blaxploitation films considered to this point.

The saga revolves around John Henry Brooks (Leonard Jackson), a barber by trade and domineering head of his household. He is an Army veteran and staunch advocate of capitalism who is wholly dismissive of black liberation ideology and symbolism and takes great pride in his status as a small business owner. His wife, Gladys, is the prototypical docile, frumpy, obedient housekeeper who obeys her husband's every order (she is expected to address him as "Mr. Brooks") and is completely devoted to their children, Booker T., Gideon, and Gail. As suggested by his name, Booker T. is closely aligned ideologically with his father, although he works in an antipoverty program and is rumored to have a white girlfriend. His younger brother, Gideon (Glen Turman), is in rebellion against his father's insistence that he major in business rather than archaeology. Gail is the character most directly aligned with black power ideology and symbolism. Her bedroom is decorated with various examples of African-inspired clothing, Afrocentric posters, and other BPM symbols. She is engaged to Marvin, a Vietnam War refusenik, and their "African" wedding is eminent. Her father is, of course, not supportive of the "mumbo jumbo" wedding plans, but feels the need to respect Gail's wishes.

The exploration of the family dynamics plays out within two heavily gendered spaces—John Henry's Barbershop and Gladys's kitchen. The name of John Henry's enterprise is the "Black Star Barber Shop," an obvious riff on Marcus Garvey's "Black Star Line." Within the walls of the shop the barbers and regular customers express a chorus of misogynistic views and behaviors. No women are allowed to enter the shop. The colorful monikers of regular customers pay homage to the diversity of African American culture, including "Sweetness," "Rolls Royce," and "Fun Loving." When an unwelcome visitor entreats John Henry to display a black liberation-oriented poster, John Henry rips up the poster after the corn-rowed visitor departs, declaring that it is crazy to go around yelling "I'm Black and I'm Proud!" This act firmly establishes the shop as an anti–black power sanctuary.

The liberation of Gladys is accomplished through the intervention of two friends, Ruby (Clarice Taylor), and especially the vivacious "Stormy Monday" (Ja'net Du Bois). Through a series of consciousness-raising discussions in Gladys's kitchen she is convinced to issue a set of demands to John Henry intended to achieve "peace, liberation, and self-determination"—an extension of BPM values to the individual level. However, Gladys inveighs that her real objective is simply to get John Henry to relax and "let me love him." Gladys and her compatriots don military gear and wage protests outside the Black Star Barber shop. Her forces eventually storm the shop, erasing its heralded status as a monument to black patriarchy. Her liberation efforts spark conflict among her children, but Gail's fiancé, Marvin, intervenes using the ideology of Malcolm X emphasizing the need for a spirit of "we-ism" to quell the tensions.

All of the guests at Gail's and Marvin's wedding are brightly attired in African-oriented clothing, except John Henry and his barber colleagues. By this time John Henry has been forced reluctantly to submit to Gladys's demands but their relationship is in question. The wedding ceremony itself is problematic because it reinforces the idea that a wife is expected to submit unquestioningly to her husband's will, a curious construction given the film's emphasis on Gladys's liberation. Suspense is created during the celebration following the wedding when John Henry, who has obviously been uncomfortable throughout the ceremony, unexpectedly disappears. However, it is clear that all is well when he returns proudly clad in a dashiki and actively participates in the closing scene during which attendees form a Soul Train dance line that actually features dancers from the *Soul Train* television show.

In summary, in addition to its other dimensions, *Five on the Black Hand Side* explores the complexities associated with efforts to expand the scope of African American culture to encompass broader acceptance of the values and objectives of the BPM. This treatment of black power clearly represents an alternative to the dismissive posture found in other blaxploitation-era films. The prominence of Romare Bearden's painting, "The Block," in several scenes underscores the film's emphasis on community cohesion, a critical value espoused by black liberation proponents.

Returning to the critical role of music in reinforcing or neutralizing the overt and subliminal messages embedded in films, *WATTSTAX*, originally released in 1973, was a music-based counterforce to the 1970s blaxploitation films. Produced by Mel Stuart, the film is a retrospective on the Watts riots of 1965. The primary focus is the Watts Summer Festival's 1972 concert held at the Los Angeles Coliseum. The concert featured various "soul" artists including Isaac Hayes, Rufus Thomas, The Staple Singers, The Bar Kays, and

Luther Ingram. The concert footage is interwoven with interviews dissecting the state of black America in the early 1970s and the effects of the riots on both Los Angeles and the United States.[27] While not appealing to the type of mass audiences sought by action films and comedies, *WATTSTAX* clearly demonstrated that there were alternative approaches to the creative use of popular culture to explore critical sociopolitical issues beyond action films and comedies.

A Problematic Legacy

As the blaxploitation film genre lost traction black sitcoms emerged to fill the void, shifting the primary locus of cultural deconstruction to television. The foundation for modern sitcoms featuring a black cast was laid by the success of *All in the Family* (1971) leading to the spin-off of the second African American sitcom, *The Jeffersons*, in 1975. *The Jeffersons* successfully broke into mainstream television, airing over 250 shows over a ten-year run and compiling Nielsen ratings among the top twenty-five for eight years.[28]

Beginning in the 1990s there was a pronounced resurgence of de facto blaxploitation or, alternatively, "gangsploitation" films. The new genre of blaxploitation films were fueled by the growing popularity of hip hop/rap music and made possible by the success of independent black filmmakers. The exact origins are in dispute but the release of *I'm Gonna Get You Sucka* in 1988 is one important benchmark. Other significant films include John Singleton's *Boyz n the Hood* (1991), Mario Van Peebles's *New Jack City* (1991), Ernest Dickerson's *Juice* (1992), and Albert and Allen Hughes's *Menace II Society* (1993). Other representative titles include *Dead Presidents*, *Set It Off*, and *Poetic Justice*. Like their 1970s predecessors these films typically highlight drugs and violence, with a story line that pretends to say something genuine about the black experience. The destructive messages projected by this genre were reinforced by the revival of the minstrelsy tradition in various entertainment genres including standup comedy and most contemporary television programs focusing on African Americans.

In a manner reminiscent of the debilitating effect of 1970s blaxploitation films on the Black Power Movement, this neo-blaxploitation genre undercut an emerging movement associated with the revival of the legacy of Malcolm X (El-Hajj Malik El-Shabazz) fueled by the release of Spike Lee's 1992 film, *Malcolm X*. Lee provided an alternative treatment of this cultural icon to that propagated in the traditional media, which branded Malcolm X as a dangerous militant framed by his famous statement "By any means necessary." In 1993 Andrea Enisuoh claimed that 84 percent of young black Americans considered Malcolm X to be their hero.[29] The influence of Lee's film was visually documented by the prevalence of the "X" icons on T-shirts, baseball caps, and other attire, which functioned as a statement of recognition of African American oppression as well as a call for a collective movement to redress social ills. As was the case during the era of the BPM, capitalists quickly recognized the potential to commodify this renewed interest and introduced a plethora of "X merchandise," including board games and air fresheners. Regrettably, the neo-blaxploitation film genre unwittingly (hopefully) contributed to the diffusion of this emergent movement through the propagation of visions of fame, fortune, and pliant women that were presumably available through heavy engagement in the underground economy.

As the neo-blaxploitation film genre lost momentum, progressive political tendencies continued to be neutralized by the expanding popularity of comedic depictions of the African American experience integrated into the most popular type of contemporary black theatrical performances, the so-called gospel plays. These plays have been popularized by Tyler Perry, who himself plays in drag, the character of a gun-toting grandma named Madea Simmons in drag. Perry's touring plays all typically revolve around vaudeville-style church services reminiscent of Greek morality plays and choruses. There are several other producers of this type of play and the titles clearly signal the moral message, including *Real Men Pray and I'm Doing the Right Thing…with the Wrong Man*. The plotlines tend to be similar and relatively simple, typically including a wronged woman (or, occasionally, man), the no-good man (or, occasionally, woman), an easily accessible lover (milkman, janitor or mechanic), the evils of drugs or alcohol, a comically over-the-top gay man (usually a hairdresser) and a cathartic "come-to-Jesus" moment.[30]

From the vantage point of African American studies these plays perform a constructive role in providing an alternative to the degradation of traditional values that is propagated through many other popular cultural genres. The plays are especially popular among black women over twenty-five years old. At the same time, the simple solutions to life problems proposed in these presentations are not adequate to address the complex problems facing black communities, which are far more complex than those that confronted filmmakers and musicians during the 1970s.

The contemporary African American media climate is characterized by a pattern of consolidation in ownership and control that has decimated black radio news, a key complement to rhythm and blues political commentaries in the 1960s and early 1970s. The decline of black radio news has conditioned listeners to expect mundane news broadcasts, thereby dulling the receptivity of listeners to incisive political commentaries by progressive hip hop artists. *Black Commentator* argues that "the near death of Black radio news has been a major factor in the erosion of Black political organization, nationwide" and that "[c]hains like Radio One gradually eliminated news from the mix, passing off syndicated or local talk, instead, and pretending that morning news jockeys could double as news people."[31]

Community activists committed to formation of a new mass liberation movement must confront these realities. Hopefully they will be able to enlist as allies a cadre of filmmakers and musicians who understand the potential of popular culture as a vehicle for conscious raising and empowerment and are willing to forego the glitter of bling and commit to the vision outlined so long ago by W. E. B. Du Bois.

Notes

1. Brian Ward, *Just My Soul Responding, Rhythm and Blues, Black Consciousness, and Race Relations* (Berkeley: University of California Press, 1998), 5–6.
2. James Stewart, "Message in the Music: Political Commentary in Black Popular Music from Rhythm and Blues to Early Hip Hop," in *Journal of African American History* 90, no. 3 (Summer 2005): 196–225.
3. William L. Van Deburg, *New Day in Babylon* (Chicago: University of Chicago Press, 1992), 215.
4. Ward, 316.
5. Ibid., 317.
6. Melba Boyd, *Wrestling with the Muse, Dudley Randall and the Broadside Press* (New York: Columbia University Press, 2004), 126.
7. Ibid., 152.
8. W. S. Tkweme, "Blues in Stereo: The Texts of Langston Hughes in Jazz Music," *African American Review* 42, nos. 3/4 (Fall 2008): 503–12.
9. James Smethurst, *The Black Arts Movement: Literary Nationalism in the 1960s and 1970s* (Durham: University of North Carolina Press, 2005), 370.
10. Smethurst, 370.
11. Ibid.
12. Ibid.
13. David Kraemer, C. Neil Macrae, Adam E. Green, and William M. Kelley, "Musical Imagery: Sound of Silence Activates Auditory Cortex," *Nature* 434 (March 10, 2005), 158.
14. Samuel Floyd, *The Power of Black Music* (New York: Oxford University Press, 1995), 227.
15. Ibid., 226–27.
16. Josiah Howard, *Blaxploitation Cinema: The Essential Reference Guide* (Surrey, England: FAB Press, 2008), 7.
17. For celebratory information about this genre see http://www.blaxploitation.com/.
18. In *Across 110th Street* actors Paul Benjamin and Ed Bernard play two Harlem residents driven by desperate circumstances to steal $300,000 from the local mob. In *Superfly*, actor Ron O'Neal plays Youngblood Priest, a Harlem coke dealer who wants to get out of the business but must outwit the cops who have a vested interest in the Harlem dope trade.
19. Yvonne Sims, *Women of Blaxploitation: How the Black Film Heroine Changed American Popular Culture* (Jefferson, NC: MacFarland, 2006).
20. Ibid., 193.
21. *Superfly*, Curtom Records CBS 8014-ST, 1972, 33⅓ rpm; and *Across 110th Street*, United Artist Records UAS-5225, 1972, 33⅓ rpm.
22. Curtis Mayfield, vocal performance of "Freddy's Dead," 1972, on *Superfly*, Curtom Records CBS 8014-ST, 33⅓ rpm.
23. Bobby Womack and Peace, vocal performance of "Across 110th Street," by Bobby Womack and James Louis Johnson, 1972, on *Across 110th Street*, United Artist Records UAS-5225, 33⅓ rpm.
24. Curtis Mayfield, vocal performance of "No Thing on Me," 1972, on *Superfly*, Curtom Records CBS 8014-ST, 33⅓ rpm. Thanks to Perry Hall for this recommendation.
25. Howard, 10.
26. Sims, 8.

27. A review of the *Wattstax* film by George Singleton can be found at http://www.reel-moviecritic.com/movies20034q/id1947.htm. My thanks to Tom Poole for suggesting this source.

28. G. Gutierrez, "American Sitcoms: A Diversity of Flavors in Society," *Contribution to English Media Culture* (University of California, Santa Barbara), http://www.uweb.ucsb.edu/~monicamd/gloriapaper.html.

29. Andrea Enisuoh, "The Life and Legacy of Malcolm X," SocialistAlternative.org (1993), accessed August 4, 2010, http://www.socialistalternative.org/literature/malcolmx/

30. Tony Brown, "'Mad Black Woman' Draws from Gospel 'Chitlin' Circuit,'" *The San Diego Union Tribune,* March 24, 2005, http://www.signonsandiego.com/uniontrib/20050324/news_1c24black.html

31. "Many Ways to Pressure Black Radio," *Black Commentator*, E-Mailbox, Issue 46, http://www.blackcommentator.com/46/46_email.html

8

A Silent Protest: The 1968 Olympiad and the Appropriation of Black Athletic Power

Jamal Ratchford

"Good day everyone, on behalf of ABC Sports I would like to welcome nearly four hundred million people who are glued to their seats for this one. I am Jim McKay, my partner is Keith Jackson and we are anticipating a high level of competition in today's 200 meter men's final featuring Americans Tommie Smith and John Carlos."[1] Before the race, all was not well in the American camp. Tommie Smith, who won his semifinal heat by six yards in the time of 20.1 seconds, cramped up and was listed as doubtful for the finals. Smith said, "When I crossed the finish line, I slowed down too fast, pulled a leg muscle and fell flat on my face."[2] To make matters worse, the stadium announcer mentioned to a vibrant crowd of 80,000 at the Estadio Olímpico that the injury might prevent Smith from competing in the finals.

Nevertheless, Smith refused to let an opportunity of grandeur pass him by. "I waited too long and come too far to allow a leg injury stop me from running,"[3] Smith said. Rather than drug his leg, Smith's coach, Lloyd C. "Bud" Winter, told the doctor to apply ice so that his leg would be mobile while also numb from the pain. During warm-ups, he jogged lightly and feigned major injury for two reasons. On the one hand, he wanted to keep the pressure off his leg; on the other hand, he wanted his competitors to psychologically believe that he would not run. Make no mistake about it, Smith said, "The Olympics is strict competition and is no place to think about friendship."[4] Not everyone was fooled, and the stadium announcer mentioned that Tommie Smith would run despite injuring his leg only an hour prior. American Broadcasting Company's (ABC) Jim McKay called the race. "John Carlos is in lane four and should burst out of the blocks quickly and if he doesn't take the lead early then he may be in trouble. Tommie Smith, injured in the semifinals, usually starts kinda slow but makes his bid down the stretch." The starter said, "Runners come to your marks, get set" and, at the sound of the gun Smith said, "Carlos took off like a jet," and took an early lead. Australian sprinter Peter Norman also started well and threatened to win the race. "Tommie Smith is running pretty well so far but its John Carlos right now followed by Peter Norman in lane two…but here comes Tommie Smith…and Tommie Smith wins, I don't know who finished second."[5] Amidst a continual roar from the crowd, Smith flew past Carlos with about fifty meters left and never looked back. Smith ran so quickly that it appeared that the field briefly was in a state of slow motion, as a stunned Carlos looked over his shoulder with forty-five meters to go, only to see his friend, teammate, and rival pass him. With fifteen meters remaining, Smith raised his arms in victory and crossed the finish line in world record time at 19.83 seconds. Carlos's mistake of looking back would cost him the silver medal as Peter Norman placed second with a time of 20.06, while Carlos finished third at 20.10.[6] The crowd was enthralled by the race and the men later took a victory lap in appreciation. So what happened? For a minute, the race captivated the Mexico City crowd and television audience, and about twenty minutes later, the cheers became boos, and the Olympic community officially depicted the heroes as troublemakers.

Times sure have changed. Forty years after critics blasted the 1968 Olympiad black-gloved, silent protest, white journalists, spectators, athletes, and administrators honored Tommie Smith and John Carlos at the Excellence in Sports Performance Yearly (ESPY) Awards. In 2008, the Entertainment Sports Programming Network (ESPN) held their annual gala at the Nokia Theater in Los Angeles and numerous sports and entertainment dignitaries celebrated the apex of athletic accomplishments. Singer Justin Timberlake entertained the audience and hosted the sports premier award show. The tone for the evening was jovial—a lighthearted attempt to recapture the best athletic achievements from the calendar year. The Arthur Ashe Award for Courage, an honor presented to one that made the most significant humanitarian contribution to sports and society, shifted the tone from playful to a serious and reflective remembrance of the moment captured. Actor Samuel L. Jackson and National Basketball Association (NBA) all-star and two-time most valuable player Steve Nash gave the opening remarks. For Jackson, the silent protest remained fresh in his mind. The year 1968, he recalled, "may have been forty years ago but for many of us, like me, a nineteen-year-old student at Morehouse College at the time, the events were so vivid, so personal, that they could have occurred yesterday."[7]

The festivities did not end. Actor Tom Cruise narrated a nine-minute clip that documented events leading up to the silent protest. When the film concluded Tommie Smith and John Carlos were introduced and received the award. The audience erupted into a standing ovation. A crowd that included racer Danica Patrick, National Football League (NFL) all-time great Jerry Rice, and internationally renowned soccer star David Beckham rose and cheered the two men. They gave another silent protest in appreciation of the audience. Smith spoke of sacrifice and Carlos reminded current athletes to use sports as a vehicle for social change. ESPN honored them three years after San Jose State College (SJS), their alma mater, erected a statute in their memory. In 1968, after the silent protest, the reception was different. *Chicago Daily News* sports writer, and later ABC play-by-play man, Brent Musburger, ferociously criticized the protest. He said "Smith and Carlos looked like a couple of black skinned storm troopers (Nazis), holding aloft their black gloved hands during the playing of the National Anthem. It's destined to go down as the most unsubtle demonstration in the history of protest...and it insured maximum embarrassment for the country that picked up their room and board bill in Mexico."[8] In other words, how dare these black athletes rebel against a country that Tommie Smith said, "treated him like just another nigger off the track." How and why were Smith and Carlos blacklisted in 1968 but appreciated in 2008?

This research investigates black and white definitions of black athletic power specifically as they pertained to the circumstances surrounding the 1968 Olympiad grandstand protest. Scholars typically break up twentieth-century African American sports history into three categories —segregation, integration, and the revolt of the black athlete. Two positions, though, are highlighted here: double consciousness in segregated sports and American culture, and a two-pronged revolt of the black athlete embedded in a continuous twentieth-century black freedom struggle. Historian David Wiggins uses W. E. B. Du Bois's notion of double consciousness to explain that black athletes were proud of their race for overcoming assumptions predicated on scientific racism. On the other hand, the successes of black athletes and their ability to assimilate into American culture were predicated on adhering to the values upheld in dominant society. Therefore, sports for African Americans represented race pride and American citizenship for black athletes who faced racism regularly.[9]

Twentieth-century sports, unlike politics, labor, education, or legislation, represented racial equality for African Americans and a platform to stabilize their claims for American citizenship by their performances and later, protest. The revolt of the black athlete must be examined within these two overlapping points. First, black athletes overcame segregation in sports by earning spots on previously all-white teams, and they often did this using direct action and nonviolence. Second, as depicted in the 1968 Olympic Games, black athletes used revolutionary activism with the intention to confront racism in sports and society. In this regard, the black-gloved protest demonstration is rooted in a continuous African American freedom struggle in which black athletes regularly and intentionally used sports as a protest strategy against racism. "A Silent Protest" traces the continuity in the revolt of the black athlete from the direct action phase of the Civil Rights Movement in the mid-1950s at SJS to the revolutionary activist phase of the mid- to late 1960s.[10] Politicians, journalists, and administrators, moreover, also attempted to define black agency and athletic potential. The gloved salute perplexed and flustered whites. To them, how dare black athletes reveal their frustration through sport. To them, sport best represented American democracy. Athletic integration meant national integration. To blacks athletic integration, which in some ways was a fallacy, only deepened the paradox of American democracy.

The Idea of Blackness in Sports

There are numerous historical examples and contexts that alluded to a legacy of white appropriation of black athletic potential, agency, and freedom prior to the 1960s revolt. To build on activist H. Rap Brown and historian Howard Zinn, white appropriations of black identity and agency were as American as American pie.[11] In 1790, President George Washington signed the Naturalization Act. This law reinforced racial distinctions in the Constitution and prohibited black citizenship. Race-based clauses also were promoted and reinforced alleged black inferiority. *Dred Scott v. Sanford* further defined racial parameters of black agency by denying citizenship and the rights associated with such. In the antebellum period, white appropriations of a limited black identity and agency were advanced by popular culture and enforced by the executive, judicial, and legislative branches of government. Despite the passage of Thirteenth, Fourteenth, and Fifteenth Amendments after the Civil War, blacks were denied full participation as American citizens. Since racism permeated all forms of American life, African Americans, to paraphrase historian Hasan Jeffries, readily understood the possibilities of "freedom rights" or the restoration of black dignity and attainment of civil and human rights in antebellum and postbellum contexts.[12]

Although African Americans certainly were not passive or reactive to attempted white appropriations of their identities, they were according to W. E. B. Du Bois cognizant of American racism and contradictions of freedom, all while creating their own spaces as citizens. Sports historian David Wiggins asserts black athletes doubly felt proud because of their ability to sustain and overcome constructions of black inferiority amid burdens that their success predicated on a willingness to assimilate and reinforce hegemonic white values.[13] Wiggins argues that more than white athletes, blacks typically had to uphold the status quo by showing passivity and obeying coaches in order to attain glory. They, as a whole, were not socially or politically conscious and negotiated their identity to achieve athletic success and reconstruct a positive black image.[14] Black athletes were cognizant of the term, the "tripartite framework of black sport history." First, blacks understood sport was, in theory, a space that allowed for integrated competition. Second, black athletes lived through and were aware of constructed stereotypes intended to define their identity.[15] Finally, black athletic participation reinforced the contradiction of sport and freedom in the United States. Thus, black athletes used performance as a protest mechanism that confirmed their humanity, reasserted racial pride, and defined citizenship. Desegregation of sport was merely one goal that was used by black athletes. Indeed, some black athletes and administrators discussed strategies to use sports as a catalyst for racial advancement. Sport then, was situated in a legacy and struggle for black freedom that was acted on and utilized differently by black athletes.

Early American sport also was situated in complicated race-based contexts. Historians Elliott Gorn and Warren Goldstein confirmed the importation of English games and sport to the American colonies.[16] To the British, work aligned with pain, toil, and servitude—play with freedom and gentility, a necessity and sin juxtaposed against pleasure and ease. The Puritans opposed sport because of theological assumptions that games led to indiscretions, sin, and separation from moral obligations. For elite white men in colonial America, sport confirmed honor and masculine empowerment. Work then coincided with arduous labor and an inferior social status, and granted space for white constructions of inclusivity and exclusivity in sport and society. Virginia gentry emulated English gentleman and showcased ostentatious displays of sport and games that reasserted their status as the ruling class. Blood games or the violent involvement in sport for patriarchal empowerment often included gambling on cockfighting, bearbaiting, fighting, and gander pulling.[17] Blood games and early sport were not enacted for the profit motive. On the contrary, elite whites used it exclusively in seclusion to confirm their class status.[18]

American sport shifted between the Reconstruction and Progressive eras. Gorn and Goldstein implied that urbanization and immigration contributed to the growth of modern American sporting culture. Businessmen such as Albert Spalding learned that huge profits could be made from charging admission and developing new technology for sport. The intellectual class promoted the value of sport. Ralph Waldo Emerson connected it with power; Harriet Beecher Stowe loved speed; Thomas Wentworth Higginson feared effeminacy; and Oliver Wendell Holmes craved heroic strength. President Theodore Roosevelt boxed, wrestled, ran, and believed that sport instilled courage, resolution, and endurance—all necessary traits of good leaders. Even the Young Men's Christian Association (YMCA) adhered to the elevation of man's physical state to equality with his mental and religious condition; its 1895 emblem signified the three components of the fully developed man—mind, body, and spirit.[19]

For African Americans, white supremacist doctrines of the late 1800s also attempted to define their agency and freedom in sport. In 1874, Richard Kyle Fox and his *National Police Gazette* became a framework for sensational sports journalism. His paper openly promoted nativism, racism, and anti-Semitism. Organizations such as the Amateur Athletic Union (AAU), the San Francisco Olympic Club, the United States Lawn Tennis Association, the National Collegiate Athletic Association (NCAA), and the National Association of Baseball Players formed. These organizations defined their rules and determined inclusive and exclusive race-based policy. In 1867, the African American Pythian Baseball Club of Philadelphia was denied entry to the Pennsylvania Association of Baseball Players. For white athletes and administrators the landmark case *Plessy v. Ferguson* doubly reinforced exclusion and provided glimpses of how they perceived American citizenship. To them, the shift to modern sport confirmed their definition of American citizenship and who could access and reap its full benefits. To them, black athletes were not American citizens and should not be accepted in any capacity.

The Olympics were an oddity for discussions on race, sport, and politics. The man responsible for implementing conflicted rules and regulations on Olympic space and politics was Pierre de Coubertin. Born on January 1, 1863, as the son of an immigrant Italian family that had lived in France for nearly five hundred years, Pierre de Fredy, Baron de Coubertin, grew up in Paris. He witnessed the French defeat in the Franco-Prussian War and certainly understood that Europe was rapidly changing in the late nineteenth century. He studied ancient history, was captivated by the Olympics, and proclaimed "Olympism" as an ideal that could transcend national differences through sport. By June 1894, meetings were held that led to the formation of an International Olympic Committee (IOC). That IOC, similar to the founders of numerous athletic organizations, consisted of elite white men from European countries.[20] In many ways, the IOC was naïve to the potentially hostile interplay of race, sport, and politics. Although overly simplistic, de Coubertin's ideals strongly influenced Avery Brundage, the fifth IOC president and stalwart during the 1968 Olympic Games.[21]

The IOC pledged to uphold the Olympic ideal over nationalism. Brundage was keen to "preserve the ideal": a utopian belief that individuals can and must separate their own values from the shared and equal competition of the Olympic Games.[22] Born on September 28, 1887, in Detroit, Michigan, Brundage lived by the mission of de Coubertin. At age twenty-five, Brundage competed at the Stockholm Olympic Games and placed sixth in the pentathlon.[23] As president of the United States Olympic Committee (USOC), Brundage professed that "Olympism" and its message of fair play may succeed where others failed. However, even he could not avoid controversy. Leading up the 1936 Berlin Games, Brundage toured Germany applauded the host country's efforts. He opposed pressure from the AAU, black and Jewish groups, and opposed an American boycott of the Games. Despite claims from a Nazi paper that black participation would taint the sacred grandeur of the Olympics, Brundage did not refute those claims or vouch for black athletes in opposition to the racist propaganda promulgated by Nazi Germany. Brundage saw the Olympics as a manifestation of freedom. Just as the ancient Greeks viewed the Olympic Games as civilization in its purest form, Brundage believed that competition rooted in solidarity would disassociate individuals from global conflict and unify the world. Historian Richard Espy stated that sports were seen as an ideal vehicle to instill spirit and social values in the individual. It was an opportunity to broaden the athletes' horizons and expose them to diverse peoples and cultures that generally did not interact. To the IOC, political acts during the Games defeated the purpose of "Olympism," and ran counter to freedom.[24]

Perhaps the most relevant examples of white confusion and appropriation of black athletic power before the 1960s stemmed from debates that were rooted in scientific racism. Despite white supremacy, black athletes flourished. In 1875 when the Kentucky Derby began, fourteen of the fifteen jockeys were black, and in the first thirty years half of the victors were black. In the 1890–91 racing season, Isaac Murphy became the first jockey to win consecutive derbies at Churchill Downs.[25] During the Progressive Era, E. B. Henderson, educator and writer, created avenues for African Americans to participate on the field and in athletic organizations. His work on black athletes appeared in The Crisis, and Messenger, and influenced prominent African American newspapers such as the Chicago Defender and Pittsburgh Courier.[26] Rube Foster was the entrepreneurial spirit behind the Negro Leagues—the black baseball entity that infused race pride in black communities. When permitted, black athletic participation advanced

American democracy in international competition. Jesse Owens, Eddie Tolan, Alice Coachman, the Tennessee State Tigerbelles, and numerous others earned gold medals in Olympic competition.

Black athletic successes perplexed many white journalists, politicians, athletes, spectators, and politicians. They found it necessary to study black athletes and used Eurocentric methodology in their examinations. Many of these debates reinforced essentialist claims that black athletic superiority stemmed from innate physical characteristics. They studied skull size, facial angles, skin color, hair, and body lice. Black sprinters were said to have longer heel bones and stronger Achilles' tendons than whites. Their narrow hips and longer arms, argued scholar Eleanor Methany, allowed them to run faster than whites. Laynard Holloman, a clinical psychiatrist, espoused that black athletic success emanated from their hatred of whites and desire for revenge. University of California at Berkeley (UCB) professor Arthur Jensen argued that blacks were intellectually inferior to whites but still capable of physical greatness.[27]

Even white coaches of internationally acclaimed black athletes voiced opinions on the pseudoscience. Dean Bartlett Cromwell was a track and field legend. By 1938 he developed more world record holders and Olympic champions (thirty-six) than anyone in American history. His University of Southern California (USC) teams won twelve NCAA championships, nine Intercollegiate Association of Amateur Athletes of America (ICAAAA or IC4A) titles, and set fourteen individual records. USC only lost three dual meets from 1939 to 1948 and his athletes won thirty-eight AAU titles. [28] His peers revered him as the "Maker of Champions." Similar to his nationally renowned peer Brutus Hamilton, head coach at Berkeley, Cromwell attracted black athletes from the South to compete on his teams. On the surface, Cromwell seemed to advocate sport as a site for integrated participation. However, in 1941, he continued a long-standing debate on why black athletes were successful. "It was not long ago," Cromwell asserted, "that his ability to sprint and jump was a life-and-death matter to him in the jungle. His muscles are pliable, and his easy-going disposition is a valuable aid to the mental and physical relaxation that a runner and a jumper must have."[29] Cromwell was situated in an era when white scientists, journalists, administrators, coaches, and politicians attempted to understand and define the parameters of black intellectual and physical ability. Many whites often constructed and used essentialist traits to confirm their idea of a true black identity and potential. These historical examples and contexts allude to a legacy of white appropriation of black athletic potential, agency, and freedom prior to the 1960s revolt.

Jesse Owens and Jackie Robinson both illustrate debates on the transformative black athletic revolt. Both men defied racial barriers in sports. Their accomplishments informed white masses that blacks and whites could compete athletically—although remain socially separate and unequal. As college students, they excelled at majority white institutions, Ohio State University (OSU) and the University of California at Los Angeles (UCLA) respectively, similarly to Tommie Smith, John Carlos, and Lee Evans who would be involved in forms of athletic protests and at the center of negotiations about the possibility of boycotting the 1968 Games. Unlike the latter track and field stars, however, any challenge against racism in sports was done on the field, but rarely off it. Before 1965, the Negro athlete was expected to compete and keep his or her mouth shut.

Jesse Owens best represented this mold. In November of 1935 Owens told a radio station that blacks should boycott the upcoming 1936 Berlin Olympic Games if they were discriminated against. His comments were denounced by his Ohio State coach Larry Snyder, and by executive secretary of the National Association for the Advancement of Colored People (NAACP) Walter White. Owens reneged on his comment and never committed to a boycott. On the track, blackness was viewed as weakness to some whites. Hitler declined to shake Jewish or "black auxiliary" hands. After defeating Adolf Hitler's Nazi propaganda machine by winning four gold medals, the AAU booked Jesse Owens on a European exhibition tour where he was forced to compete in at least eight competitions over ten days without compensation. Because of the grueling physical stress, Owens lost eleven pounds and refused to continue. He protested to USOC president Avery Brundage who, in return, criticized him for being ungrateful to the American team. The AAU answered his refusal by banning him for life from amateur sports and denying him for consideration of the Sullivan Award, given annually to the most outstanding amateur athlete.

Owens had to scrape to make a living by running against horses and cars, and reinforced scientific racist assumptions to white masses that the black athlete was an enhanced physical specimen. Owens activism should not come as a surprise. In the 1930s his alma mater continued an ignoble reputation against black student-athletes. In 1931, football player William Bell was benched in a home game against Vanderbilt, and in 1933 the Ohio State Supreme Court upheld a university ruling to deny housing to Doris Weaver. University president Dr. George Rightmire claimed to know the feelings of Ohioans, at least white Ohioans, and concluded that race mixing was harmful. The Chicago Defender urged Owens against attending or supporting an institution that majored in prejudice. He enrolled anyway. His student life typified black athletes up until the 1960s. He was denied on-campus housing and lived with other black students off campus. Only one movie theater allowed black patronage and restaurants refused him service. Owens's story detailed the overlap between racism, housing, administration, and athletics.[30] Despite his earlier activism, Owens is often viewed later in life as a team player. Harry Edwards however reported that he lamented, "I've never been in the mainstream. They won't put me on any key Olympic committees, the policy committees. I've been used."[31]

Jackie Robinson, the youngest child born to sharecroppers in Cairo, Georgia, moved to Pasadena, California, after his father abandoned his mother and his parents' subsequent divorce. Always a sports enthusiast, he excelled in baseball, track, football, basketball, and tennis, and used sports to escape the more negative aspects of life that confronted black youth. With an amiable personality and standout athleticism, Robinson nonetheless encountered racism at Pasadena Junior College and was arrested under questionable circumstances.

He received probation for the offenses, but used the incident as well as other to internally build a barrier that would serve him well in his future endeavors. He transferred to UCLA, and again garnered attention because of his phenomenal athletic abilities. Robinson, however, did not graduate from UCLA; he had to withdraw just short of graduation because he had to work to help support his family. The army drafted him for service after the United States entered World War II and he encountered southern-style racism after being sent to Texas to train. Unaccustomed to such blatant displays of discrimination, Robinson could not acquiesce to Jim Crow customs and, when forced to ride in the back of the bus, protested and faced arrest and military court martial—which was reduced to insubordination and eventually overturned. After an honorable discharge, Robinson engaged in baseball by playing with the Negro League's Kansas City Monarchs. Eventually, he caught the eye of Branch Rickey the general manager of the Brooklyn Dodgers who wanted to desegregate baseball using an African American player. Rickey knew that he needed a certain kind of player and personality for this feat: someone who could persevere in the face of the tremendous backlash he would face. After leaving baseball, Robinson continued his involvement in civil rights issues by supporting the NAACP and the Southern Christian Leadership Conference (SCLC), participating in southern campaigns and the March on Washington, and using his influence with politicians to affect change.[32]

Since American sport also was situated in complicated race-based contexts, white misappropriation of black athletic agency, freedom, and potential was featured alongside a racist status quo. Some white critics, players, and managers praised Moses Fleetwood and Welday Wilberforce Walker, the first black professional baseball players. When Wendell Smith and the *Pittsburgh Courier* staff attacked racism in major league baseball, a cadre of white writers supported their efforts. When all-star, all-black teams played white players and defeated them, the latter were convinced blacks could thrive in major league baseball. Even though Branch Rickey envisioned a nonconfrontational black player to de-segregate the lily white league, his vision allowed for gradual integration of major league baseball. With regard to debates on black athletic superiority, John Wooden asserted that black success was not due to innate physical skills. Rather, black athletes were ambitious to work hard and thrive because of racial and social inequality. An anonymous writer proclaimed:

> Perseverance, determination, and great effort allowed many of them (black athletes) to reach the top in world competition and brought their country (the United States) a rich collection of Olympic medals....Even those Negro sportsmen who are able to obtain security, due to success in sports, are subjected to degradation and race discrimination. Such is the fate of Negro sportsmen in America.[33]

Athletes as Activists

Born in East St. Louis, Illinois, in 1942, Harry Edwards described his early life as surviving on "beans and spaghetti and...[watching] neighborhood kids freeze to death."[34] Defying the odds by graduating from high school as a black male in 1957—he reported that he was the first from his area—and winning an athletic scholarship to the University of Southern California for football, he found that his education did not prepare him for college-level work. Therefore, he enrolled in junior college at Fresno City, dropped football for basketball and track, and transferred in 1960 to San Jose State College. This experience opened his eyes to the possibility of intellectual pursuit as well as athletic prowess. At 6 feet 8 inches tall and about 250 pounds, Edwards epitomized the ideal of black athletic structure and excelled in sports.[35] Two professional football teams expressed interest in him, but after graduating he decided that an academic career would prove more beneficial and earned graduate degrees in sociology from Cornell University. "As I moved toward graduation, it dawned on me that there was no serious sociological literature on sports. People saw sports and society as somehow insulated and isolated from each other."[36] Upon receiving his master's degree and while studying for his doctorate, he returned to his alma mater to teach and counsel other black athletes and students attending the college. African American athletes were a commodity for the mainstream teams for which they played. Recruited for their athletic abilities, but oftentimes treated as second-class citizens at the amateur and professional level, teams and institutions exploited these individuals for their honed skills in order to prevail in competitions and bring in revenue. In exchange for the opportunity to compete, black athletes should be team players and grateful for the opportunity. Harry Edwards's own experience and research showed that athletics for African Americans resembled a "plantation system." Moreover, these elite players "function[ed] as little more than 20th century gladiators." Blacks seriously involved in sports saw a bleak future once their playing days ended with little opportunity for lucrative endorsements of employment in mainstream coaching or sports administration. Therefore, he had an eye on educating athletes and attempting to change the corrupt American sports system.

> I felt it was imperative that we defend our own definitions relative to the politics of sports. . . . So long as Black Africa was squirming under the heel of British, French, German, and Portuguese colonialism, Black athletes who did well in international sports reflected the ideological position that Blacks do well under the guidance of White domination and colonialism. If they failed, it reflected the White Supremacist position that Blacks, irrespective of circumstance, are inferior to whites physically, morally, and otherwise.[37]

In the 1960s, Seventh Street was the epicenter of campus activity at San Jose State. Similar to Sproul Plaza at the University of California at Berkeley, students, administrators, and on occasion, public figures gathered and spoke on a variety of topics. Chinese national and student body president Vic Lee used Seventh Street to confront discrimination and the Vietnam War; SJS president Robert Clark refuted resignation threats made by conservative opponents; and Congress of Racial Equality (CORE) national director James Farmer gave impromptu speeches on black power and challenges faced by black people. It was no coincidence that former SJS student-athlete and instructor of sociology and anthropology, Harry Edwards, chose Seventh Street as the location where he publicly introduced white masses to a unique component of the broader 1960s student and black freedom movement: the black athletic revolt. San Jose State was the seventeenth largest university in America, but black students were in the numerical minority. In the late 1960s, out of 23,000 students, approximately 200–300 were black. Of the African American students fewer than a hundred were full time, and most of those full time students were athletes.[38] If black students at SJS were to rise, then athletes would have to assume leadership roles. Edwards and, former SJS athlete-turned-graduate student, Ken Noel struggled for the restoration of black dignity and attainment of civil and human rights, or what historian Hasan Jeffries terms, "freedom rights."[39] Noel and Edwards centered their protest on five broad and interlocked local issues: student and faculty admission and recruitment, housing, Greek organizations, campus administration, and athletics. The impact of their organized protest swept the country and their activism shifted university life at the college. President Robert Clark acted swiftly in favor of the black athletic revolt and implemented antiracist measures in all facets of the university. By early 1968 and throughout the 1970s, collegiate black athletes built on the initial activism sparked by SJS athletes and used sports as a mechanism to achieve freedom rights.

It all started over lunch. On Friday, September 15, 1967, Harry Edwards and twenty-nine-year-old Ken Noel met at the SJS cafeteria and discussed differences between historically black Greek organization Omega Psi Phi and majority white Greek organizations on campus. They identified preferential treatment in regards to race and pledging. They confirmed ways in which black athletes were forced to live in motels because of discriminatory housing practices and acknowledged university regulations that allowed 2 percent of the student body to be enrolled without proper academic qualifications. They viewed little difference or progress in the plight of the current black undergraduate students with regard to racial discrimination and their own past campus experience.[40]

From his athletic experience, Edwards understood the impact of sport as a vehicle for social change. He saw athletics as an American religion. It became ritual "on Saturdays from 1 to 6 to find a substantial portion of the country: in the stadium or in front of the television set. We want to get to those people, to affect them, to wake them up to what's happening in this country, because otherwise they won't care."[41] Edwards believed that the only way to engage the white masses was by "showing them all is not well in the locker room. Then maybe they'll see beyond the locker room. No one attempts to change anything he's not in love with, and the Negro loves this country, fights for it in war and runs for it. The tragedy here is that the country the Negro loves doesn't love him back."[42] Edwards also refuted a nonviolent course of action. If people, as Edwards saw it, were attacked with "bottles and garbage as if they were dogs,"[43] then they would reciprocate violence. Accordingly, "if any Neanderthal type decides to throw garbage on us or get smart like that, he'd just better have his hospitalization papers in order."[44] Many whites were concerned with the prospect of militant blacks burning down SJS Spartan Stadium, and certain sorority and fraternity housing that practiced discrimination. The United Black Students for Action (UBSA) sought "help in this because if you have discrimination in the elite sub-culture of this college campus, then how can you hope to eliminate it in places like Detroit, Newark, Hunters Point and East Palo Alto?"[45] The issue was of national consequence. Some questioned if "those opposing any issue choose sports events as their targets of dissent?"[46]

Black athletes were not immune to this movement. Edwards and Noel tapped into the broader black freedom movement and publicized racism against black athletes. Although they introduced the black athletic revolt, athletes used a plethora of tactics to attain freedom rights— many of them disagreed with Edwards and aspects, if not all, of his agenda. On the other hand, for black athletes, the 1960s revolt marked new activist possibilities and responsibilities for them.

Moments after Edwards and Noel finished their lunch, they were approached by a local news reporter who was on the hunt for them. The reporter asked them about the living situations of black athletes and gave Edwards his first taste of publicity—recognition that catapulted him onto a national stage. Word spread quickly and later that night about forty black students met at the Omega house—a gathering that became the first unofficial meeting for the UBSA.[47] The meeting was productive and Edwards and Noel, members of the UBSA executive committee, met with dean of students Stanley Benz. Benz was not inexperienced to charges of racial discrimination in housing, administration, and organizations at SJS. In 1954, Benz responded to allegations that the SJS administration was complacent toward racial discrimination in housing. Thirteen years later, Benz, at least to Edwards and Noel, seemed biased and unchanged in his approach. When the two men informed Benz of their concerns, he grinned, faintly smiled, and chuckled in their faces. To Edwards, Benz crossed the line. So, the UBSA took to the street.

At 11:00 a.m. on the first day of classes Monday, September 18, 1967, approximately thirty-five to fifty students rallied at Seventh Street amidst the chaos of opening day registration. The onlookers, which included President Clark, Dean Benz, and nearly 700 others, did not see the "Welcome back to SJS" signs. Rather, the protesting black students charged racial discrimination and proclaimed, "If it can't be done at SJS then where?" They demanded "racism at SJS must end now!" They reminded students that "racism kills the mind and destroys the nation."[48] Edwards spoke through a bullhorn and Noel passed out documentation. In his animated oratory style, Edwards attacked discrimination in housing, categorized white Greek organizations as racist enclaves, and trivialized an apathetic administration on racial equality. To some, the speech by Edwards influenced the "Black Panthers to act like a Greek Chorus." They shouted, "Sock it to 'em, Brother!'[and] 'Run it on down, Brother!" After Edwards, groups from San Jose City College and San Francisco State College offered support and "warned against trusting white liberals."[49] Edwards concluded, "You heard what he [the Panther] said. That's where it's at. If things don't get better than this, Uncle Tom won't be able to cool it any longer."[50]

They demanded change by any means necessary, and listed four concentric goals: (a) end racism in student organizations, (b) outlaw racial discrimination in housing, (c) disrupt segregation and bigotry in athletics, and (d) increase black enrollment, faculty, and staff. After the demands came a threat. If progress was not made by Friday, then "there would be no football game at SJS this week."[51] The Black Student Union from San Francisco State informed the crowd of their support. President Clark then took the bullhorn and confirmed his administration would take action against discrimination. Edwards, Noel, and the UBSA did their homework in anticipation of the new school year. They conducted numerous interviews with local media five days before the new school term. Thus, the *Spartan Daily* was aware of the issues and printed "faculty member charges discrimination in housing," on the front page of the student newspaper on the first day of classes. The rally was successful for two reasons: it organized black students and pressured the Clark administration to act.[52]

The UBSA made inroads quickly and decisively. Student body president Lee legitimized claims made by the USBA and "heard of instances of racial discrimination within the community." He argued that "until this mess is cleared up for everybody, it is cleared up for nobody."[53] His fellow councilpersons also supported the USBA. They unanimously upheld "deliberative and constructive action programs to insure equality of opportunity to all students." The student council went on record and "condemned all types of religious and racial discrimination on campus and in the community."[54] However, beyond strengthening communication they were initially unsure of concrete ways to battle local racism. Even faculty members conceded to Edwards that they were complacent but supported the current goals of the UBSA. The seven-member academic council passed a resolution and called for the enforcement of rules against discrimination at SJS. They resolved that all forms of "discriminatory practices based on race, religion, or ethnic grouping reprehensible and unequivocally supports efforts of minority groups on campus to further their fundamental rights to equality and justice."[55] Dr. John A. Galm, president of the SJS chapter of the American Federation of Teachers (AFT) was "prepared to act quickly to help end any current abuses of students' civil rights at this college." They called on President Clark to examine all charges and if "substantiated, we will demand immediate corrective action and a continuing program to ensure that such abuses do not arise in the future."[56] On the surface it seemed President Clark was cornered. Thanks to the swift action by the USBA and subsequent support from other Bay Area black community groups, SJS was forced to confront its own racism. He immediately appointed an ombudsman to "conduct a continuous campaign against racial discrimination."[57] In addition, he encouraged his campus to learn more about black people. Clark requested displays at the library and Spartan bookstore. He asked his community, "how are we going to understand this critical problem or deal with it if we do not know what the people most deeply concerned are thinking, feeling, and saying?"[58]

The lip service and inaction forced the administration's hand. In the end, the public demonstrations and demands compelled Clark to cancel the upcoming opening football game against the University of Texas at El Paso (UTEP). Though the athletic departments of both schools threatened to participate in the contest even if officially canceled, many of the black athletes on both squads were prepared to sit the game out if played as originally planned. Moreover, the threat of violence loomed large. San Jose State College and the surrounding community lost approximately $100,000 in revenue because of the cancellation, but the black athletes and students along with concerned others learned that they could organize and have their demands considered if not completely met. Edwards deduced that "we had learned the use of power—the power to be gained from exploiting the white man's economic and almost religious involvement in athletics."[59]

Prior to the 1960s, black athletic protest was not new. Blacks often used their participation in sport as a protest strategy against racism, athletically and in society. Some blacks used activism as a strategy to gain freedom rights. In these contexts, the revolt of the black athlete represented an extension and the culmination of black athletic protest in the twentieth century. For black athletes, the distinctiveness of the 1960s was marked by social movements and rooted in their unified activism. The black athletic revolt signified the first time in American history that collegiate black athletes publicly and collectively used their position in sport to attain freedom rights.

As earlier mentioned, Jesse Owens voiced the possibility of an Olympic boycott in the 1930s. In 1960 Rafer Johnson, the gold medal decathlete, did not act on the suggestion that he boycott the games in response to the violence that black civil rights workers encountered in their southern campaigns. Despite the inaction, the press carried the story and influenced some African Americans to contemplate such an idea. Comedian and activist, Dick Gregory, led a failed boycott of black athletes for the 1963 Russian-American Track and Field meet but still called for a boycott of the 1964 Tokyo Olympics. The African American Olympians noted various forms of discrimination concerning certain athletic and social accommodations while in Japan. After Tokyo, track and field athletes in particular discussed the validity of boycotting Mexico City. At the University Games in Tokyo in the fall of 1967, sprinter and SJS undergrad, Tommie Smith, answered a Japanese reporter's query about the likelihood of an upcoming Olympic boycott. Smith had a quiet demeanor, but found the voice of protest when questioned on this occasion. He stated, "Some black athletes have been discussing the possibility of boycotting the games to protest racial injustice in America."[60] This incident along with the demonstrations at SJS would plant the seed that germinated into the birth of the Olympic Project for Human Rights (OPHR).

This research further asserts two positions about mainstream viewpoints concerning the appropriation of black athletic power: to whites that may have disregarded black concerns, integrated sport best represented the possibilities of American greatness, and, black protest was interpreted as antithetical to the assumption of sport as a nonpolitical space. Furthermore, the black athletic revolt was defined as un-American. Perhaps a useful example of the conflicted interplay between race, sport, and politics was Tommie Smith and the ways white perceived him prior to the athletic revolt. Tommie Smith gradually developed a critical lens on race and human rights. Although his upbringing was poor and rural (his parents were sharecroppers and itinerant workers in Texas and California before his father landed a job as a janitor with the California school system), he rarely questioned the potency of racism on his life. At SJS, that changed. He possessed a demure demeanor and often learned by observing others. He learned from Harry Edwards and other black students when they discussed race relations on campus. Smith joined the black Greek fraternity Omega Psi Phi during his junior year. His employment with the Oakland Public Schools introduced him to conditions in local schools. Aware of the consequences of the Vietnam War, he joined the ROTC for two reasons: his love for the United States and his eagerness to avoid the draft. He even participated in an antiwar and civil rights march to San Francisco. Although his attendance at such events is unknown, notable speakers that visited and spoke at SJS might have enlightened Smith.[61] Even though Smith enhanced his intellectual development on race alongside his athletic career, at the time he was not considered as a threat to whites.

Prior to 1967, neither administrators, coaches, or spectators regarded Smith as an activist or a menace to the social order at SJS. On the contrary, they revered him. In intercollegiate athletics, track and field was a second semester sport. So, most members of "Speed City" the aptly named SJS men's track and field team typically used the fall semester to prepare for the spring season. Not Tommie Smith: In his first year he competed on the freshmen basketball team. Coached by Danny Cline, Smith bragged about his ability to dunk the ball in practice and outrun his teammates to any loose balls. In the first game of the season, the 6 foot 4 inch, 175-pound Smith was eager to prove his talents on the court. Cline decided not to start Smith and instead went with an all-white lineup. This decision confused Smith. Whether or not Cline's decision to bench Smith at the start of the game was a watershed moment in Smith's ideological development on racial issues, he certainly was not immediately impacted by the decision. Smith entered four or five minutes into the game and became a starter for the rest of the season.[62] Cline quickly changed his mind about freshman and that season Smith, the only black player on the team, dominated nearly every statistical category. In twenty games played Smith shot 42 percent from the field, averaged 13 points a game, and grabbed 10 rebounds a contest.[63]

On the track, Smith's ascension to international acclaim coincided with his intellectual growth specific to human rights and the needs of black people. On the one hand, white administrators, coaches, and the public at large prescribed high expectations for black athletes in sports. On the other hand, many whites in the 1960s did not have high expectations for blacks outside of sports.[64] Similar to black athletes before him, his use of performance in sport elevated humanity, asserted racial pride, and fomented black engagement with American citizenship. By April 1966, the nation had noticed. Tommie Smith ran the nation's best time in the 220-, 440-, and 100-yard dashes and he also anchored the nation's best 440-yard relay time to a mark of 39.9 seconds.[65] Although other Spartans earned glory, Tommie Smith was in a different league. His records put him in the public spotlight. He became the golden boy of SJS athletics and Coach Bud Winter vouched to "make Tommy [sic] Smith the greatest sprinter in history."[66] At the luncheon for Northern California Track Writers Winter said, "I believe you should set goals for all your athletes, and our goal for Tommy is that he will better, equal, or at least approach world records in all three sprints, the 100, the 220, and the 440...but I think Tommy has a chance to be the best man who ever drew on a spike."[67] Winter's colleague Coach Sam Bell of the University of California Golden Bears agreed. Bell asserted, "I've seen three great 440 relay anchors in my time, including Bob Hayes at Tokyo [1964 Olympic Games], but Smith's 110 yards Saturday, in which he shifted gears four or five times, was the best of all."[68] Ron Clarke, arguably the top distance runner of his era, believed that "[t]here are only two supermen in track, Jim Ryun and Tommie Smith."[69] In March 1966, Smith finished second to Kansas star Jim Ryun in voting for the Sullivan Award, annually given to nation's best amateur athlete.[70] In early May the Northern California Track and Field writers named Smith the "Athlete of the Week" for the fourth time that season and at SJS the *Daily* named him person of the year. White writers, spectators, and administrators viewed him as an "All-American" athlete—*Sports Illustrated, Track and Field News*, and the *San Francisco Examiner* wrote feature stories in his honor. The "Tommie kick" or Smith's ability to sprint from his competitors caught the attention of the National Football League. By the end of the 1965–66 academic year, Smith contemplated a career in professional football. NFL recruiters lured him with financial stability but Smith decided against mixing sports. He committed to track.[71]

John Carlos, of Cuban ancestry, called Harlem, New York, home, but left to attend East Texas State University. During the 1966–67 school year he decided to leave Texas and transfer to San Jose State, making him ineligible to run for the college until the 1968–69 season. Edwards recounts that Carlos had some of the same complaints of discrimination that athletes experienced at SJS. Carlos talked to Edwards and voiced his disillusion with the situation and interest in doing something to elicit change, and the mentor convinced him to transfer to SJS. "Come…work with the brothers to end all this racist bull. Join us in this movement to liberate black people through the use of athletics."[72] So, he moved his family to the Bay Area in the summer of 1967 and became immersed in an emerging, campus-driven black athletic revolt. Lee Evans, like Tommie Smith, was central to student leadership after he transferred to SJS in 1966. Prior to that he ran track at San Jose City College. A native Californian, Evans shared a similar background with Smith in that their families worked in the California agricultural fields.[73]

The Olympic Project for Human Rights

In *The Revolt of the Black Athlete* Harry Edwards points to Bill Russell's book *Go Up for Glory* as the signal for the possibility of organized athletic revolt. In that work Russell delineated the racism inherent in organized sports as it specifically related to his basketball career. Russell's story correlated to many instances of racial discrimination in sports where athletes chose to fight back such as black players refusing to play in the 1965 American Football League's East-West All-Star game because they were not welcome in many of the host city New Orleans's social establishments. The league decided to move the game rather than risk boycott by the black players. Prior to that, the press picked up the story that Rafer Johnson had been approached about boycotting the 1960 Rome Olympics. Johnson did not entertain such a thought, but the spread of the story inevitably gave credence to the possibility of boycotting. As previously mentioned, Dick Gregory tried to organize a boycott by black track and field athletes against a Soviet-American track meet. Though unsuccessful in this venture, Gregory tried again in 1964 in light of the Tokyo Games. He convinced a small group to protest at the US Olympic trials, but again failed in mobilizing black athletes to threaten to walk. Some African American Olympians awakened to their mistreatment in Japan and voiced concern over perceived slights that the press, in turn, covered up. This, however, sparked a new activism. Specifically, the possibility of a boycott became the topic of discussion at "every major track meet that followed the games"[74] with Mexico as the targeted Olympiad.

At the World University Games held in Japan in September 1967, Tommie Smith, when asked by a reporter about the possibility of a forthcoming boycott, replied that this was a viable option. Upon his return to SJS, Smith was pressured to revoke his previous statement. Instead, he issued a response of his own stating that he could not speak for all black athletes, but that "if a boycott is deemed appropriate, then I believe most of the Black athletes will act in unison."[75] For such comments Smith received hate mail. To Ralph Brubaker of Los Angeles, Tommie Smith became "Nigger Smith," an "irresponsible black ape."[76] Perhaps the most striking example came from Willie Williams, a white infantry solider. Williams admitted the ways the army required whites and "niggers" to work together—they ate, slept, and attended the wounded together. Blacks and whites fought in the same company and were as good as the next soldier. However, as Williams asserted, "they are still niggers and that is as far as it goes—when I have free time I want to get as far away from a nigger as I can get. The other whites feel the same way."[77] To Williams, race and sport was bigger than any proposed protest—rather, that protest elucidated what American identity was not. The "nisei [sic—pronounced Ni-say in Japanese] is a fine American...[and] have suffered as much discrimination as the next one, but they are very good Americans. You don't hear of them rioting, burning, looting, stealing, knifing."[78] Williams reminded "Nigger Smith," his title for the gold medalist champion, "I am sure that at least 98% of whites (north and south) (and I am from the north), feel the same way."[79] Smith realized that he and other athletes commanded an audience whether they sought one or not. They were athletes, but also wanted to make a difference. "We began to really reach down for statements that would make our point but also be generic and not alienate us from the world."[80] Then the events occurred at San Jose State, which organized the students to protest against long-standing discrimination at the university.

By 1967, the black athletic revolt and implementation of black power as a protest strategy were in full force. In July 1967, Newark, New Jersey, hosted a conference on black power and Dick Gregory lamented that black athletes should protest the Games in retaliation to the stripping of boxing title from Muhammad Ali.[81] World-class black athletes would be queried about the proposal and their attitudes toward a boycott gauged. "We found...that [black athletes] had given a great deal of serious thought to the idea of boycotting the 1968 Olympic Games in order to dramatize the racial injustice in America."[82] Edwards began to mobilize and held a meeting at his home in October attended civil rights activists, athletes, and student leaders. They formed the Olympic Committee for Human Rights (OCHR), an advisory body, which would progress into the OPHR. They emphasized human rights over civil rights—similar to the larger freedom movement. Tommie Smith stressed the independent focus of the group. In hindsight he recollected that it was not a subset of the Black Panthers or necessarily a proponent of black power, though others might disagree. He emphasized that the struggle supported "human rights, not civil rights, nothing to do with the Panthers or Black Power—all humanity, even those who denied us ours.[83]

The upcoming Los Angeles Black Youth Conference to be held at the Second Baptist Church with the theme "Liberation is coming from a black thing" seemed the perfect setting to launch the movement. Aside from raising money, the most difficult task was contacting the targeted athletes since mail typically was forwarded through athletic departments that censored what the athletes, African American athletes in particular, received. Though the OCHR attempted to control information about any proposed plans and members, Edwards reported in an article for the *Saturday Evening Post* that renowned athletes such as Lew Alcindor, Otis Burrell, John Carlos, Lee Evans, Henry Jackson, Jerry Proctor, and Tommie Smith had agreed to boycott the Games. While a final vote had not occurred at the time of print, Edwards asserted that any of the named athletes "knows he may be hurting his own career, but is prepared to sacrifice his personal opportunity at the Olympics in order to win some recognition for the plight of his race."[84] Moreover, Edwards forecasted, "The members of the Olympic Project for Human Rights see this as a simple problem. Negroes have been relegated to an inferior status because society feels we belong there." The former athlete-turned-sociologist continued, "Our refusal to accept this has led the U.S. to the edge of revolution. Too many athletes have sold out to whitey in the past." And finally, "If we can show that our sense of personal worth and obligation is more important than any rewards we might be offered, and that we few represent the many, something may finally be accomplished."[85]

Despite the obstacles of finances, contacting athletes, and information control, a workshop on the Olympic boycott was scheduled for the conference and attended by Alcindor, Carlos, Evans, Smith, and Mike Warren. Before the meeting, Smith said that "he would not sacrifice his manhood or the dignity of his people to participate in the Olympic Games. I am quite willing," Smith noted, "to not only forgo the Games but also my life, if necessary, in order to open doors for the advancement of black people in America."[86] Harry Edwards revealed that the United States should be exposed for what it is, especially since its actions were similar to the apartheid nation of South Africa. Furthermore, the Negro athletes have been exploited and will take their plight to the United Nations.[87] This particular conference highlighted the complexities of black radical thought in the late 1960s. Black public figures also present at the conference included Huey Newton, the leader of the Black Panther Party (BPP) and Martin Luther King, Jr. Carlos, whose father fought in World War I, was so moved by both men that he gave an impromptu speech on the advantages of black power and solidarity in sport. Lew Alcindor also spoke about the inequalities he experienced even as one of the most recognizable college basketball players. He recounted an incident with a police officer and a shooting, with him as a bystander, that almost ended his life. "After all we were just niggers. I found out last summer that we don't catch hell because we aren't basketball stars or because we don't have money. We catch hell because we are black."[88] By November 23, a group of more than 200 participants nearly unanimously voted at the youth conference to possibly boycott the Games.[89]

The mainstream press and sports power structure immediately vilified the OPHR and any athlete thought to be associated with it. They surmised that a black boycott would not happen because true athletes would not jeopardize their status nor pass up the opportunity to compete in the Olympics. Mirroring the progression of the Black Power and Black Arts movements, the Negro athlete associated with the proposed boycott transformed into the black or Afro-American athletic competitor. Edwards confirmed that the media had it wrong. "Confronting them now was the new black athlete and a new generation of Afro-Americans."[90]

Shortly after the conference, Edwards with the consultation of Louis Lomax contacted Floyd McKissick of CORE and Dr. King to spearhead a plan to promote an all-sport boycott that would push white administrators to deal with blacks on the basis of equality. They held a press conference to articulate the demands of the boycott movement. Floyd McKissick stressed, "An athlete is only on the field two or more hours, after which he becomes a black man again subject to the same discrimination other black men must live in." Dr. King said, "The boycott marked a protest against racism and injustice and the athletes who sacrificed for the greater good of society should be praised."[91] Particularly, along with the removal of Avery Brundage from the head of the IOC, the boycotters sought the following structural changes:

1. An end to discrimination against Negroes and Jews at the New York Athletic Club
2. The reinstatement of Muhammad Ali as heavyweight boxing champion
3. Appointment of a second Negro coach to the United States Olympic team
4. Appointment of a Negro to the United States Olympic Committee, and finally,
5. [R]efusal by the United States team to compete against teams from Rhodesia and South Africa.[92]

The uses of black power leading up to the 1968 Olympic Games infused people socially and historically defined as violent and nonviolent in ways that inspired them to collaborate on national and transnational issues.

"So what," lamented Bob Hayes, a former black Olympian at the 1964 Tokyo Games and star for the Dallas Cowboys. "I don't know what they are doing because nothing would have kept me from participating in the Games." Ralph Boston, a world-class long jumper who competed in both the 1964 and 1968 Games, stated that the whole boycott idea was manipulated by people who were not athletes. He said, "Politics should not be mixed with the Olympic Movement," and "I will not support it."[93] Ironically, Boston later became a central organizing voice for black athletes considering the 1968 boycott.

Each participating athlete prepared a statement to demonstrate his support of the movement. In his remarks, Tommie Smith articulated that he certainly wanted to participate in the Olympics as well as other track and field meets, but would forego such if necessary since he "recognize[d] the political and social implication of some black people participating for a country in which the vast majority of black people suffer from unthinkable discrimination and racism." This was bigger than simple competition and proving one was the best in the world in a particular feat. Smith resounded that "it is my obligation as a black man to do whatever is necessary . . . to aid my people in obtaining the freedom that we all seek."[94] Still Edwards and many of the athletes received hate mail. California governor Ronald Reagan argued, "Young athletes are being victimized, and Edwards is not contributing nothing toward harmony between the races."[95]

Charles Maher, a white journalist for the *Los Angeles Times*, clarified that an athletic boycott of the 1968 Olympics would anger not encourage the white majority. He saw Negro athletes, as he called them, as "shameful in boycotting their own country and humanity."[96] He questioned if "the white majority in the United States be disposed to grant equal rights pending no black participation in the Games, or will it anger them more and thus resist future Negro demands."[97] He noted inconsistencies against star UCLA basketball player Lew Alcindor. How, cited Maher, could Alcindor disregard the Olympics and compete for the "white establishment"[98] at UCLA? Maher asserted if Alcindor wanted to make a splash, then he should forgo all basketball regardless of financial penalties. He concluded that Negro militants should learn from the gradual emancipation approach exhibited by baseball, of which blacks were slowly included into rosters over a twenty-year span. His insistence to solve the proposed boycott for black athletes stifled individual agency and overlooked the very purpose of black power protest. The flexibility of self-determination allowed black athletes to use sport for individual and collective gains—their activism in struggle for marginalized and racially oppressed peoples. White journalists did not understand black power protest or the downside of gradual integration. A *Chicago Tribune* editorial claimed, "All of this chatter is silly as it is intemperate."[99] The *Tribune* revealed that every major league baseball team and most college teams all were integrated. Additionally, Negro stars not only are applauded for their efforts, but their salary checks rewarded their successes. The author wrote, "It is a shame that Negro athletes would boycott their own country and humanity."[100] *U.S. News and World Report* confirmed 177 black players or 28 percent of the total in the National Football League and 105 athletes or nearly 30 percent in the American Football League were black. The article cited the high salaries of basketball greats Wilt Chamberlain, Oscar Robertson, and Bill Russell as examples of racial equality in sports.[101] Whites were clear—sport allowed for black social mobility. Thus, black manipulation of that enterprise was deemed inappropriate and un-American. To whites in the late 1960s, black political activism carried two goals: uplift the country through victory, and remind people of color of American democracy as the prototypical way of life in a contested Cold War world. To whites, black athletic power and protest were bad politics because it criticized rather than uplifted the United States.

In December 1967, the Olympic Committee for Human Rights met in New York City to start the planning to mobilize for the issued demands. The New York City Athletic Club held an annual track meet in February. Though spectators came to see the top track and field athletes, many of whom were black, the club did not admit African Americans. The OCHR did not want to desegregate the athletic club per se, but rather wanted discriminatory policies ended so that the black and Jewish athletes competing in the event were treated with the respect they deserved. The committee and its allies contacted high schools, colleges and universities, and foreign athletic delegations and enlightened them, if they were unaware, of the policies of the club. Following the example of their African American counterparts, many white athletes and mainstream collegiate teams pulled out. The OCHR informed the Soviet national team that black protestors would picket the meet and that the safety of the athletes could not be guaranteed. The team declined to participate "to avoid interference in a conflict involving the internal integrity of the United States."[102] Though officials did not cancel the track meet, the mobilization by the OCHR to contact athletes and organizations, and organize boycotters and protestors proved successful.

Time magazine published a biased report of the boycott of the New York Athletic Club's racist practices. Calling Edwards a "brainy Negro," the article linked the sociologist to the Black Power Movement and suggested that he either "cajol[ed] or corerc[ed]" black athletes into boycotting the event: that somehow these individuals could not decide for themselves that the club deserved such a protest. *Time* claimed that Edwards's efforts to that time had "drawn more scoffs than support from Negro athletes." Instead, he received endorsement from H. Rap Brown, chairman of the "militant Negro" group "ill-named" the Student Nonviolent Coordinating Committee. According to the article, Edwards threatened any black athlete who crossed the picket line of about 500 protestors. Though long jumper Bob Beamon and nine other black track and field athletes participated and quickly left, Jim Hines and John Thomas reportedly received threats (from Edwards or his allies if either participated). Specifically with regard to Hines, Edwards supposedly stated, "I hear he wants to play pro football. Some cats in Texas have personally said they'd fix it so he'd be on sticks if he's crazy enough to run in that meet." More than likely, instead of threats Edwards contemplated the plight of the African American athlete in that, "They are only being used to further the racist attitudes of the U.S.A."[103] Still the dismal showing at the New York Athletic Club's meet forced the IOC to rethink inviting South Africa to compete in Mexico City.

In June 1968, over 250 athletes converged at the Los Angeles Coliseum and competed in preparation for the Olympics. John P. Carmichael, sports editor for the *Chicago Daily News*, inaccurately categorized Jim Hines, Tommie Smith, Ronnie Ray Smith, Lee Evans, John Carlos, and others as militants that stifled American athletic hegemony with their pending boycott.[104] Carmichael was not unique—his view reflective of many white critics in majority presses that confused black power cultural expressions with armed militancy. Historian Jeffrey Ogbar noted the ways the Black Panther Party and cultural nationalism in the late 1960s influenced many black youths. Student-athletes wore black leather jackets, powder blue shirts, black pants, black shoes, and black berets. Some grew afros and kept their hair natural. The Reverend A. Sherwood Nelson, a white minister that lived in a predominate black community in Inglewood wrote to John Carmichael, "The very premise that the [Olympic] boycott rests on is self-identification, human reconstruction, cultural awareness and dignity...To have a rosy Olympics reveals but a frosting for the hypocrisy that is underneath."[105] In sum, these student-athletes and advocates for black athletic power were not proponents for black separation or propagandists for armed resistance. They embraced slogans "Black is Beautiful" and "I'm Black and I'm Proud," and at times tenets of black nationalism. On the other hand, they intimately believed in an American potential that welcomed and provided for all citizens. They attempted to redefine blackness in a society that ostracized them—a country they constructively criticized.[106]

According to Smith, the USOC held two sets of track Olympic trials: the meet in Los Angeles "to make sure the real trials...were not disrupted by a protest or a bunch of controversy," and the official competition in Lake Tahoe. The USOC reported that leaders of the OPHR sent letters threatening and harassing black Olympians to boycott the upcoming Games. In reality, the athletes received correspondence from the committee threatening them if they attempted the proposed protest with immediate dismissal from the Olympic team, or being sent home if any incident occurred while at the Games. Furthermore, perceived leaders like Smith received hate mail. "Nobody, competing or not, boycotting or not, could relate to how much hate mail and death threats those of us most deeply involved were receiving.... [W]e were never going to live to run in Mexico City; we had only 48 hours to live; and we were only niggers living in the white man's land." People called his home, where he, his wife and young son lived, and hung up; others shouted threats as they drove by, or knocked on the door or windows and disappeared. At times, Smith feared for his life.[107]

Still, no definitive boycott vote was confirmed. Shortly before the Olympics in September 1968, black athletes met in Denver for final preparations for the Games and discussed the prospects of a boycott. Boston, instead of Edwards who was not present, presided over the meeting. Many did not want to jeopardize professional contracts or the prospect of financial gain that participation in the Olympics should garner. In the end, they decided to do what each felt individually compelled to do in the fight against racial discrimination. For maximum impact, any personal demonstrations should take place during medal ceremonies. Alcindor, Warren, and other UCLA basketball players technically boycotted; they did not try out for the team and thus were spared any repercussions if an actual boycott or demonstration happened. [108]

Rafer Johnson, viewed as the nation's greatest decathlon star and broadcaster for the National Broadcasting Company (NBC), reminded black athletes that he made the team on ability and if an athlete possessed the ability to go then they should go. Johnson claimed that the Olympic Committee remained fair to the

Negro and that black athletes should not forget such a past. Charlie Greene, a six-time NCAA sprint champion, renewed his patriotic alliances with the US Track and Field Team. "It comes down to whether you're an American or if you're not. I'm an American and I'm going to run."[109]

Jessie Owens, the track legend at the 1936 Berlin Games, deplored the use of the Olympic Games by certain people for political aggrandizement as there was no place in the athletic world for politics. "The Olympics bridged gaps of misunderstandings for many people in this country," added Owens, and "individual reward elucidated the essence of freedom, the essence of American life."[110] Owens publicly purported that athletics helped bring racial understanding and top African American athletes commanded the respect of both whites and blacks. Jackie Robinson originally opposed the boycott. After much contemplation, Robinson posited that a boycott could be constructive if leadership motives were correct. "When a kid is willing to give up his right arm for a Gold Medal and also realizes that life offers more than material success, then it is important to admire that kid." Robinson foresaw the benefits of racial collaboration and believed that some whites would support a boycott similarly to the ones who voted for black mayors in Cleveland, Ohio, and Gary, Indiana. "The struggle for decency in America is no longer just the struggle for Negroes," said Robinson. Although Robinson's views did not entirely coincide with those of Harry Edwards, he was able to find beneficial aspects of black power as a protest mechanism.[111] Owens and Robinson's engagement with the boycott debate elucidates a central rhetorical question about tactics and philosophies. Both men contributed to the black athletic freedom struggle though Owens disagreed with black power protest in sports as opposed to Robinson.

Black Power, Mexico City, and the Aftermath

The Civil Rights and Black Power movements cannot simply be viewed as radical and conservative, integrationist and self-empowerment, violent and passive, as people embraced and opposed multiple frameworks in order to achieve racial, economic, social, and political equality.[112] Such ideological diversity on black power as expressed by black activist-leaders also was debated among black athletes. Sociologist Douglas Hartmann argues that Smith and John Carlos interjected blackness in an Olympic space not designed to recognize oppressed peoples. Accuracy aside, Hartmann does not see blackness as a fluid concept often debated internally by black athletes who seemingly embraced black power as a protest strategy. For black athletes, black power protest was often misunderstood.

Despite Brundage's vision of a nonpolitical Olympic movement, many blacks sought solutions to the problems that burdened their communities. In response to the American melting pot, which caused blacks to assimilate despite racist resistance into the mainstream culture, and blend into the white community on their terms, black power provided an avenue for self-worth. Student Nonviolent Coordinating Committee executive secretary Stokely Carmichael, who popularized the term "black power," believed that it was pertinent for blacks to organize themselves politically and find the power to affirm and control their own communities. Rather than accept the status quo on face value, political self-determination became a facet of black power. Second, Carmichael urged blacks to understand the importance of defining their own culture and to also separate from the demeaning definitions and limitations placed on them over centuries of conditioning by a racist culture. Thus, cultural and psychological self-determination became the second critical feature of black power. Black power stabilized the power to affirm black humanity, to defend black institutions and culture, and to politically organize and economically develop black communities. This ideology also reinforced pride, self-respect, and autonomy, of which it connected with a larger universal human struggle for self-determination. The black student-athletes at the 1968 Olympic Games channeled into this energy and expressed themselves in diverse ways.[113] Although black athletes recognized (figuratively, symbolically, or literally) the viability of black power for collective (racial, humankind) struggle, the praxis and manifestation of it lacked a unified purpose and was carried out individually by them.

Moderates such as the Urban League's Whitney Young and Martin Luther King originally took a cautious approach with regard to the tenets of black power, but by mid-1968, their views changed. After a 1967 march in Chicago, King argued that integration may not be the solution with whites who either fled to new areas or enacted hostile violence against them. Since the Negro, as King said, was in dire need of dignity and cannot seem to succeed in the mainstream, black power became relevant. Black people should never be ashamed of being black, King later espoused. By mid-1968 Whitney Young argued that black power doubly captured the imagination of blacks and above all conveyed pride and community solidarity for them. He embraced it as a positive, constructive concept. Young not only was cheered by the majority black audience, but also by whites such as James Linen, president of Time, Incorporated. Linen affirmed his advocacy for black power but not for black terrorist power. "I am not for Black Power for vengeance but Black Power for vindication.... Only Black political power, black economic power, black social power, and black educational power can ensure progress toward a truer democracy."[114] Linen's statement reflected a common belief shared not only by moderates such as Jackie Robinson but also by quasi-radicals like Tommie Smith and John Carlos who did not want to separate from the contours of American life. Hence, the major difference between the moderate and radical camp drew from the variations of cultural expression by the individuals in these camps in addition to the immediate urgency to enact social change.[115]

After winning the race, Tommie Smith remembered a dream by teammate Lee Evans. Evans said that several bullets hit Smith's chest causing him to collapse on a wooden surface, covered in blood. When Evans attempted to pick up Smith, he was shot in the back and head, the dream then was over. While in the locker room, Smith remembered that he did not want to embarrass himself or his country. "I do not want to dishonor the flag...Blacks fought and died for this country and we are a part of the American dream. The clenched fist will remind all that I ran for both the United States and for black people."[116] Smith wanted to do something significant because he knew of the hypocrisy that plagued sports and politics. Although the Olympics were intended to be a nonpolitical event, he grew tired of being a puppet. Smith would not allow Olympic official Avery Brundage, whom he viewed as "the biggest racist in the world,"[117] to call him a boy during the obligatory congratulations, and decided that the medal ceremony would be his opportunity to stand up.

"What should I do?" Tommie Smith contemplated what should be done after winning the 200-meter dash at the 1968 Mexico City Olympic Games. Smith recalled the tense moments of waiting in the locker room located in the bowels of the *Estadio Olímpico*. Smith remembered a letter from his then wife Denise. "Dearest Tommie, I got your letter today and it was all the inspiration I needed to keep me going a few more days. I've told you this before, but I have all the confidence in the world in you and that I love you." Denise Smith informed her husband of the fear she felt for his life. "Tommie, the British newspaper said you would be shot. Oh, Tommie, I just read it and I want you to come home! Don't listen to anyone, John [Carlos], Lee [Evans], the newspapers, nobody. Don't be brave, be alive."[118] Needless to say, Tommie Smith's eventual protest was not a set-in-stone phenomenon that was finalized months or days before the race. Smith was torn but knew that he had to do something. Before he left for Mexico, his wife had bought him a pair of black gloves and Smith wondered what it would mean to wear them.

Smith grew tired of being viewed as a passive black athlete and decided to do something significant. So, he reached into his track bag, grabbed his black scarf, and tied it around his neck. Next, he took off his Puma warm-up shoes and rolled up his sweatpants so that his black socks showed. He followed this procedure by putting a black glove on his right hand and told Carlos, "Here, you can have this glove. I'm only going to wear one." After Carlos put the glove on his left hand, Smith said, "You can watch me, and do what I do." Carlos instantly removed his shoes and rolled up his socks. Peter Norman, the Australian sprinter who placed second asked, "Is there anything I can do, I really sympathize with you guys…If there's anything at all."[119] Smith then gave Norman an Olympics Human Rights Project (OHRP) "Freedom-Power-Equality" button that he had worn during the Olympics. Norman would further support the black medalists by wearing black socks.[120]

Once Lord Burghley of the International Olympic Committee gave all three contestants their medals, and the "Star Spangled Banner" played, Smith lowered his head and raised his right arm and Carlos did the same with the opposite one. For Smith, "that was total freedom."[121] After the medals were given out, the raised fists of Smith and Carlos simultaneously made them instant villains to some, icons to others, and forever engrained in the memory of the nineteenth Olympiad. Smith recounted, "The black glove on my fist was for them and for black people everywhere who had no power. It stood for freedom. The black scarf around my neck symbolized black pride and the black socks with no shoes stood for black poverty and neglect in racist America." He continued, "The American flag represented the black man who had worked so damned hard all his life and gotten nothing out of it but racism and oppression. The Stars and Stripes represented all the black people who had shed their blood for this country and never received equality. It represented all the blacks who were thrown onto ships and sold into a life of slavery in the United States." Therefore, on that "day in Mexico City, the flag represented a white racist America. I hoped my demonstration would represent black America. These thoughts flashed through my mind as the song played and then I began to silently pray. I knew when the Anthem was finished because that's when the booing began."[122]

Smith negated the idea of a black power salute, though the gesture and historical moment might beg to differ. "This was not the Black Power movement. To this very day, the gesture made is described as a Black Power salute; it was not.... It was more than civil rights; that's why it was called human rights."[123] Edwards characterized the movement as one that forced athletes to think about more than their particular sport and to place the struggle of African Americans, in particular, in a larger context. He did not divorce it from the larger struggle for black liberation. He stressed that "the black revolution in America has not been carried into the locker room... What has happened is that the black athlete has left the façade of locker room equality and justice to take his... place as a primary participant in the black revolution.[124]

Harry Edwards did not go to Mexico City. He had received several death threats and did not want to be a distraction to the event. Since each competitor had to decide what action, if any, to take, he did not coach Smith and Carlos in their gloved protest. After their medal ceremony display, Lee Evans, who set world records in the individual 400 meters and as the anchor of the relay team, along with Larry James and Ron Freeman, wore black tams during their medal ceremony (though many thought Evans should have done more); Bob Beamon, after shattering the long jump record, rolled up his pant legs to show his black socks and stood shoeless as he received his gold medal; and Ralph Boston who placed third also displayed support for the gloved salute on the medal stand by also removing his shoes to reveal black socks. US Olympic officials wanted to revoke the medals awarded to Smith and Carlos, but neither gave them back. They immediately moved out of the Olympic Village, and the US delegation suspended them, soon took their visas, and informed them that they had to leave Mexico within forty-eight hours. White administrators also co-opted and misinterpreted black athletic power. USOC president Douglas Roby said, "The Committee does not believe that the immature behavior of two athletes of the U.S.O.C. warrants any formal action because it was an isolated incident."[125] His views were closely aligned to IOC president Avery Brundage who had asserted prior to the opening of the Games that not only were there enough white athletes to replace Negroes after their boycott, but that these misguided young men also deprived themselves of a once in a lifetime opportunity for Olympic glory. For many black athletes, Brundage became the prototypical, old, racist white man. Black athletes were so perturbed that twenty-one athletes signed a petition for the removal of the IOC president.[126] Even Stan Wright, the often criticized black American coach, questioned Brundage. Wright, a man viewed as too passive by some black athletes, stressed that if Brundage was against nonviolent protests such as the wearing of arm bands, then people should question his sympathies and understandings. Brundage replied that his comments on dismissal were distorted—the fundamental basis of the Olympic movement was no discrimination of any kind regardless of racial, religious, or political affiliations.[127]

One particular majority white group, the Harvard Heavyweight Eight turned US Olympic crew team at 1968 Mexico City Games, supported that black athletic revolt. Their support for the protest grew as they endured pressure from American Olympic authorities. At the 1967 Pan-American Games, the USOC made two things clear: politics and sport do not mix (at least athletes should not be political), and American athletes must defeat the Cuban communists. This did not sit well with the well-to-do crewmen. Ironically, the USOC inspired the Harvard team to support Edwards and the OPHR. Soon after the Olympic trials, Edwards was scheduled to visit Boston. The team was emotionally exhausted and debated their stance. Six of the eight men agreed not to boycott the Games but to support the black athletic revolt.[128] To their surprise, head coach Harry Parker gave them his blessing. Captain Curt Canning prepared a statement for the press. Their goals were threefold: to inform all Olympians about the black freedom struggle, stimulate discussion, and identify methods to support black athletic revolt at the 1968 Olympic Games. The media chose to portray white athletes that supported black agency, freedom, and potential as counterculture dropouts. *Newsweek Magazine* identified the team as "the grubby crew," "the shaggies," and "the hippies." In actually, as coxswain Paul Hoffman asserted, the team was not radical but merely Yankees that understood the language of white civil rights workers and what was right. After the silent protest, USOC officials speculated a conspiracy. They questioned Hoffman, sent him to a hospitality room, but eventually cleared him for competition.[129]

Following the silent protest, white students theoretically and historically had much ammunition against their fellow peers. In actuality, San Jose State College was divided. From October 20 to November 3, 1968, President Clark received twenty-four letters in favor of the silent protest and ninety-two against it.[130] Indeed it was Clark that provided the statement that sparked SJS engagement with the black-fisted salute. Clark regretted that "our [American] treatment of our black athletes has been such to prompt them to feel they must use the Olympic Games to communicate their real concern for the conditions of blacks in America."[131] Clark hoped the "silent protest would be interpreted properly and that Smith and Carlos do not return home in disgrace but as honorable young men."[132] Clark often responded to his critics. In a letter to A. Ray Freeman he asserted, "while I personally cannot agree with some of the tactics utilized by Mr. Edwards and feel that the press coverage has frequently been misleading if not downright inaccurate, I am strongly sympathic [sic] to this cause—justice for the Black in America."[133] Not all SJS students agreed with Clark. Student body president Dick Miner believed they "caused irreparable damage to the cause of inter-racial understanding and indeed human dignity by virtue of a hasty, emotional and surely ill-advised action which can only reflect discredit on them and our country."[134] *Spartan Daily* staff member Tim Garcia believed the silent protest ruined the spirit of Olympic goodwill.[135]

Garcia was not alone. A staff editorial depicted Smith and Carlos as "propagandists at the moment of their greatest triumph."[136] Harrison F. Heath, professor of psychology, clarified that the series of sounds emitted was not random rather, "it was Tommie's flag being raised and his anthem played... if he does not recognize that then something is wrong with Tommie Smith."[137]

In the aftermath of the Olympic demonstration, many whites characterized Harry Edwards as a professor that taught "racist bad poison" to his students. The white Texas Western athletic director George McCarty, who led the department that was highlighted by the victory of five black basketball players over the all-white University of Kentucky in 1966, said that "he did more for his niggers than Harry Edwards."[138] The derogatory comments did not stop. Robert Allen, a white spectator, threatened, "your two Negro students can brag about Black Power all they want, but a few more acts like they put on at the expense of U.S.A & they might find out also that their such a thing as *Real White Power* left here in America."[139] Dr. Sammy Lee asked Harry Edwards to "Show me another country which has as many colored Olympic champions as our country does."[140]

Indeed sport and society were interchangeable to black athletes—a link often criticized by the white masses. Much of the proof was found in newspapers and personal letters written by white journalists, spectators, administrators and politicians, and Edwards was a prime target. An anonymous letter from Riverside, California, sent prior to the gloved salute asked SJS president and silent protest supporter Robert Clark, "Sir, why don't you commit this thing to some zoo before it infects the minds of more young people than it already has?"[141] An unknown writer from St. Charles, Illinois, questioned, "You must have a shortage of teachers to employ a person like Harry Edwards. Why don't you ship the baboon back to Africa?"[142] At least Alejandro Medina gave his name. He asked Clark, "Why don't you trim this nigger Edwards, down to his proper [*sic*] size, so he can be a respectable Negro?"[143] To whites Harry Edwards was unfit for academia. They looked at a man and saw, god forbid, "a beard, beads, cap and glasses"[144]— all characteristics of an unworthy professor. Perhaps the best part of that anonymous letter from Portage, Indiana, was the mythical colorblind ending. The writer said, "This is the first letter of this type I have ever written, so you know how some people—and I'm not a racist either, think."[145]

Edwards was not the only victim of racist hate mail. Tommie Smith and John Carlos, whose careers and personal lives faltered after they raised their fists in the air, also bore the brunt and were classified by, arguably, one of whites' favorite racial adjective. To Ralph Brubaker of Los Angeles, Tommie Smith once again became "Nigger Smith," an "irresponsible black ape."[146] An anonymous postcard asked them, "If you Smith & Carlos don't like the U.S.A. why don't you go to Russia? They love you NIGGE [*sic*] LOVERS there. AFRICA WOULD LOVE YOU MORE???"[147] Harry Jackson connected the silent protest with a failed educational system. It "proved that a free college education does not do much to civilized people out of apes such as Smith and Carlos."[148] To many whites he was right.

When Smith and Carlos returned home and told a predominately white crowd of 1,500 students that "We'd Do It Again Tomorrow," many supported them. Certainly all white Americans were not opposed to the silent protest but many were.[149] Students widely expressed their support in the *Spartan Daily*, criticized the editorial staff, and called the student body president Miner a racist.[150] Faculty such as Dr. Al Rutherford, president of the local American Federation of Teachers, and Dr. Hobert Burns, SJS academic vice president, praised the silent protesters.[151] Clark even received his share of support. Lewis E. Ward, professor of mathematics at the University of Oregon, and M. J. Lunine, dean of the Honors College at Kent State University, expressed their support for Clark, Smith, and Carlos.[152] In the 1960s, black agency toward grasping an American identity and citizenship was real and reverberated in ways that transcended race. The impact and dedication of black athletes involved in their revolt empowered some of their white peers to support the broader freedom struggle.

The 1968 Summer Games were troublesome for the International Olympic Committee, and not solely because of Smith and Carlos. Rather, the potential for a politicized games fueled by the black freedom struggle loomed as a constant gadfly for leaders such as Avery Brundage. Similar to the global anti-apartheid movement, the Civil Rights Movement involved many unique individuals in one way or another. Black collegiate and high school students across the United States dynamically engaged in this movement and fought to reshape the framework of their particular milieus through vigorous grassroots activism. Black power provided unique opportunities for expression and self-determination during the late 1960s. Plagued by poor wages and unemployment, segregation and unequal opportunities to social mobility, many blacks not only engaged the Civil Rights Movement, but they also lived it and sought to eradicate these injustices. Black student-athletes were intimately connected to a larger, national energy of which they did not separate sports from a politicized daily life. The actions of Tommie Smith and John Carlos thus symbolize a movement that was larger than they, and begun before their participation. Similarly to the actions of Rosa Parks, Smith and Carlos provided an iconic moment that elucidated ongoing problems faced by blacks.

Although many black student-athletes were involved in the Civil Rights Movement, they were not a monolithic, united group in their struggle for equal rights. Divisional factions were as common as segregated public spaces as black people struggled for diverse interpretations of civil rights. Additionally, the 1968 Olympic Games, like the larger Civil Rights Movement, was not simply a white against black issue, as various races collaborated, opposed one another, and often vouched for mutual understanding during this conflicted time. On the other hand, the IOC abided by a utopian vision of sport free of politics and full of humanity thus, any such uprisings were deemed intolerable. The patriotic sympathy for soldiers fighting in Vietnam also shaped the critical framework by many Americans who viewed black power protest as insensitive to the nature of the Olympic Games. Finally, black athletes were problematically constructed as natural athletes and due to individual yet overly seen as racialized gains in sport, black student-athletes should not complain of any injustices. Black power at the 1968 Olympics and its subsequent protests were not separatist or even militant acts of rebellion but rather were pleas for equal rights. [153] Black athletes did not separate sports from their ideological values or political realities that shaped their lives. Nevertheless, expressive self-determination at the games countered status quo decorum of nonpolitical action thus providing for conflicting rivalries between distinct peoples and interest groups.[154]

Legacy of Black Athletic Protest

Basketball player Christopher Wayne Jackson became Mahmoud Abdul-Rauf after converting to Islam (1991) and changing his name (1993). Drafted by the Denver Nuggets in 1990, the point guard emerged as a team asset and league leader in percentage free throws. In a flashback to the previous era, during the 1995–1996 National Basketball Association's regular season, Abdul-Rauf refused to stand for the playing of the national anthem. For more than sixty games, he sat during the anthem without incident. Then, Nuggets fans started inquiring as to why he did not conform and a maelstrom ensued. Abdul-Rauf objected to standing for the anthem because it conflicted with his religious beliefs and he felt that the flag and accompanying anthem represented oppression and tyranny. Many fans and sportswriters labeled him unpatriotic and suggested that if he did not want to honor the flag—and in their eyes the country—then he should leave. Moreover, anyone making his salary ($2.6 million that year) should be grateful for the opportunity afforded. Alex English, representing the NBA's Players' Association, supported the player's right to opt out of the anthem. "We support Mahmoud Abdul-Rauf and we support the American flag, which symbolizes Mahmoud's right to precisely [take] the action he is taking."[155] However, the NBA suspended him under a rule that obligated coaches and players to stand "in a dignified posture" in acknowledgment of the national anthem. He compromised by agreeing to stand at the appropriate time, but recite prayers rather than recognize the patriotic symbolism.[156]

On June 15, 2004, Rasheed Wallace won his only NBA championship when the Detroit Pistons defeated the Los Angeles Lakers in five games. For Wallace, occasionally referred to as "Sheed," the title was only a fraction of his professional legacy. The four-time all star, drafted fourth by the Washington Bullets in 1995, was 6 feet 11inches tall and could run the fast break, defend post players, and knock down the outside jump shot. He also was passionately outspoken and infamously earned the title NBA all-time technical fouls leader. After a loss by his then Portland Trailblazers, he responded at the postgame press conference that "Both teams played hard…both teams played hard my man…God bless and goodnight." The interview became an Internet sensation on YouTube and is still found on numerous ESPN sport highlight reels. However, fans and critics did not adore all of his commentary. In 2003, Wallace condemned NBA commissioner David Stern and the league for treating black players like slaves on a plantation. He claimed, "They don't know no better, and they don't know the real business, and they don't see behind the charade. They look at black athletes like we're s——. It's as if we're just going to shut up, sign for the money and do what they tell us."[157]

Similar to reactions from the 1960s and before, reactions by white commissioners, writers, and the general public were not sympathetic. Why? For many whites, an African American athlete cannot be rich and also perceive the world as racist. To them, Wallace became the prototypical oxymoron. Indeed, Wallace, like fellow Tarheel and NBA star Vince Carter, majored in African and Afro-American studies at the University of North Carolina—a discipline rooted in the 1960s black freedom struggle that espoused academic excellence, cultural grounding, and social responsibility. Wallace had this educational grounding well before he became a millionaire. Despite the fame of numerous black athletes, sportswriter William Rhoden argues, they still are on the periphery of true power in multi-billion dollar American sports industry.[158] The implicit argument was the same that Edwards and others had espoused. Racism remains dynamic and its institutional component became the standard form of racial injustice.

Commenting on Tiger Woods's progress at the 1997 Masters golf tournament, Fuzzy Zoeller derided, "That little *boy* is driving well and he's putting well. He's doing everything it takes to win. So, you know what you guys do when he gets in here? You pat him on the back and say congratulations and enjoy it and tell him not to serve fried chicken next year. Got it?" Then Zoeller smiled, snapped his fingers, walked away, turned and added, "Or collard greens or whatever the hell they serve."[159] Furthermore in 2008, Golf Channel anchor Kelly Tilghman joked with former golf champion Nick Faldo that young players should, "lynch him in the back alley."[160] Both instances received public criticism, but then were quickly pushed aside and forgotten. In the twenty-first century it is not politically correct to be overtly racist—when applicable keep it behind closed doors. Even if Wallace made mistakes, and he certainly did, the former NBA star was conscious of the gravity of institutional racism and journalist William Rhoden situated that argument in a broader historical context. One need not be spat upon, verbally abused, or lynched to understand or experience racism. While much of the overtly physical racial abuse has subsided, institutional racism continues to exist.

Enter LeBron James. For nearly a year, sportswriters, administrators, fans, and fellow athletes anticipated the 2010 NBA free agency period highlighted by megastars LeBron James, Dwayne Wade, Chris Bosh, Amar'e Stoudemire, and Dirk Nowitzki. Nearly ten million people watched his televised hour-long decision. When the Akron, Ohio, native left his Cleveland Cavaliers (Cavs) for South Beach and the Miami Heat, chaos ensued. Cleveland fans cried, shouted at television screens, and burned jerseys. They anticipated removal of anything connected to James as "the Witness" or "King": with signs removed from Quicken Loans Arena days later. Some journalists charged conspiracy and said Wade, Bosh, and James colluded during and after Team USA won gold in men's basketball at the 2008 Beijing Olympics.[161] The Cavaliers owner Dan Gilbert incited anti-James propaganda. His once beloved king and savior of Cleveland basketball became a "coward narcissist" that turned his back on his hometown. Gilbert used the team's official website to make the disparaging remarks against his once franchise player and his decision to leave. Commissioner Stern then fined him

$100,000 for lewd conduct as a team owner. Many fans, however, agreed with Gilbert and some sold lemonade in opposition to the commissioner when he fined the owner. One local brewery sold a new beer, described as leaving a bitter taste, called "quitness." White and black Cavs fans made a parody film of the Nike LeBron James video, "What Should I Do?" Gilbert certainly had his critics. Some sportswriters pondered the irony in Gilbert who wanted James a day prior but crucified him when he chose Miami. Without hesitation, James rebuilt the Cleveland Cavaliers into a national and internationally acclaimed franchise. The Reverend Jesse Jackson claimed "His [Gilbert's] feelings of betrayal personify a slave master mentality. He sees LeBron as a runaway slave. This is an owner employee relationship—between business partners—and LeBron honored his contract."[162]

The public was outraged. How could Jackson insert race in what was popularly perceived by many in the mainstream as a seemingly nonracial situation? There he goes playing the "race card" again, many spectators and journalists lamented. Commissioner David Stern, a good friend of the civil rights activist, carefully crafted his response and politely disagreed with him. Many found fault in Jackson and to them, with the public's ever present avoidance of racial matters, he was the racist. Colorblind proponents made Jackson the bigot and Gilbert the sympathetic owner, racially criticized because of his condemnation of a former employee that *happened to be* black. On the ESPN television show *Outside the Lines*, two of the three panelists, Dennis Manoloff and Chris Sheridan, agreed that Jackson was out of line. However the third guest Bomani Jones differed. First, the general public extrapolated meaning from Jackson's words and interpreted his message as a criticism of Gilbert as a racist. In actuality, Jackson referred to a "slave master mentality" in which Gilbert's letter assumed ownership of a "less than human piece of property that he lost"[163] to free agency. Second, Gilbert, Jones argued, incited public rage by posting his letter on the front page of the Cavaliers's website. A ploy that cemented the owner's message as the voice of the franchise and instantly put the safety of James at risk—police units patrolled James's house. Manoloff asked, "If LeBron James were white would Jackson make the same comment?" Jones replied, "A better question is if the slavery statement were semantically clumsy then why are we discussing it and not the rest of Jackson's statement...much of which was accurate."[164] To Jones, the bigger issues were twofold: assumptions from fans and ownership that players owe them loyalty, and Gilbert's letter as the instigator of public rage and the voice of the Cavs's website—a member of the broader NBA family.

Cultural change is dynamic and racism remains an integral aspect of American culture. First, institutional racism, white privilege, and colorblind ideas shape American realities and possibilities of what discrimination is, who experiences it, and when they face it. This is merely a shift in a legacy of American racism and cooption that extended from the Colonial and Early Republic eras. Second, racism and specifically attempts by white spectators, fans, writers, administrators, and politics to define black freedom and agency remain a subplot in the legacy of American racism. Manoloff assumes common race histories and goals from slavery to freedom and believes a racially reverse argument clarifies a complex freedom struggle, past to the present. Indeed this is a benefit of white privilege. More importantly, for black athletes, the LeBron James "Decision" symbolically represented two shifts. First, the spectacle that surrounded his hour-long special and his ultimate decision reinforced the empowerment and influence that black athletes indeed have in American and global cultures. Second, his commentary on financial support to Boys and Girls Clubs reinforced the potential of economic, social, and political black nationalism. To build on Malcolm X, the LeBron James decision signaled the impact black athletes could have on spearheading efforts related to social and economic development in black communities. Historically, numerous African Americans struggled for socioeconomic empowerment in black communities. In some ways, the "Decision" reinforced the importance of individual and collective agency and uplift as a primary concern for black athletes with white attempts at appropriation of black rights only contextually relevant in understanding the dynamism of American racism and ways to counter it.[165] The freedom struggle continues and African American athletes should recognize the ongoing battle and how best to combat it whether through collective action or individually, despite monetary gain and fame. In the meantime as "Sheed" advised, "Just play hard my man…God bless and goodnight."

Notes

1. Avery Brundage Papers, University of Illinois (Box 335, Films in Oversize File, XIX Olympic Games, Mexico City, 1968).
2. Tommie Smith, as told to Bruce Henderson, "Why I Raised My Fist at Uncle Sam," *Sepia*, July 1973, 28. Also, ratings were compiled from Amy Bass in *Not the Triumph but the Struggle: The 1968 Olympics and the Making of the Black Athlete* (Minneapolis: University of Minnesota Press, 2002), 235.
3. Smith and Henderson, 28.
4. Ibid., 29.
5. Brundage Papers.
6. David Miller, *The Official History of the Olympic Games and the IOC, 1894–2004* (Edinburgh: Mainstream Publishing, 2003).
7. Samuel L. Jackson remarks, ESPY Awards, July 16, 2008.
8. Brent Musburger, "Bizarre Protest by Smith, Carlos Tarnishes Medals," *Chicago Daily News*. For more see C. D. Jackson and John Carlos, *Why? The Biography of John Carlos* (Los Angeles: Milligan Books, 2000); David Steele and Tommie Smith, *Silent Gesture: The Autobiography of Tommie Smith* (Philadelphia: Temple University Press, 2007); Frank Murphy, *The Last Protest: Lee Evans in Mexico City* (Kansas City: Windsprint Press, 2006); Harry Edwards, *The Revolt of the Black Athlete* (New York: The Free Press, 1970); Kevin B. Witherspoon, *Before the Eyes of the World: Mexico and the 1968 Olympic Games* (DeKalb, IL: Northern Illinois Press, 2008); Douglas Hartmann, *Race, Culture, and the Revolt of the Black Athlete: The 1968 Olympic Protests and Their Aftermath* (Chicago: University of Chicago Press, 2004); and Bass.

9. See Michael Lomax, "Bedazzle Them with Brilliance, Bamboozle Them with Bull: Harry Edwards, Black Power, and the Revolt of the Black Athlete Revisited," in *Sports and the Racial Divide: African American and Latino Experience in an Era of Change*, ed. Michael Lomax (Jackson: University of Mississippi Press, 2008); Ron Briley, "The Black Panther Party and the Revolt of the Black Athlete: Sport and Revolutionary Consciousness," in Lomax, *Sports and the Racial Divide*; Kurt Edward Kemper, "Dark Spirits: The Emergence of Cultural Nationalism on the Sidelines and on Campus," in Lomax, *Sports and the Racial Divide*; Patrick Miller, *The Sporting World of the Modern South* (Urbana, IL: University of Illinois Press, 2002); and John Bloom and Michael Nevin Willard, *Sports Matters: Race, Recreation, and Culture* (New York: New York University Press, 2002).

10. David Wiggins, *Glory Bound: Black Athletes in a White America* (Syracuse, NY: Syracuse University Press, 1997). See also W. E. B. Du Bois, *The Souls of Black Folk* (Chicago: A.C. McClurg & Company, 1903; New York: Bantam Books, 1989).

11. Howard Zinn, *A People's History of the United States* (New York: Harper & Row, 1980).

12. Hasan Kwame Jeffries, *Bloody Lowndes: Civil Rights and Black Power in Alabama's Black Belt* (New York: New York University Press, 2009).

13. See Wiggins.

14. Ibid., 200–20.

15. Ibid., 177–99.

16. See Elliott J. Gorn and Warren Goldstein, *A Brief History of American Sport* (Chicago: University of Illinois Press, 2004).

17. Bear baiting was the act of pitting a bear against dogs or a bull. Gander pulling was the act of greasing the head of a goose, tying its legs to a tree, only for an individual to ride a horse toward it and attempt to rip off its head.

18. A useful film that in some ways tackles race, slavery, and blood games was the 1973 film *Mandingo*.

19. Gorn and Goldstein, 103.

20. South Africa won medals at the 1908 London Summer Games, but their victory was racially tainted because of apartheid.

21. For more see David Miller, *The Official History of the Olympic Games and the IOC, 1894–2004* (Edinburgh: Mainstream Publishing, 2003); and Kristine Toohey and A. J. Veal, *The Olympic Games: A Social Science Perspective* (Oxfordshire: CABI Publishing, 2000).

22. "Brundage Defends Ideals of Olympics," *Santa Barbara News-Press*, Monday Evening, October 7, 1968.

23. The Stockholm Games also featured Jim Thorpe and George Patton.

24. Allen Guttmann, *The Games Must Go On: Avery Brundage and the Olympic Movement* (New York: Columbia University Press, 1984); Richard Espy, *The Politics of the Olympic Games* (Berkeley, CA: University of California Press, 1979).

25. Wiggins, 21–34; and Martin Kane, "An Assessment of Black is Best," *Sports Illustrated* (January 18, 1971): 72–83.

26. Wiggins, 221–40.

27. Ibid, 177–99.

28. Cordner Nelson, "Track Talk," *Track and Field News* (May 1953); "Sport: Cromwell's Crop," *Time Magazine* (June 13, 1938); and "Dean Cromwell," United States Track and

Field Hall of Fame, http://www.usatf.org/HallOfFame/TF/showBio.asp?HOFIDs=36, accessed December 8, 2009.

29. Wiggins,180. See also, Dean B. Cromwell and Al Wesson, *Championship Techniques in Track and Field* (New York: Whittlesey House, 1941), 6.

30. For more on Owens see Randy Roberts and James Olsen, *Winning is the Only Thing: Sports in America since 1945* (Baltimore: Johns Hopkins Press, 1989); William J. Baker, *Jesse Owens: An American Life* (New York: Free Press, 1986); and Jeremy Schaap, *Triumph: The Untold Story of Jesse Owens and Hitler's Olympics* (Boston: Houghton Mifflin, 2007).

31. Harry Edwards, "Why Negroes Should Boycott Whitey's Olympics," *Saturday Evening Post*, 10. Ebscohost

32. For information on Jackie Robinson, see Jackie Robinson and Alfred Duckett, I Never Had It Made: The Autobiography of Jackie Robinson (New York: Putnam, 1972; New York: HarperCollins, 1995).

33. "The Negro Becomes a Champion...Why are Negroes Frequently the Winners?' " *Physical Culture in School* 11, no. 47 (1966): np, in *Yessis Review of Soviet Physical Education and Sports* 3, no. 2 (1968): 47.

34. Harry Edwards, "Why Negroes Should Boycott," 6.

35. Aldore Collier, "Doctor of Sports and Psychology," *Ebony*, October 1987, 102; and "The Black Boycott," *Time*, February 23, 1968, 75, Academic Search Premier.

36. Collier, 102.

37. Ibid, 106.

38. See Melvin Durslag, "New Area of Rebellion—No Easy Answers—A U.S. Problem The San Jose Threat," *Los Angeles Herald Examiner*, September 29, 1967; Melvin Durslag, "Grid Cancellation Saved Blood Bath," *Seattle Post Intelligencer*, September (nd) 1967. Harry Edwards in *The Revolt of the Black Athlete* puts the number of black students at seventy-two (50).

39. For more see Hasan Kwame Jeffries.

40. Joyce Augustin, "Campuswide Discrimination Issue Born Over Cafeteria Lunch Talk," *Spartan Daily*, September 28, 1967.

41. Robert Lipsyte, "Sports of the Times, Striking Nerves," *The New York Times* December 16, 1967.

42. Ibid.

43. Dick Egner, "Militant Anti-Prejudice Move Threatens SJS Sports Program," *San Jose Mercury News*, September 15, 1967.

44. William Chapin, "Angry Negroes at San Jose State," *San Francisco Chronicle*, September 19, 1967.

45. Ibid.

46. Durslag, "New Area of Rebellion," np.

47. Joyce Augustin, "Lunch Talk," *Spartan Daily*, September 28, 1967.

48. Photo and caption, *Spartan Daily*, September 22, 1967.

49. Chapin, np.

50. Ibid.

51. See *Palo Alto Times*, September 19, 1967; *East San Jose Sun*, September 20, 1967; and "Lee Promises Protestors Immediate Investigation," *Spartan Daily*, September 20, 1967.

52. For more see Joe Palermo, "Black Power on Campus: The Beginnings," *San Jose Studies* 14 (1988): 31–48; David Gray, "A Prelude to the Protest at the 1968 Mexico City Olympics," (master's thesis, San Jose State University, 1997); and Lomax.

53. "Lee Promises Investigation," np.

54. Don Cox, "ASB Council Supports Negroes as Discrimination Tension Grows," *Spartan Daily*, September 22, 1967.

55. John Wallak, "Faculty Group Passes Discrimination Policy," *Spartan Daily*, September 20, 1967.

56. "AFT Blasts College Racial Discrimination," *Spartan Daily*, September 20, 1967.

57. Francine Miller, "President Clark Creates New Post in Effort to Alleviate Racial Tension," *Spartan Daily*, September 22, 1967.

58. "Clark Request: Book Store Display Airs Black Feelings," *Spartan Daily*, September 26, 1967. Books displayed included *Discrimination* by Wallace Menderson, *Crisis in Black and White* by Charles E. Silberman, *The Negro Mood* by Lerone Bennett, and *The Negro Challenge to the Business Community* edited by Eli Ginzberg.

59. Edwards, *Revolt of the Black Athlete*, 47.

60. Ibid., 40–42.

61. Numerous notable figures in the 1960s freedom struggle visited SJS when Smith was a student. The list included Bill Cosby, Dick Gregory, James Farmer, Saul Alinsky, Ivanhoe Donaldson, Don Warden, Anne Braden, and numerous others. Since the OPHR connected activists in the Bay Area, Smith also might have learned from students, activists, and leaders from regional schools and perhaps the local Black Panther Party chapters.

62. Edwards, *Revolt of the Black Athlete*, 77.

63. *La Torre*, 1963–1964 (San Jose State yearbook).

64. In his autobiography, *Silent Gesture*, Smith describes the ways in which black athletes were not regarded as intellectually gifted students by peers and instructors. In addition, the lack of black professionals and nonathletes in the academy during the 1960s signaled a hindrance to feature or train blacks for success outside of the realm of sports. Harry Edwards draws the same conclusion in much of his writing; see *Revolt of the Black Athlete*.

65. Paul Savoia, "Three Best-in-Nation Marks: Smith Dominates the Sprints," *Spartan Daily*, April (nd) 1966.

66. "Winter Lays Plans to Make Smith Best," *Spartan Daily*, April (nd) 1966.

67. Ibid.

68. Ibid.

69. Ryun was the first high school runner to break the four-minute mile and won the silver medal in the 1500 at the 1968 Olympic Games. He also set the world record in that event and the mile.

70. "The Round Up," *The Amateur Athlete* 38, no. 3 (March 1967): 27; Ryun earned 86 votes and Smith came in second with 69 votes.

71. Jeff Stockton, "Decision Due—Football or Track for Sought-After Spartan Sprinter," *Spartan Daily*, June 1, 1966. For more on Tommie Smith's track and field career at SJS see, "SJS Trackmen Travel to L.A. for Invitational," *Spartan Daily*, February (nd) 1966; "Tom Smith Wins Three Events to Lead Trackmen in Open Meet," *Spartan Daily*, February 21, 1966; "Trackmen Run Today," *Spartan Daily*, February 18, 1966; Lee Juillerat, "Tracksters Run at Stanford Tomorrow," *Spartan Daily*, March 4, 1966; Paul Savoia, "Smith Aims for 220 Mark," *Spartan Daily*, March 11, 1966; Paul Savoia, "Trackmen Try for 9 in a Row over Cal," *Spartan Daily*, March 18, 1966; Paul Savoia, "Spartan Trackmen Rip Cal; Smith Takes Three Firsts," *Spartan Daily*, March 21, 1966; Paul Savoia, "Oregon Nips Spartans in Triangular; Tommy Smith Clocks a 9.2 Century," *Spartan Daily*, April 18, 1966; Paul Savoia, "The Old Professor," *Spartan*

Daily, April 22, 1968; "One More Time—Smith Top Athlete," *Spartan Daily,* April/May (nd) 1966; Lee Juillerat, "Smith Runs Record 19.5 in Mercurial 220 Sprint," *Spartan Daily,* April/May (nd) 1966; Lee Juillerat, "Smith's Performance: 'Greatest Effort Ever," *Spartan Daily,* April/May (nd) 1966; "Smith Runs for Hometown Followers in Three Fresno Relays Tomorrow," *Spartan Daily,* May (nd) 1966; At Golden Gate Invitational, Undefeated Relay Team Goes for Fifth Win," *Spartan Daily,* February 17, 1967; Jim Street, "Smith, Relay Team Set World Records," *Spartan Daily,* February 20, 1967; "Track Is Back," *The Amateur Athlete* 38, no. 2 (February 1967): 30; "Kip's Korner," *The Amateur Athlete* 38, no. 2 (February 1967): (np) ; Bill Kipouras, "Big R Busts Loose in Big D," *The Amateur Athlete* 38, no. 3 (March 1967): 4–6; "Ryun, Clarke Dominate Men's All Comer Records," *The Amateur Athlete* 38, no. 3 (March 1967): 15; "Tommie Smith, Ron Clarke Dominate World Records Officially OK'd by IAAF," *The Amateur Athlete* 38, no. 3 (March 1967): 38; Jack Stevenson, "Record Assault At Oakland," *The Amateur Athlete* 38, no. 4 (April 1967): 4–6; Hank Ives, "World Class Athletes L.A.-Bound," *The Amateur Athlete* 38, no. 6 (June 1967): 6–7; Shavenau Glick, "U.S. Rules British Again," *The Amateur Athlete* 38, no. 8 (August 1967): 4–5; "Southern Cal Reaps Provo Harvest," *The Amateur Athlete* 38, no. 7 (July 1967): 15; NCAA Track and Field Performances, Track and Field Outdoor File, July 6, 1966,Walter S. Byers Collection, NCAA Library, Indianapolis, Indiana; and Track and Field 6/66–9/67, Walter S. Byers Collection, NCAA Library, Indianapolis, Indiana.

72. Edwards, *Revolt of the Black Athlete,* 41
73. For information on John Carlos and Lee Evans see John Carlos and Dave Zirin, *The John Carlos Story: The Sports Moment that Changed the World* (Chicago: Haymarket Books, 2011) ; and Murphy.
74. Edward, *Revolt of the Black Athlete,* 41.
75. Tommie Smith with David Steele, *Silent Gesture: The Autobiography of Tommie Smith* (Philadelphia: Temple University Press, 2007), 160.
76. Ralph Brubaker to Tommie Smith, September 27, 1967, Los Angeles, CA.
77. Willie Williams to Tommie Smith, September 29, 1967, San Francisco, CA, UCLA Record Series 277, Administrative Files of Robert Fischer 1945–1983, Box 41, Folder NCAA 1975. See also An Ex-Veteran to Robert Clark, October 23, 1968, Robert Clark Papers.
78. Ibid.
79. Ibid.
80. Smith, *Silent Gesture,* 161.
81. "Negroes May Boycott: Sprinter Smith Tells of Talks," *Chicago Daily News,* September 23, 1967, 45.
82. Edwards, *Revolt of the Black Athlete,* 49.
83. Smith, *Silent Gesture,* 161.
84. Edwards, "Why Negroes Should Boycott," 6.
85. Ibid., 10.
86. "Negroes Vote Ban on Olympic Games," *Chicago Daily Tribune,* November 24, 1967.
87. Ibid.
88. Edwards, *Revolt of the Black Athlete,* 53.
89. Only three people voted against the boycott. Dan Toweler, who had played professional football attempted to dissuade the participants from supporting a boycott. The audience shouted him down as he tried to speak about the attributes and monetary gain that black participation in sports garnered. See Ibid., 53–54.

90. Ibid., 57.
91. "CORE to Study Negro Boycott of Olympic Games," *Santa Barbara News-Press*, November 30, 1967.
92. Ibid.
93. "Negro Ex-Olympians Rap Proposed Boycott," *Chicago Daily News*, November 25, 1967.
94. Edwards, *Revolt of the Black Athlete*, 63–64.
95. "Don't Put off Medi-Cal Cut, Reagan Warns," *Chicago Tribune*, November 29, 1967.
96. Charles Mayer, "Boycott Would Bring More Grief than Good," *Los Angeles Times*, November 25, 1967.
97. Ibid.
98. Ibid.
99. "Olympic Boycott?" *Chicago Tribune*, November 25, 1967.
100. Ibid.
101. "Where Negroes Have 'Struck it Rich,' " *U.S. News & World Report*, December 11, 1967.
102. Edwards, *Revolt of the Black Athlete*, 68.
103. "The Black Boycott," 75.
104. John P. Carmichael, "Olympic Grind Begins," *Chicago Daily News*, June 28, 1968. See also, George Strickler, "Olympic Track Trials to Open Today: 250 Athletes to meet in Los Angeles Showdown," *Chicago Tribune*, June 29, 1968.
105. John P. Carmichael, "Views on Olympic Boycott," *Chicago Daily News*, July 6, 1968.
106. Jeffrey O.G. Ogbar, *Black Power: Radical Politics and African American Identity* (Baltimore: Johns Hopkins Press, 2004), 65, 75, 149–53.
107. Smith, *Silent Gesture*, 163–65.
108. Ibid., 166–68.
109. "Negro Ex-Olympians," np.
110. Ibid.
111. Ibid.
112. Historian Peniel Joseph and other scholars of Black Power studies do not necessarily temporally separate civil rights and black power as completely distinct movements. Instead, they belong on a continuum of civil rights history as well as situate both as part the "broader black liberation movement." Harry Edwards echoed similar sentiments in his recollection of the black athletic revolt. "The revolt of the black athlete in America as a phase of the overall black liberation movement is as legitimate as the sit-ins, the freedom rides, or any other manifestation of Afro-American efforts to gain freedom." See Peniel E. Joseph, "Black Liberation without Apology: Reconceptualizing the Black Power Movement," *The Black Scholar* 31, no. 3–4 (Fall/Winter 2001): 2; and Edwards, *Revolt of the Black Athlete*, 38.
113. Ibid., 527, 531–32.
114. "He's for Black Power," *New York Amsterdam News*, August 10, 1968, 1.
115. Ogbar, 65, 75, 149–53.
116. Smith and Henderson, "Why I Raised My Fist," 32.
117. Ibid.
118. Ibid., 29.
119. Ibid., 32.
120. There are discrepancies in various renditions of the stories surrounding the events that led to the medal stand protest. For instance, see Caroline Frost, "The Other Man on the Podium," BBC News, October 17, 2008, http://newsbbc.co.uk/go/pr/fr/-/2/hi/uk_news/magazine/7674157.stm. Paul Hoffman claims to have given Norman the

OPHR button. See David W. Zang, "Rowing on Troubled Waters," in *The Rock, The Curse, and the Hub: A Random History of Boston Sports*, ed. Randy Roberts (Cambridge, MA: Harvard University Press, 2005), 112–31.

121. Smith and Henderson, "Why I Raised My Fist," 32.

122. Ibid., 24. Edwards wrote that Smith relayed to him that the bowed heads symbolized fallen martyrs like Malcolm X and Martin Luther King, Jr. See *Revolt of the Black Athlete*, 104.

123. Smith, *Silent Gesture*, 22.

124. Edwards, *Revolt of the Black Athlete*, xvi.

125. Avery Brundage Papers (Box 85, Folder 67th Session of the IOC; Mexico City Press Statements Released).

126. Twenty-one athletes signed the petition including Jim Hines, Norm Tate, Mel Pender, Charlie Mays, Charlie Greene, Vincent Matthews, Erv Hall, Larry James, Ed Caruthers, Ronald Ray Smith, Art Walker, Ron Freeman, Lee Evans, Ralph Boston, Louis Scott, John Carlos, Leon Coleman, Willie Davenport, Tommie Smith, Dave Smith, and Coach Wright.

127. "U.S. Olympic Official Says Athletes with Armbands Will Be Dismissed," *International Herald Tribune*, September 9, 1968; "Olympic Trials: Black Athletes Compete for Slots on U.S. Team," *Ebony*, October 1968, 186–92; "Negroes Call for Removal of Brundage," *Chicago Tribune*, September 25, 1968; "Olympic Blacks Ask Brundage Removal, " *Chicago Sun-Times*, September 25, 1968; "Athletes Call for Ouster of OAC Head: Brundage Denies Negro Racial Charges," *The Register*, September 25, 1968; "Brundage: Quotes Were Distorted," *Chicago Daily News*, September 25, 1967; "Negroes, Avery Patch up Dispute," *Chicago Daily News*, September 25, 1968.

128. Steve Brooks, Art Evans, and Fritz Hobbs decided not to support Edwards and the OPHR.

129. For a detailed discussion on the historical development of the Harvard crew team and their activism at the 1968 Olympic Games see Zang, "Rowing on Troubled Waters,"112–31.

130. Robert Clark Papers, Box 7

131. Hurschmann, np.

132. "Dr. Clark Praises Smith, Carlos in Olympic Fuss," *San Jose Mercury News*, October 19, 1968; and Robert D. Clark, "Honorable Men," *Spartan Daily*, October 24, 1968.

133. Clark to Mr. A. Ray Freeman, July 10, 1968

134. Hurschmann, np.

135. Tim Garcia, "Just Punishment?" *Spartan Daily*, October 22, 1968.

136. "The Olympic Spirit," *Spartan Daily*, October 23, 1968.

137. Harrison F. Heath, "Thrust and Parry, Mixed Reaction to Smith's, Carlos' Ouster, Piece of Metal?" *Spartan Daily*, October 22, 1968.

138. Jack Olsen, *The Black Athlete: A Shameful Story: The Myth of Integration in American Sport* (New York: Time-Life Books, 1968).

139. Robert Allen to Clark, October 19, 1968, Salt Lake City, UT.

140. Eddie West, "West Winds: From the Mail Bag," *The Register*, December 7, 1967.

141. Anonymous letter to Clark, July 2, 1968, Riverside, CA.

142. Anonymous letter to Clark, July 3, 1968, St. Charles, IL.

143. Alejandro Medina to Clark, July 1968, Guadalajara, Mexico.

144. Anonymous letter to Clark, July 2, 1968, Portage, Indiana.

145. Ibid.

146. Ralph Brubaker to Tommie Smith, September 27, 1967, Los Angeles, CA.

147. Anonymous postcard to Clark, October 1968.

148. Harry Jackson to Clark, October 19, 1968, Saratoga, CA.

149. Sue Amon, " 'We'd Do It Again Tomorrow' John Carlos Tells SJS Crowd," *Spartan Daily*, October 23, 1968.

150. See "America Out on Bail," *Spartan Daily*, October 21, 1968; "Thrust and Parry, Olympic Ouster, Aliases and Recruiting," *Spartan Daily*, October 21, 1968; Susy Lydle, "Black Protest Powerful Act," *Spartan Daily*, October 21, 1968; Sue Amon, "Smith, Carlos Back in San Jose after 'Too Exciting' Time," *Spartan Daily*, October 22, 1968; Kenyon Jordan, " Pres. Miner, Editor Stone Called Racists by MASC," *Spartan Daily*, October 22, 1968; "Daily Clarifies Out-of-Context Miner Quote," *Spartan Daily*, October 22, 1968; Jim Brewer, "ASB Machine?" *Spartan Daily*, October 23, 1968; "Thrust and Parry, Council Cut Debated; Column Angers," *Spartan Daily*, October 23, 1968; Robert M. Strouse, "Thrust and Parry, Miner Arrogant?" *Spartan Daily*, October 24, 1968.

151. Hobert Burns, "Dr. Burns Criticizes Brundage," *Spartan Daily*, October 21, 1968; and Al Rutherford, "Thrust and Parry, Mixed Reaction to Smith's, Carlos' Ouster, Actions Insulting" *Spartan Daily*, October 22, 1968.

152. Robert Henshel to Clark, October 24, 1968; Lewis Ward to Clark, October 23, 1968; and M.J. Lunine to Clark, October 31, 1968.

153. There are epistemological differences between militancy and ideological radicalism. While militancy has connotations for armed resistance, the latter explains a willingness to separate self from a conservative-liberal scale of thought and instead adhere to values that would not be considered tolerable in the status quo. In this case, some of the student-athletes were closer to a pseudo-form of radicalism as they appropriated cultural expressions of Black Power that were misinterpreted as militant.

154. For works on black power, see Ogbar; Stokely Carmichael with Ekwueme Michael Thelwell, *Ready for Revolutions: The Life and Struggles of Stokely Carmichael* (New York: Scribner, 2003). For an overview of the Civil Rights Movement see Townsend Davis, *Weary Feet, Rested Souls: A Guided History of the Civil Rights Movement* (W.W. Norton & Company, 1998). For works on the politicized nature of the Olympic Games see the following unpublished dissertations: Udodiri Paul Okafor, "The Interaction of Sports and Politics as a Dilemma of the Modern Olympic Games" (PhD diss., The Ohio State University, 1979); Robin Tait, "The Politicization of the Modern Olympic Games" (PhD diss., University of Oregon, 1984); and Robert Alan Mechikoff, "The Politicization of the XXI Olympiad" (PhD diss., The Ohio State University, 1977).

155. Nat Hentoff, "Abdul-Rauf: Rights and Respect," *Washington Post*, March 25, 1996, A15.

156. Robert Lipsyte, "Athletes Standing Up as They Did Before," *The New York Times*, March 17, 1996; and Peter Steinfels, "March 10–16; Anthems, Islam, and Basketball," *The New York Times*, March 17, 1996.

157. Jon Saraceno, "Keeping Score: Despite Wallace's Rant, NBA Remains a Players' League," *USA Today*, December 14, 2003; and "Blowing Smoke," *Washington Times*, December 12, 2003.

158. William Rhoden, *Forty Million Dollar Slaves: The Rise, Fall, and Redemption of the Black Athlete* (New York: Crown Publishing Group, 2007).

159. "Golfer Says Comments about Woods 'Misconstrued,' " *CNN*, April 21, 1997.

160. "Tiger OK with 'Lynch' Joke, Sharpton Isn't: Golf Channel Anchor Tilghman Suspended over Comments about Woods," *Associated Press*, January 9, 2008.

161. J. A. Adande, "King and Co. Guilty Only of Dreaming Big," *ESPN*, July11, 2010; Marc Stein, "Sources: No Probe from Cavs, Raptors," *ESPN*, July 12, 2010; Chris Broussard, "Time for Cavs Owner to Act his Age," *ESPN*, July 9, 2010; Scoop Jackson, "LeBron's Big Move? Been There," *ESPN*, July 10, 2010; Tom Withers, "LeBron's Mural Coming Down in Cleveland," *Yahoo Sports*, July 10, 2010; "LeBron's 'Decision' Watched by Nearly 10M People," *Yahoo Sports*, July 11, 2010; and Tom Withers, "Cavs Owner Defends Stance on LeBron," *Yahoo Sports*, July 12, 2010.

162. Jason Whitlock, "Jesse Jackson Way off Base on Lebron," *Fox Sports*, July 12, 2010.

163. *Outside the Lines*, ESPN, July 14, 2010, http://www.youtube.com/watch?v=JihcOovA15k.

164. Ibid.

165. In the summer of 2014, despite the acrimonious words and behavior of Cavalier management and the fans concerning his decision to depart Cleveland, LeBron James decided to leave the Miami Heat and once again play for his hometown team.

9

Imagining a Strange New World: Racial Integration and Social Justice Advocacy in Marvel Comics, 1966–1980

David Taft Terry

"A Real Live Negro Super-Hero!!!"

High above New York City, in a gleaming futuristic jet, three of members of the superhero team Fantastic Four head to their next adventure. As they start out, however, something is different. Benjamin Grimm whose codename is "Thing," asks team leader, Mr. Fantastic, "When did you have time to dream up a jazzy flyin' fastback like this baby?" "I didn't Ben! It was an unexpected gift sent to me by an African chieftain called, 'the Black Panther'!" Cynical, Grimm smirks, "Never heard of 'im," adding, "how does some refugee from a Tarzan movie lay his hands on this kinda gizmo?"[1] Black characters were unknown in mainstream comics at the time. As part of a broad endorsement of racial integration, writer Stan Lee and artist Jack Kirby, two creators at upstart publisher Marvel Comics, determined it was "time to end that lunacy." They set out to create "a new major character strong enough to stand on its own."[2] Thus, the July 1966 issue of the *Fantastic Four* (no. 52) presented a black character as a bona fide superhero for the first time ever in comics.

The Black Panther proved a perfect fit for Marvel at the time. Kirby, his primary creator, liked the character very much, and confessed that he saw a role for this character in the social justice movement against racism. "If we can wander about in his bigger-than-life experiences enough to gain the satisfaction of triumph," Kirby wrote, "who knows, we might even find ourselves winning in the real world!"[3] Stan Lee was more philosophical about fictional superheroes advocating real-world social justice: "Perhaps a comic mag isn't the proper place for this type of discussion," he mused soon after the Black Panther's debut, "[but] there's just a chance that these pages, which are so widely perused by thinking readers throughout the world, are possibly one of the best places of all [for socially relevant discourse]!"[4] A reader, however, was much more to the point: "This is good...this is good! A real live Negro Super-hero!!!"[5]

Of the mainstream comic publishers in the late 1960s and into the 1970s, Marvel represented the most progressive, the most hip. At the height of its appeal, Marvel had solidified an audience of "true believers," as they were called, "who thought that they were reading cutting-edge literature."[6] Beginning in 1961, Marvel ascended to the top of the industry by presenting a new approach to the superhero genre—creating an expectation of social, political, and cultural relevancy. Early-on, at least, the approach was a hit with a large segment of readers, which included an increasing number of older teens, college students, and young adults. They seemed to welcome story lines on everything from communism, to poverty, to bigotry; "the idea of bringing modern problems into focus," wrote one reader, "is something I enjoy seeing."[7] Following its own editorial line (and commercial imperative), as the social and political movements of the period proliferated—black power, antiwar, women's liberation—Marvel attempted to speak to these issues. Marvel was "selling more than just comic books," one scholar points out, "they were selling a participatory world for readers, a way of life for its true believers."[8]

Yet, by the late 1960s, despite its self-bestowed claim to relevancy, the American Civil Rights Movement, for example, had gone uninterpreted—unreferenced, even—in the pages of Marvel's comic books. Indeed, only as the Civil Rights Movement approached crescendo—as the implementation of hard-wrought gains remained—only then, did Marvel get the civil rights religion. "Let's lay it right on the line," opined Marvel's Stan Lee in December 1968, "bigotry and racism are among the deadliest social ills plaguing the world today....The only way to destroy them is to expose them—to reveal them for the insidious evils they really are." At the time, Marvel was selling fifty million comics each year.[9]

This chapter essay something of an interpretive chronicling of the years during which Marvel Comics functioned as an advocate for social justice, especially on race. In pursuing these thematic interpretations, it traces a rather linear chronology in four parts, periodizing the years of approximately 1966–1969 as the time of Marvel's greatest advocacy for integration. From the beginning of the decade through about 1973, Marvel broadly pursued a sincere (if only problematic) advocacy for reform of the persistent black ghetto, which it held out as an obstacle to integration. The middle years of the decade, roughly 1974–1976, witnessed the popular and pervasive rush to commodify black power's vernacular and aesthetic qualities emerge fully at Marvel. Social justice relevance gave way for a time to base blaxploitation. Finally, this chapter's chronology concludes as the 1970s draw to a close, and Marvel narratives developed a post-ghetto framework, which sought to restructure the interpretive context for integrating blacks, by moving away from social justice issues pointedly relevant to antiracism in favor of more allegorically anti-discrimination narratives (mutants rather than race). In the process, Marvel's black characters are dispossessed or de-raced. Related to such editorial departures, changes in the retailing aspect of the comics industry see black consumers as an ever-shrinking segment. By 1980, in fact, despite fifteen years of presence, black characters in Marvel narratives, like black Americans in the real world, were shunted into almost wholly disconnected or deracinated states of cultural being as an entry fee of sorts into an amalgamated society in which whiteness is not necessarily normative, but is nonetheless presented as a logical, accessible, pidgin culture.

"I'd be Sharp, Sharp, Sharp!"

The 1970s began by finding the fictitious Clark Washington working as a janitor, cleaning floors at the *Daily Planet*, a Metropolis newspaper. Though his work was menial and he was privately angered by the fact that others at newspaper disregarded him personally, and devalued his contributions to the company, Clark was known generally by colleagues as "mild mannered." To get along well in this environment, he "shuffled" a bit. This work persona had been just a ruse, however, no more than a mask developed long ago to protect who he really was. The true Clark Washington was more than a janitor, and as the decade pressed on, the possibilities of his nation accepting him honestly had never seemed more promising. Given a chance, Clark knew he and those like him might soar. Just few years later, a similar scene found Lloyd and T. C. taking a momentary break from the duties at a fictional car wash in Los Angeles. As he was known to do, T. C. got right back into an ever-running monologue about his favorite fantasy, The Fly, a black superhero. With a twangy, melodic, jive cadence, he worked himself up: "[But] I wouldn't be like Superman, Jack—that square sucker! Man...I'd be sharp, sharp, sharp!" Getting more excited still as he visualized out loud, he created a picture for his colleague: "I'd have me a bad black cape, man, and a helmet that looked like two big eyes! Dig?...Wit' a brim on it, man." Unimpressed, Lloyd bluntly muses: "You full o' s——." T. C. could not be dissuaded from his dream, however. "Awe, come on, Lloyd, man! I would be able to walk up the side of buildings, man! And nobody would mess with me—I mean, no-bo-dy!" Shifting his voice now to the authoritative "hero" octave, T. C. concluded "because I would be 'The Fly'—Bzzzzz!" T. C. had his dream, his hero-self. It was an attitude insistent with a faith that served him well by the end of the day, when he finally got the girl. In this scene, however, only Lloyd remained unconvinced: "You still full o' s——." Nevertheless, by the mid-1970s, it was getting easier for black people to see themselves and to imagine each other as something special, as something "super": as heroes. The confidence of Clark Washington, from a skit by comedian Richard Pryor, and later the exchange between fictional characters T. C. and Lloyd, from the film *Car Wash,* spoke directly to their aspirations and sense of new freedom that integration in America seemed to hold out, even to young inner-city guys who exhausted their youth cleaning floors, or shining other peoples' rides.[10]

The racial integration era of American history, from the Voting Rights Act in 1965, through the election of the transforming conservative, Ronald W. Reagan, to the presidency in 1980, proved a defining period of the twentieth century. Like films that played upon their audiences' familiarity with heroic iconography and motifs, comics published during this era function now as cultural artifacts of a sort. Indeed, as one historian has asserted, "any scholar seeking to test how deeply popular assumptions about issues…penetrated into the American consciousness ought to consider what comic books had to say."[11] In their visibleness, text, and subtext, they reveal what the largely male, largely white, largely northeast-based comic creators attempted to reflect and promote about the strange new world of racially integrating America. Comic books as artifacts inscribed with the real-time perspectives of comic creators (and their audiences) witnessed and recorded authentic reaction to the climate of the 1970s.

Few social historians have taken comics for their full value. Those who have interpreted comics do so largely without regard to specific historical contexts. Thus accepting comics as cultural artifacts, interpretations of real-world developments and the pacing of racial integration, in particular, will be considered here as context for the narratives in Marvel comics published during that same time. Analyses of characters will be drawn in support of the broader themes, as will analysis of fictitious geographic locales for their interpretive reflection of actual historical places and settings. Reading backward from the twenty-first-century vantage, it is easy—perhaps, tempting, even—to see only Marvel's missteps. For, as liberal and progressive as was its creative team, during most of the period it was also a de facto closed-shop, racially and gender-wise. As in other genre of pop culture media, Marvel's efforts with superhero comics from the late 1960s through the 1970s suffered greatest from the absence of black creative input on their staff. They moved slowly toward filling this void—evidence that they recognized it, if nothing else—but indeed never quite effectively got there: neither did society at large. As such, what white men at Marvel produced about black life, what they imagined, "often reflected a patronizing attitude." At best then, these creations can only be received as a well-meant approximation of black life, and by consequence an appropriation of what was perceived as authentically black.[12] White male creators' monopoly over the interpreting voice caused too much of black life to be lost in the translation. These failings should not wholly define the effort, however, for it is clear that they believed they were doing their part to push the thing along.

Meanwhile as stated above, as late as 1966 Marvel had no black characters—T'Challa, the Black Panther was the first. Slowly, however, new characters were developed and introduced into the "Marvel universe" (the multiple, overlapping, and ongoing story lines, which connected all Marvel superhero comics to a common reality and therefore a history). In its stories, Marvel approached superhero-ing as something of a matter of profession, and a manner of work. Marvel's earliest steps toward integration of its universe saw more blacks "hired" to civilian offices, and to super-teams of heroes and villains. Though a lagging indicator more than a real-time reflection of change, black characters entering the fictional workplaces of the Marvel universe during the 1960s and 1970s faced the ideological battles of colorblind "opportunity" versus race-conscious "quotas." As such they came to service debates over genuine acceptance versus mere racial tokenism.

Of course, in the real world, by the time Marvel actually took up the African American struggle for equality, that struggle was shifting as calls for black power injected a new energy into a movement at its crossroads. Clearly unsure of what to make of black power, preferring if nothing else to hold it and all other "militant" and "extremist" expressions of whatever political stripe at arms-length, Marvel's early interpretive runs at black power came only as part of a larger acknowledgment of campus unrest from about 1968 through 1971.[13] However, by the early 1970s, "black militant" became a stock character in the Marvel universe, and the locales of action came to include black spaces—namely "the ghetto." Indeed, for most of this period, Marvel would employ a ghetto-focused strategy for inclusion of black characters and story lines that sought to highlight and elevate relevant discourse on the black condition. This approach achieved varying impacts with Marvel readers and fans. In its presentation of ghetto life, for example, Marvel claimed authenticity. And yet, on that point, many readers, particularly newly won blacks, challenged Marvel's view as inappropriate, obstructed, and flatly disinformational. "Your ghetto depictions are somewhat impressionistic," a black reader observed, "something you've imagined rather than something you've known."[14]

Ultimately, Marvel's creators, its mainstream audience, and the marketing environment for the industry all combined to remake race, if only, fictionally. While African American characters were included after 1979 (and even a sprinkling of black creators), they were often advanced as individuals unconnected, or rather disconnected, from the persistent, problematic racial contexts of the times. And more so, if black heroes were still included, in many ways black identity was forced very much to the periphery. As the 1970s drew to a close, Marvel had embraced a post-ghetto framework for dealing with race that supported visions of a diverse America if not so much an integrated one. Marvel's America after 1980, of course, remained as functionally segregated as ever before. Reflecting the real-world views on race, Marvel had largely abandoned its advocacy role.

The New Guy at the Office

On July 2, 1964, President Lyndon Johnson signed the comprehensive Civil Rights Act of 1964, which included under its Title VII: federal prohibitions against employment discrimination on grounds of race, color, religion, sex or national origin. For his part, President Johnson expressed several months later that he saw such comprehensive legislative achievements as only part of a broader program. "We seek not just freedom but opportunity," he told a commencement audience, "not just legal equity, but equality as a fact and a result."[15] His administration pushed "contractors to hire" at least the best and brightest minorities. Yet, the goal remained only qualitative, and "did not attempt to say how many more such people an employer should hire." As such, the Civil Rights Act touched only the largest companies right away—businesses with more than 100 employees. Those with twenty-five or fewer employers, as one historian phrased it, "did not have to stop discriminating until 1968." As a result, 60 percent of Americans were not affected by the revolutionary new law for several years more. The full desired impact of anti-employment discrimination efforts remained debatable and hard to define, and race integration of the American workforce proceeded slowly. [16]

In the federal government support for the idea developed during the decade. Its first urgings, however, amounted simply in "directives calling for race-neutral actions," as one scholar noted, meaning "recruit more widely, offer job training, rid employment tests of racial bias." By the mid-1960s antiracism in employment was not yet about the goals and timetables for which such reform would become (in)famous in just a few years. Reform sought more simply to ensure that public funds should not support racial discrimination against many of those very same taxpaying citizens. Tying government funds and lucrative contracts to fair employment and antiracism, however, encouraged many of the larger players in the private sector to "began to take their first, if only tepid, steps toward racial integration of their workforces."[17] For whites this period produced a watershed moment of liberalism, but that feeling would not last. When Watts exploded in July 1965, it not only fragmented the movement, but also fostered resentment among whites formerly sympathetic to black civil rights. A national poll the following year revealed that three-in-four whites thought that blacks were "moving too fast" in their demands. Indeed, it seems that Watts had confused white liberals. A flabbergasted President Johnson could only ask incredulously, "what [more] do they want?"[18]

With a longer view, however, Watts convinced Johnson that the nation's persistent racial problems had deep economic roots. Economic transitions of the nation's industrial economic had impacted blacks severely; black unemployment was twice that of the nation as a whole. Such disparities had only emerged in the preceding decade as the escalating impact of de-industrializing cities. The Kerner Commission appointed in 1967 to determine the underlying causes of urban riots confirmed this belief, framing the episodes as the culminating result of entrenched white racism. To the president, a full-faith pursuit of the spirit of the Civil Rights Act seemed the only honest response. He set an administrative course toward more jobs and job training, as well as more comprehensive school desegregation.[19]

If before 1968, civil rights reform in economic practices, including access to jobs, had meant opening doors wider to the black best and brightest, that day had passed by the closing years of the decade. "Special considerations" would inform public and private policies aimed toward increasing participation by historically excluded groups, and affirmative action became its catch phrase. The challenge it presented was profound, yet "the Johnson administration knew that challenge could be met only with the help of the business community," one historian explained.[20] Generally, through the late 1960s, most white-owned and mainstream firms adhered to an older principle of "equal opportunity" for the best and brightest when hiring minorities. However, "the growing body of civil rights bureaucrats in the state fair employment practices commissions (FEPCs) and government compliance agencies had discovered that simply removing discrimination, or being color-blind, did not lead to racial integration." One scholar has demonstrated, "actual integration would require seeing and seeking out color, not ignoring it."[21] Moreover, in "a short-lived burst of social responsibility," American companies revised earlier hiring policies, instituted new job-training initiatives, and resolved to recruit, "the hard-core unemployed, the unemployable, or the disadvantaged, the majority of who were imagined as black." By the 1970s, at least among the nation's large firms, this approach was having its impact. [22]

While President Johnson had begun much of this momentum, his hand in implementing affirmative action was actually limited. Indeed by 1968, an overwhelmed Johnson administration would "lose focus" on employment discrimination as war raged in jungles of Vietnam and on the streets of Chicago. Not seeking reelection, the task of defining and securing economic opportunity for blacks as a civil right would have to await his successor, Richard Milhous Nixon. Numbers, quotas, and timetables became the evaluation metric for affirmative action under Nixon during the early 1970s. And as they did, as the question shifted from whether a black could get a job to whether he actually had a job, the new policy raised questions of fairness and ultimately divided the nation. Turning the actual letter of the Civil Rights Act against its undeniable spirit, some began to argue that, goals, quotas, and timetables violated Title VII insofar as it equated to reverse-racism as it was phrased (Nixon, however, maintained hard quotas were never intended, only vaguely defined, process-driven, goals). And yet, for a time, Nixon pressed on. By executive orders, President Nixon established the Office of Minority Business Enterprise (no. 11458, 1969), and also dictated that the Small Business Administration (no. 11625, 1971) "consider the needs and interests of... members of minority groups seeking entry in the business community."[23]

At any rate, the implementation of the economic components of civil rights sired a visual reality. That image of black business and business people venturing boldly to compete in the national and global markets resonated as expressions of black power, capturing the imagination as it would any actual market share. The national publication *Black Enterprise* first appeared in 1970, tapping this phenomenon. Similarly, members of the Congressional Black Caucus (CBC), which formed in 1971, took up the cause of minority-business enterprise as a centerpiece of the group's mission. Nixon had emboldened and empowered the federal agencies most connected with investigation and enforcement of antidiscrimination employment policies, the Equal Employment Opportunity Commission (EEOC). When his administration became bogged-down and distracted by Watergate and other scandals, a period of salutary neglect commenced for the EEOC. "Armed with the power to bring corporations to court, buoyed by increased funding and more attorneys," explained historian Terry Anderson, "the EEOC began the most aggressive enforcement policy in its history," and expanded the protections it offered to a wider segment of the populace, including those historically marginalized.[24]

As Jimmy Carter's presidency began, for those seeking to affix pejorative meaning to affirmative action in employment, the context had been established by the early 1970s. And yet, for those concerned with quantifiable outcomes, affirmative action was having an impact. "Between 1970 and 1980 the percentages of black union workers and apprentices had doubled," one scholar points out, and "African American officials and managers, professionals, and skilled workers increased 70 percent, twice the national rate of growth for those positions.[25] Each of Carter's predecessors had put a stamp of some sort on the push for antiracism in employment. And while his term labored from the start with an extended economic recession, and became burdened in several foreign affairs crises, Carter nonetheless added to the decade's legacy on affirmative action in governmental agencies: minority set-asides on federal public works projects.[26] Indeed, "by the end of the Carter years," as Anderson has characterized it, "affirmative action had reached its zenith."[27] Public sector jobs represented more than half of all jobs held by African American in management and the professions. "Between 1970 and 1980, as the total of federal civilian employees rose by 13 percent, to 3,762,000," for example, "the number of blacks among them increased by 24 percent, to 693,000."[28]

It is more difficult, however, to assess with specificity the impact of federal affirmative action efforts during the 1970s toward improved job opportunities in the private sector, as historical barriers were easily maintained. "White mangers had long complained about the dearth of 'qualified' blacks," as Jennifer Delton has written for example, "but researchers found that their definitions of 'qualified' were informed by traditional assumptions about black work and white work."[29] Working-class white men, who saw such initiatives as directly threatening their economic viability, did not support such policies, and upholding affirmative action policies reduced Carter to a pariah. In his reelection bid against Republican Ronald Reagan, President Carter lost every state but six, thanks largely to the defection of economically disgruntled white Democrat men. This would be the end of the era. Back at its beginning, in the late 1960s, just as black men in suits and ties invaded the nation's corporate spaces, black superheroes also donned masks and capes in the culture's comic books for the first time.

Costumed Professionals

African Americans' efforts toward greater economic justice and job opportunities in the real world, as an extension of the Civil Rights Movement, resonated in the superhero comic book genre. By the mid-1960s, just as blacks in real life began to trickle into the offices and environs of corporate America, through themes related to work and labor, Marvel created moments in their fiction for similar examples of acceptance, participation, and contribution. In the real world blacks came at first in small numbers, almost never overwhelming to the culture of the workspace. By this manner, so too did Marvel's blacks come into the fictional world and workplaces of superheroes. At first only promoting the mantra of teamwork and tolerance, of leadership and sacrifice, Marvel can be seen revealing to its audiences the challenges faced by these individuals seeking to assert self-identity within these new environments. It can also be said that these early efforts reflected the sensibilities and fears of whites, insofar as the black voice in these workplaces was always a singular voice; black inclusion was never plural at any given moment. And yet, the first blacks of the Marvel universe (like those in the real world) possessed unqualified skill and irreproachable character, even if they were all not always "super."[30]

As a character in the Marvel universe, T'Challa, the Black Panther, was the hereditary King of Wakanda, a fictional nation in Africa. Wakanda had achieved a global-leading level technological development, and also possessed great wealth, including an abundance of the planet's rarest natural resource, vibranium (which fell to Earth as a meteorite several millennia ago). Wakanda had managed to fend off the imperial treachery of other nations, near and far, mainly to the warrior-cult traditions centered on their "Panther God." T'Challa received an education abroad, not in any deference to foreign capacities, but to prepare for leadership (to know one's enemies). T'Challa trained his body as an ultimate weapon, and the rite of passage to the throne involved the use of rare herbs that produced heightened human senses, strength, and peak stamina. Combined with "Wakanda-Tech" and weaponized vibranium, whenever T'Challa donned the mantle of the Black Panther, he became arguably the most dangerous man alive. Shortly after the character debuted, of course, the term black panther took on an entire fresh connotation in the American lexicon, as the black nationalist group of that name burst on to the scene. Marvel's Stan Lee expressed concern once the name was appropriated by the radical group, yet Marvel decided to keep the name as it was. Though T'Challa, the Black Panther, appeared in several issues of *Fantastic Four* in the months after his 1966 debut, he was not a new member of that team, or any other team for that matter. As a consequence, his appearance remained sporadic. He would need his own title book, or at least a team affiliation to appear with any consistency in Marvel comics.

Within weeks of the Black Panther's debut, Marvel introduced its first black civilian character. "I know you've been trying to help me and I appreciate it," a frustrated Henry Pym, aka the Avenger, Goliath, confessed to his fiancé and teammate Jan Van Dyne (the Wasp), "but...I keep tripping over you every time I turn around! You've got to leave me alone." Van Dyne senses that his rudeness stemmed from desperation at his inability to figure what has gone wrong with the chemical formula that allows him to be Goliath—he was "stuck" at fifteen-feet tall! Rather than bicker, she took the high road: "You need an assistant."[31] Pym agreed, but later lamented to his friend Tony Stark, the brilliant head of Stark Industries, whose alter ego was the Avenger, Iron Man, "I haven't been able to locate a single bio-chemist who's qualified enough to assist me in my work!" Stark's reply was quick and assured: "I've got just the man you need, Pym! Bill Foster works in the plans and research division of my Baltimore factory!...I'm sure he'd be glad to help you."[32] Shortly thereafter, Foster arrived at Pym's laboratory in suburban New Jersey. Like minds, Pym and Foster hit it off immediately. "No wonder Stark recommended you so highly, Bill," Pym admitted glowingly, "It's a pleasure to work with a man who catches on so quickly—and who darn well knows what he's doing!" Legitimized for his ability, other than his brown-faced appearance, no comment is made of Dr. Foster's race. He's a smart guy, nothing less; he belongs.

Similarly, in the following year, 1967, another recurrent black civilian character, Joseph "Robbie" Robertson, was introduced as senior management at the *Daily Bugle*, the leading newspaper of Marvel narratives, and the main employer of a freelance photographer, Peter Parker, whose alter ego was Spider-Man. Robertson's credentials as a professional were established by the mere fact that the irascible editor of the *Bugle*, J. Jonah Jameson, would hire him. So established, Robertson asserted his authority and leadership in only his second appearance. In the plot of the issue, Jameson has gone missing. Suspecting foul play, Robertson calls his editorial team into his office, all of whom are white. "I figure [Jameson's] been abducted, and we gotta figure out why!," he barks. "I'll hold down his desk while you see what you can uncover." When one of the reporters doesn't move with requisite urgency, Robertson insists: "Let's GO, Boy!...There's no time to waste!"[33] In both instances, Bill Foster and Robbie Robertson, Marvel's message was clear. Tony Stark was an accomplished corporate head, whose genius allowed him to see what others could not, a fellow genius named Bill Foster, who just happened to be black. Naturally Stark took advantage of his competitors frailties, by looking past race, which readers were to believe was insignificant to him. Likewise, though an overbearing blowhard at times, *Daily Bugle* chief, Jameson, was revealed to have had a keen sense of talent, having hired the excellent (if only black) Robertson.[34]

The Comic Hero Workspace

In the Marvel universe, fictional corporations play a significant role in society. Many have been central to character development, or have functioned as recurrent scenery for narrative arcs unfolded: Roxxon Oil Company, OSCORP, and of course, Stark Industries. The hiring of excellent and deserving black civilians to these and other companies played well to the day's model of progressive race thought, for, "by the 1960s, the climate of opinion among corporate executives, as among white people in general, was favorable to equal employment opportunity" in the form of rewarding black excellence (as opposed to cultivating it).[35] Similarly, while the driving force of the genre, hero-ing, had never been presented as a revenue-generating economic segment within the universe, or even a true livelihood for that matter, metaphors presenting superheroes as workers appeared regularly. Thus, the idea of bringing excellent and qualified superheroes to the superhero corporate structure, superhero teams, seemed in-step within that tradition. And, since as late as 1968, there was only one black superhero in the entire Marvel universe—T'Challa, the Black Panther—and, for that matter only one corporate-model super team, the Avengers; the pairing seemed obvious.

In all of the Marvel universe, the Avengers best represented the corporate model organization (the team leader was chair and the team functioned at under a government sanction), as essentially a security services company, "to fight the foes no single superhero could withstand." Perhaps encouraged by Foster's and Robertson's receptions in the previous two years, as much as the Black Panther's own, Marvel's creators had him integrate the Avengers. Late in *Avengers* (no. 51,

April 1968), a panel reveals the chairman, Captain America after a hard-fought victory crouching in tall grass, "on an island near Africa." Next to him is a brown-skinned, black-clad ally. Speaking into a high-tech communication device, "Cap" reports in to his Avengers teammates back at headquarters in New York. He tells them of his location, and that he has with him at that moment, "a special friend." Unspoken, but understood, Cap's friendship was earned in battle and based upon professional respect. Authenticating the legitimacy of both the locale and the colleague, Cap says, "With your permission, I've suggested he join the Avengers...as my replacement!" "He calls himself...the *Panther*!!" Clearly expecting the affirmative, his confidence is rewarded when the voice on the other end replies, "If *you* vouch for him, Cap, he's as good as *in*!"[36] This issue, in poetic coincidence, perhaps, appeared at newsstands only days following the assassination of Rev. Dr. Martin Luther King, Jr. Black superheroes and white superheroes, for the first time, were now on the same team, "an historic moment," as Marvel recognized.[37]

At about the same time, ironically, writers at Marvel's chief rival, DC Comics (publishers of characters such as Batman, Superman, Wonder Woman, etc.), had reportedly developed that its first black character for one of its team titles, *Teen Titans*, but its editorial staff reacted poorly to the pitch: "Do you think we're going too far? Should we be doing this?...Oh my God, we're doomed! We'll never sell our magazines...anywhere south of Toledo!" DC scrapped the character, and revised the story for a white character." Several years more would pass before a black superhero came to the DC universe.[38] One can easily imagine in the real world, the early days for first-blacks in countless companies and office space during the 1960s, who upon arrival, must deal with questions from security guards about being in the wrong place, or from new colleagues who mistake them for the janitorial crew. Indeed, when T'Challa arrives in New York to join his new team, he finds that the squad has been attacked (apparently murdered) and he is immediately accused and arrested as the prime suspect.[39] To clear his name, he becomes a fugitive for the law, discovering and pursuing the true attacker (the superheroes were in fact, not dead), all while eluding the authorities, a group all-too-eager to assume his guilt. He soon clears his name and is united with his grateful new team. Yet, for a time thereafter, T'Challa found he must defend his honor against teammates who doubt his merit and are perhaps unaccustomed to black men of his sober and regal demeanor; "you self-centered, second-rate Tarzan," quips one of his teammates in a moment of frustration.[40] Yet, in the battles, the Black Panther proved their equal in ability leadership, intellect, and comportment under fire. Ultimately, he commanded the professional respect of his Avengers teammates.

In the mode of superhero-making at the time, it was appropriate that Bill Foster and T'Challa were men of science. Both possessed unqualified credentials (Foster's as vouched for by his boss, Tony Stark; T'Challa as in evidence by the technological wonder that was Wakandan society). Put another way, Foster and T'Challa were by no means affirmative action hires in the pejorative, 1970s sense of the phrase—implying goals, and timetables—they were impeccably qualified, and appropriately presented as the best examples of the fair employment and equal opportunity approaches popular through at least the mid-1960s: the best fictional impersonations of reality's first-black phenomenon. "There was nothing radical about opportunity," as one scholar noted, as "it affirmed white American's fundamental beliefs about their nation and themselves."[41] As with Foster a few years earlier (who worked as a sort of civilian attaché to the Avengers), the Black Panther became the vehicle through which the issues of the nation's integrating workforce played out in the pages of the comic. Though some readers found the character as "not immediately friendly," many others "wholeheartedly agree[d]," with T'Challa's addition, and welcomed him to the Avengers. "It's another big step forward by mighty Marvel."[42]

The Black Panther's hire by the Avengers was touted as more colorblind than conciliatory. If white racial integrationist of a more remedial approach had a pitch-man within the Marvel universe in the late 1960s and early 1970s, it was Captain America. More so than any other character Cap was an icon: a symbol of American aspirations, ideals, and conviction. As a character, Cap emerged in early 1941 as a genetically engineered "super-soldier" produced by the US Army to combat rising Nazism and fascism. A victim of the consensus culture, however, Captain America was no longer needed by the 1950s, and his title (indeed most superhero comics) ceased publication for a time. Reality of the early 1960s left consensus debunked. As the Cold War escalated, and the Civil Rights Movement approached crescendo, Marvel revived Cap to function not simply as a super-hero, but more importantly as a moral compass and icon. Tapping the market in nostalgia for so-called traditional values, Captain Marvel promised (if only fictionally) to help restore the nation to its historical course of unending progress. As the 1960s pressed on, however, Marvel's writers (most of them only in their twenties and thirties at the time) had Captain America quickly realize, that he, himself, would be changed by the strange new world of radical protest and racial integration. Given his presentation as an altruistic man championing the values of an altruist past-America (ahistorical though it were), he "had to determine what those values now meant." One method for accomplishing this was advocacy of racial integration. [43]

Shortly after he engineered the Black Panther's coming to America to join the Avengers, Captain America discovered and trained a talented African American, Sam Wilson, to be the next black superhero: the Falcon. Several readers saw the possibilities of the new character immediately, insisting that "the Falcon has opened the door to a new kind of Captain America... [one] more interested in human rights and dignity." Falcon's functionality in the narrative of Captain America stories was also understood: "Now at last Captain America can become America's Number One freedom fighter." Acknowledging this motivation for developing the Falcon character, Marvel conceded, "If Cap doesn't deal with the problems most important to the majority of Americans— well then who will?" In the first years of the 1970s, the pages of *Captain America* became a social laboratory of sorts: a forum where the characters confronted (and readers debated) issues of racism, the Vietnam War, radical dissent, urban decay, and the like. More than any other statement, however, the comic book advocated racial integration through a moderate, decidedly anti-militant, approach. And, by February

1971, Marvel changed the name of the publication from simply *Captain America*, to *Captain America and the Falcon*.[44]

Yet, as an metaphor for black economic aspirations, from the first appearance of the character in *Captain America* (no. 117, September 1969), Marvel writers created a narrative for the Falcon very much influenced by contemporaneous debate regarding access to employment as a fulfillment of earlier civil rights initiatives. If the Black Panther's joining the Avengers drew from the mid-1960s traditions for "equal opportunity" in employment, which made possible the integration of the black "best and brightest" into the corporate world, Falcon embodied much of the early 1970s anxiety over the world the Civil Rights Movement had made, and the price integration would demand as it entered its affirmative action phase full on. Rather than a "best and brightest," readers were presented with a Falcon as an apprentice in-training, and most important, from Harlem—in a way T'Challa initially was not. Interestingly, however, Marvel writers also presented a Falcon who did not see himself as in need of remedial training. Though grateful to Captain America for opportunities afforded, Falcon was ever eager to demonstrate his capacity for independent action/work. Shortly after his training with Cap ends, Falcon pledges to protect Harlem, and Cap pledges to help him when needed. Yet, he was afforded very few solo story lines; every issue of *Captain America and the Falcon* that was more about the Falcon, was by consequence less about Cap—readers would grumble. In form and function, then, Falcon served only as a conduit to Cap's presence in the black community.

"What a Black Super Dude Would Do with His Powers"

As Falcon would struggle to self-identify, by 1972 Marvel debuted its most polarizing character to that point in the ongoing series, *Luke Cage, Hero for Hire*.[45] Pulled from contemporaneous dialogues about criminality in black ghettos, police oppression, and criminal justice malfeasance (brought to public light dramatically in 1971 by events at California's San Quentin Prison and New York's Attica Prison), writers developed the lead character as an antihero from the start. Though he comes to his super powers rather conventionally—through an accident of science—his specific circumstances set him apart from his super-peers. A petty criminal named Carl Lucas, he was sent to prison for a crime he did not commit. In an act of desperation, he agreed to medical experimentation, revisiting a recurrent theme in Marvel fiction of science as both promising and dangerous, while engaging a historical black reality of being guinea-pigged. All goes wrong, of course, bestowing his powers—super strength, endurance, and near-indestructibility thanks to steel-hard, thick skin. (What black man of the integration era could not use thick skin?) He used his powers to escape prison, though authorities presumed his death while attempting escape. Thus, he became a sort of fugitive. But death allowed Carl Lucas to reinvent himself as Luke Cage. Inevitably, he found himself driven to the superhero role less by volunteerism, or even vigilantism, and more by economic necessity. His prospects were otherwise limited given his very circumstance. Thus, the enterprising Cage became a glorified private investigator, a minority business owner, and a hero-for-hire.

The black guy as hero-for-hire in many ways carried forward the relevancy and social commentary editorial bent, as Marvel attempted to speak to both the limited economic prospects of the growing urban underclass, and to the persistence of unmet needs of black and poor communities. In one issue, for example, Cage is called to the scene of a construction accident in the slums—"preparation for yet another round of urban renewal." When a building collapsed, the foreman saw no hope to save his crew, but thankfully remembered the card he has in his wallet from the "Hero for Hire" (yes, Cage had business cards!). Public services in the decaying cities were a controversial topic in the 1970s. The poor needed heroes, too. But, having been theretofore underserved by the "supers," many accepted having to pay for the service. Marvel writers were aware that this proved a difficult structure to support; one of his early clients mistakes his overly concern with collecting fees and throws a wad of money in his face in disgust. "[I]f you want money, Mr. Cage, you can have it!... but I think you're a snake." The unarticulated subtext betrays the social tensions over racially and economically disparate social services, if superhero services might be seen as such. Thus, though he lacked the traditional heroic approach, he nonetheless produced truly heroic outcomes. [46]

Meanwhile, in the early 1970s, existential inner-turmoil drove many other Marvel characters (though not, ironically, the very pragmatic Luke Cage). For characters of color, racism was constant. If it did nothing else, persistent and lingering racism thwarted black aspirations and challenged morale. Several talented and skilled individuals expressed frustration in their inability to win employment commensurate with their merits. Given a fair chance and afforded opportunities to develop themselves, they believed they could be and do as any other American. Without that chance, blacks felt boxed in. How the individual responded was often the only line between the good guys and the bad.[47]

In juxtaposition, African American characters in the role of villain emerged in the Marvel universe beginning in the late 1960s, just as black superheroes appeared. As a testimony to the now-famous ad campaign that the United Negro College Fund began running in 1971, which warned "a mind is a terrible thing to waste," the early 1970s brought many new black villain geniuses. The character development of African American rogue geniuses revealed that most had turned to crime only after experiences with race discrimination. For example, Hobie Brown, a bright, inventive, but frustrated young man, wasted his days away (or at least he felt so) as a window washer. He possessed a healthy ambition in life, but felt hemmed-in by dead-end jobs, and bigoted white bosses who lacked his vision. Brown searched his soul: "Just being a nutty superhero isn't the whole answer...It can take too long." On the other hand "a super villain can go into action right away!...so which'll I be? Heck—it ain't even a contest!" So motivated, the super-villain Prowler was born. Developing gadgets, and a bad-guy costume, he soon attempted to steal payroll from the *Daily Bugle*, but was thwarted by Spider-Man.[48]

This precedent established, the 1970s brought a parade of brilliant but criminal black characters. The demented young chemist, Tilda Johnson, aka Deadly Nightshade, first challenged Captain America and the Falcon in 1973. That same year Luke Cage tussled with another rogue chemist, Chemistro, and T'Challa's nemesis, the MIT-trained genius (and criminal) Erik Killmonger, debuted. The villain Thunderball appeared in 1974 as the alter ego of a genius-level physicist who had been jailed following a botched attempt to recover intellectual property that had been stolen from him by a large corporation. Several months later, in 1975, the brilliant Ethiopian-American arms dealer and terrorist, Moses Magnum, first appeared, followed two years later by the Rocket Racer, another genius inventor gone wrong.[49] Thus, it was intimated in the characterization of black baddies that as their brilliant minds were wasted to racism, a terrible price was paid by society in the form of crime and villainy. Ironically, in the real world, Marvel itself was slow to recognize the value (moral, economic, or otherwise) of hiring African American creators to any great degree. In fact, only a few would be allowed in at a time at the publisher, and none before 1972. Instead, Marvel chose to appropriate blacks as subject matter, perhaps even in pursuit of readers of color as an audience segment.

Look Out, Whitey! Black Power (Man)'s Gon' Get Your Mama!

Having emerged in the heat of the late 1960s, black power determined to ideologically reenergize the struggle by restating the basic claim to freedom: freedom cannot be given, but rather it must be claimed. Many facets of life in black America, from protest culture to performative and popular culture, resonated with this claim-staking. Soon, however, this sociopolitical expression had blossomed into a full-blown cultural emancipation of sorts. By the early 1970s black power's most surface tenets were commodified in the mainstream, so much so that black became a mode across many genres of media. Having appropriated and commodified these cultural expressions of black power, mainly white producers, then presented this to black consumers as spectators. On the one hand, questions of authenticity and exploitation (blaxploitation) naturally abounded. On the other hand, the scale of presence and the focus on black life, real or simply approximated, as subject matter and consumer base had never been approached before. For better or worse, everyone could see that a new day had arrived.

Despite the intentions of popular modes, at its base, this renaissance was real. "Now blacks are beginning to study their past, to learn those things that have been lost, to re-create what the white man destroyed in them," observed writer Julius Lester in 1968, "and to destroy that which the white man put it its stead." For Lester, a new day had arrived for his kinsmen, the historical moment when "they have stopped being Negroes and have become black men," and had accepted this development as "their real identity."[50] Iconic (if for no other reason than the ability of its title to capture the spirit of the time), Lester's 1968 book *Look Out, Whitey! Black Power's Gon' Get Your Mama* spoke for the moment of rebirth at hand that would soon lift up black America, and embolden her to historic, self-determined strides. Lester's broad-based call to the black masses returned to a familiar refrain when it suggested that true advancement of the race would only be possible through an appropriate awareness of the black self. "Black consciousness is...fundamental to Black Power," he wrote. "It is the foundation for Black Power."[51]

Black power energized participation in government, for example, and not simply as electorate, but also as the elected. Although a few cities outside of the South had sent African Americans to Capitol Hill prior to the late 1960s, part of the implementation of black power's promise was southern black political empowerment, which came earliest from the Upper South (St. Louis in 1969, Baltimore in 1971, and Memphis in 1974), and then the Deep South (Houston and Atlanta in 1973). Meanwhile in 1972 at Gary, Indiana, organizers convened what was billed as the first National Black Political Convention, where delegates shaped a "National Black Political Agenda": in essence a black power–inflected manifesto toward still greater self-determination in matters politics, education, and health care. Local politics, too, would reflect the developments of the 1970s, as mayoralties in major cities were claimed by black candidates running on platforms promising, in the coded language of black power, to effect self-determined participation in the American political life.

Many hopeful politicians responded to the undeniable cultural development that arrived symbiotic with the black power worldview. That development was captured in a single word: soul. More than just heritage-conscious stylized approaches to cuisine and music, soul captured the self-liberated vantage with which blacks of the day (especially younger blacks) presented themselves to the rest of American society. Though some of its polemic voices phrased a separatist ideology, most blacks continued to push for access to mainstream American life, though on their terms, in their way, and without apology. The power of soul expression can be no more clearly demonstrated than by the pace at which mainstream elements attempted to appropriate and approximate it, representing soul as true expressions of their own. The music fad, blue-eyed soul for example, was the most easily recognizable appropriation (reminiscent of rock 'n' roll's appropriation of blues culture a generation earlier). And yet, this imitation was received by many blacks as an acknowledgment and homage.

As black and white thinkers worked to articulate the import of the Black Power Movement, they often turned to its impact on aesthetics. As African Americans began to proclaim that black was beautiful, mainstream America took notice: blacks were trendsetters. This, too, owed much to black power. The icons of soul style for many were the political black nationalists, especially the Black Panther Party for Self-Defense (later simply the Black Panther Party as the focus changed from armed self-defense to community programs and political involvement). Indeed, Angela Y. Davis has acknowledged, with some regret, that despite all that her voice advocated, her presence in the popular memory owes as much to her iconic hair style as her message.[52] Far from a rejection of her message, or even a reduction to Davis to a mere icon, her image in the popular mind attests, instead, to the visuality associated with everyday Americans' interpretation of black power. The visual, that is, had a wide-ranging impact. "The ideology of Black Power gives supreme importance to the problem of the Negro's image of himself," one sociologist writing at the time concluded. Whereas traditional civil rights groups (the NAACP and Urban League, to name two) were concerned with presenting blacks aesthetically in ways that made them, "more acceptable to whites," the new directives of black voices sought aesthetics, "ultimately capable of giving the Negro direction in his fight for cultural freedom and economic equality." Thus in "one sense, Black Power advocates are professional image-makers."[53]

In one of the climatic moments of the 1970 film, *Cotton Comes to Harlem* (based on a Chester Himes novel and directed by Ossie Davis), the black crime lord, Casper, tries to impress upon his Italian mafia counterpart just how much of an economic impact has been caused by the social changes underway in the Black Power era, concluding finally, "seems like there's a whole 'lotta money in just being black these days." Indeed, by the late 1960s, in fact, "Black is Beautiful" had taken its first steps on Madison Avenue. Black women began to appear on the covers of theretofore white-only national fashion magazines. In August 1968, for example, model Katiti Kirondi graced *Glamour*. *Life* magazine followed in October of the next year and announced provocatively, "Black Models Takes Center Stage," as a brown beauty, Naomi Sims, peered from the cover. Increasingly, others would follow—even the gentlemen's magazine, *Playboy*, featured a black woman model, Darine Stern, on its cover for the first time (October 1971). And yet, if there was a true moment of crossover for black women as mainstream supermodels/sex symbols, it came in 1974, when *Vogue* offered readers its first brown-faced cover girl, Beverly Johnson. For a time after that, one observer recalled "[fashion show] runways were almost dominated by black girls."[54] From the college campuses to the corporate workspaces, from the church pews to the streets, a cultural black-ness resonated within the broader society.

Yet, of all popular media genres available in the 1970s, popular films were largely the most transforming mode for perspectives on black life. Where they had been largely absent from mainstream offerings of the 1950s and 1960s, after 1970, at a time when the industry struggled to find viable markets, suddenly black characters and black films were everywhere in Hollywood. The new inter-est would be dubbed (pejoratively) by the NAACP as an era of black-stereotype proliferation and exploitation, or simply blaxploitation. Yet, in mainstream Hollywood, the action film formula—especially gritty crime-dramas—were very prevalent in the early 1970s, rendering such iconic white American characters as "Dirty" Harry Callahan, Don Vito Corleone, and Frank Serpico. Black characters like John Shaft, Youngblood Priest, and even Cleopatra Jones were seen in a simi-lar vein, and garnered a strong black following. Even fictional British super spy, James Bond, came to Harlem in the action thriller *Live and Let Die* (1973), which sought to capitalize on the crossover appeal of so-called blaxploitation action films. Thus, where the NAACP saw only exploitation, many others received the new visibility as a result of the historical moment. "Black Power continues to flourish at the film box office," wrote *Jet* magazine, reporting that African Americans, alone, were spending in excess of $150 million at this time to see movies. That the blaxploitation audience also represented those most receptive to the black power political and economic tenets, suggested, perhaps, why the NAACP found itself on the wrong side of the blaxploitation films debate. [55]

Blaxploitation was more a production, marketing, and distribution ploy than a true genre, as it sought to capture predominantly African American audiences—especially young, urban segments—by creating, "a sense of identification." Ultimately, however, historicity of the blaxploitation film rests with its absolute dominance as a popular medium for presenting "authentic" black life in America, to the near-total exclusion for any other representation or interpretive lens for most of the 1970s.[56] Coupled with a number of television programs debuted during the 1970s, despite some variance, these fictional representations established the popular image of urbanity and poverty—the ghetto—as the enduring theme of black life. [57]

The Black Superhero and the Black Ghetto

Meanwhile, with a scene tinted by drab, dark hues, revealing despondent and sullen people, amid worn out and uninviting urban-scape, the narrator of *Avengers* (no. 78, July 1970) implores readers: "come with us now…for a short ride on the uptown subway [to] a world distant…to New York's Harlem, down whose mean streets blow last week's newspapers and yesterday's dreams!" Few white Marvel superheroes had ever come to Harlem. And yet while Captain America's approach was always well-meaning, always outwardly deferential, it still felt nonetheless complicated, troubled even, like that of a religious missionary in a wholly foreign land. In this way, it appeared as if the writers intended Falcon to be nothing more than a his man Friday, to allow Cap to "become more closely involved in the lives and circumstances of the people" in Harlem.[58]

When Marvel's creators rendered Harlemites in the early 1970s, they could only produce images of desperate men forced into desperate acts by circumstances not of their making. Some readers attempted to take Marvel to task for this, to which the editors responded, "We suspect…you've never taken a walk through Harlem…We have!" The Harlem of their comics was the Harlem they knew, supposedly: "unheated, unplastered, unsafe, unsanitary." Furthermore, this realistic depiction of the black ghetto complicated matters for any white superhero, including the Captain America character, who "in the eyes of the ghetto…represented the establishment."[59]

Generally, Marvel's interpretive statement on Harlem responded to the upheavals of the Watts, Newark, and elsewhere in the late 1960s, and aligned with the conclusions of the Kerner Commission and Moynihan Report. Marvel, then, presented a Harlem that was not simply a racial ghetto, but was in most ways irredeemable—not simply foreign to mainstream sensibilities, but lost. Indeed, the splash (first page) of the inaugural issue placing Captain America in Harlem shows him and the Falcon on the street, shaking hands, preparing to part ways for the day, amid a crowd—no doubt amassed by the sheer spectacle of their costumes. The visual cues in the artwork, however, leave readers with the impression of something unknowable—perhaps an African village, perhaps something else—something uncivilized even. A man in the immediate background, for example, appears to be squatting on the rear deck (trunk) of a car. It looks primitive, in a word, like Captain America is among the natives, on safari. And though everyone in the panel seems excited and happy at the spectacle of the two supers, one critic later described the setting (meaning black Harlem) as depressed. Whatever the visual impact from such a perspective, Marvel creators built a foundation upon which the majority of black characters, major and minor, would operate throughout the 1970s. [60]

Racial integration in comics had always meant blacks coming into previously white-only space, but never the opposite. In the real world, as the civil rights coalition searched for new footing, and as the call of "Black Power!" articulated a growing disaffection with liberalism's returns, those blacks who had achieved some measure of integration in their professional experiences were presented as conflicted by feelings of having left "their community" un(der)served. Thus, if white superheroes in the ghetto seemed uneasy interlopers, black heroes were drawn there. The roughest edges of this phenomenon were reflected in the Marvel universe as black superheroes experienced social and psychological tugs-of-war. "There are a few things we feel strongly and surely enough about to applaud and augment in the pages of our magazines," Marvel editors announced during the summer of 1970, "and one of these is the attempts of right-minded people throughout the nation who are attempting to fight a war against bigotry and racial hatred on all sides of the color line."[61] More so than with other black characters, through the Black Panther, Marvel would crusade against intolerance.

Indeed, almost instantly upon joining the Avengers, T'Challa finds something stifling about being too long at team headquarters in Lower Manhattan. He takes walks to locales described only as "some blocks north," where he can be "free to think." For T'Challa (an African foreign national), African American responses to seeing him in action with the Avengers provided a revelation of sorts at the very moment he seemed to be searching for existential meaning. "I became an Avenger...hoping to find fulfillment in ridding the society of those who would ruthlessly destroy it!" he thinks to himself. "Yet, even that is not enough! I must do more." In his superhero persona, the Black Panther races himself (even while maintaining the anonymity of a mask) by self-indentifying as "a soul brother." When a woman who does not know him as T'Challa, asks why he had not previously made his race, at least, known to the world, he responded, "I thought it was enough to be just a man!...but now I know it's time to stand up and be counted [as a black man]."[62] Soon after, while in action against some baddies, he overhears a young black boy nearby, speaking elatedly to a friend—"Man, that Black Panther is somethin' else!...We could sure use 'im on my block!"[63] The boy inspired T'Challa with new purpose: to serve Harlem.

His role in Harlem would not be confined to superhero work; T'Challa sought to serve the community as a teacher. Establishing the civilian secret identity, Lucas Charles, T'Challa secures a job teaching in a "ghetto high school," Andrew Jackson High, "some blocks uptown."[64] Thereafter, and throughout the early 1970s, readers encounter Mr. Charles giving lessons on African culture—a nod to the emergent black studies movement of the era.[65] Once, in a moment of introspection about his new avocation T'Challa admits to his Avenger colleagues that he was struck by the irony being a superhero in a community much more in need of a crime fighter—basic law enforcement, and protection from little more than hoodlums—"no gaudy masks, no colorful costumes...just a creeping, insidious evil, which corrupts everything and everybody it touches!"[66] "Right now it's waging battles every day for the minds, the bodies—the very souls—of kids like the ones I teach—and it must not win!" So profound was the experience, that later, in the middle of a tussle with criminals, he finds himself mentally distracted, contemplating his divided soul. "Now," he admits while throwing a well-placed punch, "I keep thinking of myself as a teacher...on his lunch hour!" [67]

In coming to the defense of blacks, T'Challa often acted solo, often by choice as statement of honor—"those are my people that the [racists] have been beating and killing! And I claim my right to take them...alone!" [68] Fans applauded the Black Panther's "coming to grips with one of the worst evils in the world since the dawning of time—bigotry." Others, however, did not welcome interpretation of the race issue, believing it settled, believing the continued debate over the evils of the "establishment" a straw man—"the so-called 'Establishment' hasn't done a thing to his people since 1965." This theme, the Black Panther versus the white bigots, would be revisited again and again throughout the decade. While appreciating its qualities as "pure, thought-provoking entertainment," fans also acknowledged that Avengers "didn't toy around" in confronting the nation's continued struggles with race. [69]

It may be inferred, as well, some of these fans were black, drawn to Marvel by relevance, and race, and T'Challa. The liberal political and social views were reportedly not universal. "We represent virtually every shade of opinion," Stan Lee wrote 1971. "If we can make you think—if we can anger you, arouse you, stimulate and provoke you, then we've served our purpose."[70] Once the Black Panther was added to the Avengers roster, several key creators, especially writer Roy Thomas, used the character, "to reflect [their own views on] certain aspects of the race situation." In truth, however, Marvel took on, not everyday racism, but rather demagoguery and manipulation by ideologues on both the Left and the Right, especially those espousing violent solutions to social problems (an ironic position to assume, as one historian pointed out, "since superheroes tacitly endorse violent means to solve problems every time they slugged it out with the bad guys"). Sticking to this shared-blame perspective, in several key story lines during the early 1970s, racial flames are revealed as having been fanned by black and white baddies in cahoots.[71]

Actually, the year before T'Challa's fateful decision to moonlight uptown, Harlem gained its first champion. Sam Wilson, a Harlem social worker, debuted as the Falcon in September 1969 and was promptly established there as a sort of superhero-in-residency training. The potential for his character created some excitement. "You have a good setting for him, in the ghetto," one self-identified black reader wrote following Falcon's debut. "What I really liked...was the pride and hope you had drawn on those brown faces," referring to the street scenes of Harlem and the people who greeted the new hero upon his arrival. "Pride means a lot to us."[72] Early-on, Falcon is sensitive to being viewed as a potent hero figure by "his people." At the heart of this quest for respect was a desire project himself as more than simply Cap's "sidekick," a position of ignobility and with a history for black superheroes. In one storyline, for example, discovering Spider-Man swinging through Harlem—"that cat's way outta his territory... It's bad enough I gotta compete with Cap"—Falcon attempts (unsuccessfully) to take him down, just for the "rep." Similar to positions the Black Panther expressed to his white Avengers teammates about his prerogatives in protecting Harlem "alone," in Falcon's mind, he would be shamed should he allow Cap to assume the mantle of Harlem's savior.[73]

Pursuing this line, and coming into narrative form during the height of Marvel's social relevancy phase, the burdens of the moderate/centrist black voice on race often fell to Falcon. Through the Falcon, whose ideological orientation was integrationist, Marvel attempted to navigate the intraracial politics of inner-city black life through presentation of the dynamic yet contested ideologies. Marvel regularly got this aspect spectacularly wrong, however, as in an issue of *Captain America* when the giant-sized villain, Bulldozer—while proclaiming "Power to the People" no less—leveled a housing tenement with his fists, as the residents stood around and cheered. "Right on, Bulldozer!" they shouted, as he apparently represented some great liberating force. "'Baloney!'" cried one reader; "Do you honestly think that the black people are really that blinded by hate and fear?" A similar exploration, this time of the intergenerational politics, occurred for a time in the *Amazing Spider-Man,* when the relationship between "integrated" Robbie Robertson and his son, a radicalized college student, who tells his father, "I have to be more militant... because of you! You've become part of the Establishment, the white man's Establishment [and] I've gotta live that down!" In other Marvel titles, the antiwar movement of the early 1970s is racialized through presentations of the ideological and physical battles between radical black militants and politically moderate black vets. And, ideologically consistent though he was, Falcon/Sam Wilson's message of moderation often rang empty in the ears of Harlemites. Even his girlfriend, Leila, habitually called him, "Uncle Tom."[74]

Falcon more than any other character in the Marvel universe was presented as consciously and consistently negotiating the unmapped terrain of post-Movement racial integration during the early 1970s. Racially, he seemed perpetually in search of place and meaning. He often struggled as found himself asked to occupy the moderate-center time and again, amid the opposing forces at play: perceived white indifference and malaise on one side, actualized black frustration and militancy on the other. Ironically, the middle was the ground white superheroes always occupied on race matters, as Marvel and other publishers rejected white racism, but also "made it clear that militant black power was not the remedy for racial injustice."[75] In fact, Spider-Man, Captain America, and others moved in and out of moderator roles at will. They were not compelled in the same way Falcon was to constantly be on point, betraying the creators' sense the race problem was chiefly a black problem.[76]

Meanwhile, the black superhero, Luke Cage, knew exactly who he was. Possessing the qualities of the antihero superhero most appreciated by readers, toughness, incredible power and strength, and courage, Cage seemed in-step with American popular culture for its appropriation of the Black Power era's vernacular language. Cage was "a new kind of black superhero," as he would later be described, "who had greater 'street credibility' than his predecessors." Indeed, *Luke Cage, Hero for Hire*, represented the advent of the blaxploitation comic, for as one reviewer noted, "Luke Cage was really John Shaft in long underwear."[77] Whereas the films, however, were geared toward largely black movie-goers, it is unclear whether Marvel intended *Luke Cage, Hero for Hire* to serve mainly a black reader segments, which surely had been building since the late 1960s. *Luke Cage, Hero for Hire* represented a departure from Marvel's previous approach to black superheroes, and would not function as a vehicle for social proselytizing. Cage was neither militant, nor moderate, he was morally independent and economically pragmatic. As Marvel explained, "though he's been a real victim of white oppression, [Cage] still manages to judge people on an individual basis."[78] Whereas *Captain America and the Falcon*, intended to be cerebral and contemplating, the point of *Luke Cage, Hero for Hire* was simply action.

Moving away from the black superhero as social messenger, Marvel creators also relocated the black geographical space—or at least expanded that space. While many story lines found Cage in Harlem, many others did not. In fact, borrowing directly from the 1971 classic film *Shaft* (about a black private detective whose office was in Times Square), Luke Cage opens his office, not in Harlem, but in a space about the Gem Theatre, on West 42nd Street, which by the 1970s, had "degenerated into one of the tawdriest areas of the city." That Cage could afford to rent there suggested that the unintended consequences of the 1960s social change spurred white flight, urban decay, and the spread of Harlem-like ghetto trappings and black vernacular culture. "Theaters fell into disrepair or were turned into porn-movie houses. Drug dealers and thieves prowled the street. Shootings were not uncommon."[79]

From its "hero-for-hire" orientation, to its (mis)appropriation of jive vocabulary, readers registered a range of responses, to the Luke Cage publications. Some recognized Cage as a conscious and "striking contrast" to previous approaches to black superheroes, the Falcon and the Black Panther. Others used *Hero for Hire's* readers' page as a space for dialogue about the perceptions and stereotypes of race and place in the 1970s. "He belongs in a slum," one reader insisted, "fighting syndicates and minor super-thugs." Another put it more bluntly: "Cage presents a bit more logical conclusion [than the moralistic Panther and ideological Falcon] toward what a black super dude would do with his powers." Readers' responses to the use of jive were also mixed. Some rejected it wholly: "[the vocabulary] made you think he came from Watts or Harlem...I mean, who can identify with that?" Others enjoyed it, but the basis of their appreciation no doubt revealed to Marvel the hazardous terrain upon which they operated: "Luke Cage should be [even] more jive, more black." After a couple years in publication (and with sales apparently sagging), Marvel pushed the Cage character toward a more conventional stance, at least in title, renaming him "Power Man" and aligning him more with conventional superhero-ing. And, as the series continued into the 1970s, Marvel creators toned down the jive in Cage's vocabulary.[80]

By the mid-1970s, a time when Marvel was unabashedly committed to the mantra, "follow the trends," kung fu comics were added to the blaxploitation ones.[81] In film, both genres had enjoyed considerable popularity with young black audiences. Interestingly, *Enter the Dragon* (1973) featured a tri-racial team of protagonists (Bruce Lee, Jim Kelly, and John Saxon), and *Three the Hard Way* (1974) starring Kelly with Jim Brown and Fred Williamson brought a black kung fu hero to the streets of Harlem. The following year, then, Marvel debuted the blond-haired, blue-eyed martial arts mystic, Daniel Rand, aka Iron Fist, in the second-tier publication, *Marvel Premiere*, before launching the eponymous *Iron Fist* in 1975. Three years later he was teamed with Luke Cage as *Power Man and Iron Fist*.[82]

Black Power as Pop Aesthetic in Comics

Marvel generally advocated against ideological extremes on both the Right and the Left. In fact, its writers attempted to reveal black nationalists as frauds. At the same time, however, Marvel's narratives also often acknowledged a symmetry between black nationalism's call for greater self-determination and basic American values. Whatever its catalyst, story lines during the Black Power era reflected a dislocation of liberal whites and the divestment of whites from the black struggle. Something had happened.

If comics captured aspects of white thought at the time, they seemed to betray that whites did not seem to know or believe they truly understood black people anymore. They suspected that even the blacks they knew as their friends, were not who they appeared to be. By and large, that is by the mid-1970s, many of Marvel's blacks became angry. Overwhelmingly, the angry black people were not criminal; they were legitimately discouraged, if only occasionally duped—"We've been suckered by somebody even worse than the whiteys!"—or tragically drawn to the extremes of political militancy and racist ideology.[83] Other times they were presented as the pawns of manipulative leaders whose only motivation was greed.[84] All of the work of liberal reform since World War II, that is, seemed to be undermined in a matter of a few years, and all in the name of black power.

Angry black people in the ghetto appeared regularly in *Captain America and the Falcon*. In a surely unintended homage to the Black Panther Party's imprint upon American self-perspective, by the early 1970s the "brothers on the block" were "valorized," as one scholar ably observes, in the minds of many blacks. The angry black man represented "the authentic repositories" for black life and culture, which had dramatically come to mean urban life and culture in the black power era.[85] Against this militant ascendancy, Sam Wilson, the Falcon, struggled in issue after issue of the publication to hold the middle ground for black moderates. In his social circle, Captain America was the liberal white voice.[86] Politically opposite Cap, however, was Leila Taylor, the self-professed black nationalist with whom Sam shared a sincere if only turbulent love affair for most of the 1970s. Leila and Cap engaged in an ideological war for Falcon's soul. "What makes you think I'm your enemy?" Cap asked Leila in 1971. "'Cause you're white!" she replies flatly.[87] Through Leila, specifically, Marvel attempts to capture black power for its self-determined essence with grounding in the American essential right to freedom of speech. Leila also stands in the role of women as leaders, and as a voice of dissent within the emergent subculture (in the likeness of Kathleen Cleaver, Elaine Brown, and Angela Davis). They are strong, smart, and sincere, but also outspoken, independent, and therefore dangerous. From her first appearance, she is the consistent voice speaking out in fiery, blunt defiance against integrationist presumptions. Leila is angry. She is the surrogate of young blacks in the ghetto during the 1970s.

Black dissention came to dominate Marvel's ghetto after 1971, and the ghetto came to be populated by angry black people, almost to the exclusion of all other voices. The veil of earlier interracialism, of the double-consciousness and polite society, had been tossed away, had been reconciled. Now, these angry black characters only sought to speak a truth, as they understood it, whether whites wanted to hear it or not. Unflattering at times, but deemed necessary in pursuit of authenticity, Marvel's white creators appropriated a range of anti-white pejorative dialogue: "honkey," "whitey," and "Mr. Charlie."[88]

Vehicles of juvenile male fantasy as they ultimately were, superhero comics did not just make the likes of Leila Taylor ideological and angry, she also had to be beautiful and sexy. She was not alone in that regard. Just as black women began to appear as models in mainstream fashion publications, so too did they emerge as characters in Marvel comics. Leila debuted in 1971, followed the next year by Claire Tempe, a physician who ran a clinic in New York's Chelsea District, and was the long-time love interest of Luke Cage. Three years later, Marvel introduced Gloria "Glory" Grant, a former fashion model, who moved into the apartment down the hall from Peter Parker/Spider-Man. Of the Marvel leading ladies, two in particular emerged, Mercedes "Misty" Knight, a private detective, and Storm, the first black woman character to be fully developed as a superhero.[89] In these characters, especially, shades of the black action film genre popular at that time can be clearly gleaned, most obviously the film character Cleopatra Jones, a protagonist renowned for an "unapologetically majestic, cool, chocolate, regal, and diva-like 'tude."[90] Cleopatra Jones inspired the character of Misty Knight in her competence and toughness, and Storm shared her "regal and diva-like 'tude." As a representation of black women's beauty, however, Storm's features were "exotic"—long white-hair and blue eyes. However, Storm's visual impact was also balanced by a wide range of additional visualizations of the other black women in the Marvel universe. Against Storm's flowing locks, that is, Claire Temple, Leila Taylor, and Misty Knight all wore perfectly maintained abundant afros, while Glory Grant kept her hair short and "natural."[91]

As black women characters emerged in a superhero universe dominated by white male ones, though still somewhat taboo in the 1970s, interracial sex was at least subtly teased. For example, in a scene from *Captain America and the Falcon* (no. 164, August 1973), at a pensive pause in the action, Cap "tenses himself for expected peril." However, at that moment, he at last gets an eyeful of his nemesis, a new villainess called Nightshade. In that instant, however, the man only sees a woman—a gorgeous woman, in a revealing costume. "His eyes widen," the narrator tells readers, "as his mind whispers... 'Wow.'" That she is a black woman is the unspoken subtext.[92]

Generally, beyond mild representations, sexual situations of any nature—even between members of the same race—were only delivered through coded visuality of flirty grins and inviting stares. In this way, for example, various white women characters responded to the strapping and "dangerous" black hero, Luke Cage. In 1973, in fact, a few months before Cap is smitten by Nightshade, the character Medusa was drawn sexually, if only momentarily to Cage. In one scene, Medusa actually uses here "living hair" to grope Cage's shoulders and thigh as he strides confidently past her. For the black man Cage and the white woman Medusa to have been more than coded still seemed a challenge to comics' creators, and perhaps their main readership. Ironically, however, in that same year, Marvel developed a romance between a white woman heroine and an android—they would eventually even marry and produce children. But androids are robots and robots are not a race. Two years later, across several issues of *Captain America and the Falcon*, a supposed love affair between Gabriel Jones (black), and Peggy Carter (white) is inferred but never actually depicted. At one point, in fact, they embrace passionately but deny themselves the kiss.[93]

It was later divulged that influential voices on Marvel's editorial staff were adamantly against going "too far" in presenting any interracial relationships. Reportedly, in 1976, for example, writer Don McGregor submitted a story for *Luke Cage, Hero for Hire* that featured an interracial relationship—"it had a white guy married to a black woman." On those grounds, "I got called into the office [at Marvel]; they did not want an inter-racial couple in the story," the writer recounted: "How can you take this Nordic blood and taint it," someone asked rhetorically (as some have recalled, Marvel's staff in the 1970s and 1980s was quite permissive by modern standards of workplace decorum). Determined that, "you can't have a black woman as the white guy's wife," the editors rejected the story.[94]

Yet, whatever transpired in the meantime, by late 1977, writer Chris Claremont and artist John Byrne presented what amounted to the first interracial kiss in the mainstream Marvel universe, for which they received accolades from some readers sensitive to fact that, "it's a difficult thing to carry off." Through Claremont and Byrne, the black woman character, Misty Knight, openly takes a white male lover, Daniel Rand, the secret identity of Iron Fist, and their relationship was accepted without remark by the rest of the Marvel universe. In many ways, Knight and Rand reflected a contemporaneous social trend as away from parental control and community gaze. Many young Americans in the 1970s identified with the fictitious Marvel characters, and like them revolted against traditional values and rejected the taboos on dating across racial lines. Indeed, black–white interracial marriage was a feature of American life emergent with a much increased occurrence, nearly doubling between 1970 and 1980. [95]

Morning's Approach

By the mid-1970s, the outcomes of two decades of race reform were mixed. Affirmative action policies in the work space, and in governmental contracts, had been joined by efforts to complete schools desegregation. Title IV of the Civil Rights Act of 1964, for example, reaffirmed the federal government's commitment to school desegregation. As with employment and economic matters, it seemed that school desegregation had become a numbers game. At higher levels of politics, the southern response to continued desegregation mandates was to force the burden of racial integration upon the entire country, insisting for example that the school busing remedy put in play by the US Supreme Court target the de facto northern varieties of school segregation, as well as the de jure southern kind. "School suits erupted across the North [as] city after northern city was hauled to federal court." By forcing northern liberal politicians to face the hypocrisy of their policies—and to face the angered white constituencies those policies brought finally into race reform—saw the limits of northern liberalism laid bare. Much of the white north and west, that is, rejected integration through busing as vociferously in the 1970s as had their white southern counterparts in the decades prior rejected other forms. School busing brought enthusiasm for racial integration to a screeching halt by decade's end.[96]

Meanwhile, after the mid-1970s, a silent majority of Americans, that President Nixon had once identified as not in league with the political radicals and cultural dissenters, began to push back. In their minds, affirmative action laws in the 1970s represented a departure from simple pledges for future "fairness." These were remedial. These seemed retributive and unfair. These laws amounted in the minds of many whites to "reverse racism." Similarly, after having functioned as a near-activist advocate for affirmative action and desegregation through the late 1960s and early 1970s, the US Supreme Court, too, revealed its ideological limits.[97] In *Regents of the University of California v. Bakke*, for example, the Court struck down as unconstitutional an affirmative action admissions plan for a medical school, which reserved a predetermined number of seats in each incoming class for minority students, and held them to meet different (comparatively lower) admissions criteria. To the benefit of an aggrieved white male applicant refused admission to the school, in the majority opinion of the five-to-four decision, the Court found that the admissions process discriminated against non-minority students. It was reverse racism.[98] While *Bakke* reflected the mood among rather large majorities of whites by the late 1970s, as some observers argued at the time, for blacks the ruling confirmed suspicions of white social justice fatigue.[99]

The economic challenges of the 1970s also tested the limits of white liberal largesse. As such, a decade that began somewhat promisingly for social reform agenda quickly turned instead toward a new birth of social and political conservatism.[100] As a voice of this New Right, California governor Ronald Reagan made an influential, though unsuccessful bid for the presidency in 1976. He came back stronger, however, in 1980, bolstered by continued and persistent white male backlash against social justice reforms. Reagan took the Republican nomination that summer, and the wave of enthusiasm for conservatism moved across the white American middle class and landed him in the White House by the fall. More women had voted for his opponent, incumbent Jimmy Carter, than men. Carter had also taken the overwhelming majority of black and Latino votes. And yet, the defection of working-class northern white men—the so-called "Reagan Democrats"—handed Carter an unqualified electoral thrashing.[101] Social justice fatigue, and its many contributing factors, like an economy many believed made weak through regulations and affirmative action mandates which slowed productivity and hampered efficiency, had proven enough to mount an electoral revolution.

Of course, for blacks, this fatigue seemed designed only to thwart their momentum as it "became increasingly clear that the things African Americans had taken for granted during the previous two decades were no longer so."[102] In their coded reversal, Reaganites posed as standing against discrimination. They purported," We must not allow the noble concept of equal opportunity to be distorted into federal guidelines or quotas, ratios, and numerical requirements to exclude some individuals in favor of others," when in actuality they hoped only to accomplish freezing historically ill-gotten gains in their place. [103] Reagan's tenure proved significant, as "for the first time, a presidential administration joined other critics in opposition to affirmative action."[104] Under Reagan, the Justice Department's Civil Rights Division "became the principal opponent of blacks seeking relief through the course in matters pertaining to affirmative action."[105] Across the board, it seemed, the administration sought to pull back its enforcement duties, intimating ultimately that the federal government had no role, and that enforcement of civil rights were matters better left to the states. He even slow-walked support for renewal of the Voting Rights Act, which was set to expire early in his first term.

As the middle of the decade approached, and Reagan prepared for a reelection bid, he sought to taut his remaking of the American mood since coming to office. Speaking clearly and directly to those voters who had worried over the lasting, and perceivably irreversible impacts of social justice efforts, and to those who fretted that the sun had set on the America of their values and their ways of life, Reagan was reassuring. "It's morning again in America," he told them. The long night of 1970s-style social justice would never return. For his confidence, white working-class voters delivered a victory to Reagan more decisive than his first, giving him the most lopsided electoral posting in history.

"It's Pretty Obvious That You're Black": De-Racing Marvel

In 1975, after years in oblivion, one of Marvel's earliest black characters, Bill Foster, reemerged as a superhero called Black Goliath. The new Foster appeared in a few issues of *Luke Cage, Power Man* before his own ill-fated eponymous title, *Black Goliath*, was launched. Marvel canceled it after just five issues.[106] The character remained a part of the universe, however, making occasional appearances in a range of publications. In one such instance, late in 1979, Foster wonders aloud what Marvel editors were likely discussing amongst themselves: was the "black" in "Black Goliath" holding him back? In step with a broader transformation, he determined to re-brand himself as hero. "As long as ya got yerself some new duds," suggested Thing, of the Fantastic Four, "why not complete the overhaul with a new name?" Relatedly, Marvel had been getting flack from readers for its convention of using "black" qualifiers for its characters of color—"Why isn't it White Thor, Green Hulk, or Yellow Shang-Chi?...I resent this discrimination," several of the complaints read.[107] Thus inspired, perhaps, Marvel creators had Thing offer this: "It's pretty obvious that you're black—and if I remember my Sunday school lessons, Goliath was a bad guy...why don't ya just call yourself Giant-Man?"[108]

Marvel approached the late 1970s with a good deal of trepidation. Not only was readership declining (an industry-wide reality), but their marketing profile actually worked against many of those wanted greater access to comics. The company reworked its marketing, taking up a revolutionary distribution model. By distributing directly to its core fan base, through comics-dedicated retailers, profit margins could be restored. Fresh platforms for building-out business could be thereafter developed. As a consequence of this new approach, Marvel's still-broad audience became increasingly no longer a truly "mass" audience, as comics progressively shed the casual reader in pursuit of the dedicated comic fan. Meanwhile, editorially, it was determined that "superheroes ought to spend less time proselytizing and more time punching."[109]

Issues of access to product, with its cultural and demographic implications, saw Marvel's readers for a long while after 1979 become even whiter and less urban. This audience, in turn, demanded different measures of "relevancy." It became clear that the new core fan base had bored of race. The crusades "to bring about a more just society," one scholar observed, "had taken superheroes too far from their basic appeal as escapist entertainment."[110] As part of a broader effort to satisfy the new appetite, Marvel began to de-race its universe. This was accomplished not by killing-off black characters, but rather through a more subtle de-emphasis racism and "blackness" as determination factors in their lives. Black characters, then, spent less time "being black," less time in Harlem, and more time being culturally nondescript, singular, and in support roles to whites. This development echoed white Americans' broadly communicated social justice fatigue of the late 1970s. Marvel superhero comics, always a lagging indicator, simply reflected these transformations.

The transformation was stark when compared to just a few years before. For example, beginning in 1973, while still being featured in an ongoing manner in *Avengers*, the Black Panther concurrently became the lead character of a second publication, *Jungle Action*. Such exposure in two ongoing publications simultaneously had only been known by the likes of Captain America, Iron Man, Thor, and Spider-Man. The majority of white characters would never be featured in this way. It seemed that as late as 1977, the Black Panther's place amid the stars of Marvel's heroes was secure. Indeed, even as the Marvel universe began to steer away from social relevance on race, some of the creators, like writer Don McGregor and artist Billy Graham, who worked with black characters and, "wanted those stories to be about something," attempted to push back a bit against the emerging trend.[111] With their earliest *Jungle Action* story arcs, McGregor, who was white, and Graham, black, set T'Challa, the Black Panther, in his native country, the fictional African country of Wakanda. Marvel's editorial leadership remained unconvinced that a Wakanda-based Black Panther would build its audience. Bluntly, "editorial wanted white people in the storyline." By 1976, McGregor and Graham returned *Jungle Action*'s story lines to America, but not to New York. Instead, the Black Panther found himself in the Deep South—small-town Georgia—taking on the Ku Klux Klan. "Hey!" McGregor responded to Marvel's editors, "You asked for white people!"[112] Critically acclaimed, *Jungle Action* did not sell well enough, especially among the core of Marvel fans. This made it vulnerable to the mood shifting Marvel away from social justice advocacy. *Jungle Action* was cancelled in the middle of the Klan arc.

Marvel leadership moved immediately, not so much to reinvent the Black Panther, as to return him to his roots—as iconic creator Jack Kirby had imagined him back in 1966 when he debuted. A new title, *Black Panther*, was launched in January 1977, with Kirby given full creative control—similar to the latitude he had been granted a year earlier with *Captain American and the Falcon*. Yet, of all his responsibilities, however, *Black Panther* seems to have been the least important to his bosses, who if nothing else, hoped that the legendary creator could bring commercial success.[113] A shot at previous writers' placement of the character's narratives in Africa, and later in the American South, Kirby once quipped, "my character is neither Kunta Kinte nor Chicken George, but he can open wide the door to the most interesting area of [life]."[114] As Kirby worked to reclaim "his" T'Challa—whose social advocacy came subtly, in metaphors and allegories—he created "bigger-than-life experiences" for the character, launching cosmic, time-traveling, science fiction-laden tales, which threw "the Panther into a simplistic, even goofy tale of straight super-hero action [that] was jarring to say the least."[115] Kirby's Panther, that is, was be a total departure from socially relevant storylines created by writers since in *Avengers*, and *Jungle Action*, and he shifted the storylines abruptly, "without even a single reference to what McGregor had been doing only weeks before," as if the ten previous years of continuity had never happened—"such an attitude didn't endear him." In fact, readers howled with disapproval from the start: "to take Marvel's first black character and depersonalize him so severely is criminal," and too "comic-bookish."[116]

By the time Marvel separated Kirby from the assignment, after nearly two years in control, the moment had been lost. *Black Panther* ended with issue 15, May 1979. As the character was also already simultaneously being written out of *the Avengers* story lines, the Black Panther—Marvel's first black character, and by far its most classically heroic black superhero—ended the 1970s without a home for his fans to find him. The last appearance of the character during the decade came in the second-tier publication, *Marvel Premiere*, which ironically attempted to tie together the loose strings of the "Panther v. the Klan" arc Don McGregor had begun years earlier in *Jungle Action* before it was canceled (although with an ending, "other than the one McGregor had in mind.")[117]

The handling of the Black Panther spoke to Marvel's struggles to choose an appropriate contextual setting for the competing visions of race as subject matter held by whites on staff. In the end, it was determined that race only complicated superhero storytelling. A black presence was desirable in comics, but race as blackness, was unnecessary.

As mentioned above, a year prior to coming to *Black Panther*, Jack Kirby took over *Captain American and the Falcon*, promising to return the book to its glory, though, in the end, he met only the same disapproval as he had for his handling of the T'Challa narratives. However, the "Kirby Kontroversy" in *Captain American and the Falcon* unfolded to reveal a somewhat unexpected wrinkle. Not only were readers not interested in Jack Kirby's 1960s-style Captain America, but they seemingly had also tired of the Falcon as well. This latest return to the book saw Kirby give more of an edge to the Falcon's character, making him more pronounced, and a less contented sidekick (at the same time, his strong and independent companion, Leila, became domesticated, doting, and fragile). Readers disapproved. "I buy Captain America regularly to see the red-white-and-blue Avenger," complained one, "and lately I have seen too much of the Falcon."[118] Calls for Kirby's ouster, and Falcon's, grew with each issue. "[Captain America and Falcon] have outlasted their partnership," one reader declared, "he cramps Cap's style."[119] Another encouraging the split assured Marvel, "I seriously doubt that Falcon's absence is going to cut sales one iota."[120]

At first, the editors replied only coyly to the suggestion that Falcon be ousted from the *Captain America* publication that "until an over-whelming [*sic*]majority decide that they want us to deep-six Falc [he'll stay]." Though within a few months, they finally admitted "that's a story possibility."[121] Kirby would ultimately resign from the project, but in the meantime the Falcon and the ghetto came to occupy only the smallest of spaces in his vision of the book. Even with such forewarning, however, the end of *Captain America and the Falcon* as a title and team came suddenly and unceremoniously. Though Falcon had appeared in nearly every issue since 1969, the Falcon simply ceased to be included in the story lines.[122] In fact, with issue no. 223 (July 1978) the title of the magazine reverted back to simply, *Captain America*; Falcon would only appear in three issues of the comic through the remainder of the decade.[123] Similar to the contemporaneous handling of the Black Panther character, the Falcon's role in the broader Marvel universe shifted dramatically during the closing years of the 1970s. Without subtexts of race(ism), Marvel creators did not seem to have an idea of how or why to use him.

Soon after the undeclared dissolution of his partnership with Captain America, the Falcon was asked to join the Avengers to meet a racial quota. The "black" Avenger to that point, T'Challa, had resigned. The team functioned under sanction of the US government, and had to comply with federal employment law. He agreed as a personal favor to Captain America. As it took nine months or more for the average comic book project to move from the writers' desk through all of the other publication processes and onto the newsstands, this story line, which first appeared in March 1979, clearly reverberated the US Supreme Court's ruling in *Bakke* from fall 1978.[124] All of Falcon's new colleagues expressed openly that they felt Falcon was forced upon them, and that they feared he was not qualified for the responsibilities of being an Avenger. Iron Man even suggested that the

Avengers did not need a black team member as they were already in compliance with minority hiring dictates: "just what do you think androids are?" More than anything else, however, the white Avengers regretted out loud that a good white man that they knew—the superhero Hawkeye—would be denied a job so that the "under-qualified" black man could have it, superhero or not. Marvel readers' responses to the quota story line were equally impassioned, if only more divided. Some appreciated the approach to an important contemporary matter (suggesting that a market in social justice advocacy still existed): "this was one of the most perfect stories to date"; "I'm glad the Falcon is joining"; and "after reading [the quota issue], I subscribed!" Others disapproved, though mainly to the fact that the pro-affirmative action contingent appeared to have won: "I find the story to be totally and completely ridiculous"; "[this] was the first comic to sicken me"; and simply, "You stink."[125]

Soon after in the narrative, however, the government granted the Avengers an expanded autonomy, in part freeing them from affirmative action compliance (in a poor choice of words, one of the Avengers likened this development to being "emancipated"). Socially isolated, and haunted by his teammates low expectations of him, at this first opportunity Falcon resigns. Explaining his decision to leave, Falcon addressed his teammates, who claimed to be unaware that anything was the matter (they certainly at least felt no complicity). "Maybe [my resignation will] ease some of the tension I seem to have brought in with me." Leaving his supposed friend to bear the burden alone, Captain America shrinks from the moment: "I don't think anyone really noticed, Falcon. But if you've made your decision, we'll honor it." Falcon turns, takes to the sky. When next he was seen, he was swooping down 125th Street, back in the ghetto, back in his place. [126]

Storm as Mutant, Cage as Race

As cultural artifacts of the late 1970s, Marvel comics reflected much about the progress of racial integration in America, which had fallen dramatically from the trajectories of only a decade prior. By 1979, in fact, as Marvel editor-in-chief Jim Shooter proclaimed "our best [sales] year ever," the Black Panther had left the Avengers, and his own title had ceased publication. Similarly, the Falcon was no longer appearing with any regularity in *Captain America*, and would soon be written completely out of *Avengers*. Indeed, it was difficult to find many black superheroes in Marvel Comics. Only two black characters in the entire Marvel universe were being featured in any ongoing publication in the entire line of more than two-dozen titles. But these two black characters, Luke Cage and Storm, represented a break from 1970s more so than a continuation.

Since the introduction of black superheroes into the Marvel universe, they had been consistently contextualized by black spaces, particularly the ghetto. Indeed, within that time, generally from 1968 through 1978, the ghetto served as the aesthetic context and discursive structure through which black heroes and blackness were presented to readership. Blacks of the Marvel universe were drawn to the ghetto. This was what gave them their worldview; this was the location of their self-acknowledged people and their community. Beginning with the Black Panther, who sought to make his affiliation with the Avengers most relevant by serving Harlem—"I must do more!"—this was why they did what they did. Other characters followed T'Challa's form. From the period he was first "discovered" on a tropical island by Captain America and returned to America, for example, the Falcon's entire identity sprang from his desire, his need, to be grounded in the ghetto, and to be of relevance to that community. Simultaneously, however, Falcon also worked to model for that community, the successful strategies for existing beyond the limitations that unjustly restrained that community— strategies for achieving the opportunities of a racially integrated existence. Later, still, by 1972 as the group War sung "The World is a Ghetto," the character Luke Cage found opportunities amid the expansive need, opening his hero for hire office on blight-stricken 42nd Street in Midtown Manhattan. But while Harlem still served as a locus for much Cage's action, his comics represented something of a departure from the tradition rendering of the ghetto, inasmuch as they brought an interracial cast of characters uptown.

Within the context of Marvel's ghetto paradigm, racism functioned as the primary social justice issue for black superheroes, and race (meaning blackness) was the chief and recurrent reference point for their relations with, and engagement of, the world around them—other superheroes, supervillains, the civilian population. Whatever, wherever, and however they existed, they were first and always black. For Black Panther, this comes through most deliberately in his Africanness, as the King of Wakanda, his insistence on nonaligned strategies for dealing with the Cold War world, and a sense of himself not so much as a pan-Africanist, but through an awareness of himself as a man of color in a society were that characteristic had implications. For the Falcon, the ever-present negotiation of racism was the central theme. He constantly attempted to self-identify and project an image of himself as something other than the pejorative sidekick. He was also as often found promoting centrist solutions to social problems—speaking mainly to unreceptive ears. Similarly, the Luke Cage character seemed burdened by a most problematic blackness—a blaxploited blackness—confident, cocksure, and hypermasculine. Cage was neither an educated, born leader like T'Challa, nor a big-hearted idealist like Sam Wilson. Yet, his pragmatic, entrepreneurial approach to problem-solving (he needed money; Harlem needed a hero) was nonetheless rife with race as context because it reflected situations overwhelmingly faced by the black poor and dispossessed of the 1970s. Yet, in the process, Cage heard a higher calling, and came to be in-step with the broader narrative trend prevalent during the years of Marvel's ghetto paradigm, which saw black superheroes (and minor characters) function as the bearers and ambassadors to the ghetto as they used race to find footings in the community.

Drawing from subplots present throughout the period, however, after 1978, a number of social justice agendas emerged more fully in the narrative discourse of Marvel's superhero comics, challenging antiracism for hegemony. So, while a basic bent toward social justice issues remained, advocacy for a broader anti-discrimination replaced the more specific antiracism. As the age of diversity dawned in the real world, allegories of social inclusion, for example, saw the fictional society wrestle with the meaning and implication surrounding who was and who was not human, with "mutants" emerging as the new most-wretched of the earth. Corresponding to this, in turn, the narratives shifted away from racial ghetto as locus and scene, marking the end of an era in Marvel comics. As such, a single character in the Marvel universe of the 1970s, Storm in *X-Men*, can be seen as accommodative of this shift from the specific antiracism to the broader anti-discrimination.

Marvel introduced Storm in 1975, as the fourth and most powerful black superhero of the era. Like Storm, all the X-Men were mutants, and by consequence, "feared and hated by the world they have sworn to protect." Mutants drew their super powers from their genetics; they were born different than other humans. Many mutants had no unique physical traits, and looked otherwise normal, "passing" for human. More than any other setting, the focus of the post-ghetto social justice discourse in Marvel story lines found their allegorical placement most comfortably and consistently with the plight of mutants. And, as evidenced by the wild success of *the X-Men* (which dominated comic sales for three decades beginning in the 1980s) it could be argued that the superhero comic audience had not so much tired of talking about social justice, as they had tired of talking about race, specifically. They were clearly tired talking about the ghetto, and Storm facilitated the transition.

Storm wielded the power to manipulate weather in her immediate vicinity. At a whim, she commanded forth and completely controlled anything from blizzards, to heat waves, to hurricanes, to lighting, to gale-force winds. Upon her debut, Storm was one of seven new characters introduced during summer 1975 in an effort to reboot *X-Men*, new issues of which had been canceled for slow sales five years earlier. As the new character was under development in the early 1970s, its primary creator, Marvel artist Dave Cockrum, had originally conceptualized a black female to be called Black Cat: with "a cat-like haircut with tufts for ears … she wore a collar with a bell on it." Development of the X-Men revamp, however, hit a lull of at least several months. "When we came back to the project," Cockrum remembered, "all of a sudden all of these other female cat characters had sprung up … so I figured that we'd better overhaul this one!"[127] Critical for Storm's impact as the first major black woman character in Marvel's history (whether the creators realized it or not at the time), her visuality projected the first signs of her ultimate de-racing. Writer Chris Claremont, who worked on the *X-Men* with Cockrum and others, suggested that the artist's first direct movements toward Storm after the Black Cat concept were much more in the line of other black women characters at that time: "an Afro [of] black hair."[128] Cockrum, however, took the character in another direction, as Storm ultimately received long, flowing white hair, and blue cat-like eyes. "I think he was trying to create someone," wrote Claremont later suggested, "whose features were not classically black or classically white." Despite these attempts at exotica, some at the time received Storm as little more than, "a white woman dipped in brown paint." [129]

Biographically, Storm came to the X-Men most directly from Kenya, and she was the only woman among the new team, which also included foreign nationals from Russia, Canada, Ireland, Japan, and Germany, respectively, and an American Apache (Marvel's parent company, Cadence, had an interest in the overseas market for comments, and an international team held some attraction).[130] In her origin narrative, Storm was born Ororo Munroe in Harlem to American David Munroe and his Kenyan bride, N'Dare. A photojournalist, David relocated the family to Cairo, Egypt, for work in the early 1950s. A few years later, in an instant of tragedy, the Munroes' apartment complex was destroyed in the ravages of Suez War (1956). Young Ororo found herself trapped in the rubble, and suddenly orphaned. Eventually able to free herself, she spent her childhood homeless on the streets of Cairo as an urchin and pickpocket. When her mutant abilities manifested during puberty, Storm journeyed southward to rural Kenya, and spent several years there as a near-goddess to the local people who were grateful that she protected their crops from drought. Recruiting new members, the X-Men discovered her there and convinced the young woman to come to America where she learned to master her powers and serve humankind as a superhero. [131]

Through the first five years of these new X-Men (1975–1979), Storm received much authorial attention for, as one critic accurately pointed out, she was writer Chris Claremont's showpiece among the new characters. And yet, many were put off-balance as Claremont de-raced Storm, generally presented her as a woman (a gender) rather than as black (a race), or even as African (a surrogate of ethnicity). Initially, however, despite Claremont's efforts Storm's race/ethnicity was nonetheless primary with many readers and critics. "Since she has been a 'noble savage' for many years," one critic wrote, finding Storm too at ease with civilization, "she *must* be experiencing *some* sort of culture shock." Saying much about presumptions of modern Africa circa 1975, Storm was too civilized for some: "She expressed no fear or confusion at the many examples of our technological society which she has encountered, including [a] space station, various computer banks, Sentinels (robots), and mandriods (androids)." Supposedly, white characters were more believably at ease with such things. [132]

Obvious from her beginnings, Marvel's Storm set upon a path different than other, older, black superheroes. Indeed, she seemed not to have been intended as a black superhero at all. Marvel creators made no attempt to situate Storm as a black woman—other than her brown-faced appearance, and her African lineage—or even as the black member of the team (in the way, for example, contemporaneous issues of Avengers used race to contextualize Black Panther, and then Falcon). In X-Men of the late 1970s, Storm's race was literally muted. If the character had any identity beyond mutant (and perhaps woman), it was immigrant. But even there she was not set apart, as the entire team was from elsewhere. Yet, Storm had very real, very raced groundings that her teammates lacked. Slowly, the Marvel creators began to reveal these as the decade drew to a close.

In the June 1979 issue of X-Men (no. 122), against the reddened evening sky, the recently repatriated Harlem native, Ororo Munroe, moved with curious trepidation along 112th Street. With long and flowing snow-colored hair, and a full-length coat of matching color, the statuesque brown-skinned beauty cast a vision literally armored by whiteness. She searched the streets of her father's memories and walked the community she had been born into but had never even remotely known. "In my father's tales, this was a magical place," she thinks to herself, "wicked yet joyous, poor, rough-edged but alive...He was happy to leave it, yet sad also." As she moved along past the filth and the degeneration of Harlem she found it in the late 1970s, she conceded that her father's memories were of community, "long ago...the magic seems almost gone now, if it was ever truly here."[133] Ororo has come home to Harlem simply to say goodbye.

Arriving at the very building where she and her parents once lived, she found it run-down. Entering the old apartment of her parents' love and hopes from so many years before, she found only a shooting gallery (a den of heroin addicts). "Why am I here?" she asked herself. "Then, she consciously made a choice: Yes I was born here...part of my heritage is here, but is it a part I want?" Meanwhile, the racially diverse current occupants almost succeeded in accosting her. Attacked before she could respond, Storm was saved suddenly by Luke Cage and Misty Knight, who burst-in to the apartment in the nick of time. As they later revealed, the two black heroes had just been "cruising the neighborhood," when they heard "street talk about a tall, regal, white-haired sister makin' the rounds." They knew it had to be Storm, and figured she was out of place and probably in trouble. Grateful, Storm left Harlem that night, satisfied that she was leaving nothing behind. She would not be back. [134]

Returning to her native place after twenty years, and finding it foreign—coming home but feeling estranged—served Storm as a break with blackness. Functioning as the bridge between Marvel's ghetto and post-ghetto eras (black community and other black folks as context, however, disappeared), Storm was the new sort of character: one who was phenotypically black, but whose race was silenced. Likewise, the discourse of Storm's search for meaning can easily be read as the collective voice of the Marvel creators saying goodbye to the black space, goodbye to the ghetto as the dominant and enduring context for black super-heroes. The metamorphosis of the Marvel universe away from race and black-ness after 1980 through the development of the Storm character and other tactics symbolized that the black superhero was being disconnected from ghetto. The black hero was, in fact, being made exceptional. As for the ghetto, the community does not migrate toward the mainstream, nor integrate with the mainstream, only the black superhero does. By the issues of late 1980s, for example, Storm became the poster child for an all-encompassing, though quite ahistorical diver-sity in the Marvel universe, one that transcended racial classification (by sup-posedly embracing them all). "Fans of the character watched while the features [Storm]...did have in common with many young black and brown girls—brown skin, full lips, almond-shaped eyes," one critic has observed, "slowly faded from view as many colorists selected light tan hues and artists preferred sharp angu-lar features to depict Storm." And though nothing in her narrative biography ever suggested that she was anything but a descendant of Africa, one 1989 story line would have her as "not Negroid or Caucasian or Oriental—yet somehow, an amalgam of the rarest elements of them all." Ultimately through assimilation, appropriation, and silence, the integration process was declared complete, if only not universally successful. Those still outside when the gates to the Marvel uni-verse closed, it was supposed, wished to remain there.[135]

Outside, however race did remain, and interracialism functioned as its inter-pretive framework. But interracialism, a discourse acknowledging race/heritage as relevant and advocating for the type of social activity that transcended the challenges raced existences often met, was set apart in the mainstream narrative of the Marvel universe. By the end of the 1970s, race became niche, and that niche was confined to a single Marvel publication: *Power Man and Iron Fist*. Similar to the coded dictates of racial integration in the professional and social settings of contemporaneous real-world life in America at the time, black characters brought into the Marvel universe for many years after 1980 entered that world defined as some category other than race (gender, class, nationality, etc.).[136] Unless, that is, they were within the narratives sphere of *Power Man and Iron Fist*.[137] Cage's world was black-dominated integration at its purest. This was the black power space, so much so that it existed without need for doctrinal expression. *Power Man and Iron Fist* attempted affirmation of the integration era: it had apparently worked here. White characters like Daniel Rand/Iron Fist folded effortlessly into place, and without racial comment. Furthermore, in his relationship with Cage, Rand accepted that Power Man was primary, as it seemed natural, almost. Thus, the fact that *Power Man and Iron Fist* was the only comic even aware of race made it almost by default the "race" book in Marvel's lineup.

The heroes took up none of the day's great social justice issues involving race–at least no more so than ever before. And yet, finding themselves increasingly on the outside along with *Power Man and Iron Fist* stories, readers suspected they were being taken for granted, or at least misread as to their tastes: "Many of your characterizations [in *Power Man and Iron Fist*] have left much to be desired," one reader's letter to the editor's opened, "[and] at times, your characters lack dig-nity and intelligence…Luke Cage is sometimes insulting." Villains were often no more than flamboyant street thugs and crime lords. Received by many readers as "distasteful and vulgar," the villains lacked sophistication bordered on mock-ery of the readers familiar with storylines of Marvel's other titles.[138] Luke Cage battled such eccentric foes as "Cockroach" Hamilton, Mr. Fish, Piranha Jones, Wildfire, Spear, Mangler, and Cheshire Cat. None of them had appeared in any other publication, nor had they battled any other superhero. In truth, Cage was pit against such crass adversaries because Marvel creators could not image a nar-rative that would see respectable baddies like Dr. Doom, or Magneto, or even the super crime lord King Pin brought down by a black hero (or at least in a black context).[139] At a point, this reality caused some readers to bristle: "[C]an you see Spider-Man or Captain America fighting rejects like [these]?" Ultimately, read-ers chastised Marvel to, "take your black characters more seriously," but, Marvel would not.[140]

Coda: The Ballad of Clark Washington

"Those who say that we are in a time when there are no heroes," President Ronald Reagan said at his 1981 inauguration, "just don't know where to look."[141] While Reagan, spoke of the everyday heroes in American life, those looking for black superheroes in comic books would be hard-pressed to find many. Back in 1966, like most Americans, the creators at Marvel could not help but draw inspiration from the social justice activism of the 1960s, and the new visibility blacks had attained in white America's eyes. Marvel creators responded to the moment with impetus for developing comics' first black superhero. As Jack Kirby, the legendary artist, would later recall, "I came up with the Black Panther because I realized...I needed a black." Though Kirby had had black friends in his social circle, they were not at that point widely represented in his profession, or in their medium: "nobody was doing blacks...[but] I had a lot of black readers."[142] From their view in 1966 looking forward, therefore, the white men and the white male audience they reached believed themselves in some ways embracing the historical moment, and moving forward in support as they knew how: advocating integration through the speech bubbles of dialogue that filled their comics.

This study has attempted to hold those efforts against the light of their times, and to recover the broader narratives and to understand how real decisions and considerations regarding integration might have been reflected (and refracted) in the amazing, fantastic, and uncanny feats of Marvel's superhero comics. In the end, well-meaning though they were, while attempting to present authentic (and thus marketable) black voices, Marvel proceeded clumsily and with diminishing returns throughout the period. By that time, after nearly twenty years of the Marvel universe, with nearly 450 total new characters developed, no more twenty had been black, and of those, a mere half-dozen were of any resonance (Black Panther, Falcon, Luke Cage, Storm, Misty Knight, and perhaps Bill Foster/Black Goliath). Such mishandling and lack of appreciation for a potential audience largely resulted from too few black voices on the creative staff at Marvel—"the Bullpen," as visionary Stan Lee dubbed them by the mid-1960s.[143]

For most of the 1970s, as it promoted and advocated for social justice and economic opportunity, Marvel did not possess the capacity, it seems, to practice what it preached. While never a large operation by any measure (perhaps no more than a few dozen staff writers and artists, plus freelancers, at any one time), black creators were rare at Marvel—their ability the shape projects even rarer. Like many small-shop workspaces in the 1970s, Marvel moved slowly toward bringing more racial minorities and women into its fold. The first African American to work as part of Marvel's creative team, artist Billy Graham, joined the publisher around 1972, apparently in preparation for the launch of *Luke Cage, Hero for Hire*, Marvel's first title with a black lead character. While Graham played several creative roles at Marvel (writer, penciller, inker, cover artist) in nearly all of the early 1970s issues of *Luke Cage, Hero for Hire/Luke Cage, Power Man*, ultimate creative direction and decision-making rested elsewhere, as the "white creators conceived and wrote the series" (of the two issues which he received a writer credit, each is as a co-writer).[144] Graham left the Cage books for a time join writer Don McGregor on the revamped *Jungle Action*, which had become the vehicle for the Black Panther character. Graham penciled every issue of *Jungle Action* from July 1974 through July 1976, and as such the critically acclaimed (but commercially disappointing) publication is the best representation of his work during that time. He would continue to work on several projects for Marvel into the 1980s, including episodic returns to Luke Cage books. [145]

Shortly after Graham joined Marvel, artist Ron Wilson began working there. Having grown up in New York as a fan of many of the veteran creators, "I felt that as an artist—from a kid—I wanted to work for Marvel," he later admitted. Wilson got his start as a contributing penciller on vast number of projects in the 1970s, including several issues of *Luke Cage, Power Man*. [146] Wilson would be best known during the decade, however, as a cover artist, working at times on a number of Marvel publications.[147] Similarly, artist Arvell Jones began contributing to an eclectic mix of Marvel books. Though he did not work on many projects featuring black heroes, he did pencil several issues for some of Marvel's marquee comics, such as *Thor* and *Iron Man*. By the end of the 1970s he was creating for DC Comics too. Jones found Marvel an "interesting place." He recalled, "They didn't know quite how to relate to us [black creators]." "Racism was there," he contends, but of the variety familiar to those moving into newly integrating spaces at the time. "I spent a lot of time getting to know people…in some cases we had nothing in common but our love of the industry." Interpersonally he found most of his white colleagues to be collegial and supportive. Creatively, however—particularly as it related to interpretations of black life, differences remained. "People were trying to be very open minded, but they only could draw on what they knew." "The climate became a little more political once I got some assignments," Jones recalled, adding that, "I found myself in very frank discussions about stereotypes in how blacks were shown in comics."[148] A fourth creator, the artist and writer Keith Pollard, also began working with Marvel in the mid-1970s, but like Graham, the few writer credits he received in the decade were for co-writer roles (with as many as two other co-writers on any single issue). Pollard delivered a number of penciller credits for several issues of some of Marvel's flagship titles in the late 1970s, including *Amazing Spider-Man*, *Fantastic Four*, *Iron Man*, and *Thor*.[149]

Though the Marvel system gave considerable creative input to artists in shaping plot-lines, and to a lesser degree, characterization, that so few opportunities existed for black artists to pencil issues alone stunted the impact of this system. This fact made the decade's dearth in black writers at Marvel all the more impactful. The stories about black characters (as well as black interpretive views on stories about nonblack characters) had only limited input from black creators. This appropriation of black voices thus could only hope to approximate authentic black historical experiences, rather than draw from them. As the decade closed, however, legitimate questions arose about the necessity to speak with an authentic black voice, even to a black audience. Shifts in the distribution model for comics promised, for a time at least, to halt if not shrink, the black audience for superhero comics. Economics and demographics combined to make it hard for black consumers to even find comics after 1979.

"The Marvel Comics Group wishes to interview candidates for a sales manager specializing in the Collector market," a 1979 ad in *Comics Journal*, a trade publication, announced. "Interested applicants must be thoroughly familiar with existing collector shop sales and operations…[and] should possess ability to structure, instruct and assist in the opening and operation of new shops."[150] By the end of the 1970s, economic shifts in the retailing of comic books reflected both their failure to successfully broaden their audience, and the impact of the demographic relocation of the audience they actually had. In the end, Marvel convinced itself that it did not have a large enough black audience, and white boys proved unwilling to buy what so-called "black books" there were. As economics tightened, Marvel offered still fewer black characters, assuming that the black audience it did have would continue its penchant for buying superhero comics, whether black characters were in them, or not.

Relatedly, the shifts in how comics were sold, or rather where they could be bought, spoke to the shifting terrain of racial integration. Traditionally, comic publishers like Marvel had worked with distribution companies similar to those that circulated magazines and newspapers to have comic books carried on newsstands and in mom and pop convenience stores across the nation (in the iconic "spinner" carrels). These locally oriented, often locally owned businesses, however, gave way to chain retailers by the late 1970s, and competition for limited retail space for magazines and periodicals saw comics squeezed. Indeed, retailers gave comics progressively less space in their shops because of their low profit margins. Each month, in fact, unsold comics were collected from the retailer and returned to the publisher for refunds. With less space available, as the 1970s wore on, only a fraction of the titles available from Marvel (and DC for that matter) were ever carried in any one store. Retailers would pick and choose which titles they wanted to offer; many black titles did not sell simply because they were not offered for sale at the retail level.

By the end of the 1970s, however, a system had been devised that proved the savior for Marvel, but sounded the death knell for its ability to reach inner city black audiences. Rather than sell to distributors who placed comics on newsstands and in convenience stores for low profit margins, Marvel began working with distributors who sold new comics to the specialty comic book shops. Buying from the publisher directly, these shops did not return unsold copies, improving Marvel's profits. By promoting and supporting the development of the so-called direct market through specialty shops, publishers like Marvel actually thought they might grow their audience after more than a decade of reduction. Rapidly in a matter of but a few years, in fact, from the late 1970s to the early 1980s, comic books disappeared from newsstands and convenience stores almost entirely. If comic book aficionados wanted to buy books, they had to go to the local shop. The strange racial calculus that considered the impacts of school busing, white flight, and commerce in the shifting demographics of the late 1970s, however, found comic book shops mainly located in emergent suburbs, away from inner cities, away from black communities.

For several years, until that is, blacks began to experience increased instances of suburbanization themselves, most did not even have access to comics, save for publishers' subscription services. Indeed, until well into the decade (more likely, the following decade of the 1990s), blacks would be hard pressed to find comics even if they sought them. The days of African American kids and teens (like any other kids and teens) unexpectedly discovering comics by being drawn to its colorful, action-filled covers were past. The narrowing audience further dictated the de-racing nature of comics. The purposeful and missionary racial integration of the comic's universe from the early 1970s continued to be replaced by a happenstance diversity, which reflected mainstream sensibilities of Reagan's America in the 1980s.[151] The absence of discourses on the relationships between race and power accompanied depictions of a diverse America, represented by mere sprinklings of "others" amid a preponderance of white people, whose social, political, economic, and culture prerogatives were presented as normative. Through these measures, at least in superhero comics of the 1980s, it seemed consensus had returned.

The Racial Interlude Ends

"Faster than a bowl of chitlins. Able to leap a slum with a single bound. 'Look! Up in the sky! It's a crow. It's a bat. No, it's Supernigger!" With that, legendary American comedian, Richard Pryor, parodied the opening sequence for the *Adventures of Superman,* a television program from the 1950s with which many young Americans of his generation were very familiar. As his skit continued: "Yes, friends, it's Supernigger! With x-ray vision that enables him to see through everything, except whitey!" First performed as early as 1971, this politically charged lampoon was most famously released on his comedy album *Supernigger* in 1983.[152] That it was still funny more than a decade later—that the notion of a black superhero was still laughable to black audiences—spoke volumes to the failure of Marvel and other publishers to help Americans imagine something more for themselves. Spider-Man, Iron Man, Fantastic Four, Incredible Hulk, Avengers, to name but a few Marvel characters, all became American icons in the same relative time period as the publishers' troubled attempts to present even a single black character to similar result.

And despite such troubles, black readers and fans of Marvel had developed something of a historical relationship with black characters during the 1970s. As one reader of color recalled about his point of identification with Luke Cage, "[some] may not have felt as nostalgic as I did," when reading *Power Man,* "but you may not have grown up on the same movies, TV shows, and paperbacks that I did."[153] Similarly, another wrote of his appreciation for the character's narrative groundings—"he was a product of the streets, [and]...a character in step with the 1970s." Based on a historical relationship—"I've been with Luke Cage since the beginning"—this reader, too, identified Cage. "I care about him," he told Marvel editors, "to me he *is* real."[154] Appropriated, approximated, commodified, or not, black characters formed a grounding in the national culture for blacks during the integration era. Marvel's retreat from black characters and its retreat from race, followed form with the nation's broader experience with implementing racial integration after 1966. Too often, the national will fell short of meeting its lofty goals.

Finally, the release of Pryor's comedy album *Supernigger* in 1983, with previously performed material, featured its namesake skit. As the routine concluded, Pryor introduced his hero's alter-ego, Clark Washington, a "mild-mannered custodian for the *Daily Planet*." The absurdist hilarity of the skit rests with the familiarity black audiences had with the superhero motif, and their lamenting reflection upon the failure of integration in the 1970s to meet its desired ends. That is, his sobering punch lines were still tragically funny at the dawn of the age of Reagan, and perhaps seemed even more absurd—more laughable—since by then most Americans understood that the racial integration experiment would finally end.

Notes

1. Stan Lee (w), Jack Kirby (p), "The Black Panther," *Fantastic Four* v. 1, n. 52 (Marvel Comics, July 1966).
2. Rob Steibel, "The Panther: Kirby Biography Excerpt by Stan Taylor," *Kirby Dynamics* (blog), August 19, 2011, accessed Octber 19, 2011, http://kirbymuseum.org/blogs/dynamics/?s=Black+Panther.
3. Jack Kirby (w,p), "Panther Postscripts" *Black Panther* v.1, n. 1 (Marvel Comics, January 1977).
4. Eds. to Henry B. Clay, III in "Klaw, the Murderous Master of Sound!," Fantastic Four v.1, n. 56 (Marvel Comics, November 1966).
5. Henry B. Clay III to eds. in "Klaw, the Murderous Master of Sound!," *Fantastic Four* v.1, n. 56 (Marvel Comics, November 1966).
6. Matthew J. Pustz, *Comic Book Culture: Fanboys and True Believers* (Jackson: University Press of Mississippi, 1999), xi.
7. Heil to eds., Roy Thomas (w), Don Heck (p), "The Light That Failed," *Avengers*, v. 1, n. 35 (Marvel Comics, December 1966); Mortimer to eds., Roy Thomas (w), Don Heck (p), "The Light That Failed," *Avengers*, v. 1, n. 35 (Marvel Comics, December 1966).
8. Matthew J. Pustz, *Comic Book Culture: Fanboys and True Believers* (Jackson: University Press of Mississippi, 1999), 56; Bradford W. Wright, *Comic Book Nation: The Transformation of Youth Culture in America* (John Hopkins University Press 2001), 230–43.
9. Stan Lee, "Stan's Soapbox," Captain America, v. 1, n. 108 (Marvel Comics, December 1968); Peter Sanderson and Matthew K. Manning, *Marvel Chronicle: A Year by Year History,* with a foreword by Stan Lee and afterword by Joe Quesada (New York: DK Publishing, 2008),128.
10. *Car Wash* (1976); and "Human Fly," *Comicbookdb.com: The Comic Book Database,* http://www.comicbookdb.com/character.php?ID=5092.
11. Wright, xvi; Matthew J. Costello, *Secret Identity Crisis: Comic Books and the Unmasking of Cold War America* (New York: Continuum Press, 2009).
12. Costello, 91.
13. Stan Lee (w), John Romita, Sr. (p), "Crisis On Campus," *Amazing Spider-Man*, v. 1, n. 68 (Marvel Comics, January 1969); Stan Lee (w), Gene Colan (p), "Crack-Up on Campus!" *Captain America*, v. 1, n. 120 (Marvel Comics, December 1969).
14. Jacobs to eds., *Luke Cage, Power Man*, v. 1, n. 42 (Marvel Comics, April 1977).
15. As quoted in Terry Eastland, "Redefining Civil Rights," *Wilson Quarterly* 8, no. 2 (Spring, 1984), 70; Terry Anderson, *The Pursuit of Fairness: A History of Affirmative Action* (New York: Oxford University Press, 2004), 65.

16. Eastland, 83.
17. Ibid., 70; Jennifer Delton, *Racial Integration in Corporate America, 1940–1990* (Cambridge: Cambridge Press, 2009), 36–43.
18. Anderson, 91–92.
19. Delton, 225 – 28; Anderson, 98.
20. Anderson, 90.
21. Delton, 38.
22. Ibid., 225–26.
23. As quoted in Anderson,119.
24. Ibid.,140–41.
25. Ibid.,159.
26. Ibid.,147.
27. Ibid.,160.
28. The case was even more positive for white women… [as] they quickly advanced into technical and skilled positions. See Eastland, 70–71; Anderson,159.
29. Delton, 227.
30. Stan Lee and Jack Kirby (w), John Severin and Kirby (p), "The Prize Is…Earth!" *Strange Tales*, v. 1, n. 137 (Marvel Comics, October 1965).
31. Stan Lee (w), Don Heck (p), "The Sign of the Serpent!" *Avengers* v. 1, n. 32 (Marvel Comics, September 1966)
32. Ibid.
33. Stan Lee (w), John Romita, Sr. (p), "In the Clutches of the Kingpin!" *Amazing Spider-Man*, v. 1, n. 51 (Marvel Comics, August 1967); Stan Lee (w), John Romita, Sr. (p), "To Die a Hero!" *Amazing Spider-Man* v. 1, n. 52 (Marvel Comics, September 1967).
34. Interestingly, as the character was being developed, early iterations had him as a former boxer—with a cauliflower ear, no less—what then emerged had to been seen as a conscious effort to move beyond stereotypes of blacks as athletes. See Sanderson and Manning, 123. Also, in 1969, for the mildly successful *Silver Surfer* title, Marvel creators introduced a black civilian scientist, Al Harper, who helps save the day, but only by sacrificing his own life heroically. See Stan Lee (w), John Buscema (p), "…And Who Shall Mourn For Him?" *Silver Surfer*, v. 1, n. 5 (Marvel Comics, April 1969).
35. Delton, 5, 12.
36. Stan Lee (w), Jack Kirby (p), "And So it Begins," *Tales of Suspense*, v. 1, n. 97 (Marvel Comics, January 1968); Lee (w), Kirby (p), "The Claws of the Panther!" *Tales of Suspense*, v. 1, n. 98 (Marvel Comics, February 1968); Lee (w), Kirby (p), "The Man Who Lived Twice," *Tales of Suspense*, v. 1, n. 99 (Marvel Comics, March 1968); and Roy Thomas (w), John Buscema (p), "In the Clutches of…the Collector!" *Avengers*, v. 1, n. 51 (Marvel Comics, April 1968).
37. Thomas (w), Buscema (p), "Death Calls for the Arch-Heroes!"; Delton, 6.
38. Roger Slifer, "Len Wein" *Comics Journal* 78 (August 1979): 73-74; "Len Wein—*Teen Titans* (1966)—Writer," *Comicbookdb.com: The Comic Book Database*, http://www .comicbookdb.com/creator_title.php?ID=2232&cID=322&pID=1; and Neal Adams, Dick Giordano (w), Neal Adams, Sal Amendola (p), "Titans Fit the Battle of Jericho!" *Teen Titans*, v. 1, n.20 (DC Comics, April 1969).
39. Roy Thomas (w), John Buscema (p), "Death Calls for the Arch-Heroes," *Avengers*, v. 1, n. 52 (Marvel Comics, May 1968).
40. Roy Thomas (w), John Buscema (p), "In Battle Joined!," *Avengers*, v. 1, n. 53 (Marvel Comics, June 1968)
41. Delton, 27.

42. Fletcher to eds., "Avengers Assemble," *Avengers, v.*1, n. 59 (Marvel Comics, December 1968). See Hopkins to eds., and Lawhead to eds., "Avengers Assemble," *Avengers, v.*1, n. 57 (Marvel Comics, August 1968); Kowalski to eds., "Avengers Assemble," *Avengers, v.* 1, n. 56 (Marvel Comics, September 1968).

43. Wright, 244.

44. Gorman to eds., "Let's Rap with Cap," *Captain America and the Falcon*, v. 1, n. 137 (Marvel Comics, May 1971); Eds. to Gorman, "Let's Rap with Cap," *Captain America and the Falcon*, v. 1, n. 137 (Marvel Comics, May 1971).

45. A first for black superheroes, it debuted and that title in 1972, but later evolved to *Luke Cage, Power Man* (issue nos. 17 – 49), and later still *Power Man and Iron Fist* (issue nos. 50–125).

46. Denny O'Neil (w), Neal Adams (p), "No Evil Shall Escape My Sight!" *Green Lantern*, v. 2, n. 76 (DC Comics: April 1970); Steve Englehart (w), George Tuska (p), "Don't Mess with Black Mariah," *Luke Cage, Hero for Hire*, v. 1, n. 5 (Marvel Comics, January 1973).

47. Some villains were little more than accomplished street thugs, heads of organized crime (chiefly Harlem-based), with no true superpower—as was the case with Stoneface, Boss Morgan, and Black Mariah. Others had only campy special powers, like the knife-throwing crime lord Diamondback, or Cottonmouth, the drug king-pin, who could unhinge his jaw to wield razor sharp teeth. Respective first appearances: *Captain America #134 (February 1971); Captain America #152 (1972); Luke Cage, Hero for Hire #5 (1973); Luke Cage, Hero for Hire #1 (June 1972); and Luke Cage, Power Man #19* (June 1974).

48. For example, Noah Black, a renowned geneticist (and African American) becomes the villain, Centurius, and battles super spy, Nick Fury, in 1968. At about the same time Hobie Brown began his abortive criminal career, another man—one with absolutely no misgivings about the path he had chosen—plotted against the Black Panther. As such, M'Baku, the traitorous genius from the Panther's home nation, Wakanda, transformed by the mystical power of the Great White Gorilla into the Man-Ape, takes on his king, T'Challa, the Black Panther, and his new teammates, the Avengers, in March 1969—just a few months after T'Challa joined the team. Jim Steranko (w,p), "So Shall Ye Reap…Death!" *Nick Fury: Agent of Shield*, v. 1, n. 2 (Marvel Comics, July 1968); Stan Lee (w), John Buscema (p), "The Night of The Prowler!" *Amazing Spider-Man* v. 1, n 78 (November 1969); Stan Lee (w), John Buscema (p), "To Prowl No More!" *Amazing Spider-Man* v. 1, n. 79 (December 1969); Roy Thomas (w), John Buscema (p), "Lo! The Lethal Legion!" *Avengers*, v. 1, n. 79 (Marvel Comics, August 1970); Roy Thomas (w), John Buscema (p), "The Monarch and the Man-Ape!" *Avengers*, v. 1, n. 62 (Marvel Comics, March 1969).

49. Lee (w), Buscema (p), "The Night of The Prowler!"; Steve Englehart (w), Alan Weiss (p), "Queen of the Werewolves," *Captain America and the Falcon*, v. 1, n. 164 (Marvel Comics, August 1973); Tom Field, "The Colan Mystique," *Comic Book Artist*, May 2001, http://twomorrows.com/comicbookartist/articles/13colan.html; Steve Englehart (w), George Tuska (p), "Chemistro!" *Luke Cage, Hero for Hire*, v. 1, n. 12 (Marvel Comics, August 1973); Len Wein (w), Sal Buscema (p), "Power Play!" *Defenders*, v. 1, n. 17 (Marvel Comics, November 1974); Gerry Conway (w), Ross Andru (p), "To Sow the Seeds of Death's Day," *Giant-Size Spider-Man*, v. 1, n. 4 (Marvel Comics, April 1975); and Len Wein (w), Ross Andru (p), "The Fiend from the Fire," *Amazing Spider-Man*, v. 1, n. 172 (Marvel Comics, September 1977).

50. Julius Lester, *Look Out, Whitey! Black Power's Gon' Get Your Mama* (New York: Dial Press, 1968), 91–92.

51. Lester, 93.

52. Amy Abugo Ongiri, *Spectacular Blackness: The Cultural Politics of the Black Power Movement and the Search for a Black Aesthetic* (Charlottesville: University of Virginia Press, 2010), 51–52.

53. Raymond S. Franklin, "The Political Economy of Black Power," *Social Problems* 16, no. 3 (Winter 1969): 291.

54. See *Glamour*, August 1968; *Life*, October 17, 1969; *Playboy*, October 1971; Guy Trebay, "On Fashion Runways, Racial Diversity Is Out," *New York Times,* October 22, 2007; and *Vogue*, August 1974. The statement by the observer is probably exaggerated given the known obstacles faced by African American models at the time.

55. "$150 Million Spent Yearly By Blacks To See Movies," *Jet*, Nov. 1, 1973.

56. Ibid.

57. The most important television series about fictional black characters, themes, and subject matter were: *Sanford and Son* (National Broadcasting Company, 1972–1977), *Good Times* (Columbia Broadcasting System, 1974–1979), *That's My Mama* (American Broadcasting Company, 1974–1975), *The Jeffersons* (Columbia Broadcasting System, 1975–1985), *What's Happening!!* (American Broadcasting Company, 1976–1979). Similarly, two important television events and miniseries were *The Autobiography of Miss Jane Pittman* (Columbia Broadcasting System, 1974), and *Roots: The Saga of An American Family* (American Broadcasting Company, 1977).

58. Roy Thomas (w), John Buscema (p), "The Man Ape Always Strikes Twice!" *Avengers*, v. 1, n. 78 (Marvel Comics, July 1970); Chris Claremont (w), Dave Cockrum (p), "Who Will Stop the Juggernaut," *X-Men*, v. 1, n. 102 (December 1976); and Pierre Comtois, *Marvel Comics in the 1970s: An Issue by Issue Field Guide to a Pop Culture Phenomenon* (Raliegh, NC: TwoMorrows Publishing, 2011), p. 73.

59. Eds. to Nocerino, "Let's Rap with Cap."

60. Lee (w), Colan (p), "Crack-Up on Campus"; Comtois, 35.

61. Eds. to Chavez, "Avengers Assemble," *Avengers* v. 1, n. 78 (Marvel Comics, July 1970).

62. Thomas (w), Giacoia, Trimpe (p), "The Sting of the Serpent!"

63. "[T]he Panther's little episode in an all-negro section of New York City was excellent." See Marks to eds., "Avengers Assemble," *Avengers,* v. 1, n. 61 (Marvel Comics, February 1969); Roy Thomas (w), John Buscema (p), "Behold . . . The Vision!" *Avengers,* v. 1, n. 57 (Marvel Comics, October 1968).

64. Thomas (w), Buscema (p), "Lo! The Lethal Legion!"; Josh Barbanel, "Cortines, Citing Litany of Failure, Plans to Close 2 Big High Schools," *New York Times,* November 12, 1993; and Michael Pezone, "School Segregation in Queens, New York: From Andrew Jackson to Law Government," *Social Science Docket* (Summer 2011): 54–56. http://people.hofstra.edu/alan_j_singer/docket/docket/11.2.24_School_Segregation_in_Queens.pdf.

65. Roy Thomas (w), John Buscema (p), "Heroes for Hire!" *Avengers*, v. 1, n. 77 (Marvel Comics, June 1970).

66. Roy Thomas (w), John Buscema (p), "The Coming of Red Wolf!" *Avengers*, v. 1, n. 80 (Marvel Comics, September 1970).

67. Thomas (w), Buscema (p), "Heroes for Hire!"

68. Roy Thomas (w), Frank Giacoia (p), "The Sting of the Serpent," *Avengers* v. 1, n. 73 (Marvel Comics, February 1970).

69. Chavez to eds., "Avengers Assemble," *Avengers* v. 1, n. 78 (Marvel Comics, July 1970); Kuhne to eds., "Avengers Assemble," *Avengers* v. 1, n. 78 (Marvel Comics, July 1970).

70. Stan Lee, "Stan Lee's Soapbox," *Captain America and the Falcon*, v. 1, n. 137 (Marvel Comics, May 1971).

71. Hayden to eds., "Avengers Assemble," *Avengers* v. 1, n. 77 (Marvel Comics, June 1970); Eds. to Hayden, "Avengers Assemble," *Avengers* v. 1, n. 77 (Marvel Comics, June 1970); Hayden to eds., "Avengers Assemble," (Marvel Comics, June 1970); and Wright, 235.

72. Stan Lee (w), Gene Colan (p), "The Coming of... The Falcon!" *Captain America*, v. 1, n. 117 (Marvel Comics, September 1969); Johnson to eds., "Let's Rap with Cap," *Captain America* v. 1, n. 124 (Marvel Comics, April 1970).

73. Oddly the two contemporaneous heroes in Harlem—the Black Panther, and the Falcon—never seem to cross paths in the 1970s; Stan Lee (w), Gene Colan (p), "To Stalk the Spider-Man," *Captain America and the Falcon* v. 1, n. 137 (May 1971) Stan Lee (w), Jack Kirby (p), "The Human Torch Meets... Captain America," *Strange Tales*, v. 1, n. 114 (Marvel Comics, November 1963); and Stan Lee (w), Jack Kirby (p), "The Coming of... Sub-Mariner!" *Fantastic Four*, v. 1, n. 4 (Marvel Comics, May 1962).

74. Stan Lee (w), Gene Colan (p), "Madness in the Slums," *Captain America and the Falcon*, v. 1, n. 133 (Marvel Comics, January 1971); Eds. to Nocerino, "Let's Rap with Cap," *Captain America and the Falcon*, v. 1, n. 137 (Marvel Comics, May 1971); Stan Lee (w), John Romita, Sr. (p), "Mission: Crush The Kingpin!" *Amazing Spider-Man* v. 1 n. 69 (Marvel Comics, February 1969); Roy Thomas (w), Gene Colan (p), "A Life on the Line," *Daredevil* v. 1, n. 69 (Marvel Comics, October 1970); and Gary Friedrich (w), John Romita, Sr. (p), "Power to the People!" *Captain America and the Falcon* v. 1, n. 143 (Marvel Comics, November 1971).

75. Wright, 235–37.

76. Ibid., 235; Lee (w), Romita, Sr. (p), "Crisis On Campus."

77. Ruben-George Toyos, "Media Influence on Power Man," *Comics Journal* 41 (October 1979): 22.

78. Eds. to Jenkins, "Comments to Cage," *Luke Cage, Power Man*, v. 1, n. 20 (August 1974).

79. Peter Sanderson, *The Marvel Comics Guide to New York City* (New York: Simon & Schuster, 2007), 74–75.

80. Hayden to eds., *Luke Cage, Hero for Hire*, v. 1, n. 8; Weibe to eds., *Luke Cage, Hero for Hire*, v. 1, n. 6; Gilbert to eds., "Comments to Cage," *Luke Cage, Power Man*, v. 1, n. 19 (June 1974); Kanes to eds. *Luke Cage, Power Man*, v. 1, n. 24 (April 1975); and Len Wein (w), George Tuska (p), "Rich Man: Iron Man—Power Man: Thief!" *Luke Cage, Power Man*, v. 1, n. 17 (February 1974).

81. Sanderson and Manning, 78.

82. *Marvel Premiere* nos. 15–25 (May 1974–October 1975); *Iron Fist* nos. 1–15 (November 1975–September 1977); *Power Man and Iron Fist* nos. 50 – 125 (April 1978 – September 1986); and "Iron Fist (01–Daniel Rand)—Chronological Listing" Comicbookdb. com: The Comic Book Database, http://www.comicbookdb.com/character_chron. php?ID=1642.

83. Gary Friedrich (w), John Romita, Sr. (p), "Power to the People!" *Captain America and the Falcon* v. 1, n. 143 (Marvel Comics, November 1971); Steve Englehart (w), Sal Buscema (p), "Captain America—Hero or Hoax?" *Captain America and the Falcon*, v. 1, n. 153 (Marvel Comics, September 1972).

84. Stan Lee (w), John Romita, Sr. (p), "It Happens in Harlem," *Captain America and the Falcon* v. 1, n. 138 (Marvel Comics, June 1971).

85. Ongiri, 19, 23.

86. Ralph Macchio, "Steve Englehart in Transition," *Comics Journal* 63 (Spring 1981): 281.

87. Stan Lee (w), John Romita, Sr. (p), "In the Grip of the Gargoyle," *Captain America and the Falcon* v. 1, n. 140 (Marvel Comics, August 1971).

88. Lee (w), Romita, Sr. (p), "Crisis On Campus"; and Lee (w), Romita, Sr. (p), "In the Grip of the Gargoyle."

89. Toyos, 22; Tony Isabella (w), Arvell Jones (p), "Daughters of the Death-Goddess," *Marvel Premiere*, v. 1, n. 21 (March 1975); Roy Thomas (w), Ross Andru (p), "Have Yourself A Sandman Little Christmas!" *Marvel Team-Up* v. 1, n. 1 (March 1972); and Donald Bogle, *Prime Time Blues: African Americans on Network Television* (New York: Farrar, Straus and Giroux, 2001), 219–20.

90. *Cleopatra Jones* was released in summer 1973 and its sequel, *Cleopatra Jones and the Casino of Gold*, two years later. See Stephane Dunn, *"Baad Bitches" & Sassy Supermamas: Black Power Action Films* (Urbana: University of Illinois Press, 2008), 85.

91. Gerry Conway (w), Ross Andru (p), "...And One Will Fall," *Amazing Spider-Man*, v. 1, n. 140 (Marvel Comics, January 1975).

92. Englehart (w), Weiss (p), "Queen of the Werewolves."

93. Steve Englehart (w), George Tuska (p), "Where Angels Fear to Tread," *Luke Cage, Hero for Hire*, v. 1, n. 9 (Marvel Comics, May 1973); Klutey to eds., "Letters to the Living Legend," *Captain America and the Falcon*, v. 1, n. 217 (Marvel Comics, January 1978); and Steve Englehart (w), Don Heck (p), "The Measure of a Man!" *Avengers*, v. 1, n. 109 (Marvel Comics, March 1973).

94. "It was the habit in the Office," according to one staffer, to refer to *Captain America and the Falcon* as "Captain America and the Fowl Coon—Black Goliath was frequently referred to as 'The Big Nig'." See Richard Arndt, "A 2005/2006 Interview with Don McGregor!" *The Warren Magazines Interviews by Richard Arndt*, February 3, 2010, http://www.enjolrasworld.com/Richard%20Arndt/The%20Warren%20Magazines%20Interviews.htm; "The John Byrne Forum," Topic, "OT: Jesus Christ: Super-Hero?" *Byrne Robotics: The Official John Byrne Website*, February 1, 2011, 11:00 AM, accessed December 1, 2011, http://www.byrnerobotics.com/forum/forum_posts.asp?TID=37691&PN=1&totPosts=24; Catron, et al, 59; and "The Last Time Priest Discussed Race in Comics" *Adventures in the Funnybook Game: The Official Website of Christopher J. Priest*, May 2002, accessed December 1, 2011, http://digitalpriest.com/legacy/comics/chips.html.

95. Robinson to eds, "Comment to Cage," *Power Man and Iron Fist* vol. 1, n. 50 (Marvel Comics, April 1978); Chris Claremont (w), John Byrne (p), "If Death Be My Destiny...," *Marvel Team-Up*, v. 1, n. 64 (Marvel Comics, December 1977); Don McGregor (w), P. Craig Russell (p), "The Day the Monuments Shattered," *Amazing Adventures*, v. 1, n. 31 (Marvel Comics, July 1975); Arndt, "A 2005/2006 Interview with Don McGregor!"; Delores P. Aldridge, "Interracial Marriages: Empirical and Theoretical Considerations," *Journal of Black Studies* 8, no. 3 (March, 1978): 357.; Michael J. Rosenfeld and Byung-Soo Kim, "The Independence of Young Adults and the Rise of Interracial and Same-Sex Unions," Tables 1 and 2, *American Sociological Review* 70, no. 4 (Aug., 2005): 547; *Richard Perry Loving, Mildred Jeter Loving v. Virginia* 388 U.S. 1 87 S. Ct. 1817; 18 L. Ed. 2d 1010; 1967 U.S. LEXIS 1082; and Jonathan Zimmerman, "Crossing Oceans, Crossing Colors: Black Peace Corps Volunteers and Interracial Love in Africa, 1961–1971," in *Sex, Love, Race: Crossing Boundaries in North American History*, ed. Martha Hodes (New York: NYU Press, 1999), 514–30.

96. J. Harvie Wilkinson, III, *From Brown to Bakke: The Supreme Court and School Integration: 19541978* (New York: Oxford University Press, 1979),108–215; See generally David Riddle, "Race and Reaction in Warren, Michigan, 1971 to 1974: Bradley v. Milliken and the Cross-District Busing Controversy," *Michigan Historical Review* 26, no. 2 (Fall, 2000): 1–49; Richard A. Pride, "Public Opinion and the End of Busing: (Mis)Perceptions of Policy Failure," *Sociological Quarterly* 41, no. 2 (Spring, 2000): 207–25; Donald Philip Green and Jonathan A. Cowden, "Who Protests: Self-Interest and White Opposition to Busing," *Journal of Politics* 54, no. 2 (May 1992): 471–96; McKee J. McClendon, "Racism, Rational Choice, and White Opposition to Racial Change: A Case Study of Busing," *Public Opinion Quarterly* 49, no. 2 (Summer 1985): 214–33; Bert Useem, "Trust in Government and the Boston Anti-Busing Movement," *Western Political Quarterly* 35, no. 1 (March 1982): 81–91; and David O. Sears, Carl P. Hensler, Leslie K. Speer, "Whites' Opposition to 'Busing': Self-Interest or Symbolic Politics?" *The American Political Science Review* 73, no. 2 (June 1979): 369–84.

97. *Green v. County School Board of New Kent County*, 391 U.S. 430 (1968); *Swann v. Charlotte-Mecklenburg Board of Education*, 402 U.S. 1 (1971); and *Milliken v. Bradley*, 418 U.S. 717 (1974).

98. *Regents of the University of California v. Bakke*, 438 U.S. 265 (1978).

99. Derrick Bell, "The Politics of Desegregation," *Change* 11, no. 7 (October 1979): 50.

100. Wilkinson, III, 180.

101. Reagan garnered 489 electoral and beat Carter by a margin of 10 to 1.

102. John Hope Franklin and Alfred A. Moss, Jr., *From Slavery to Freedom: A History of African Americans*, 7th ed. (New York: McGraw-Hill, 1994),535.

103. Ronald Reagan as quoted in Anderson,164

104. Ibid., 166.

105. Franklin and Moss, Jr.,535.

106. Gary Groth, "Black Lightning Strikes Out!" *Comics Journal* 32 (January 1977):12.

107. Roberson to eds., "Avengers Assemble," *Avengers*, v. 1, n. 185 (Marvel Comics, July 1979).

108. Mark Gruenwald, Ralph Macchio (w), John Byrne (p), "Giants In The Earth" *Marvel Two-In-One* (Marvel Comics, September 1979); "Giant-Man (02–Bill Foster)—Chronological Listing," *Comicbookdb.com: The Comic Book Database* http://www.comicbookdb.com/character_chron.php?ID=11285.

109. Wright, 245.

110. Ibid.

111. Arndt, "A 2005/2006 Interview with Don McGregor!"

112. Ibid.

113. Kim Thompson, "An Interview with Marvel's Head Honcho: Jim Shooter," *Comics Journal*, no. 40 (June 1978): 39.

114. Jack Kirby, open letter, "Panther Post-Scripts," *Black Panther* v.1, n. 6 (Marvel Comics, November 1977).

115. Kirby (w,p), "Panther Postscripts"; and Comtois, 7; 204.

116. Comtois, 7, 204; Carlisle to eds., "Panther Postscripts," *Black Panther* v.1, n. 6 (Marvel Comics, November 1977); and Judge to eds., "Panther Postscripts," *Black Panther* v.1, n. 7 (Marvel Comics, January 1978).

117. Jim Shooter, "Comics are Alive and Well at Marvel," *Comics Journal* no. 52 (December 1979): 23.

118. Buchko, Jr., to eds., "Let's Rap with Cap" *Captain America and the Falcon* v. 1, n. 206 (Marvel Comics, February 1977).

119. Ibid.

120. Gibson to eds., "Let's Rap with Cap" *Captain America and the Falcon* v. 1, n. 210 (June 1977)

121. Eds. to Buchko, Jr., "Let's Rap with Cap" *Captain America and the Falcon* v. 1, n. 206 (Marvel Comics, February 1977); Eds. to Haskell, "Letters to the Living Legend," *Captain America and the Falcon*, v. 1, n. 214 (October 1977)

122. Ralph Macchio to eds, "Let's Rap with Cap" *Captain America and the Falcon* v. 1, n. 197 (May 1976); Farr to eds., "Let's Rap with Cap" *Captain America and the Falcon* v. 1, n. 203 (November 1976); McGreevy to eds. "Let's Rap with Cap"; Klutey to eds., "Letters to the Living Legend," *Captain America and the Falcon*, v. 1, n. 217 (January 1978); and Kaufman to eds., and eds. to Kaufman, "Letters to the Living Legend," *Captain America and the Falcon*, v. 1, n. 221 (May 1978).

123. Don Glut (p), Sal Buscema (w), "On a Wing and A Prayer," *Captain America and the Falcon* 220 (April 1978).

124. *Bakke* (1978);Tom DeFalco, "Introduction," in Sanderson and Manning, 9.

125. Michelinie (w), Byrne and Day (p), "On the Matter of Heroes"; Stiles to eds., "Avengers Assemble," *Avengers*, v. 1, n. 185 (Marvel Comics, July 1979); Weibe to eds., "Avengers Assemble," *Avengers*, v. 1, n. 185 (Marvel Comics, July 1979); Banner to eds., "Avengers Assemble," *Avengers*, v. 1, n. 185 (Marvel Comics, July 1979); Roberson to eds., "Avengers Assemble," *Avengers*, v. 1, n. 185 (Marvel Comics, July 1979); Morrison to eds., "Avengers Assemble," *Avengers*, v. 1, n. 185 (Marvel Comics, July 1979); and Farnham to eds., "Avengers Assemble," *Avengers*, v. 1, n. 185 (Marvel Comics, July 1979).

126. David Michelinie (w), A[rvell] Jones and R. Villamonte (p), "Steel City Nightmare," *Avengers,* v. 1, n. 192 (Marvel Comics, February, 1980); David Michelinie (w), George Perez (p), "Interlude," *Avengers, v.* 1, n. 194 (Marvel Comics, April, 1980); and Michelinie (w), Perez (p), "Interlude."

127. Wolverine actually debuted in *Incredible Hulk* 181 (1974). Jon B. Cooke, "Dave 'Blackhawk' Cockrum: The Marvel Days of the Co-Creator of the New X-Men" [excerpted from *Comic Book Artist #6*], *Twomorrows.com*, http://twomorrows.com /comicbookartist/articles/06cockrum.html.

128. Margaret O'Donnell, "Chris Claremont," *The Comics Journal,* no 50 (October 1979): 50.

129. Ibid., 50.

130. Cooke, "Dave 'Blackhawk' Cockrum"; and Les Daniels, *Marvel: Five Fabulous Decades of the World's Greatest Comics* with an introduction by Stan Lee (New York: Harry N. Abrams, Inc., 1993), 167–68.

131. Chris Claremont (w), Dave Cockrum (p), "Who Will Stop the Juggernaut."

132. Carol B. Kalish and Richard E. Howell, "Life among the Mutants: The X-Men under Chris Claremont and John Byrne," *Comics Journal*, no 49 (September 1979): 61.

133. Chris Claremont (w), John Byrne (p), "Cry for the Children!" *X-Men*, v. 1, n. 122 (Marvel Comics, June 1979).

134. Ibid.

135. Ibid.

136. Monica Rambeau, the new Captain Marvel, for example, debuted and joined the Avengers in 1982, though like Storm, more as woman than a black woman. Gender shapes her narrative attempts to achieve and succeed as a superhero. Her race is muted and, except for her appearance, her blackness receives little narrative exploration.

137. Claremont (w), Silvestri and Leialoha (p), "Storm Warnings," *Uncanny X-Men* v. 1, n. 253 (Marvel Comics, Late November 1989); Cheryl Lynn, "Trinity: The Black

Fantasy," *Digital Femme,* May 7, 2009, 03:08 p.m., http://digitalfemme.com/journal/index.php?itemid=1073.

138. Jacobs to eds., "Comments to Cage," *Luke Cage, Power Man,* v. 1, n. 42 (Marvel Comics, April 1977).

139. Dr. Doom actually hired Cage for a job early-on in the series, but then attempted to renege on paying the fee, for which Cage confronted him directly. See *Luke Cage, Hero for Hero,* v. 1, nos. 7–9.

140. Jacobs to eds., "Comments to Cage."

141. "First Inaugural Address of Ronald Reagan," Tuesday, January 20, 1981, *The Avalon Project: Documents in Law, History, and Diplomacy,* http://avalon.law.yale.edu/20th_century/reagan1.asp, accessed March 27, 2010.

142. Gary Groth, "Jack Kirby Interview," *Comics Journal,* n. 134 (February 1990) http://www.tcj.com/jack-kirby-interview/.

143. Compiled from referencing of *The Marvel Comics Encyclopedia: The Definitive Guide to the Characters of the Marvel Universe* (New York: DK Publishing, 2009).

144. Before coming to work for Marvel in 1972, Graham spent his first few years in the industry working for Warren Comics, publisher of horror genre offerings. Of the two issues for which he received a writer credit, each is as a co-writer. See "Billy Graham," *Comicbookdb.com: The Comic Book Database,* http://www.comicbookdb.com/creator.php?ID=589; Wright, 247.

145. "Billy Graham," *Comicbookdb.com: The Comic Book Database.*

146. Daniel Best, "Looking Back with Ron Wilson," *20th Century Danny Boy,* January 3, 2010, accessed April 22, 2011, http://ohdannyboy.blogspot.com/2010/01/looking-back-with-ron-wilson.html; "Billy Graham"; and "Ron Wilson," Comicbookdb.com: *The Comic Book Database,* http://www.comicbookdb.com/creator.php?ID=907.

147. "Ron Wilson."

148. Vince Moore, "Standing on the Shoulders of Giants: Arvell Jones," *Comic Book Resources,* February 22, 2006, http://www.comicbookresources.com/?page=article&id=6492.

149. "Keith Pollard," *Comicbookdb.com: The Comic Book Database,* http://www.comicbookdb.com/creator.php?ID=358.

150. Advertisement, *Comics Journal,* no. 49 (September 1979): 72.

151. For a useful and insightful view of black impressions through the 1980s and early 1990s of so-called fan-boy ascendency in the comics culture and industry, see Jeffery A. Brown, *Black Superheroes, Milestone Comics, and Their Fans* (Jackson: University of Mississippi Press, 2001), especially chaps. 1–3.

152. The "Supernigger" routine was performed at least a few times live in the early 1970s, and was also included in the concert/film *Wattstax* (1973). However, as the result of a protracted legal battle over publishing rights, Pryor's first record label, Laff Records, which lost the artist but continued to release his work from the 1960s and early 1970s as new material well into the 1980s—the routine did not appear on a comedy album until 1983's *Supernigger* as Laff attempted to capitalize on Pryor's costarring role in the motion picture, *Superman III* (1983). Much later, Pryor regained the rights to his earliest materials, and the "Supernigger" skit was re-released on the *Evolution/Revolution: The Early Years* (Rhino Records, 2005).

153. Toyos, 22.

154. Manley to eds., "Power/Fistfuls," *Power Man and Iron Fist,* v. 1, n. 56 (Marvel Comics, April 1979).

10

So You Think You Can Dance: Black Dance and American Popular Culture

Tamara Lizette Brown

Stuart Hall asserts that "by definition black popular culture is a contradictory space. It is a site of strategic contestation." Therefore, "it can never be simplified or explained in terms of the simple binary oppositions that are still habitually used to map it out: high and low; resistance versus incorporation; authentic versus inauthentic; experimental versus formal; opposition versus homogenization."[1] Thus, there is cause for a new and broader assessment tool than traditional prognosticators allow. Cultural scholar Harry Shaw links all black popular culture to black culture. "Black popular culture in America holds a peculiar status in that, unlike Western popular culture in general, it has no counterpart in Black high culture." Moreover Shaw concedes that all of African American "culture is to a great extent Black popular culture, for there is no identifiable Black culture that cannot be or is not readily embraced by the wide spectrum of Black society. Black culture is popular culture partly because it continually looks toward the roots of the common Black experience and draws from those roots for its creativity."[2] Finally he correctly posits that as black creativity continues to proliferate, popular forms move out of the community to be adopted and appropriated by the larger mainstream audience.

In critically assessing Shaw's limited analysis that African Americans do not possess a black high art, such an absolute cannot be corroborated. An abridgement to this with dance as the example is offered. For example, scholar Richard Long presents a more inclusive definition than the Western canon allows with regard to the distinction between high and low art. Long asserts that while all black dance evolves along the same continuum because it emanates from the people who become the impetus and/or creator, still there is a distinction between concert-theatrical dance (deemed high art) and social/vernacular dance (considered low or folk art)—and that is one of intent.[3]

In his work on how white Americans truly view their black counterparts, *Two Nations: Black and White, Separate, Hostile, Unequal*, Andrew Hacker reveals how whites misinterpret black dance, but gives compelling evidence as to why this is so. "To be white is to be 'civilized,' which brings acceptance and imposition of sexual constraints.... Still, fantasies persist that black men and women are less burdened by inhibitions, and can delight in primal pleasures beyond the capacities of whites. (The erotic abandon displayed in black dancing has no white counterpart.)"[4] This supposed erotic abandon is actually comfort with producing rhythmic movement by one's body. Historically when viewed inside of cultural parameters, the sexual nature of black social dance, when present, was not the primary factor: One's ability to dance precipitated adulation. Contemporary sexualized views of black popular music and dance, however, have reinforced such notions rather than countered them. The artists and producers share an equal blame through the promotion of such characterizations for profit. However, the globalization of black/American popular culture also is a factor. Consequently, many when partaking in the product-oriented music and dance simply revert back the stereotypical, hypersexualized view of those of African descent as perpetuated by the institution of chattel slavery and Africans as the sex-starved Other.

The problem and process discussed in this study centers on the appropriation of African American popular culture by whites and the misrepresentation and historical revision of the origins and/or impetus behind the initiative—in this case popular and/or vernacular dance. When culture is created out of certain circumstances by marginalized and, at times, commodified people, its meaning changes when it is adopted, adapted, and reinterpreted by the very community responsible for hegemonic factors contributing to that marginalization.

Black Dance Traits

African dance retained many of its motor characteristics as it was transplanted from its original birthplace to a land across the seas. In some cases, mainly in religious dance and through animal imitation, it retained some of its communicative function as an agent of the gods as well as a socialization means for communication between different cultural groups, and further as a vehicle for passing on traditions from one generation to the next. Differences must be noted, however, between the urban enslaved and those of the plantation and whether blacks lived—enslaved and/or free depending on the time period—in the North or the South. The nature of the dances performed would change if whites were either present or participants, and this caused some degree of cultural exchange, exploitation, and transformation. Generally accepted in cultural studies by scholars such as Carter G. Woodson, W. E. B. Du Bois, Melville Herskovits, Lawrence Levine, Sterling Stuckey, and Paul Gilroy is the premise that the Middle Passage and slavery did not wipe out all traces of African behaviors; core cultural forms did survive albeit in altered forms. "Culture is not a fixed, static condition but a process; a product of interaction between the past and present."[5]

When documenting Africanisms through dance, specifically, one must be concerned with not only the physical survival, but of the psychological aspect as well since this is a determining factor in cultural retention.[6] If one simply performs an act without knowing or realizing the significance behind it, then can it really be considered retentive? For people of African descent in the United States until the Civil War, at least, the practitioners of these dances did understand the significance attached to what they were doing. If not, then they would not have taken such great pains to protect certain secret aspects of it.

Despite the discrepancies in analysis, it is generally conceded that Africans, forcibly transplanted to the Western Hemisphere throughout the period known as the Transatlantic Slave Trade, also brought their cultural practices. These practices, while not always surviving in their original forms, often were forced to adapt and change to new forms though the impetus behind the mutated forms could still be traced to Africa. By viewing the enslaved Africans' culture through their dance as a basic form of communication, one can chart how the African changed from the indigenous form to the synthesized African American construct.

Many black dance traits are traditionally initiated by the lower to lower-middle class of the cultural group. These characteristics that can be seen through working-class vernacular and social dance correspond to identity, cultural integrity, ingroup–outgroup association, and political resistance.[7] Identity refers to the idea of someone feeling that he/she should be able to dance. Blacks have traditionally been seen by whites as being natural dancers. French critic Andre Levison, while writing about the black dances performed for the European audiences, said:

> This Negro ragtime, executed with such unimaginative dexterity positively dazzles European audiences. This dancing with its automation, its marvelous flexibility and rhythmic fantasy is as impossible for us to reproduce as it is astounding for us to watch. Here we see ourselves in the presence of an innate art, not a conscious art.[8]

While whites often use the deduction of natural ability to devalue those of African descents' dances as vulgar, low-class, or at another level low art as opposed to high art, blacks look at one's dancing ability as evidence of his/her "blackness."[9] The cultural integrity issue is not age-specific and crosses socioeconomic lines. It also becomes an assertion of one's blackness as opposed to a different ethnic group to which one is trying to join. "Through dance, one proves that one is a member of the cultural body, that one is truly in touch with the cultural material."[10] Ingroup–outgroup association appears on a social-psychological level. In this case, one's ability to dance can increase his/her standing and/or acceptance by peers or other social grouping. A prime example of this could be seen at Harlem's famed Savoy Ballroom. Those patrons who could really "cut a rug" were distinguishable by their presence in the Corner/Cats' Corner. Only those persons who could measure up to a particular dance standard were allowed to showcase their talents there.[11] The final trait, political resistance, corresponds to the distinction of black dance from white dance—which in this case was simply a redefinition from the black impetus—or white dancers who are trying to dance black. Zora Neale Hurston reported of the malformation in movement of whites when they try to mimic blacks. "They often have all the elements of the song, dance, or expression, but they are misplaced or distorted by the accent falling on the wrong element. Every one seems to think that the Negro is easily imitated when nothing is further from the truth."[12] Norma Miller, a dancer who grew up during the 1920s and 1930s, recalls the fast pace of the Lindy hop, "We wanted our tempos fast, and the white dancers didn't like that. It was always fast because we didn't want them taking our dance. They had everything else, so we couldn't allow them to take the Lindy hop."[13]

LeeEllen Friedland piggybacked on Hazzard-Gordon's original definitions by adding annotation, imitation, and subversion in augmenting black vernacular dance traits. These delineations represent the association with or "exaggeration of cultural symbols," replication of various steps, and social or cultural commentary about or outside of the African American community.[14]

Interdisciplinary scholar Jonathan David Jackson charts the use of improvisation in African American vernacular dance. He divides improvisation into two fields: individuation and ritualization. Jackson defines individuation as inclusive of vamping, riffing, and breaking utilized by the dancer in order to "establish a unique identity according to her or his own physical capabilities, personal style, and capacity for invention;...[It] is a matter of the constant negotiation of personal style and community expectations."[15] Along the same lines, ritualization as a process of improvisation includes competition, ritual celebration, satirical dancing, and erotic coupling. Obviously the competitive form serves as a status symbol and dancers may satirize people or actions within and outside of the black community. The meanings of the characteristics associated with individuation and ritualization can change with geographical and time considerations, but the "principles, processes, and traditions...endure."[16] The African American community praises the use of improvisation in dance; it demonstrates ability and authenticity. However, "the commodification and distortion of black vernacular dancing for mainstream white Euro-American consumption is as enduring as the traditions themselves." This cultural raiding serves to distort the original impetus and cultural context of the dance as well as the "devaluation of the dancing as 'low culture' (or as fads) and the concomitant rejection of rich cultural meaning and aesthetic intelligence."[17]

From Africa to America

At the savage Captain's beck;
Now like Brutes they make us prance:
Smack the Cat about the Deck,
And in scorn they bid us dance.[18]

This sentiment from the 1790 poem "The Sorrows of Yamba; Or, the Negro Woman's Lamentation" tells about an African woman's deep-felt unhappiness at being kidnapped from her family and village in Africa, and then transported to a life of unyielding, forced bondage in America. Dance in Africa served as an integral part of society, and those who perform it are viewed as essential to the well-being of the cultural group. In European-influenced societies, this is not always the case: dance is typically recreational or for entertainment purposes. Dance pioneer and anthropologist Pearl Primus suggested that the "role of the professional dancer was of tremendous importance in Africa. He was necessary to all ceremonies, all feasts, all occasions which involved the health and well-being of the tribe. In return for his services the tribe fed and clothed him and provided for him in his every need. He was left free to dance." Primus mused, "Is it any wonder then that dance stands with music and art at the very top of the list of cultural contributions of the African to the world?"[19]

A multitude of different cultural groups occupy the African continent with certain cultural traits that are endemic to only them. There are, however, certain general traits that can be associated with the practice and function of dance in African societies. "All African cultures express themselves through the universals of dance, music, visual arts, and graphic arts."[20] Kariamu Welsh Asante characterizes the aesthetics of African and African-inspired dance as polyrhythmic—meaning that the movement cannot be separated; polycentered—coming from a cosmological view that relates the deities, nature and the being; curvilinear—in its shape and form as well as mythical structure that holds the circle as sacred; dimensional—building upon more than just certain steps to also include the music, surroundings and the supernatural; having epic memory—not a historical recollection, but an emotional response transferred from the performer to the viewer; holistic—so that the individual or particular component is not more important than the whole; and repetitious—to emphasize and intensify a movement.[21]

A main purpose of African dance is communication. The dance "has an urgency. The dancer has direction and purpose. The purpose is to communicate.... For him and his people, the dance is life."[22] Traditional African dances are classified as social/recreational, religious/sacred, and ritualistic. Recreational dances are subject to the changing whims of fashion, music, and societal values. Ritual dances are mostly left unchanged and correspond to a specific event in the lives of the participant such as initiation into woman or manhood. The dance is a representation of the symbolic act, thus becoming an aid or tool in the socialization and communication process of dancers. "People use their bodies as instruments through which every conceivable motion or event is projected. The result is a hypnotic marriage between life and dance."[23]

Unaware and unimpressed by the complexity of the Africans' culture, oftentimes the slave ship captains were entertained by their future captives prior to the latters' enslavement. Captain Theodore Canot described one such ceremony he encountered during a slaving expedition as:

> a whirling circle of half-stripped girls [who] danced to the monotonous beat of a tom-tom. Presently, the formal ring was broken, and each female stepping out singly, danced according to her individual fancy. Some were wild, some were soft,

some were tame, and some were fiery. After so many years I have no distinct recollection of their characteristic movements.[24]

There is even an instance of slave traders using the dance as an enticement for the Africans to board their ships. Thomas Johns, a former slave residing in Texas in the 1930s, recounted the ancestry of his mother and father, which he traced back to the Kiochi tribe, and told of them being invited to dance on the white man's ship. "[M]y aunt said it was early in the mornin' when dey foun' dey was away from de land, and all dey could see was de water all 'round."[25]

The Middle Passage, part of the triangular trade, referred to the journey from the African coast to the shores of the Americas. The price of the captives garnered so much financial reward once sold that slave ship captains often opted for "tight packing" rather than "loose packing" without regard to the high mortality rate when transporting their human cargo. During the Middle Passage slavers appropriated the administering of the dance from the practitioners and instead used it as a tool of oppression. "Dancing the slaves" was an activity on many slave ships. This so-called dance was used as a way of exercising the captives on board these vehicles of human subjugation, and also as a remedy for preventing scurvy. Captains sometimes advertised for musicians for these abominable expeditions in order to provide accompaniment for the newly enslaved inhabitants. If musicians were not available, then an African was forced to beat on "a broken drum, an upturned kettle, or an African banjo."[26] Testimony in front of the Parliamentary Committee for the Abolition of Slavery recanted:

> In order to keep them [the slaves] in good health it was usual to make them dance. It was the business of the chief mate to make the men dance and the second mate danced the women; but this was only done by means of frequent use of the cat [a whipping device]. The men could only jump up and rattle their chains but the women were driven in one among another all the while singing or saying words that had been taught them...well.[27]

At other times, however, the witness remembered that "there was another time when the women were sitting by themselves, below, when I heard them singing other words and usually them always in tears. Their songs then always told the story of their lives and their grief at leaving their friends and country."[28]

Even if the indigenous Africans suffered from some type of illness, or pain because of the chains on their limbs, they were still expected to engage in this activity. Most slavers simply felt that singing and dancing were indicative of the Africans' behavior, and that they derived joy and happiness from this forced opportunity to participate. "Our blacks were a good natured lot and jumped to the lash so promptly that there was not much occasion for scoring their naked flanks. We had tambourines aboard, which some of the younger darkies fought for regularly." Under the erroneous assumption that the captives danced to entertain with such performances, the ship captain continued that "every evening we enjoyed the novelty of African war songs and ring dances, fore and aft, with the satisfaction of knowing that these pleasant exercises were keeping our stock in good condition and, of course, enhancing our prospects of making a profitable voyage." [29] Thus the purpose of the dance changed during this historical moment. Dance was still a function of the practitioners as a means of communication by way of bridging cultural gaps if ethnic groups were separated, and a further method of keeping traditions. Therefore, through their dance, Africans asserted their independence from their captors—who thought of it as exercise for their chattel and/or lighthearted recreation. The Middle Passage actually helped to forge kinship ties among the participants who looked to their "shipmates" as extended family members. Therefore, even this horrifying experience did not totally "obliterate their culture and humanity." Frequent instances of revolt further demonstrate that the enslaved peoples resisted their new status. This suggests that just as they physically fought against the enslavers for their freedom, so did they mentally resist the taking of their souls by the slave holders. To a certain degree, they would have some autonomy in maintaining cultural norms—in this instance through dance. "The slave ships carried not only men, women and children but also their gods, beliefs and traditional folklore."[30] Under the yoke of slavery, hybrids of cultural syncretisms visible through the dance survived. Although Africans forcibly brought to North America came from various cultural backgrounds, shared values and traits tended to be adopted and adapted in the form of cultural exchange between Africans for endurance in the new environment.

When delineating cultural hierarchies, Westernized thought tends to place those things derived from European sources as the paradigm or standard, while ranking other traditions on a much lower plane. Such conscious and unconscious thoughts lauded those cultural links of European descent while deriding those of anything African. Moreover, slaves were encouraged to continue some indigenous practices for the purpose of distinguishing them from the white power structure. The colonists could justify enslavement on the basis that Africans were not only physically different but inferior as well.

In defining the relationship of all African dance, dance scholar Richard Long denotes that dance is a cultural representation derived from the cultural milieu that gives it impetus. Thus all black dance originates from those cultures of sub-Saharan Africa. Consequently, "the Africanized components of Western-hemisphere cultures... [when related to] Black dance, Black stance, and Black gesture are non-verbal patterns of body gestures and expressions which are distinctively Black African or originate from their descendents elsewhere."[31]

As a result of the Stono Rebellion in 1739, where enslaved Africans attempted to secure their freedom by escaping to Florida, accompanied by the beat of the drum, through securing arms and killing anyone who impeded their progress, colonial authorities in South Carolina outlawed the use of drums. Other colonies followed by outlawing the drum and curtailing meetings of blacks. The power structure felt that the Africans communicated through these instruments: communication that could lead to revolt or rebellion.[32] But the beat of the drum did not die; Africans beat the same rhythms that would have been produced through striking animal hides—though the drum would still be clandestinely used—with other instruments, on their own bodies, or on the ground. Pattin' juba was a rhythm and subsequent dance steps that evolved because of this. African dance and music is polyrhythmic—more than one beat is played at the same time. The body manifests these rhythms through isolation of various body parts; therefore the "African dancer carries a different rhythm in each part of the body. The feet may be moving in 4/4, while the hips sway in 3/4, and the head in 6/8."[33] Other musical instruments used were the fiddle (and European violin), banjo, and tambourine. Africans on the continent and throughout the diaspora in the Caribbean and parts of Latin America utilized similar instruments.[34]

Because of the surroundings and conditions in which they lived, African dance in the United States became synthesized and flourished into a unique strand of African American dance. Dance was an outlet for the enslaved who, after performing backbreaking work in the fields all week, congregated on Saturday evenings, during holidays, or at weddings, funerals, corn-shuckings, and quilting gatherings at nearby plantations and partook in the surviving dance customs from a culture which they had been removed. Dance also was used, as in the case of the slave captains, to entertain the white plantation owners. Performing in front of them often resulted in contests where the winner received a prize in the form of clothing, food, alcohol, or bragging rights. The buck and wing— which would later be a standard tap dancing step—jig, cakewalk, ring dance, buzzard lope, and rhythms of juba were some of the dances and steps performed. These dances required much skill and agility to be executed well. Dr. John Wyeth recalled the dance of slaves on his Alabama plantation as "steps which required not only a keen sense of keeping time with the music, but agility and muscular power of a high order."[35] Of course, at times, owners and authorities often frowned upon gatherings like dances of the enslaved for fear that insurrection would be planned. On other occasions, however, dance was encouraged to entertain whites and as a requirement to boost a sale on the auction block.

Jump Jim Crow

During the slavery era in US history cultural exchange would occur during dance ceremonies where whites were present, since black musicians would play for both the white and black events. Though the musicians played European instruments like the violin, they kept their own unique rhythm that would be transferred to the dancers as they kept time with the music. Some whites, when possible, would join in the dances of the bondsmen, and the enslaved blacks would borrow some of the floor patterns of their white enslavers.

The earliest minstrelsy was performed by whites and originated in the North. They built a performance tradition on their perception of how they conceived black Americans, not how they actually were. Whites had professionally performed as blacks in blackface as far back as prior to the American Revolution, and by the 1820s white dancers imitating blacks in blackface "were all the rage and beginning to create a new blend."[36] For instance George Washington Dixon, the "first uniquely American clown" that utilized blackface in his New York City routines beginning in 1828, became famous for his rendition of the derogatory love song "Coal Black Rose," which promoted the stereotype of blacks as insatiable and foolish in love.[37] Englishman Charles Matthews, however, may conceivably be the precursor to the blackface performers of the 1820s. While visiting the United States in 1822, he meticulously studied blacks (in New York and Philadelphia) and documented their speech, songs, stories, sermon cadences, and mannerisms. He even attended performances of the fledgling black stage troupe, the African Company—a theatrical group that performed Shakespeare and other classics interspersed with comedic acts and song and dance. Though the semi-professional theater company performed mainly for blacks at their African Grove site, whites were welcomed, but often attended in the form of hooligans looking to disrupt the show. When Matthews attended, white hecklers in the audience demanded that the actor portraying Hamlet sing "Possum up a Gum Tree" rather than the classic play. Matthews would use that very song in the performance he created for English audiences entitled, *A Trip to America*. This became a documented "first certain example of a white man borrowing Negro material for a blackfaced act."[38]

The often repeated standard story centers around Thomas Dartmouth "Daddy" Rice who, also around 1828, put burnt cork makeup on his face and imitated a physically challenged, enslaved black man he had encountered in Kentucky named Jim Crow.[39] Often this black man danced a step while singing the ditty, "First on the heel tap, Den on the toe, Ebry time I wheel about, I jump Jim Crow. Wheel around, turn about, Do jis so. An ebery time I wheel about I jump Jim Crow."[40] He called this jumping Jim Crow. "He was very much deformed, the right shoulder being drawn high up, the left leg stiff and crooked at the knee, giving him a painful at the same time laughable limp. He used to coon a queer old tune with words of his own, and at the end of each verse would give a little jump."[41] Rice added more lyrics and put the song to a popular English tune, but reviews of the time suggest that the movement rather than the song entertained the audiences.[42] Thus Rice helped usher in the performance medium known as American minstrelsy while creating a name and making a living for himself by imitating the singing and dancing of a black man. In fact he spread this entertainment form to England where he continued to reap the benefits as the European audience embraced this professional degradation.[43] And as he profited from this negative depiction, he was not celebrating black culture or dance through this portrayal. The caricature and stereotypical performance of black song, dance and dialogue became the standard for the minstrel clown. "Thomas Rice created an image from a handicapped individual and this ridiculous caricature was imposed upon a race of people."[44]

After the War of 1812, many advocated for a cultural independence to match the political autonomy that victory symbolized. This cultural uniqueness would further distinguish Americans from their English antecedents and promote a "common man's culture" to promote "American democracy and the average white man" rather than any aristocratic elements. The average white man, though, would look toward the enslaved black as an anchor for this emerging popular culture. Andrew Jackson was elected to the presidency in 1828 ushering in a more democratic era. Theater and blackface reflected this change. In New

York City specifically, public spaces for the common folk "were increasingly restricted by municipal regulations." This crackdown on public space forced the public into the theaters, typically reserved for the elite, where when offered they often enjoyed blackface performance.[45] Typically, however, those inclined to partake in this entertainment found lower tiered theatrical venues willing to service the desires of this type of patron. Therefore, audiences for antebellum blackface performance in the North "tended to be male, youngish, and lower class."[46]

The first minstrel troop (though short-lived) to form and perform in blackface, beginning in 1843, called themselves the Virginia Minstrels and consisted of Dan Emmett, Frank Bower, Billy Whitlock, and Dick Pelham. These former circus entertainers were the first to term themselves minstrels and offer a complete show rather than simply a circus act or as diversion in a larger theatrical work.[47] White minstrels "undoubtedly incorporated actual elements of black dance, stance, gesture in their performances, for there is abundant evidence that they observed black recreational activity, which included dancing," but they also added elements from mainstream American culture to round out these performances.[48] This profiteering mimicry, however, did not fool or entertain everybody. The British actress Fanny Kemble who resided in Georgia during 1838 and 1839 recorded in her journal that "I have seen Jim Crow...all the contortions, and springs, and flings, and kicks, and capers you have been beguiled into accepting as indicative of him are spurious, faint, feeble, impotent—in a word, pale Northern reproductions of that ineffable black conception."[49] Still white onlookers did not necessarily question the artistry or authenticity of this recreated African performance culture and more than likely felt more comfortable viewing this recreated exaggeration rather than the real thing. Frederick Douglass regularly attacked whites in blackface pilfering black culture for capital gain. In October 1848, he printed in his North Star that "the filthy scum of white society, who have stolen from us a complexion denied to them by nature, in which to make money, and pander to the corrupt taste of their white fellow citizens."[50]

White minstrels performing in blackface supported existing notions of racial inferiority and the proscribed social hierarchy. The performance medium served as "the first formal public acknowledgment by whites of black culture," and invariably helped to affirm whiteness particularly by working-class people in the urban North.[51] However, the root of minstrelsy came from the behavior of enslaved Africans on the plantation. After completing backbreaking work from sunup to sundown enslaved blacks used time they had to themselves to reaffirm cultural traits through song and dance traditions. Fortified with handcrafted instruments such as the bone clappers, jawbones, scrap iron, and the banjo, they conjured historical memory through body movement. Plantation owners did not necessarily discourage this behavior since many rationalized that this time for merriment kept slaves "happy [and] faithful" and thus less likely to rebel. "Every plantation had its talented band that could crack Negro jokes, and sing and dance to the accompaniment of the banjo and the bones...When the wealthy plantation-owner wished to entertain his guests, he needed only to call his troupe of black minstrels."[52] Owners could also make money from their enslaved artists by hiring them out for other venues and pocketing the fees. Historian Cecelia Brown deduced that this is how "the minstrel show developed."[53]

A black performer William Henry Lane, better known by his performing name Master Juba, began his career as a master jig dancer by perfecting the moves of the Irish dancers he interacted with in the Five Points section of New York City. Lane was born free in 1825, reportedly in Providence, Rhode Island, and learned to dance from another black dancer named "Uncle" Jim Lowe who was known as a jig and reel dancer.[54] His emphasis on rhythm and percussion would be the basis of tap dancing. Juba and Lowe were forced to perform in dance houses, saloons, and other areas outside of the legitimate theatre though minstrel performance could be viewed as part of legitimated theatrical performance as diversion between acts or as afterpieces.[55] In his *American Notes* written after visiting the United States in 1842, Charles Dickens enthusiastically described what many perceive as Juba's dance. "Single shuffle, double shuffle, cut and cross-cut: snapping his fingers, rolling his eyes, turning in his knees, presenting the backs of his legs in the front, spinning about on his toes and heels like nothing but the man's fingers on the tambourine; dancing with two left legs, two right legs, two wooden legs, two wire legs, two string legs—all sorts of legs and no legs—what is this to him?" Dickens continued with the description by querying, "[A]nd in what walk of life, or dance of life, does man ever get such stimulating applause?" Once finished with the performance, the dancer, in a challenge to all competitors, reacted "with the chuckle of a million counterfeit Jim Crows, in one inimitable sound."[56]

Juba performed, throughout the United States and England, from 1840 until his death in 1852 and was hailed as the "King of All Dancers." He received this accolade after competing in various dance contests against Master John Diamond (aka the King of Diamonds). Prior to that time and while still an adolescent, he had replaced Diamond as the blackface dancer of note for P. T. Barnum. Barnum accused Diamond of embezzling money and engaging in disreputable conduct (alcohol and women). He then hired Lane whose act consisted of imitating all of the well-known dancers of the time and culminating with a finale of his own dance style.[57] Thomas Low Nichols, an editor at the New York *Aurora*, wrote about Lane's performance for the Barnum entertainment emporium. Barnum dressed Lane in a wig; blackened "the little 'nigger's' face and rubbed it over with a new blacking of burnt cork"; and exaggerated his lips to enunciate the African-descended features not to distort his racial composition necessarily, but to disguise the fact that he was a black man. "Had it been suspected that the seeming counterfeit was the genuine article, the New York Vauxhall would have blazed with indignation."[58] At the time of the dance challenges or "trial dances," Diamond "prided himself on his skill at negro [*sic*] dancing," but Juba ridiculed him and other white dancers in blackface in his dance performance.[59] Therefore in 1844, he engaged Juba in a series of dance challenges that took place at John Tryon's Amphitheatre, the Chatham Theater, and the Bowery Theatre. Prior to these competitive matches, Diamond only competed against "any other *white* person."[60] Perhaps pride and the lucrative prize money led to this change of course, but the black man claimed victory. The *New York Herald* proclaimed that there would be a "Great Public Contest" taking place between "the two most renowned dancers in the world, the Original JOHN DIAMOND and the colored boy JUBA for a Wager of $200." Moreover, the winner would hold the "Title of Champion Dancer of the World."[61] Though the first may have ended in a victory for Diamond, Juba convincingly won the second and third.[62] The win helped Lane take top billing as he toured with three white minstrels. He later performed with White's Serenaders and then in 1848 toured London with Pell's Ethiopian Serenaders. A critic for the *Illustrated London News* proclaimed that the

> Nigger Dance is a reality. The "Virginny Breakdown," or the "Alabama kick-up," the "Tennessee Double-shuffle," or the "Louisiana Toe-and-Heel," we know to exist. If they did not, how could Juba enter into their wonderful complications so naturally? How could he tie his legs into such knots and fling them about so recklessly, or make his feet twinkle until you lose sight of them altogether in his energy.[63]

Master Juba died in London at the age of twenty-seven. Unlike Rice and Diamond, he did not have to appropriate another's culture into his act, though it can be construed that he exaggerated elements of African/African American derived dance and performance to appeal to the tastes of the audience. "White entertainers North and South literally made millions of dollars from Negro material. The Negroes themselves, barred from most theatres as spectators and segregated in others, could seldom see a minstrel show, and at that time they were not allowed to perform in them."[64]

Antebellum southern novelists, dramatists, and journalists helped to solidify the stereotype of the southern slave and thus the person of African descent generally through their various caricatures of blacks in the media and popular culture. Persons encountering such portrayals tended to apply such derogatory depictions to all African Americans despite their station in life. Historian John Blassingame, however, pointed out the fallacy of these stereotypes in his seminal work *The Slave Community*. "[T]he slave did not necessarily act the way white people expected him to behave or the way they perceived him as behaving."[65] Southern whites championed these stereotypes because they assuaged fears of slave uprisings and possible rebellion. "If whites really believed that a majority of slaves were Sambos [the docile, happy loyal slave], how could they also believe that these pathetically loyal and docile blacks would rise up and cut their throats?...The white man's fear of the slave was so deep and pervasive that it was sometimes pathological."[66] Abolitionists helped to promote such stereotypical portrayals as well. By depicting black women ravished by white men as mulatto women with features closer to those of Europeans rather than Africans, they perpetuated the European/white American notions of the standard of beauty. Southern whites answered this criticism with the caricature of mammy: their version of the complete opposite of the Europeanized black female. These prolonged slave stereotypes manifested into sustaining derogatory characterizations of all blacks.[67]

Blacks provided whites with the material they could use to make money. Since blacks had limited professional performance opportunities prior to emancipation some deemed this lopsided relationship as a form of cultural exchange rather than exploitation. And while the exaggerated imitation of enslaved blacks formed the basis of this genre, blackface minstrels did not hesitate to proffer any skit, joke, or song from various cultural sources to entertain. "He [the blackface minstrel] was willing to find his profit in the past and to translate into negro [sic] dialect any farce, however ancient, which might contain comic situations or humorous characters that could be twisted to suit his immediate purpose."[68]

Between 1870 and 1890 the minstrel show, an early forerunner of musical theater that combined elements of theater, comedy, music, and dance, was the primary source of entertainment for the American public in general and a substantial part of the black community, specifically. Depicting black plantation life—shows typically centered around stories occurring during slavery or remembering times of slavery—these portrayals were based on stereotypical views of blacks. Nevertheless, the performers needed to be adept at dancing, singing, and comedic acting for a successful show. In the decade before the Civil War a few blacks began performing in minstrel shows and organizing some short-lived troupes. After the war, with the formation of the black troupe the Georgia Minstrels, organized by James Drake in 1865, a distinct strain of black minstrelsy emerged, which placed more emphasis on dancing elements such as the performance of the cakewalk. Dancing, typically, was a highlight of the show. Black troupes generally performed for black audiences though whites were not prohibited from attending, and whites performed for white audiences that did not admit African American patronage. Though black troupes performed across the nation and at times internationally, northern white audiences typically viewed whites in blackface rather than black minstrels. However, for a certain segment of the white population, it became "in and daring to attend the black minstrel show performances."[69] In this performance realm the performers, though copying the derogatory blackface presentation and many of the stereotypical negative beliefs about African Americans, utilized authentic source material for the music and dance numbers. In this sense, the audience was laughing with the performers rather than laughing at them—an important difference when considering the audience and performer segregation factor. James Weldon Johnson and Langston Hughes pointed to the positive performance aspects of black minstrels despite the continuation of performing in blackface and perpetuating detrimental stereotypes. Johnson surmised that black minstrels brought "something fresh and original." Furthermore, "They brought a great deal that was new in dancing, by exhibiting in their perfection the jig, the buck and wing, and the tantalizing stop-time dances."[70] Finally, this became a training ground for those seeking theatrical experience and training when other avenues remained blocked. After minstrelsy, this could be translated into more legitimate performance pursuits. Along similar lines, Hughes denoted that black performers "brought with them their indigenous qualities and the genuine basic beat. They revealed new dances, songs, and comedy routines that the whites had not yet appropriated."[71]

By the 1850s, the typical minstrel show had developed a standard format and contained three distinct acts: the First Part, the Olio, and the Afterpiece. The beginning featured the ensemble cast seated in a semicircle and featuring the endmen Mr. Tambo (with the tambourine) and Mr. Bones (with bones or caste-nets), comedians that played the foil to the straight-man interlocutor, or the master of ceremonies. This portion ended with the walk-around where, eventually, the entire cast danced. The walk-around had a connection with the ring shout (in its spatial formation), and challenge dances of the breakdown and juba. Though minstrelsy began with the exaggerated imitation of blacks, Arthur Todd reasoned that this portion of the show harkened back to elements of African dance. "The chorus sang for the dancers, as they first had in Africa, while the rest of the group clapped their hands and shook tambourines and everyone in the company was given the opportunity for a solo bit of some sort."[72] The Olio middle portion consisted of various performance acts that showcased dancing, singing and acting. The final act, the Afterpiece, often was a take on some popular dramatic piece and reprised the walk-around. Carl Wittke in *Tambo and Bones* reported that the three-part minstrel show was indicative of early minstrelsy, but as it progressed into the latter half of the nineteenth century only had two parts—the afterpiece had been collapsed into the Olio. "For some years there was a third part, consisting of farce, comic opera, or burlesque, but this was gradually merged with the other acts of the olio."[73]

The cakewalk originated as a dance that while using African-based steps was a parody of the mannerisms of whites. It evolved from the chalkline dance where dancers danced in a straight line while balancing water on their heads, and the elaborate balls and cotillions given by southern whites that would end with a type of grand march or promenade. A formerly enslaved woman remembered, "Us slaves watched white folks' parties where the guests danced a minuet and then paraded in a grand march ... marching down the center together." But when blacks developed their rendition, they utilized the form "*but we used to mock em*, every step. Sometimes the white folks noticed it, but they seemed to like it: I guess they thought we couldn't dance any better."[74] According to historian Brooke Baldwin, the plantation whites who witnessed this parody became unwitting participants by accepting their supposed superiority against the inferiority of the enslaved, but not recognizing that they were not being praised but were actually the butt of the joke.[75] Dance scholar Katrina Hazzard-Gordon (Donald) pointed to the fact that this dance did not stop at simple mimicry, but actually was a derisive dance that commented on the institution of slavery and the social hierarchy that it emphasized. Moreover, participation in the special plantation dances was not a given and was utilized to build community and preserve African culture. "Dance was an essential element in reinforcing the fragile normative structure in the slave quarter community."[76] The cakewalk would be a standard dance form during the minstrelsy period and a dance craze at the turn of the century. Southern whites had performed the dance and plantation owners had, at times, danced it prior to the Civil War. Near the turn of the twentieth century, northern whites that frequented entertainment venues where ragtime was played became familiar with the dance as well. Once the dance moved out of the black community and into mainstream popular culture, whites attempted to co-opt it.[77]

As part of the cast of Sam T. Jack's *The Creole Show* in 1889, which included men and women performers without blackface makeup, Dora Dean and Charles

Johnson helped to popularize the cakewalk with their finale rendition. Eager cakewalkers participated in various contests and Madison Square Garden hosted the first national competition, or Cakewalk Jubilee, in 1892. Fifty couples participated and the winners claimed the $250 prize purse. The production team of Will Marion Cook with Paul Laurence Dunbar (though much of Dunbar's book was not used) created the show *Clorindy—The Origin of the Cakewalk* in 1898 originally for the comedic dance team of Bert Williams and George Walker, but eventually starring Ernest Hogan. This show brought the cakewalk to the legitimate stage where it was readily viewable by whites.

Following Johnson and Dean, Williams and Walker had introduced the cakewalk in a more professional manner to a mainstream audience, two years prior to *Clorindy* in 1896, through a show produced at Koster and Bial's Theatre. They and their female partners were so popular that they appeared in several advertisements doing the cakewalk.[78] The comedic duo capitalized on their and the cakewalk's popularity by challenging wealthy railroad magnate William K. Vanderbilt to a cakewalking contest. Vanderbilt had taken lessons from black performer Tom Fletcher and then performed his version in public. This proposed dancing duel likely satirized whites' growing fascination with this plantation dance, but on a more serious level fought for their livelihood and against "the white race's attempted ultimate usurpation of this black cultural form."[79] In their hand-delivered challenge letter, they proclaimed that since Vanderbilt had been such a hit in his dancing and commanded the public's attention that they "hereby challenge you to compete with us in a cake-walking match, which will decide which of us shall deserve the title of champion cake-walker of the world."[80] They bet the nominal sum of $50 because they knew that Vanderbilt probably would not accept the challenge (he did not), nor compete with them if he did. High-society whites, as personified by Vanderbilt, catching the momentum of the fad and performing the dance catapulted it to its standing as a ballroom dance. But although high society embraced this dance craze, not everyone was convinced of its innocence as harmless fun. An editorial in the *Music Courier* lamented, "Society has decreed that ragtime and cakewalk are the thing, and one reads with amazement and disgust of historical and aristocratic names joining in this sex dance." It continued to lambast people taking part in the black-derived dance trend excoriating that the "cakewalk is nothing but an African danse du ventre [sexual type dance], a milder edition of African orgies."[81]

Williams and Walker helped spread the dance to England and France when they toured *In Dahomey* beginning in the spring of 1903. They had played the London music halls previously, but without success. According to Johnson, the "English appeared not to be able to understand or appreciate their particular brand of humour [sic]."[82] At a command performance for the Prince of Wales's ninth birthday, Walker and Williams helped popularize the dance for the European audience as they exuberantly hammed it up for audiences and even taught it to the young prince. This marked the beginning of black social dance being internationally recognized.

When the dance caught favor with whites, many tried to profit from it. White musicians, including John Philip Sousa, composed songs to accompany cakewalks, but the public seemed to crave the more authentic black original. Similarly, white cakewalkers did not satisfy the public's interest either. In this instance, black artists were able to somewhat protect this cultural form from complete amalgamation. The cakewalk was associated with blacks, and when whites could not fully appropriate the dance and accompanying music, they depicted blacks as gauche, poor imitators of whites. In the advent of modern advertising, cultural artifacts such as postcards, product advertisements, prints, cards, photographs, and toys presented an exaggerated and stereotypical image of black Americans and their popular dance, which became etched in the historical memory of Americans. Instead of a depiction of graceful and innovative dancers, "they were made to appear ludicrous." Such representations and reinforced imagery, then and now, equate the cakewalk solely with minstrelsy and the portrayal of the "cakewalk clown" rather than the dance that inspired a worldwide dance sensation.[83]

Dances of the 1920s and 1930s[84]

Social/vernacular dance is an expression of the society that practices it. It is also a reflection of economic, cultural, and political forces that affect it and vice versa.[85] Social dance is in fact dance that is done for pleasure and is also indicative of a society's values such as proper sex roles, class distinction, and appropriate behavior. In Western dance culture the image portrayed through the dance is that of the encounter with an enchanted stranger.

Mainstream couple dancing began with the American Revolution, but it was not until the early nineteenth century and the arrival of the waltz that men and women were permitted to dance face to face. While this presented a semblance of intimacy, the dance was still regulated by the basic form of the dance—the partners' bodies did not touch—and the etiquette of the ballroom, which suggested that the participants dance with people of the same class and who had only the most honorable of intentions.[86]

By the early twentieth century, dances were popularized in Broadway or dance shows. For blacks, African dance gave way to African American dance as European dance customs were incorporated into African forms. For example, in traditional African dance, men danced together and women danced together, but as they adapted and adopted traits, men and women danced in couples. Certain ballroom dance patterns would be utilized, but the essence of the dance would remain African.

Vernon and Irene Castle (dancing from 1912 to 1915)—the epitome and essence of what mainstream ballroom dance should be—borrowed most of their dances from blacks, and further danced to the music of James Reese Europe's all-black orchestra. One example of this was their famous fox trot, which came from the black and "more vulgar" turkey trot.[87] Therefore they utilized black culture for their own economic salvation without always crediting the source. Additionally, they also modified the "Negro" forms to make them more acceptable and easier to master by the whites. [88]

By the end of World War I America, on the whole, had changed. Women's skirts and hairstyles were shorter, the use of cosmetics was on the rise, and they had won the right to vote. Due to the Volstead Act, the country was supposedly "dry," and radio and talking films were definitely all the rage as the 1920s ushered in the Jazz Age a time of "undiscipline and excess which was exhibited in such social phenomena as crowded theatres, nightclubs and speakeasys [sic] and dande [sic] marathons."[89]

The Charleston helped define the era of excess and the search for unending entertainment. However, white America's fascination with black popular culture resulted in not only the appropriation of black dance forms, but the revision of the historical origin as well. Composer Will Marion Cook lamented the purposeful dishonesty with regard to the real genesis of the Charleston and black bottom, which the paper attributed to George White's Broadway show, *Scandals*.[90] Ann Pennington's watered-down version of the black bottom is what popularized the dance in the white community. "I wish to take exception to one or two statements in the article in [the] Sunday Times lauding George White and his scandals [sic]. Among other accomplishments Mr. White is credited with the creation of the 'Charleston' and 'Black Bottom' dances." Cook attempted to mitigate the situation by praising the producer's work. "I have the greatest respect for Mr. White, his genius as an organizer and producer of reviews." Nevertheless, he queried, "[W]hy do an injustice to the black folk of America by taking from them the credit of creating new and characteristic dances?" The dances emanated from the South and found their way to the northern, urban communities by way of the waves of the Great Migration. The movements from these dances had been in the black community for a long time and similar movements surfaced in Caribbean and African dances.[91] In fact, the African root most likely explains why West Indian immigrants, also a part of the black migration to the United States (especially to Harlem), had the same Charlestonian rhythmic meter in their dance and music.[92] As White explained, "From 'Old Jim Crow' to 'Black Bottom,' the negro [sic] dances came from the Cotton Belt, the levee, the Mississippi River, and are African in inspiration." Moreover, the "American negro [sic] in search of an outlet for emotional expression, recreates and broadens these dances." But as it moves out of its original environment and is exposed to a wider audience, it is reinvented and historicized/reclassified.

> Either in their crude state, or revised form, in St. Louis, Chicago or New York, the dance is discovered (?) by white theatrical producers and sold to the public as an original creation. The "Charleston" has been done in the South, especially in the little islands lying off Charleston, S.C., for more than forty years to my knowledge. The dance reached New York five years ago.... Similarly, for many years, the "Black Bottom" has been evolving in the South.... Messrs. White et al. are great men and great producers. Why, with their immense flocks of dramatic and musical sheep, should they wish to reach out and grab our little ewe lamb of originality?[93]

The *New York Times* published the results of the 1926 Committee of Fourteen's findings on conditions of vice in Harlem. Citing prohibition as a prime reason for the emergence of so many underground nightclubs and speakeasies, the report stated that these amusement venues were under-policed and "virtual rendezvous of vice." It further contended that with the publication of Carl Van Vechten's provocative *Nigger Heaven*, more and more whites were frequenting Harlem and thus subject to this moral degradation. City planners purposefully located urban vice districts in black areas. Usually, however, whites had their own exclusive places, like Connie's Inn, the Cotton Club, and (to some degree) Small's Paradise (though blacks were grudgingly admitted here), in which to view black entertainment without having to actually associate with Negro patrons.[94] There were other ballrooms and clubs that did cater to black clientele—often, depending on the geographic area, only on certain nights of the week—but with the opening of the Savoy Ballroom on March 12, 1926, blacks had their own arena in which to express their cultural dance tradition. Here, though it did not discriminate, the whites would have to take a backseat. Charles Buchanan, the black (of West Indian descent) manager and part-owner with Caucasian Moe Gale, sought to produce a dance establishment that would serve the local community. Dancers Frankie Manning, Norma Miller, and Ernie Smith all recall the atmosphere and allure of the Savoy. Manning stated, "You hear this music. Before you even reach the ballroom, you're already in the mood. You say, 'Oh wow, listen to the music!' "[95]

Commenting on the sociological aspects of the opening of this palais de danse, Miller relayed that: "Here was now a place that opened that belonged to black people. Our ballroom had opened in the heart of Harlem. This is our social center: our community center. And of course I didn't know it at this stage, but those doors opened in 1927 [*sic*], blacks walked through those doors like whites. Whites came to our ballroom. So, consequently, there was a mixture of black and white at that social level that had never existed in America before."[96] White dancer Smith said, "I wanted to go to the Savoy Ballroom because I had read about it by now, and I had heard about it. So when I was sixteen, I had saved up enough....I came to New York with a friend of mine, and the first thing that I wanted to do was to go to the Savoy Ballroom."[97] Smith explained this allure that black culture possessed. "Those white folks with a developed taste for hot music or some other aspect of black culture, made frequent visits uptown, to experience the real thing on home ground....A cynical observation by many Harlem residents at the time was that 'Harlem was ours during the day but belonged to white folks at night.' "[98]

Pepsi Bethel, a professional dancer whose traditional jazz dance style comes from the dances of the period, remembers the difference between the Savoy and another of Harlem's large ballrooms, the Renaissance. The "Renny" really was a place where a slightly younger crowd went to dance. The dance was different—possibly more authentic—since whites did not frequent this ballroom like the Savoy. "The Savoy was more of a tourist place. The Renaissance was not a tourist place because very rarely [were] there Anglos there—very rarely in the Renaissance." The competing, lesser known (to whites) ballroom served "practically [a] high school group. They had their own style that you never, never...[saw] it danced in the Savoy. I mean this is how different it was."[99] Though not necessarily detracting from Bethel's observation, Lindy legend Manning also denoted the difference in the Renny and the Savoy, but characterized it more as a training ground for the Savoy where an older and more professional crowd danced. Norma Miller agreed and described this ballroom as preparing her for a professional dance career. [100] Bethel continued:

> At the Renaissance [there] was one [dance] that [they] did there: a dance called the Mooch.... It was like the girl's back was gonna break.... They didn't ever do it [the Mooch] in the Savoy. And so in the Savoy, you had your...contest night like that at the Renny.... I don't think that they had any kind of contest, in fact, cause it was just such an atmosphere at the Renny.... They had their own style and format at the Renny.... It was a different crowd. [101]

All different groups had their special night at the Savoy. "Mondays, Tuesdays they [the dancers] came early because the admission price rose at 6 p.m. from 30 cents to 60 cents and rose again at 8 p.m. to 85 cents. " Mondays were "Ladies Night" and Thursdays were referred to as "Kitchen Mechanics Night"—reserved for those in domestic occupations. Wednesdays and Fridays were usually rented out to various social and fraternal organizations. Saturday was "Square's Night" because "the middle-aged white squares showed up to watch the dancers," so the club was usually very crowded and the "real" dancers would not have a lot of room to perform up to par. [102] On Sundays, celebrities patronized the Savoy and the best dancers could garner good money. "For the Savoy 'regulars,' dancing became a way of life. They earned money from tips and contests sponsored by the management to entertain the 'square' customers." Tuesdays were reserved for "dancers" only. At this time, serious dancers—the 400 Club—would hone their craft in order to practice for the other nights of the week. There were not any crowds, so there was plenty of dance space in which to move. [103]

Herbert "Whitey" White (aka Mac), a former boxer, became a bouncer and floor manager at the Savoy and later organized the dancers and acted as a some-time choreographer and agent: booking them for outside dance events. White realized that the high-flying, acrobatic moves of the Lindy hoppers proved to be a financial windfall. Tourists and celebrities came to the Savoy, an integrated ballroom, to watch the dancers, or pick up a few moves. Single males could purchase a dance with one of the hostesses, but the real attraction was the dancers who perfected their craft for their audience. "When the tourists came to the ballroom, they saw what they thought was a spontaneous exhibition by a regular group of dancers, simply in a ballroom to enjoy social dancing. But that wasn't the case, what they were watching was rehearsed and choreographed dance." [104] While the Savoy made a significant amount of money from those who came to watch the dance and not necessarily to participate, manager and part-owner, Charles Buchanan emphatically denied that anybody but the black dancers were the primary focus. "Our business is the volume of dancers." Other New York ballrooms like the Roseland did not admit blacks, but their patrons sometimes frequented the Savoy. "We never encourage the downtown trade. We're not partial to white people who come to gawk. They must sit down and behave themselves or out they go. Besides we're not geared to make money out of them. They can't spend more than the admission fee and the price of a couple of drinks."[105]

The dancers reserved, in 1928, their own Corner/Cats' Corner located in the northeast corner of the dance floor. "Only the elect were allowed to sit or dance there," and one way of dealing with an "intruder" was to break his shins with Charleston kicks. Moreover, no one was allowed to copy another's steps.[106] Frankie Manning disputes the naming of the designated area of the dance floor as Cats' Corner. He recollected that it was simply called the Corner and further that "Whitey" White persuaded Charles Buchanan to create a special section specifically for the best Lindy hoppers so that the other patrons would not get hurt by flying kicks or other dance moves. Manning recalled that when first honing his skills as a Lindy hopper, he and his friends would steal steps from the older, more experienced dancers, and if they had the gumption, take a spin in the special area.[107]

> It wasn't like that section was prohibited to us when we first began going to the Savoy. Anybody could dance there if they had the nerve. Some couples had the attitude that they were good enough—kids from the Bronx or Staten Island or Jersey—so they'd get out there. Maybe they didn't look like much, but it wasn't as if anything would happen to them. Nobody told them to get out of the circle. At worst, another couple might swing out on the floor to show them how it was supposed to be done, then look back and say, "That's the way you do it."[108]

Still Leon James, a member of the older set that Manning emulated, remembered his acceptance into Cats' Corner a bit differently. "When I went up there, Shorty Snowden was the all-time greatest. One thing: Nobody copied anybody else or did somebody else's specialty, because he'd get whipped up, tromped in the middle of the crowd by all the others." Therefore, he made his steps noticeable of unique in order to get noticed. "I could never do steps like the other guys anyway. I'd just wiggle my legs and it came out different—Clock Clock they called it sometimes legomania—so they accepted me in Cats' Corner." Similarly Albert Minns was unconventionally accepted into the selected Corner dancers. He had learned the virtuoso steps of the Corner from a girl that had been secretly taught by Chick Hogan. When "King" Leon James entered the ballroom one night, he had commanded the attention of most of the patrons because not only had he won the Harvest Moon Ball dance contest, but he also had just returned from appearing in a Hollywood movie. As was the custom, everyone waited "until the King appeared, and then, starting with the scrubs and working up to the King, each couple was supposed to perform in turn. After the King danced, a respectful intermission took place." Minn's then seized the opportunity after James had danced to grab a partner and perform some standard routines and new steps of his own: totally breaking tradition. Instead of being mauled by the group, he was congratulated by James who was impressed with his dancing ability.[109]

One reason why people danced was to forget the hassle and hectic pace of everyday life. Though the stock market crash of 1929 ushered in the Great

Depression, economic trends generally affect those in marginal groups first. By the time that the Savoy had opened, many of those economic trends that eventually contributed to the Depression had already surfaced in Harlem. A night at the Savoy, however, was an affordable way to spend an evening and forget one's troubles.[110] "The depression [sic], strangely enough, brought an increase in ballroom dancing—probably because the public had more time on its hands for frivolity and a yearning for anything that was cheering."[111]

In an atmosphere such as this, it is no wonder that one of America's most popular and enduring dances was born. The Lindy hop, so named for Charles Lindbergh's triumphant flight across the Atlantic, was actually an evolved form of the Texas Tommy.[112] Ethel Williams, who along with John Peters, performed the Texas Tommy in the 1913 show *Darktown Follies* said, "It was like the Lindy, but there was a basic step—a kick and a hop three times on each foot." The Lindy's basic step is a syncopated two-step with the accent occurring on the off-beat and a "relaxed and ebullient quality." As Williams noted, the main difference between the two is on the breakaway. "You add whatever you want there."[113] Though Ray Bolger, of *Wizard of Oz* fame, alleged to have invented the Lindy in 1927 at the Hotel Coronado in St. Louis, and John Banting traced its origins to Philadelphia, Shorty Snowden is credited for its rediscovery.[114]

> We used to call the basic step the Hop long before Lindbergh did *his* [his emphasis] hop across the Atlantic. It had been around a long time and some people began to call it the Lindbergh Hop after 1927, although it didn't last. Then, during the marathon at Manhattan Casino, I got tired of the same old steps and cut loose with a breakaway. Anything you could dream up was okay for the breakaway, you tried all kinds of things. Everybody did the same starting step, but after that, look out, everybody for himself. For example, the Shorty George, a step which was well known in Harlem, I just made it up during a breakaway in the Lindy.[115]

The breakaway move really was a throwback to the challenge dances of African origin. Marshall and Jean Stearns clarified the association and determined that the breakaway, "is a time-honored method of eliminating the European custom of dancing in couples, and returning to solo dancing—the universal way of dancing, for example, in Africa." Katherine Dunham reported that she saw similarity in the movement of the Lindy and the popular urban Jamaican dances—the sha-sha or mento.[116] Frankie Manning posited a trilogy of dances that contributed to the formation of the Lindy: the Charleston, the collegiate, and the breakaway. Manning first encountered the collegiate, which had a similar count to the Charleston and breakaway, at Harlem's Alhambra Ballroom. Partners faced each other in a rigid hold and performed the main step in the dance by turning the leg inward and kicking the leg backward similar to the Charleston. Manning likened it to the shag and mused that it was like "doing the Charleston, but with your partner, and without swinging your legs so much." The breakaway was the strongest link among the three dances and the Lindy. "Originally, the Lindy and the breakaway were really the same dance. However, it took a while for the new name to take hold." He figured that he had witnessed "a very flashy version of it [the breakaway] with some variations, a different style..., and more energy." The swing-out was longer and the partners released their hold. [117]

The Lindy had two distinct styles of performance: the floor school and the aerial school. The date of this separation has been placed in June of 1937, after Al Minns broke the tradition of the Cats' Corner. The "old guard" Leon James, Leroy James and Shorty Snowden objected to these acrobatic moves, but Minns, Joe Daniels, Russell Williams, and Pepsi Bethel took the dance to new heights with their breathtaking dance style.[118] The old guard had moved on to more professional jobs, but had heard that the younger Savoy Lindy hoppers were wowing the crowds. They decided to hold a contest to see who danced the best. In reality, Manning admitted that Snowden and his dancers were better at that time and that a contest was not necessary, but Herbert White picked the teams, Manning and his partner Frieda Washington included, that would compete. Manning figured that he and Washington would need to perform completely new steps in order to have a chance against Snowden. He came up with a play on the signature step that Shorty Snowden performed with his partner Big Bea where she carried him off the floor. It was comical since there was an obvious height difference with Big Bea standing nearly a foot taller than Snowden. Frankie Manning thought that instead of Washington trying to carry him off, she could instead flip over his back. They practiced the move for nearly two weeks and were ready to unveil it during the contest. Manning relayed the first performance of an air step. "I swung her out and did a jump turn over her head.... Then I jumped so we were back to back and flipped her." They executed the move perfectly to Chick Webb and his band's rendition of "Down South Camp Meeting," and when they finished the crowd was in awe. "Their mouths opened, but no sound came out. It was as if people weren't sure they had really seen what they'd seen, like they were trying to figure out what we had just done. They were awestruck. Then all of a sudden, the house *erupted*!"[119]

The addition of flight in the dance literally took it to new heights. The dancers confessed that these steps "had to be carefully worked out. They required great physical ingenuity and utmost trust between partners, since they were acrobatic, and often dangerous." As the steps caught on, many dancers incorporated the moves into their routines. "Most couples had a repertoire of aerial maneuvers, which included such moves as the Hip to Hip, Over the Head, Over the Back, and Back Flip." Creativity and improvisation ruled as the dancers did not abide by "any rule governing their appearance within the framework of the dance. This happened by the 'feel' between partners and the music."[120]

As for whites trying to perform the intricate steps of the Lindy, Frederick Bond stated, "Whites have marveled at the dance...and have had it taught to them by Negro dance teachers; but because of its difficulties of performance, it has not been widely taken up by whites. [It is a] most facetious spectacle to see whites trying to do the dance."[121] And though Ray Bolger tried to lay claim to inventing the dance, Ernie Smith commented that since culture is expressed through dance movement, "even when whites are doing it, it's a black dance." Actually, when the Lindy moved into the white communities, it became known under a new name, the jitterbug. "The Lindy hop swept the country, but as it moved into the white community, the style changed. People learned the Lindy from people in dance studios creating new steps and a new name." Smith denoted that the jitterbug moved up and down instead of side to side like the style of the Lindy; therefore, it was "not as smooth. Instead of all this hopping up and down, everybody was very smooth. It's [lindying] effortless looking dancing."[122] Moreover,

> the white jitterbug is often than not uncouth to look at...but the Negro original is quite another matter. His movements are never so exaggerated that they lack control, and there is an unmistakable dignity about his most violent figures...there is a remarkable amount of improvisation...mixed in with...Lindy Hop figures. Of all the ballroom dances these prying eyes have seen, this is unquestionably the finest.[123]

Dance during the Depression decade served as more than simply the physical release of energy to absolve the performer of the pressure of daily life brought on by the economic downturn; it was an identifying factor that helped to affirm blackness and group solidarity. The dancers influenced white Americans who were eager to learn the new dance crazes as an escape from their everyday woes and a flirtation with the supposed hedonism that black culture and people represented—even if they did not have to in some cases socially interact with blacks while utilizing their dance moves. Dances that originated in Africa, the Caribbean and the southern states evolved into something uniquely African American. And why did the whites rant and rave over this black cultural expression, and even try to claim that it came from their own European background? "These Negro dances invariably become the rage with white people months and sometimes years, after colored people have waxed enthusiastic over them."[124] Though they were quick to downplay any contributions made by blacks, obviously they were attempting to capture through the dance something that was lacking in their own traditions. Was it solely the dance—by nature a pressure releasing physical activity? Probably not, but they could see even if they would not admit, positive traits in African American culture that the blacks were either sometimes unaware of, or too busy trying to define themselves by another's cultural standards that they were not aware of their own worth and/or impact. These cultural traits were exported through the dances of the period to all parts of the world. Soldiers during World War II transported the Lindy hop or swing dance around the globe.

The resurgence of the Lindy hop and various swing dance forms in the 1980s and 1990s corresponded to the promotion of neo-swing music and emanated from various motives and viewpoints of the practitioners. Those who had danced these forms in their youth continued to do so; however, now it became popular with a youthful crowd that rediscovered and redefined the dance. In his study of predominately white swing dancers in southern California, ethnomusicologist Eric Usner provides insight into how popular culture helps to perpetuate certain historical misinformation, and why these white dancers embrace the swing era and define it in terms of white American ethnicity. "I argue that it is within the American past of the swing era—known through its representations in popular culture as a predominately white phenomenon—that the American [read white] youth in neo-swing are able to connect to a heritage that implicitly fosters a sense of identity akin to ethnicity."[125] The white youth that embraced this music and dance, even to the point of wearing period clothes, idealized the popular remnants of the original time period, as the stylized products of a hegemonic Hollywood ideal of Americaness and thus whiteness. This reinterpretation and reevaluation of the swing era reinforced whiteness and forgot "the fundamental blackness of 'American' culture. Seen in this way, it is clear why swing culture represent[ed] the desirable moment in American culture for these largely white youths to turn to, for in turning to an American culture represented in popular representations of swing, they adopt[ed] an America that looks like them."[126]

In the District of Columbia, two groups, one white and the other black, strive to perpetuate the art of hand dancing, the District's version of swing, to future generations. The National Hand Dance Association, predominately African American, and the D.C. Hand Dance Club, white, continue the social segregation tied to the incarnation of the dance and the nation's capital. "We were segregated, so it gravitates like that," explained white dancer Andy Anderson. The black dancers, spanning the generations tend to frequent many of the nightclubs that cater to the hand dance crowd, while the whites attend dances at lodges and similar venues outside of the city in the suburbs. Race plays a role in the way the dancers hand dance. Whites tend to incorporate more ballroom moves, while blacks use more social dance steps. Moreover, the Caucasian advocates dance to rock 'n' roll music and African Americans have more of a variety of music from which to dance. This may have implications on the continued preservation of the dance form. "It's hard to get younger people into it. If nobody comes in four or five years from now, it's going to vanish," lamented Ron Carroll, a white deejay specializing in hand dance music. "The white clubs are a little sticky with their music. The black clubs aren't."[127] In this particular scenario, white youth are not clamoring to reinvent and thus claim D.C.'s version of swing, but the whites continue to appropriate the form first introduced for the most part during their segregated youth. Blacks, on the other hand, are making a concerted effort to save this black dance form for future generations. As in the above documentation, whites of varying ages in the Washington, D.C. metropolitan area do participate in the larger swing dance community.

Television and Popular Dance: "It's got a great beat and you can dance to it!"

Television came to the American popular culture scene in the early 1940s, but was suspended during the US involvement in World War II. Most of the limited stations (only a few dozen) were located on the either the East or West coasts. By the 1950s, the Federal Communications Commission had granted licenses to several stations representing numerous communities across the country which helped to popularize the medium. At least 50 percent of American homes contained a black and white television set by 1955. Many of the initial popular television shows had been well-received radio shows. Talk shows and sitcoms distinguished TV from radio and the movies. Radio stations took to playing records (especially rock 'n' roll records as they gained popularity) since the new industry of television took sponsors that had once financed various radio programming.

Television dance shows ushered in a new era for music and dance. *Bandstand* (later known as *American Bandstand* after its national launch) personified this phenomenon, mainly because it was broadcast nationally. *Bandstand* started in Philadelphia as a radio show hosted by Bob Horn (at radio stations WPEN, WIP, and WFIL), and then moved to WFIL's television component, which debuted the teen dance show, as *Bob Horn's Bandstand*, on October 7, 1952, with Lee Stewart acting as cohost until his departure in 1955. Dick Clark took over the reins of the radio show and the television show (July 9, 1956) just prior to its national premiere, sponsored by WABC-TV, the following year on August 5, 1957.[128] It broadcasted from Philadelphia until (February 8) 1964 when it relocated to California. It ceased to be a daily show in August 1963, when only a sixty-minute Saturday version was produced. For six years any teenager with access to a television and a penchant for popular music and dance could tune in daily to *American Bandstand*. Eventually *Bandstand* went into syndication in 1987 and stopped broadcasting in 1989, a few months after Clark stepped down as host.[129]

White teenagers became fascinated with what disc jockey Alan Freed would brand rock 'n' roll, or black dance music. As this music steadily permeated popular culture in the 1950s, black songs often were altered from the original production and sung by whites to make them more acceptable to the growing audience. With the advent of dance shows, this youth music gained a measure of respectability because it presented a more sanitized version of what had been essentially race music. Prior to this televised proliferation of the music, white Americans saw this watered-down version of rhythm and blues as something undesirable: coming from a common and indecent place. *American Bandstand*, and the local teen dance shows that attempted to emulate it, married dance with music through the medium of television.

In interviews and approved biographical accounts, Dick Clark, until his death on April 18, 2012, often glossed over the racial history of his beloved television show. He claimed to have integrated the show once he stepped into the host's spotlight. In reality, the show promoted exclusionary policies from the beginning and "regularly blocked black teenagers from its studio audience until it moved from Philadelphia to Los Angeles."[130] In *Bandstand's* inception when there was still concern about whether it would be a popular venture, the staff grudgingly allowed a select few blacks to participate and show off their latest dance moves, popularizing their performance and making their dancing stand out. An early black *Bandstand* dancer Walter Deleall recalled: "When the music came on we were confident dancers, and we'd take over the floor. The white kids were intimidated. We were confident and we danced so well that people looking at the show thought it was a black TV show; there were so many of us there." Not soon after the policies changed so that the black dancers were excluded. For instance, a dress code of a coat and tie was imposed. This impacted the African American dancers because the participants typically came from school, and the black students' dress code did not include a coat and tie while their white counterparts' did—effectively dismissing the black dancers. The dress code as well as many of the attributes of the show which made it legendary, such as rate-a-record, the musical programming, age limitations, membership cards, the regulars and the über-elite Committee, were implemented under host Bob Horn.[131]

As reported by the *Philadelphia Tribune* in October 1957, black teens, inspired by the attempt at school desegregation demonstrated by the Little Rock Nine and discouraged because they could not attend the performance of a local singer, mounted a campaign against the television dance show and the de facto prohibition against African American dancers. Clark often purported that black teens did not want to dance on the show. Besides the dress code, producers distributed membership cards needed to participate, and any black dancers that did venture onto the show generally were not shown on camera and thus were "discouraged...from returning."[132] A 1958 *New York Post* article supported such a claim, and stated that WFIL limited the number of blacks invited to the show and their subsequent camera time. Executives pointed to the furor that erupted when singer Frankie Lymon danced with a white girl on Alan Freed's dance show, *The Big Beat*, as a reason to attempt to quell any racial situations before they escalated. Lymon's actions enraged some southern affiliate stations and forced the show's cancellation, and WFIL feared similar reprisals or a loss of advertising if the show truly integrated. The *Post* reported, "Observers believe the presence of Negroes as *Bandstand* guests...is controlled to the point where few even bother to go." At the time Clark steadfastly refuted such discriminatory claims by stating that the show was "open to anyone who wants to attend." [133] In rebuttal, the African American periodical, the *New York Age*, espoused its views on the "question of Negro participation on the various bandstand programs." The paper determined that though one might glimpse a fleeting black face or form, an "unspoken rule operates—Negro kids simply have been quietly barred from the *American Bandstand*."[134] Some determined black teens thwarted efforts to exclude them. In order to get the membership passes, guests had to write for the tickets. Personnel scrutinized these requests by studying the names and addresses of the applicants to determine if they were black. Walter Palmer sent in fake last names to gain entry. "I...gave them Irish, Polish and Italian last names. They mailed the forms back to our homes, and once we had the cards, we were able to get in that day."[135]

Bandstand may not have wanted black dancers, but it did not have a problem mining black music and dance. In fact, many black artists made their television debuts on the teen dance show, but they were to limit their fraternization with the audience members to signing autographs—certainly no interracial dancing. Interestingly enough though the show's most popular dance duo Bob Clayton and Justine Carelli embodied the ideal of clean cut American teens (ethnic, but blond), many of the dancers were of Italian descent (the Puerto Rican Jimenez sisters also became fan favorites). Philadelphia's demographic patterns often had blacks and Italians living in close proximity. "It is this ethnic diversity and juxtaposition that allowed Philadelphia to become one of the first cities to embrace black-derived...music, and thus put *Bandstand* in a unique position to...become as successful as it did."[136] The teens introduced the latest dances to the viewing audience. While Horn was still host, one of the first dances to catch on was the bunny hop. But as the teens embraced rock 'n' roll, their dance choices evolved as well. Dances that originated in the black community (albeit subject to Clark's approval and devoid of any objectionable movements) suddenly were introduced by the white regulars as their creations. Former dancer Jimmy Peatross recalled that when he and his partner Joan Buck demonstrated "the strand" in 1959, a dance they had learned from black classmates, they "weren't allowed to say that black people taught us." Clark denied such accusations and claimed that *Bandstand* credited dance styles with their African American origins. Buck simply stated that at the time the pair "didn't want to say" where they learned the dance when presented with the opportunity to demonstrate it on national television. In this realm it was easy for the white dancers, who danced to approved popular music whether altered black forms or the authentic composition, to further appropriate the dances as well as receive accolades for their creativity and dance prowess. All the while, "young America watched and danced with enthusiasm, oblivious to the debt of gratitude owed the black community."[137]

Though *Bandstand* was not even the first televised Philadelphia dance show featuring teens, Paul Whitman's *TV-Teen Club*, which featured a young Dick Clark in commercial advertising, started in 1949 and ran through 1954, it quickly emerged as the model to follow.[138] Local teen dance shows played in cities all across the country such as New York (*The Big Beat*), Detroit (*Teen Town*), Baltimore (*The Buddy Deane Show*), and Washington, D.C. (*Milt Grant* and *Teenarama*). Estimates point to hundreds of local shows that launched in the wake of *Bandstand*'s popularity during the 1950s and 1960s. These appeared to be somewhat formulaic with a local host or deejay, and advertising support from local businesses. The dancing teens became neighborhood stars and teens tuned in to learn the latest dances. Local, regional, and at times national acts performed, generally by lip-synching, their popular hits. Typically, however, these shows were either segregated or had few black dancers. In some instances, special "Negro Days" were set aside to accommodate black teens and ensure that race mixing did not occur. For example, Baltimore's teens did not have access to *Bandstand*, which made *The Buddy Deane Show* that ran from 1957 through 1964 extremely popular. Once a month, black teens could dance on Negro Day, but when adolescents threatened to cross the color lime by dancing together, as popularly presented in the Hollywood and Broadway productions of *Hairspray*, producers decided to cease production rather than desegregate.[139]

Motown: Hitsville USA

The Motown sound defined the era of the 1960s. Popular lore reinforces the notion of the possibility of the American dream illustrated by Berry Gordy's founding of his hit-making empire in 1958 with an $800 loan from his family entrepreneurial fund. With hard work and the ready availability of local talent, including musicians, songwriters, and singers, he created a sound that drove an industry. Motown is noteworthy not only because of the iconic sounds that form the soundtrack of black lives in the 1960s especially, but also because of its large crossover appeal, a goal of Gordy's. After attempting to promote his brother Robert's short-lived singing career, an artist who sounded white on records, the music mogul committed to producing black popular music that whites and blacks would purchase. Motown's first bona fide crossover hit was Smokey Robinson and the Miracles, "Shop Around," which led to an appearance on the widely popular *American Bandstand*, the arbiter of cool for what was in for white teenaged America. "Berry wanted to make crossover music. Crossover at that time meant that white people would buy your records." He proffered his business philosophy to the *Detroit News*. "I don't like to call it black music. I call it music with black stars." Berry Gordy followed a model of making rhythm and blues music palatable to a large white audience. Abraham Silver, a Motown vocal coach, deduced that Gordy discovered the winning formula. "Gordy milked it down so it was acceptable to whites."[140] Before white teens and radio stations played Detroit's distinctive sound, black stations and deejays championed the music. As Detroit disc jockey Ken Bell recalled, "At first, we broke the records before the white stations did.... And the black disc jockeys helped Motown get its sound across to the white stations."[141]

Motown's temporal progression parallels that of the direct action phase of the Civil Rights Movement. The label released an album of Martin Luther King, Jr.'s speeches, which forever links it to the protest movement's iconic charismatic figure and the promotion of the Southern Christian Leadership Conference's (SCLC) goals. Historian Suzanne Smith states in her book *Dancing in the Street*:

> Most studies on Motown and its music attempt to analyze how and why the black company achieved the success that it did—especially with white audiences. The larger historical perspective of these works usually involves the recognition that the national civil rights movement, which so tangibly heightened America's awareness of racial inequality during the 1960s, contributed to the popularity of the Motown sound.[142]

Smith argues that the Civil Rights Movement allowed for the broader appeal of Motown as whites encountered the music.[143]

Still when the Motown Revue, the live singing and dancing acts that performed to help boost record sales, and played to majority black audiences in many black theatres that were holdovers of the Chitlin' Circuit, rolled into Birmingham, Alabama, in (November 9) 1962, tension was high as the performers defied southern tradition by playing to an integrated audience in a baseball stadium. Though there were no incidents during the actual concert, the performers got a wakeup call in the ways of the South after the show. "Gunshots rang out as the singers and musicians began to board the bus to leave town. Everyone escaped without injury, but the... brush with violence would leave its mark on all of the participants, many of whom had previously believed that Motown's mystique would shield them from racial attack."[144]

Gordy's main goal was commercial success, so he was cognizant of how his business and artists were viewed, with whom they were affiliated, and how such affected his bottom line. Still, his "procurement of the Graystone Ballroom and the revue's attempts to perform before integrated audiences in the South provide two examples of how the company and its music participated albeit sometimes unintentionally, in the larger campaign toward racial equality." Thus, once the record label recorded and released the speech King made from the Great March to Freedom "the company directly affiliated itself with the potential objectives of the SCLC civil rights campaign."[145] The music of Motown was popular because it was good dance music, whether it supported the latest dance craze or the romantic interlude characteristic of the basement blue light party and the slow drag or the grind.

Cholly Atkins, a former tap dancer with the duo Coles and Atkins, was an important cog in the artist development wheel of Motown. He was the choreographer that mapped out the smooth and intricate steps of the performers. This choreography drew from popular dances that black youth naturally created and recreated, but it would also influence the type of dance they did because they would want to emulate the smoothness, sophistication and hipness of these entertainers. Atkins's staging and stylings ushered in the style of dance known as vocal choreography. Whereas Elvis Presley's hip gyrations were designed to shock, Cole's choreography was not necessarily sexually suggestive, but incorporated fancy footwork like what he was known for during his tap dance performing days. The duo of Coles and Atkins was a class tap dance act—one that emphasized the smoothness of tap dance and performed in formal or upscale attire to counter stereotypical images of black tappers as holdovers from slavery days.

By investing in artist development, Gordy was promoting middle-class values that the elite class of blacks had advanced since emancipation. This notion of respectability in a world that viewed people of African descent as savage and uncivilized was paramount to counter racist images, and advance the race in a time of increasing violence against and degradation toward African Americans. Along this same continuum, Gordy wanted to promote a clean, wholesome image of his artists. "Motown's preoccupation with public image, proper etiquette, and general decorum stood in direct relation to these older philosophies about black respectability and black culture." Despite the focus on business acumen and crossover appeal, Motown had a commitment in selling its palatable black music cloaked in a noncontroversial image that did not support centuries of racist stereotyping. As Du Bois and others had touted during the New Negro Renaissance, that art should be a tool for the advancement for attaining civil rights, "Motown marketed a product that proved that black popular culture could 'uplift the race' on a mass scale; it could be both 'of the people' and dignified."[146]

Teenarama

Teenarama premiered on WOOK-TV in the District of Columbia March 7, 1963. This station, developed by broadcasting businessman Richard Eaton (1899–1981), built upon his earlier efforts (May 1947) of starting Washington, D.C.'s first black-oriented radio station. Newspapers reported that the "Nation's first all-Negro television station" would begin broadcasting in February. [147]

Eaton's venture into the black television market did not necessarily meet with acceptance from the District's African American residents, though many expressed their desire to tune into this new, black-oriented station in letters to the editor sent to the black newspaper, *Afro-American*. District resident Paul Bedick supported the new black station. "Regardless of what many of us, as colored people, may have against Mr. Richard Eaton, WOOK's TV president, we should stand on his side for the new colored TV station. There are a great number of whites against WOOK's TV. They realize better than the colored person, it will benefit the colored race. Therefore, the colored community has been brainwashed in being against such a station." Bedick likened those protesting the station to southern segregationists fomenting a plan to remove the majority black population out of the nation's capital. "When the colored community attacks the new colored TV station, they are playing on the side of Sen. Eastland of Miss. and all the other Southerners who want the colored race in Washington, D.C. to slowdown, back-up into a corner, and make room for the white race to move back into Washington, from Virginia and the Maryland suburbs." [148]

However, a vociferous contingent existed that felt that this ethnic-specific programming promoted segregation. That group of twelve included civil rights activists Walter Fauntroy of the SCLC, Julius Hobson of the Congress of Racial Equality (CORE), Sterling Tucker of the Urban League, and the *Afro*'s editor Ralph Thompson. They met with the Federal Communication Commission (FCC) to discuss not only WOOK-TV, but the District's other radio and television outlets as well. The representatives lamented that the stations did not present a favorable view of the District's black population, which by that time was the majority, and that they did not hire African Americans either. The FCC indicated that WOOK's license was provisional and if the community objected, then "[t] hey could file a protest with the FCC and demand a hearing." [149] Eaton attempted to counter this protest by meeting with certain members of the committee. The challenge to the station as well as the late arrival of necessary equipment and a problem with a transmitter helped cause a delay in its initial broadcasting. [150]

The *Afro*'s editorial staff while in support of a broadcast station geared toward a black audience nevertheless questioned the direction of its proposed programming. "However the fact does remain that WOOK-TV does insult the colored race's intelligence by advertising itself as nothing but a station programming plain ol' music and dancing. As colored people, we've been plagued with that image ever since we were freed from slavery. WOOK-TV only perpetuates this image." The commentary continued to point out the pitfalls of the television medium and the ramifications to African American empowerment.

> About the only way to sum up the harm WOOK-TV is doing us is to point out that it appeals to the lowest common denominator of people's intelligence and passions. It does nothing to uplift them, help them, or make them proud of themselves as a group of people. It will in no way increase our political power, our economic potential, and our dignity.... Colored people are going to be the objects of programming

that not only demeans them, but does nothing to help them attain first class citizenship.[151]

By the 1960s, the former burgeoning medium of television had arrived as a staple of entertainment in many households; however, the portrayal of blacks in this entertainment realm was limited. To see a black face was a rarity and the stereotypical imagery of African Americans as a holdover from slavery and the days of minstrelsy perpetuated the American psyche. Unlike the editor's prediction, WOOK-TV with *Teenarama* as the station's anchor would present a positive image of young blacks that influenced viewers in the viewing area (D.C., Maryland, and Virginia). Still, competing black groups filed to take WOOK's parent company's, the United Broadcasting Company, license when it came up for renewal in 1966.[152]

Teenarama grew out of the radio show that preceded it on Eaton's radio station WOOK-AM. This dance show initially aired in a one-hour time slot, but proved so popular that it expanded within three months to an hour and a half format and two hours on Saturdays. The revenue from this show is what kept the station afloat. *Teenarama*'s premiere followed the demise of the *Milt Grant Show* which aired on WTTG. It started as a weekly show in July 1956, but within a year had evolved into a daily show by March 1957. Teens loved the *Milt Grant Show* and longed to be one of the featured dancers. Black teens could only dance on this program on Tuesdays. These days when blacks took the floor became known throughout the black community as "Black Tuesdays." A dance contest was held daily and the winners would come back to compete in a weekly dance off. Tuesdays' contest winners never won in the weekly competitions.

The show amidst a plethora of criticism left the air in 1961. Many believe this was racially motivated. The show was taped out of the Glen Echo Amusement Park's Spanish Ballroom (located in nearby Maryland). Because of protests by both blacks and whites, the racially segregated park was forced to desegregate in 1961. Thus, after five successful years, WTTG canceled the *Milt Grant Show* in March 1961. The official statement from management claimed that the show had run its course. The more likely cause was the distinct possibility of forced integration of the show since the park was forced to desegregate with the new season slated to open in April 1961.[153]

The all-black *Teenarama* drew teens from all over the District and promoted the "regulars," similar to *American Bandstand*'s "committee." These regulars were the best dancers and appeared regularly on the show. They were expected to help police the behavior of other dancers appearing and introduce the latest dances. Rules included no gum chewing; the dancer must be neatly dressed; one could not talk while the host Bob King was on the air; they had to move out of the camera's way at the end of a dance sequence; and they had to generally behave. Former regular Raynell Fletcher commented, "Sometimes, the new kids get upset when one of the regulars tells them what to do. They think we are being bossy. But we explain that if they don't act right, they can't be on the program." Dancers who were not regulars needed to be invited or picked to appear onscreen. "Bob is very strict on who is seen on the show. If a kid does something, we get him to apologize to Bob. But everyone enjoys the show. The kids like the comments they get when they are seen on television, and it helps them stay out of trouble."[154]

Being a regular gave one celebrity status in his/her neighborhood. Probably about 65 percent of the District's entire teen population (white and black) watched the show. Because of television, white teens could watch black dance styles to which they would otherwise not have access. Many white teens would not readily admit that they watched or enjoyed the show. Host Bob King stated that *Teenarama* had an "open-door policy." He professed, "I wish more white teen-agers would come [on the show]. [155] Though King publicly stated this senti- ment, privately whites were not encouraged to dance on the show. Producer Tex Gathings admitted, "There were thousands of white kids wanting to get in, but the management would not allow it."[156] Though this appears as what some may refer to as reverse racism, management was fearful of negative reprisals if whites were viewed dancing with blacks. Running throughout the decade of the 1960s, there is little doubt that black pride was also a factor. *Teenarama* left the air on November 20, 1970. Its spirit would live on in another locally produced, soon to be syndicated dance show known as *Soul Train*.

The Hippest Trip in America: Love, Peace & Soul!

If the 1960s were known as the Motown era, the 1970s belonged to *Soul Train*. Don Cornelius created the idea for *Soul Train* while working as a part-time radio personality on Chicago's black radio station WVON. He announced the news and sometimes filled in for disc jockeys—his real ambition. Frustrated at presenting the news when he knew that his creativity could thrive elsewhere, he came up with the idea for a televised black dance show to run locally in the Chicago area. He interested a local Chicago station WCIU-TV in airing the pilot, which he produced at his own expense ($400), though the station provided a small studio. He failed at getting financial supporters for the show, but assured WCIU that he would find the backers. On August 17, 1970, the show that he named *Soul Train* premiered in the local Chicago market. It aired five days a week in a one-hour afternoon time slot. Though geared to a black audience of not necessarily teenag- ers, early advertisements of the dance show portend that "teens and young adults of all races" tuned in. As with similar earlier televised shows, Cornelius targeted high school students to supply the talent—a main attraction of the show—and hinted that the age requirements were negotiable. Furthermore, show applica- tions were placed in the inner-city Sears stores, an early backer, where interested dancers could access them and attempt to get on the televised dance show. The host did not receive a salary for the first few months that the dance show aired, but always the businessman he not only hosted but owned and produced the show as well.[157] Cornelius would continue to exert this type of control as the *Train* chugged forward.

The idea and name for *Soul Train* came from the music and dance shows that Don Cornelius previously had produced using Chicago's high schools as venues. Several musicians had used the same name for the title of their songs prior to the launch of the show. Cornelius chose the name because of the popularity of soul music at the time. Soul "became synonymous with African American self-empowerment."[158] In his way, he linked his entertainment venture to the cultural aspects of the Black Power Movement, by producing a product for blacks by blacks. William Van Deburg states that during the Black Power Movement, African Americans sought to promote a distinctly black culture that developed in concert with and distinctly from mainstream culture. "While black Americans both contributed to and imbided from the mainstream, they continued to retain and to cherish black cultural distinctive."[159] Therefore, soul represented black popular culture's adherence to a "black aesthetic" and "perceived as being the essence of the separate black culture."[160] Soul was something intangible that black could and did possess, but was out of reach for those outside of the racial group; it defined a certain group cohesiveness. *Soul Train* played soul music to which the dancers danced. The music embodied the elusive aesthetic as something from the cultural storehouse of African Americans. "Soul music was claimed as the aesthetic property of blacks."[161] Cornelius's embrace of the term soul for the title of the show demonstrated his commitment to blackness as well as a catchy phrase that his young adult audience would appreciate.

The popularity of the show "attracted the attention" of George Johnson, the founder of Johnson Products Industry that manufactured Ultra Sheen/Afro Sheen products. Solidifying his financial backing and the popularity of the show would propel it forward to national syndication only a year after its start (Johnson Products sales doubled after its sponsorship). Sears, Roebuck and Company also financially backed the Chicago version of the show. Cornelius scouted around production sites in Los Angeles because of the limitations of the facilities he had access to in Chicago, the necessary personnel, to be closer to the music industry and to recruit dancers.[162]

Soul Train debuted as a nationally syndicated show on October 2, 1971, but was only carried in seven of the initially targeted twenty-five cities (Atlanta, Cleveland, Detroit, Houston, Los Angeles, Philadelphia, and San Francisco). "Many other station program directors conceded that the show was well produced and very entertaining, but said that they had no open time periods." Sometimes every station in a city would turn down the dance program. Almost invariably, as *Soul Train*'s reputation and popularity grew rapidly in the cities that had accepted the show the syndicator gradually began to pick up more stations. Even in Chicago where the show began, the syndicated version of *Soul Train* did not debut until the end of October. John E. Johnson introduced the national show to the Chicago audience, which still viewed the daily show as well. The *Chicago Defender* reported that the ratings for the show continued to grow and at one point only came second to the World Series.[163]

Cornelius secured Gladys Knight and the Pips for that syndicated premiere. This was no easy feat since the popular music group did not have to do this, at the time, no-name show. This buoyed Cornelius who figured that he would be able to score up and coming artists who needed the publicity and airtime. It was thought that *Soul Train* targeted a black audience though in estimation a large number of whites watched the show as well. Cornelius surmised in a 1976 interview that "If

70 per cent of blacks are watching *Soul Train* and 20 per cent of the white viewing audience, they outnumber us 20 to 1, so it's probably actually more white people watching." Cornelius, however, did not cater to his hypothesized demographic. "*Soul Train* is still a black-oriented show directed at blacks all the way. We do feel that we have as much right to direct our show to blacks as say the producer of *Hee Haw* has to direct his show to whites. Since the beginning of television, shows have been always based on what whites want."[164] By 1972, a year after going national, the *Train* was the only black syndicated show on network television. Cornelius lamented that because of "general market programming" Hollywood did not want to cultivate shows geared toward a black audience. "To me that's an insult. But you can't convince advertisers to sponsor a program geared just to the black viewer." Even if the program garnered a large viewership, executives only spent "about 1 per cent of their advertising budget in black media." Cornelius voiced the opinion that sponsorship of Johnson Products was paramount to the success of the show. "In spite of the show's success, I believe that if Johnson pulled out, there would not be anyone willing to fill his spot."[165]

Interestingly enough, Don Cornelius reflected in several interviews that there was a dearth of black entertainment programming—that only shows with a civil rights, public affairs, or historical perspective served the black viewing population. He sought to fill that void with the music and dancing on the *Train*. "Blacks want the same thing from television whites want. They want to be entertained. One hour about listening about how hard it is or what The Man is doing to us does not entertain blacks.[166] He also expressed his distress that although television was primarily an entertainment outlet and *Soul Train* carried the market at the time, that there still should be a wider representation of African Americans in the industry. For the most part he adhered to a black power mentality with regard to the direction of television and entertainment programming; blacks should control the content and production of such offerings, not simply portray the vision of others as actors or commentators. The former deejay always maintained control over the content and use of *Soul Train*. "Whites see a potential danger in having any type of Black show which brings Black people together."[167]

Writer Warren Foulkes likened the black dance show to ritualistic behavior. The symbol of a grooving train became a symbol indicating a place "to go and a means of getting there"; the host embodied a priestly figure with the responsibility of leading the ceremony; and the dancers, the ritual participants, performed the ceremonial procedures, often pantomiming scenarios that illustrated situations or conditions in the black community such as historical racism and the striated position of African American males in the United States. Many of the dancers spent hours rehearsing and perfecting their craft for the performance ritual, which helped them to secure air time as a regular or featured dancer of the Soul Train Gang. The show, like most rituals, was meant for a specific audience and not for the viewing or participation of outsiders. Journalist Clayton Riley concurred with much of this analysis. *Soul Train* featured soul music and dancing, creating a synergy that fed off of one another. The music was meant for dancing and the cast of young artists did not disappoint. He stated that show embodied "a grooving, swinging, moving thing of beauty, a video sampler of soul carried into a spirited collective ritual where human feeling is extended, is contained within but also carried without the body…the brain."[168] Using Frantz Fanon's theory on communal exorcism to explain the actions of oppressed people to extricate themselves from the source of that oppression, Foulkes theorized that *Soul Train* represented an expression of the black community to combat the entrenched prejudicial bias that African Americans faced. In fact, the show "created a reservoir (e.g., ritualistic dance) to control the release of our pent up energy until it can be directed toward successful liberation of frustrated ambition."[169]

Reflecting his commitment to black music and artists, Cornelius stated, "But I have to be honest and say that I have a specific responsibility to black artists and that has to do with the fact that many black artists you see on my show are not seen on any other major television show. So it's kind of difficult to justify putting whites on. Black artists see *Soul Train* as their show and that's something I have to respect."[170] Though some erroneously would assume that *Soul Train* patterned itself solely after Dick Clark's *American Bandstand*, which aired nationally on ABC- affiliated networks, *American Bandstand* more than likely tried to infuse some of *Soul Train*'s "flavor" to appeal to a broader audience. In comparing the two dance shows, Riley stated that it was like comparing champagne to seltzer water. Moreover, by dancing to popular music and attempting to incorporate the latest dances *Bandstand*'s predominantly white dancers patterned themselves after black youth. "Dick Clark's grim groups of teeny wonders were trying to dance to a music that bore no real relationship to their cultural and social frames of reference." White American adolescents rebelled against their parents by embracing rock 'n' roll music. In this way, they adopted and adapted aspects of black culture to fuel and represent their defiance. "White kids [could]…whip their parents with the lash of ultimate middle class defiance—acting like outlaws, in this case like America's original and lasting criminal class, niggers."[171] Don Cornelius verbalized the obvious correlation, "I think I looked at Dick Clark the right way. I watched him and my trip was: 'Clark went this way and I'll go that way'—the opposite way." In producing his niche dance show, Cornelius responded to such comparisons with, "I never made the mistake of trying to imitate either Clark or his show. Not to say my style is better, but it is my own. If I'm going to call myself a creative person, then I've got to create something."[172]

As the ratings for *Soul Train* climbed, *American Bandstand*'s share of the audience declined.[173] Cornelius, on occasion, did compare the *Train* to *Bandstand*, but did not attempt to emulate the show. Dick Clark did. In fact in 1974 realizing the obvious competition, he attempted to copy the show and take it off the air in some markets. "Look, I don't dig black people not liking white people. I've been seeing too much of that for too long already," offered Clark when queried about his new show *Soul Unlimited* and the backlash spearheaded by Cornelius ally, the Reverend Jesse Jackson. This new creation mirrored *Soul Train* with an African American host (who received producer credit), music, dancers, and artists, and ran for a short time one Saturday out of the month in *Bandstand*'s standard timeslot garnering twice the ratings as its sister show. "That's my time period," TV's oldest teenager blustered. "They want to put a black *Bandstand* on, then I'll do it." In some markets, *Soul Unlimited* preempted *Soul Train*, causing Jackson to accuse Clark of "endanger[ing] *Soul Train* not because it is a better show, but because ABC, as a power, is able to outspend *Soul Train* in promotion, production and talent recruitment." Jackson countered that after *Soul Train*'s rise in popularity, Clark attempted to attract black viewers by enticing *Soul Train*'s dancers to perform on *Bandstand* and then purposely giving them airtime to highlight their moves and fashion sense. When this still did not help in the declining ratings, Clark introduced the true black version of *Bandstand*—his own creation. When questioned about the motive of unveiling a new show aimed at black audiences, Judy Price, a producer for *Bandstand* and *Soul Unlimited* unequivocally stated that Cornelius and his supporters promoted racism since "they're talking about an all-black show. That's segregation!" After Clark bolstered that "Don avoided me for three weeks; he was so in his guts—so riled up, so put upon, the ghetto paranoia put him into this thing about racism," Cornelius, Clark, and Jackson met and Dick Clark Productions cancelled *Soul Unlimited*.[174]

Of course people tuned into *Soul Train* to see the latest dances performed by talented dancers. Don Cornelius cited the Los Angeles style of dance versus that of Chicago as another reason behind relocating the show to the West Coast. Chicago dancers exhibited a type of coolness and smoothness that was a staple in their dance style, while the LA dance gang danced much more flamboyantly, which would translate better on television.[175] Unlike the white kids who copied their dances, the African American youth were not necessarily rebelling with their music or dances. "Black social dancing remains a way of living out of a set of historical realities that have always been at once as familiar to Black grammar school kids as it is to their grandparents."[176] Before Cornelius could score regular big name musical talent on a regular basis, he depended on the dancers, the Soul Train Gang, and dancing to carry the show.[177] The *Soul Train* dancers performed and created some of the latest dances: the get down, hi low, breakdown, PA (Pennsylvania) slaughter, penguin, bump, hustle, and mechanical man (robot). In fact, Cornelius premiered the "Create-a-Dance" segment for the 1972–73 season, which featured some of the aforementioned dances.

Prior to this national show (and subsequent music videos), popular dances could have a local or regional feel or popularity and take a while to travel around the country. Now, adolescents and young adults could tune in on Saturdays for the latest dances that they could then take to parties and get-togethers. Dancers often put their own twist on current dances to make themselves stand out in a sea of talent. The time to shine was of course gliding down the *Soul Train* line. Talent scout Chuck Jackson recruited dancers from all over, including high schools, upscale discos, and round-the-way joints. At the time in the mid-1970s, four shows were taped on the weekend and good behavior was expected. Like its *Teenarama* predecessor, producers enforced a policy against drugs or alcohol, and additionally banned "gum chewing, fidgeting or clowning." Moreover according to Jackson, the dancers received no salaries, instead they got lunch from a local Kentucky Fried Chicken. "They come in droves dying for a chance to just get down in front of the camera. All of them are talented kids who are damn good dancers with a lot of class and heart. To some of them *Soul Train* is their way of life." Cornelius justified the lack of pay with the opportunities the show provided the dance talent.[178]

Dancer James Phillips part of the gang in the 1970s (the guy who always wore the headband for show aficionados) illustrated this phenomenon. Phillips wanted to become a doctor when he started on *Soul Train*. "Most of the time people notice me. It's kind of a funny feeling, especially when they ask you for autographs. I don't consider myself a star, but people do." Their favorite dances and dance style influenced those across the nation.

> Our favorite dances are of course the Bump, the Hustle, the Popcorn, the Four Corners and the Campbell Lock, but every week, the gang or individual couples come up with their own new steps, and boom, it catches on and becomes the new dance craze around. I guess each of us has our own individual styles. I hope some day I have my own show.[179]

An anonymous couple admitted, "We work hard all week and it's a gas to flaunt in front of the camera." Consequently, "Our parents go wild when they see us and it makes us happy, too. We sort of set trends for the kids."[180] And set trends they did: Damito Jo Freeman, a fan favorite with her partner Jimmy "Scooby-Doo" Foster, impressed a young Michael Jackson so much that he invited them and others to his house to raid their dance arsenal. Freeman would later perform and choreograph for television, movies, and Broadway. Jeffrey Daniels, the dance partner of Jody Whatley, both of whom became part of the 1980s musical group Shalamar, often performed the backslide on the show. Jackson later made this dance famous but called it the moonwalk. Professional dancers often came to the set to study the latest dances.[181] Fred "Mr. Penguin" Berry who played Rerun on the 1970s television show *What's Happening!!* started his professional career as part of the dance group the Lockers and a Train regular. The Lockers specialized in a form of dance called locking or the Campbell lock after the originator, Don Campbell, also a member of the Gang. Adolfo "Shabba Doo" Quinones, another Locker, found fame in the 1980s breakdancing cult classic, *Breakin'*. White professional dancer, later turned pop star, Tony Basil discovered locking, and became part of the Lockers—their only white, female member. Whatley considered herself a dancer before becoming a member of Shalamar. She moved to Los Angeles in 1974 with her family and longed to be on *Soul Train*. She got her wish when Glen Stafford, a dancer on the show, met her at church and asked her if she wanted to be his temporary partner. At the time, her looks, not her dancing ability, interested Stafford. Whatley determined to become a regular member of the Gang and often snuck into the show in order to be a part of it. She did become a regular and extremely popular with partner Daniels and they embodied the style and creativity of *Soul Train*. They "set the standard for the '70s and '80s Soul Train dancer. They were very creative, their dancing abilities were undoubted and they always seemed to know what to wear."[182]

At the time Don Cornelius, labeled as a black nationalist in television, lamented about the lack of blacks in key positions in the field of television. "These people are forgetting that there are still scores and scores of all-white shows on television. And for anyone to assert or even imply that any black person can actually practice discrimination against whites in this culture today is an insult to everyone's intelligence."[183] Ultimately, the launching of Black Entertainment Television (BET) in 1980 would probably help to signal the end for the popularity of *Soul Train*. Music Television (MTV) began August 1, 1981. In their inception, both networks aired music videos, relatively cheap programming, but MTV refused to play black music videos until Michael Jackson's *Thriller* album and followed that first with the musical visualization of Shalamar. Prince's *Purple Rain* also garnered airplay on the music station. The official policy was that the video jocks played primarily what the audience demanded, which was generally pop and rock music at the time. As rap became more popular and entered the mainstream, programming such as *Yo! MTV Raps* and *Club MTV* emerged. At one point before switching to more of a reality show format, it was hard to distinguish between the offerings of MTV and BET as the network that once shunned black-oriented music played it in heavy rotation. By this time it was what the white audience wanted. *Soul Train* endured under various hosts, after Don Cornelius stepped down in 1993, until 2006. It remains "the longest-running syndicated black music show on television."[184]

You Should Be Dancing, Yeah!

By the 1970s, African Americans, Latinos, and homosexuals popularized disco music, which was simply extended play dance music in their respective communities. Music critics emphasize that the music was producer-driven rather than artist-driven, but what made it popular was the fact that it made people want to dance. The times—the Vietnam War, Watergate, attempting to take advantage of the civil rights and black power struggles—dictated that people needed to feel good. Niles Rodgers of Chic fame proclaimed, "We wrote about happy stuff—not because life around us was happy, but because we chose sort of to pretend that life was happy. I grew up in very political times and then I realized that music provided me a place where I could go and escape from the realities of my normal life."[185]

Disadvantaged groups jumped on the disco bandwagon. Who more than these communities needed the escape and elation that dance for pleasure provides? Gay rights advocates like to lay claim to the origin of disco since the evolution of disco coincides with the materialization of the gay rights movement and these fans helped popularize the music, particularly in the venues they frequented. Producer Jellybean Benitez downplays any cultural claims to disco justifying this stance by stating that the music and dance had no color bounds. Typically when people want to disassociate skin color with some entity, they are downplaying black agency or whitewashing blackness.

Enduring dances included the bump and the hustle in partner dance and line dance forms. Studio 54 was the embodiment of the disco era's link to excessiveness and hedonism. The first owners Steve Rubell and Ian Schrager opened this club April 26, 1977. With over the top celebrities and personalities, sexual freedom, and recreational drug use, this Manhattan disco was the place to see and be seen—the then equivalent with a twist of the 1920s black and tan clubs except without the race or sexual orientation limitations. The other legacy of the era that brought the American public the mood ring and the pet rock was the movie *Saturday Night Fever* (1977) starring John Travolta. A magazine article titled "Tribal Rites of the New Saturday Night," detailing the life of a fictional, composite character of Vincent, became the basis of the movie, and the Bee Gees signed on to do the soundtrack.[186] *Saturday Night Fever* was mainstream America's embracement of the fad that was passing in the communities that had propelled it to its heights. Author and scholar Camille Paglia gushed: "John Travolta's performance in that movie is just brilliant. First of all the way he showed that it was possible for a white man to be a virtuoso of dance in a way that has always been accepted in black culture. He put choreography and graceful moves into the mainstream."[187] In the movie, Travolta's character, Italian American Tony Manero, and his partner, Stephanie Mangano played by Karen Gorney, beat a Puerto Rican and black couple in the climatic dance contest. The racial overtones are obvious as Tony and Stephanie perform their tepid hustle while the other couples out-dance them, prompting Manero/Travolta to give the trophy to the Latino dancers whom he felt should have won.[188]

After the movie, disco record sales at least doubled and, of course, the soundtrack went through the roof. The record industry and artists had to sit up and take notice. For example, people from the rock and punk rock worlds made disco or disco-influenced songs: think Rod Stewart's "If You Think I'm Sexy" and Blondie's "Heart of Glass." Blacks who would not have necessarily purchased these artists liked the songs. Still, the white male rocker, cognizant of the threat to his livelihood and popularity, fought back against this racially influenced music. Amid slogans of "disco sucks," a Chicago disc jockey burned disco records at Comiskey Park. Many felt that this was an overtly racist act since by targeting the music that had long been enjoyed by disaffected groups, and now embraced by whites, which cut into the bottom line of rock sales, the protestors were really reacting against those groups and the creativity and profits they could procure.

Throw Your Hands in the Air!

The anything goes 1970s hit the wall of the conservative 1980s, which would see the emergence of two cable channels that would change the way the public experienced music—BET and MTV. As rap, the musical backbone of what becomes hip hop, hits as the black urban youth music of the late 1970s into the 1980s, its dance counterpart, breakdancing or b-boying also emerges. The author can remember as a dance student in middle and high school in Northern Virginia, it does not get more suburban than that, wanting to learn how to break dance. Some larger dance studios in the area actually offered classes, but the white kids in the author's school did not embrace rap or its accoutrements until the Beastie Boys came out in the mid-1980s. However respectable and/or embraced by the larger rap community, the Beastie Boys were somewhat parodying rap while making whites feel comfortable with the music.[189]

Dances usually resurface about every decade or two. B-boying/breaking is popular once again. The difference this time around is that more people have access to it. A 1999 *Washington Post* article details a night at Soul Camp, a former hip hop club in Washington, D.C., aka Chocolate City.

> Brent Talley stands outside a huge circle, a "cipher," that has opened up on the dance floor. Break dancers from the Lions of Zion and Arrive to Defy, are hitting power moves. Suddenly the energy of the dancers combines with an ominous bass line, giving Talley something he can feel, and he sheds his gray fleece hoodie. He starts head spinning and up-rocking and then hits a nice freeze as the crowd waves and hives him mad love. Weekdays, Talley installs gas lines in Northern Virginia. But Thursday nights, he's Vortex, the spinning and flava specialist for his break-dancing crew. A *nappy-headed* (emphasis added) b-boy with red hair. A crowd favorite. A white guy, dancing to beats played by a white guy, in a room filled with white guys.[190]

The article dutifully questioned whether any one race has the proprietary rights to hip hop and its cultural components (rap, breakdancing, graffiti, lingo), especially since at least 70 percent of all rap is purchased by whites. Some argue that it is a colorless, youth culture—not black or white. One white participant spoke for many of the whites interviewed for the article when he posited that "Hip-hop is mainstream right now. A lot of stuff has blown up. [Whites' involvement is] good for hip-hop. If it wasn't for the white kids in the suburbs, these cats wouldn't be going platinum."[191]

The learned black voice of Dave Cook, who grew up in New York during the beginning of rap, summarized the dilemma, "We [the black community] have creative resources, they have economic resources, so that should be an even match. But it isn't. It's a pimp/ho situation, so I'm being constantly pimped." Music executives are in a position to dictate what they feel will sell in the market place—basically revising the cultural expression born of certain political and economic realities that speak of marginalization of blacks in the larger society. When blacks start selling out for the economic benefit, they "abandon creativity and political expression in order to get record deals." But what happens when white aficionados start to spit rhymes and tap into a market comfortable with seeing a face that looks like theirs—read Beastie Boys, Vanilla Ice, or of course Eminem? When white America embraces hip hop and appropriates it, they can lay claim to their own hip hop aspirations. They make the leap from hip hop consumer to hip hop creator.

In the second season of Fox Television's summer hit *So You Think You Can Dance (SYTYCD)*, Travis Wall and Martha Nichols, early favorites, performed a krumpin' routine. Krumpin' is a dance style created and made popular by Tommy the Clown, a Los Angeles dance personality, who used dance as a deterrent to the streets. Most people outside of the black community in California did not know what this kind of dancing was until the feature film documentary *Rize*, released in 2005, documented this West Coast phenomenon. The judges gave Wall, who is white, all kinds of praise while barely acknowledging Nichols, an African American, who like Wall was considered a contemporary/modern dancer (though tap and hip hop completed her repertoire). Shane Sparks, one of the hip hop choreographers who was moved up to judge in that second season, actually dissed nineteen-year-old Martha Nichols and gushed over eighteen-year-old Travis Wall, who continuously refers to the dance as animalistic and bringing out the gorilla in him. Travis ended up making it to the finals of that season but did not win.[192]

Meanwhile when hip hop/street dancer Musa Cooper was voted off the show, prior to making the top ten and thus not eligible to participate in the lucrative national tour, and after dancing for his life in his own style to curry the judges' favor in the hopes of a save, series producer and personality Nigel Lythgoe said to him that he danced one of the best solos that the panel had seen up to that point, and that he had the talent to win the show. However, the judges wanted him to progress faster in other dance disciplines, even though he had adequately performed the choreography given him. In his parting words, Lythgoe concluded that Cooper did not have the strength as an overall dancer to continue on the show. Cooper, twenty-eight years old from Camden, New Jersey, previously had unsuccessfully auditioned for the show and had gone home after the first season's stint and took dance classes to be considered more of an all-around dancer. The judges still wanted to cut him, but Sparks fought for him to be a part of the second season. When granting him his acceptance into the twenty finalists, Lythgoe warned him that while he was an exciting dancer, he would still be cut from the show if he did not nail the routines. Cooper had gotten as far as he had in the competition by having the natural ability to pick up the various dance disciplines (namely contemporary, ballroom, jazz, Broadway, and hip hop) and remembering the choreography, but from the viewpoint of the judges, his raw talent seemed threatening.[193]

Out of the other street dancers who auditioned for the dance reality show, three (Steve Terada, Victor Kim and Hokuto "Hok" Konishi) members of the same crew (SickStep) progressed to Las Vegas week and Konishi, from Japan, probably would have made it onto the show, but he confessed to immigration issues that disqualified him. White hip hop dancers Ashlee Nino and Ivan Koumaev (whose family emigrated from Russia) did make the show and were nowhere near as dynamic as Cooper. Ivan lasted into the top ten and participated in the sold-out national dance tour. Jaymz Tuaileva and Jessica Fernandez, studio trained dancers, were the alternates on the tour though they were cut before Cooper, who narrowly missed making it into the top ten. Now America put Musa Cooper in the bottom three couples that particular week in question by not voting for him: part of the reason was his partner Natalie Fotopoulos—a capable dancer but one who just strutted around the stage while the focus was on him. Even though they performed a routine where they were "dancing for their lives" the judges decided at that point who should go home.

Different from the first season, the show was billed as finding America's favorite dancer so a likeability factor played into why and how Benji Schwimmer, a good ballroom dancer who became proficient in other disciplines, ultimately walked off with the top prize. Musa Cooper was cut because he was raw. The dancer cannot be better than the person choreographing the routine. When he had to dance for his life, the judges had nothing but praise for him. This is where the political and economic aspects of popular culture are at play and are further reflective of the appropriation and misrepresentation of popular culture when embraced by the larger community. Just think of the absurdity of most of the judges critiquing Cooper's performance when they knew that they, with the exception possibly of Shane Sparks at that time, could not come up with a routine reflective of that level of creativity, ability, and performance.

Music Television's *America's Best Dance Crew (ABDC)* debuted in February 2008. The show aimed to promote and showcase street dance crews, and like its dance cousin *SYTYCD*, relied on the votes of the fans and judges to decide which dance crew is eliminated. The first season's finale pitted the multiracial Jabbawokeez (or JabbaWockeeZ) against the all-black Status Quo. The Jabbawokeez with their trademark gloves and facemasks, akin to something that Jason from *Friday the 13th* would wear, outpaced the underdog Status Quo. The mostly California b-boys dedicated their performances that season to a member who had recently died from meningitis.

Formed in San Diego, California, by Kevin Brewer, Joe Larot and Phil Tayag, the group began performing under the name the Three Musky in 2003. The three-man group grew to seven by the next year and named themselves after the Lewis Carroll poem, "Jabberwocky," which depicted a dragon-like creature—"that's what the Jabbawockeez are, mystical and free." Varying accounts denote the origin of the gloves and facemasks, but member Eddie Gutierrez stated, "The idea of the mask is to remove all ethnic and social barriers when we perform."[194] This is a noble thought of the group, which originally had Filipino, Korean, Vietnamese, Mexican, and one African American member; however, it speaks to the racial politics of the growing hip hop industry. Created by black and Latino (primarily Puerto Rican) youth, b-boying like its musical counterpart came from the streets of the South Bronx, and was influenced by the popular martial arts movies of the 1970s. The Jabbawockeez credit Bruce Lee's martial arts philosophy with impacting their dance style infused with various body beats, Beat Kundo—a mix of popping, locking, and freestyle. The predominately Asian American crew maintains linkages to their ethnic roots, through family and language, but stress their Americanization and fortitude, through eschewing Asian-centered stereotypes of the model minority and strict career-mindedness, by expressing themselves through their art of dance. "There is an artistic side to us—we're Americanized, and we're fourth and fifth generations in America."[195]

Though they had garnered the most votes to secure a spot in the finale, Status Quo, aka the Legendary Seven, obviously did not win season one's competition. They knew that the format of the show, creating choreography to various music and dance challenges, would hinder their chances no matter how much raw talent they exuded. Their opposing groups often had experience with creating choreography. Their lack of experience in this realm forced them to compete in a dance off during week three's show in order to stay on the competition. Crews losing the all or nothing battle find their banners dropped from the rafters and then are forced to "walk it out" or off the stage. Jayjion Green, Joshua Green, Dwayne Hines, Ernest Phillips, Darvis Rutledge, and Jamal Weaver performed on the show while other members of their crew stayed in Boston. Often mixing gymnastics with their dance, that the judges once described as "authentic street, athletic, and amazing," the Boston natives seemed to leave their hearts on the stage after most performances. "We're not really performers; we're more entertainers," offered Phillips, a founder of the group. He initially wanted to form a rap group, but did not have suitable skills. He then figured that dance would be his way to impress the ladies and steer clear of gang violence and other antithetical behavior. Jamal Weaver, a football and basketball player who had been expelled from several schools, found solace in music and dance. He planned to study music at the Berklee College of Music. At the beginning of the show, Dwayne Hines freely admitted that all of his friends outside of the dance crew belonged to gangs and hoped to serve as an inspiration.[196]

Where the Jabbawokeez had style, Status Quo exuded heart—the kind of heart that comes when one is intimately connected to the art presented. The Boston crew beat out nearly 750 other groups (auditions were held in New York, Atlanta, Chicago, and Los Angeles) to make it to the national show and their shot at stardom. MTV vice president Drew Patton explained why the show had invested so much in the ragtag bunch that used the street as a practice venue instead of a dedicated space or studio like many of the other competitors. "Status Quo represents the entire spirit of what the show's all about": that would be the promotion of street dance and the battles between crews in a televised setting. More importantly, "They're young, not polished professionals, with so much talent and so much heart. You can't turn away when they're onstage. They've gotten plenty of praise in Boston, I know. But this is taking them into the national spotlight." In fact, in Boston they advocated against violence by using dance and other outlets as a positive alternative. They made a name for themselves in their hometown by winning the Beantown Bounce dance competition two years in a row and also performing at the Dorchester Idol Competition and Mayor's Youth Summit. "A lot of crews have fight scenes in their routines. We like to make the crowd laugh. Because if they're laughing and happy, they're less likely to start talking and fighting."[197] Status Quo reportedly did not have enough money to get home after the New York audition and MTV paid the bills between the audition and the finale.

Blogs about *ABDC* during that first season appear to overwhelmingly favor the Jabbawokeez. While it is difficult to discern the ethnic or racial identity of the writers of the posted comments, the racial bias is apparent. The accusation that Status Quo routinely stole their choreography from New York street dancers who performed in Boston is leveled (the same posting) on more than one occasion.[198] Some of the web commentators wanted to see a finale with the Jabbawokeez and the Asian American dance crew Kaba Modern. One incensed fan called Status Quo "circus freaks" and accused MTV of rigging the votes so that the two Asian American–populated crews would not face off in the finale by theorizing that the network did not want to lose black viewers. Finally, the blog poster known as "lilbob" admonished the show for "choosing a bunch of monkeys over a very talented dance crew."[199] A hip-hop dance fan used racial slurs to defend a genre that he values and respects? A Status Quo defender said that he or she hated to bring race into the flood of hate (aka as hateration), but stressed that if the Boston crew had been white, the dancers would receive praise rather than the criticism.[200]

Since winning *America's Best Dance Crew*, the Jabbawookeez found success in the entertainment field through movie, television, and dance bookings—including their own Las Vegas production and a clothing line. Kaba Modern also parlayed their new fame into good fortune and toured internationally. Status Quo, surviving a breakup after losing another MTV dance competition, performed in much smaller venues, like halftime at a college basketball game. They were amazed when people recognized them in public, and wanted to make a movie about "hardcore street dancing." The dancers relished their position as role models; they came from the streets—the essence of the dance—and wanted to help others in the same situation triumph over their surroundings through dance. "We are also like guardians to the youth and we are trying to be role models because we are from a bad area, from a bad neighborhood where you are either dancing or you're in a gang. We are trying to get more dancers into the world than more people in gangs because a lot of young kids are dying."[201] The self-taught dancers perform anywhere they can, and try to make dance work for them by offering them a pathway to the entertainment industry and a way out of Boston. Stardom has eluded them. "When you're performing, you're doing it more for yourself. When you're entertaining, you're doing it more for the audience."[202]

According to *ABDC* results, the best street dance crews often are Asian American, since in the first six seasons such crews have won the competition four times. On the other hand, *SYTYCD* has crowned two African American male champions in its first eight seasons: both specializing in forms of hip hop (Joshua Allen from season four and krumper Russell Ferguson in season six). Contemporary dancer Sabra Johnson, who most likely considers herself biracial, won the competition in the third season. While the reality dance competition claims to promote various disciplines of dance (there have been Russian folk dance routines, stepping, krumpin', and Bollywood dances), most of the contestants train in contemporary dance. Both shows depend on input from the voting audience and the opinions of the judges. Are *So You Think You Can Dance*'s street dancers more exciting than the plethora of contemporary dancers, or is the audience amazed that the supposed "untrained" can master the choreography of different disciplines? Or have Asian Americans (and European Americans for that matter) cornered the market on hip hop dance so that in fifty to one hundred years the history of the dance will be revised to replace the roots from the black ghetto to an overemphasis on the connection to martial arts or dance that one can learn in a suburban dance studio? Again, Asian-imported martial arts movies were a part of the popular culture lore of the African American male in the 1970s and contributed to breakdancing. Carl Douglas rode this popular culture wave with the song, "Kung Fu Fighting" (1974). But other popular dances and influences like popping, locking, and even gymnastics also impacted the dance form. The art of battling or showcasing one's dance abilities against another's accompanied by the beat of the drum is an African dance tradition. There is a correlation between some hip hop dance steps and West African traditional dances in particular.

There was a time when a serious dance student only studied the theatrical forms of dance, ballet or modern, if he or she wanted a career. Jazz dance and even tap, both emanating from folk—namely black—and popular dance sources were frowned upon unless one wanted an entertainment rather than serious dance career. Katherine Dunham, the originator of the field of dance ethnography and who studied dances of the African diaspora that she then translated and transplanted to the stage (though she did not claim to recreate specifically authentic, but rather theatrically interpreted dance choreography) told her dancers not to focus on perfecting popular dances for the stage because the folk could perform them better than the trained dancer.[203] Hip hop, like various forms of swing and tap before it, was primarily something that the practitioners created, not a studio learned craft until it grew in popularity. Hip hop enthusiasts span the globe to include countries such as Turkey, France, India, Hungary, Russia, Ukraine, and Saudi Arabia. There are international dance competitions, so the culture and obviously dance are embraced worldwide. Is this a superficial association where the outward appearances are embraced without regard to the cultural foundation? Unfortunately yes. Cultural critics of the 1970s and 1980s did not believe that rap/hip hop music would endure, but it has. Like other forms of black popular culture, jazz and rock 'n' roll specifically, youth has identified with the dance because it is a somewhat safe form of rebellion. With access to the Internet and/ or most any dance studio, voyeuristic disaffected youth can learn dance moves that they may not otherwise have access—a conduit even more accessible than television was in the past. But could these wannabees exist like the members of Status Quo, using the pavement as their studio and creating (or borrowing) the next new move in order to help stop gang violence and break into show business for an alternative to the streets—similar to the original impetus of the dance? Television competition shows like *SYTYCD* and *ABDC* promote dance—a limited remunerative field like most art—to a broad audience and hopefully cultivate a future dance audience, even as they reap the monetary benefits of selling capital, cultural capital. Should this dance genre be limited to urban youth? No, but they should, as the originators and purveyor, be in control of it and utilize for their own purposes rather than at the mercy of others who are unappreciative of the history and culture of the form, and who critique it by an outside set of standards.

Stepping

The first intercollegiate Greek-letter society, Phi Beta Kappa, emerged as the British North American colonies declared their independence in 1776. Now an acclaimed honor society, it began as a literary organization as did most similar groups until 1825 when the first social college and university fraternities and sororities came into existence. While historians generally link African American fraternities and sororities to their white counterparts, a better comparison and continuum would be to the mutual aid and benefit societies organized by blacks to aid and assist members when the larger society did not. Even these have a cultural link to secret societies present in Africa. In 1904, Dr. Henry Minton of Philadelphia invited five other medical professionals to form Sigma Pi Phi, more commonly known as the Boulé, an elite male organization. The founders limited the exclusive membership to invited male college graduates. Facing exclusion and discrimination on the predominately white campus of Cornell University, Henry Arthur Callis, Eugene Kinckle Jones, Robert Harold Ogle, Charles Henry Chapman, Nathanial Allison Murray, George Biddle Kelly, and Vertner Woodson Tandy—the Seven Jewels—founded Alpha Phi Alpha Fraternity, the first black collegiate Greek-lettered fraternity in 1906. The rest of the African American Greek organizations would follow including Alpha Kappa Alpha Sorority (Howard University, 1908); Omega Psi Phi Fraternity (Howard University, 1911); Kappa Alpha Psi Fraternity (Butler University, 1911); Delta Sigma Theta Sorority (Howard University, 1913); Phi Beta Sigma Fraternity (Howard University, 1914); Zeta Phi Beta Sorority (Howard University, 1920); Sigma Gamma Rho (Butler University, 1922); and Iota Phi Theta Fraternity (Morgan State College, 1963). The original charter of Alpha Phi Alpha denotes the founding rested upon promoting "scholarship, build[ing] character, and provid[ing] mutual assistance and social activities for black students." Historically black colleges and universities originally did not support the idea of fraternities and sororities on campus because many of these had church affiliations, tied to their founding, that adhered to the endorsement of Christian doctrines. Such organizations might encourage elitism and cliques on campus. Most of the groups were formed at Howard University and by the mid-1920s, these black Greeks became a staple of campus life.[204]

Although socialization and camaraderie are factors in why people join, generally these fraternities and sororities have community service as a focal point that differentiates them from their white counterparts. Furthermore there are graduate chapters, which also focus on service to the larger community, to ensure lifetime commitment so that affiliation may continue after the collegiate years.

Song and dance rituals performed by the different African American Greek-lettered organizations evolved into full-fledged shows, which were termed block and/or step shows. For example from the 1930s to 1950s, groups would meet at noon on Fridays on the Yard at Howard University to participate in public rituals that affirmed their loyalty to and support of their particular sorority and fraternity; this practice declined once classes began to be scheduled during the noon hour. During the Civil Rights and Black Power eras black fraternities and sororities fell out of favor as a representation of elitist groups rather than people concerned with social change. By the 1970s, however, they were again en vogue and Howard University specifically sponsored Greek Shows to showcase the talents of the sorority and fraternity members. These shows and the traditional songs and dances passed along through generations of black Greeks manifested into the step shows of the 1980s.[205]

Stepping, a combination of polyrhythmic, body-integrated, percussive dance moves and chants that are visibly and audibly similar to African dance (specifically South African bootdance and West and Central African dances, juba and hambone) is a type of dance form unique to African American Greek fraternities and sororities, who first cultivated this process through singing and marching processions tied to various aspects of initiation and social ceremonies. A probate, a person in the process of pledging a fraternity or sorority, can step as part of the coming out process—introducing them near the end of the process to the campus. The pledging process has changed since the early 1990s. It is less public and officially does not last as long as it once did. The probate show allows the probates to demonstrate what they have learned about their particular organization, and manifests as a show involving stepping.

"A step...is defined as a complete choreographed sequence or series of movements. It can be verbal, nonverbal, or a combination of the two."[206] A step show typically is a fully conceptual show or show segment with an introduction, a middle section consisting of various steps, transitions and chants, and an exit. Groups do not only step at shows, they can do steps or trains (party lines) at parties or other social occasions and/or at a specified outdoor location on campus. Step shows generally occur during large campus celebrations like homecoming or founders' week. Since the 1970s onward, this ritualized performance mechanism has become a more public event and serves as a vehicle for group cohesion. Steps presented in shows whether traditional or new are choreographed and rehearsed.

Stepping while still a primarily African American form of performance adheres to the characteristics of African dance: use of the drum (with the body), polyrhythm, call and response, songs of derision or mockery, and individual virtuosity within a group cohesiveness. While the drum may not be literally used, the beats are made by striking the body and using the floor—some groups use special shoes to enhance the sound projected with their steps. The audience can be invited to participate when certain steps are performed to elicit a crowd response. The step master or mistress often demonstrates the step and/or calls out the particular cadence and waits for a response from the other members of the step team.[207] Each fraternity and sorority has its own traditional step that typically either pays homage to the founders of that organization, or exemplifies the stereotype of the member of the particular group. For example, the Alphas have the "granddaddy" and "train" steps; the AKAs perform "serious matter"; the Omegas are known for their "founders" step and other steps to emphasize their "nasty dog" persona; the Kappas step with canes and ultimately have an air step where these are tossed to one another; the Sigmas do the "nutcracker"; the Deltas have a "founders'" step; the Zetas bring the "Zeta beat"; and Sigma Gamma Rho has the "Sally" step.[208] Groups can change these steps depending on the event and choreography. The Greek groups generally joke or crack on their rivals for fun or to prove superiority. This derisiveness can occur in the form of a step, chant or both.

By the 1990s stepping had stepped off college campuses and other venues for African American Greeks and into the business arena. Teams that competed a lot could win a lot of prize money benefitting their chapters. Stepping showed up in music videos, at presidential inaugurations and in commercials. The Broadway show *STOMP* utilized similar percussive and rhythmic movement and in turn earned a large payday. Typically one can see school and religious step teams, and stepping in choreography and Hollywood movies depicting this ritualistic form, but most of these participants, with the exception of *STOMP* and professional dancers performing choreography, were, or are, black. However, school step teams are becoming more popular and moving into the mainstream.

"You would be really surprised at how many white kids love it. They don't feel like they should be doing it. They know it's a black thing, but they love it," enthused Teresa Tracy who began sponsoring step steams in majority white Loudon County, Virginia, in the early part of the twenty-first century. She began teaching this dance form after moving her children to the county and needing to provide an outlet for them, since they experienced a major culture shock. "I wanted her to have something that belonged to her, [that showed] you are different in a positive way." The team reflected the racial composition of the school, which at the time was 4 percent black, when it won the third annual Stompfest. Tracy did involve a teaching component to her sponsorship by attempting to impart African American history to the participants, but this did not stop the invariable comments from other white students about why their classmates would want to participate in this activity.[209] They wanted to be a part of something new and exciting and that to a certain extent was forbidden. However, with the helping hand of a teacher from the culture in question, they felt safe exploring this unknown world. The question to ponder is if it changed their worldview and if they placed this entrance into a different culture in the proper context? The participants were not placed in a predominately black environment where they would experience the type of isolation and culture shock that Tracy had attempted to counter.

At a high school step competition in Northern Virginia, students from various ethnic and racial backgrounds performed for prize money and bragging rights. The team representing Herndon High School consisted of students from Asia, the Caribbean, and Central America as well as cheerleaders, and sports team players. Freedom High School started its step team, the Alpha II Omegas, initially as an outlet for African American students in a predominately white environment, but membership branched out. "It crosses the color barrier," emphasized its coach, Janice Johnson, a member of Zeta Phi Beta sorority. The winner that evening, Eleanor Roosevelt High School's Dem Raider Boyz, came from predominately black Prince George's County, but also sported a diverse team with black, Asian, Latino, and African male students. Their white faculty sponsor gushed over the team and confessed that she did not know much about stepping or step teams until her son introduced her to the performance ritual. The team coach, a former member, stated, "These young men could be doing anything, but they are getting leadership skills, social skills, discipline and dedication," the same characteristics acquired through fraternity and sorority participation. Obviously, stepping as well as sports, theater and other team participatory activities build character, discipline, and teamwork skills, so why would this be controversial?[210]

At the 2010 Sprite Step Off national competition, a white sorority the Zeta Tau Alphas (ZTA) from the University of Arkansas at Fayetteville beat the AKAs from Indiana University. The win by this white sorority caused an uproar, which later resulted in representatives from Sprite announcing that a scoring error had occurred and the two step teams had tied. The footage uploaded on YouTube garnered half a million hits shortly after its posting as well as host of comments about the win. The white Zetas performed a routine centered on *The Matrix*, complete with black trench coats, boots, and a black girl bootie shake on the exit. They were not new to stepping. On their campus of the University of Arkansas, they had learned the art of stepping through a "Unity Night," where black and white Greeks exchanged various rituals and practices. When they heard about the Sprite competition, they decided to audition. In choreographing the Matrix routine, they utilized cheerleading and dance moves in addition to the traditional stepping. "Most of the girls in the group had dance or cheerleading experience," informed Alexandra Kosmitis, the step mistress. She apparently had little apprehension about performing a traditionally African American dance form before a majority black audience—perhaps because of the tradition at her university— though she admitted that she was "nervous it'd be a train wreck and we'd go too fast." But as the routine progressed, "it became more about having fun."[211]

On the other hand, the AKAs thought that they had won, and one of the judges, Rozonda "Chilli" Thomas of the singing group TLC, later stated that she felt that Alpha Kappa Alpha step team "hands-down in my opinion should have won."[212] A shocked audience turned into vitriolic Internet comments about the crowned winners. Many blacks were upset, though plenty supported the win with the general rationale that race should not play a factor, and many whites could not understand why blacks would be upset by reasoning that reverse racism fueled the ill feelings. This is an example of how a lack of historical understanding and knowledge play to the detriment of popular culture and attempt to capitalize on cultural capital. It is not enough to espouse the equality among the races when justifying the results of the competition. More than likely the ZTAs progressed to the finals because African Americans typically are flattered when others attempt to emulate black culture and succeed, until they become the model to follow.[213] The Zetas performed well and many people viewing both teams supported their win, but they were a novelty. The videographer taped the team and subsequently posted it because he could not believe how good they were. White girls imitating black style and doing it well resonated with the audience, but there is a lack of awareness in this situation. As noted in this research, black Greek fraternities and sororities come from a history of exclusion—a history born from the larger American narrative. The tradition does not simply emanate from that tradition of African American agency, but the actual art form marries black American traditions with African ancestry. It honors the history of the excluded groups who share a common past. "But remember, stepping is performed as a tribute to the founders of our organizations. We are celebrating the creation of our fraternities and sororities and, ultimately, our African roots each time we step. That is why we feel very deeply about our steps. That is why black Greeks get upset when some groups 'borrow' steps from the black Greeks."[214]

It is not a question of whether or not nonblacks should step, in fact many are members of these historically black organizations, but rather why they would want to. If they knew the history, they would be sensitive to the feelings of cultural theft. Stepping has moved out of its traditional performing context into a host of other venues. As African Americans continue to introduce this tradition to others, then the original concept will morph into alternative forms and one should not be surprised if a white sorority or fraternity wins a national competition or high school step show, or the traditional dance form shows up in professional choreography. Interestingly enough, the whites who defended the Zeta's win often compared it to African Americans winning a cheerleading competition, country line dancing contest, or the like. These arguments, though, lack some validity since blacks have those same traditions because of exclusion, albeit with their own unique interpretations, that in turn have been appropriated.

Last Dance

Now that mainstream America has taken notice of hip hop and the contributing cultural factors, industry executives seeking monetary enrichment are driving the culture to a certain extent more than the youth are creating it. However, since America is America where there is still distance between the races regardless of the application of technology and the encompassing global community, black youth will continue to create. Some will be able to capitalize on that creativity before it is eventually diluted into American popular culture and appropriated to fit the American ideal.

What is old is often new again in the realm of black popular dance. Thus, the Charleston becomes the mashed potato and the Kid 'n Play; tap dance's backslide evolves into the moonwalk; and the parts of the hustle resurface in the electric slide. Dance critic and journalist Sarah Kaufman somewhat defended Beyoncé for "the art of stealing" with regard to her music videos "Countdown," "Love on Top," and "Single Ladies." An Internet backlash erupted over the similarities with "Countdown" and the works of Belgian choreographer Anne Teresa de Keersmaeker because Keersmaeker, who has utilized the choreography of others such as Vaslav Nijinsky, did not receive credit. Kaufman noted that this form of appropriation is common in the art world, which defines it as "using borrowed material to create new work." The pop diva did not deny the borrowing of the quick dance references when called to task, but the criticism did not stop there. Beyoncé and her choreographers have regularly used various choreographed iconic dance sequences in her music videos.[215] However, what stood out in this story were the references to choreographers Bob Fosse and Jerome Robbins and their choreography being lifted by Michael Jackson and Beyoncé, or what should have been their choreographers. Fosse and Robbins were jazz and musical theater dancers and choreographers who utilized black dance for their own dance creations.

W. E. B. Du Bois defined the souls of white folk in *Darkwater: Voices from within the Veil*. "This theory of human culture and its aims has worked itself through war and woof of our daily thought with a thoroughness that few realize. Everything great, good, efficient, fair, and honorable is 'white'; everything mean, bad, blundering, cheating and dishonorable is 'yellow'; a bad taste is 'brown'; and the devil is 'black.' "[216] Thus the dominant society's culture, and popular culture specifically, reinforces hegemonic ideals and contributes to the oppressed group's continued marginalization. Manning Marable put it succinctly. "The cultural institutions that produced popular music, theater, films, professional athletics, and public amusements of all types reinforced white superiority and black inferiority."[217] These are questions of cultural capital or the "financial advantages that accrue to certain social classes due to their higher levels of education and their ability to influence popular styles and tastes in the artistic and cultural arenas."[218] In the realm of African American popular culture, this definition is particularly important and slightly skewed. While blacks become the arbiters of what is in and of the moment, they typically do not control the institutions or finances that reap the benefits of its marketing. Sociologist Katrina Hazzard-Gordon (Donald) articulated the various traits that compose a black vernacular dance aesthetic and pointed to the working and lower-classes who introduce these dances into the broader community and do not and, in most cases, cannot control the economics surrounding the creative enterprise. Similarly, historian V. P. Franklin utilizes an interpretation of cultural capital that centers on "group consciousness and collective identity...aimed at the advancement of an entire group."[219] And while financial gain always has not been the rationale behind the creative impulse, it is a consideration. Much of what has been discussed in this research is a record of community building, representation, identity, and cohesiveness, but obviously in danger of co-optation and obliteration.

Historian Frederick Jackson Turner's controversial frontier thesis concluded that the closing of the western frontier signaled among other things that a distinct American character had emerged with the settling and taming (read dislocation of the Native American) of the West. Moreover it embodied "the line of most rapid Americanization."[220] The process of Americanization previously had begun with reformers wanting to target the American Indians by extirpating their culture in favor of them converting to Christianity, learning English, and adopting to the culture of their oppressors. At first missionaries visited reservations to indoctrinate the inhabitants, but met with little success. Then the Native American children were shipped off to boarding schools away from parents and other influences to be inculcated with what could be termed American values. This model of forced assimilation would be employed to varying degrees with immigrants during various waves of immigration. Generally, while first generation migrants retain many traditions, cultural practices, and ties to their native countries, successive generations tend to be less tied to traditional ways and more heavily influenced by current surroundings—hence Americanized. African Americans with a different migration history and further separated by color as well as intense oppression and laws against intermarriage found it more difficult to acculturate and in many cases had no desire to abandon their heritage.

In his seminal work, *The Souls of Black Folk*, W. E. B. Du Bois deduced that at the turn of the twentieth century the problem confronting the United States was that of the color line—that Maginot line that separated white from black. Moreover because of the circumstances in which he or she lived, the American of African descent was uniquely aware of his or her place through this double consciousness or "twoness"—sharing some common traditions and having others particular to the race. Black folks possessed "two souls, two thoughts, two unreconciled strivings; two warring ideals in one dark body, whose dogged strength alone keeps it from being torn asunder." In this work, historian David Levering Lewis states that Du Bois offered new terrain that merged the philosophies of those that wanted complete integration and those that advocated for separatism in the larger society. Thus, "the destiny of the race could be conceived as leading neither to assimilation nor separatism but to proud, enduring hyphenation." At this crossroad, African Americans had insight into both worlds but would not "Africanize America" nor "bleach his Negro soul in a flood of white Americanism." These two competing entities forever in a tug of war for the cultural prize had to coexist. "He simply wishes to make it possible for a man to be both a Negro and an American."[221] In expressing this twoness, specific African traits, or Africanisms emerged to solidify those theories by scholars such as Melville Herskovits, Carter G. Woodson, and Du Bois that the Transatlantic Slave Trade and slavery did not destroy African culture in North America. It had to adapt and adopt to the new surroundings and circumstance. Du Bois's cultural theories resonate with the idea of pluralism or the celebration of differences rather than a forced conformity to a set of culturally biased standards.

The popular idea of the American melting pot is one of a large boiling cauldron that in theory takes parts of various cultures from the races and ethnicities that constitute the various ingredients or seasonings of the United States of America and cooks them until an authentic American culture is formed.[222] The popular idea of the American melting pot as a large boiling cauldron that are not distinctive flavors but an unappetizing glob. A more euphemistic image of delicious and filling comfort food becomes ingrained in school children's psyche and follows them throughout adulthood. This image reinforces the idea of a melting pot that produces a heavily Caucasian actualization devoid of the various non-white groups that are a part of the American narrative as well.[223] Some scholars have called for the retiring of the melting pot in favor of an image of a stew where distinct flavors come together in a tastier dish. Though the stew appears to be more inclusive, herein lies the problem. Race and racism are not welcome subjects in what is supposedly a postracial America based on the fact that an admittedly African American (he identifies as black and not necessarily as biracial) president won election in 2008 and reelection in 2012. Americans have a short historical memory and hope that the gains made since the Civil Rights Movement have leveled the playing field since overt bigotry is not politically correct. The problems of institutionalized racism and the ingrained thought that various racial groups are still inferior are not addressed. And while the term race and its derivatives are used, this is a man-made concept and problematic in many respects; the term "culture" probably is more appropriate though race is more widely understood in this particular context.

But why is this important? Because in the realm of cultural capital, black people come out with the short end of the stick: they do not reap the benefits of their cultural creativity. Does this mean that in this case black dance is off limits to whites? No, not necessarily, but it does allow for the discussion surrounding the ownership, definition, stewardship, and financial gain with regard to the commodity of popular culture. When it moves out of the initiating community, the meaning and context change. The stew with the complementing ingredients and flavors is a metaphor for cultural pluralism, or the "indefinite survival of ethnic subcultures" where the whole is comprised of several components that do not lose their individuality. Moreover, these survivals maintain the "inevitable accompaniments, suspicion and prejudice" that segregate groups at the core.[224]

Howard University philosopher and Rhodes scholar Alain Locke, the spiritual father of the New Negro Renaissance, attempted to define the impact of African Americans on mainstream American culture a decade after the publication *The New Negro*. In somewhat of a reversal from the heyday of the movement when various artists grappled with the form and function of their art, Locke classified Negro art as a by-product of racism. The mere fact of categorizing such endeavors denigrated the product through racial chauvinism rather than focusing on the endemic qualities of the art itself. In this view, the artist happened to be black rather than producing black art. "Cultural racialism and chauvinism flatter the minority group ego; cultural biracialism not only flatters the majority group ego, but is the extension of discrimination into cultural prejudices and bigotry."[225] More than likely, Locke reacted to the continual disparagement of anything coming from a black source. Locke argued that in areas such as the visual arts and literature, African Americans typically followed the European American example and classified any fare prior to 1890 as "creative but unsophisticated expression at the folk level."[226] The philosopher relied heavily on examples and documentation by white Americans for his analysis. At this time he did not take into consideration the oral traditions and historical motor memory passed along through folktales and dances recited and performed in private without scrutiny from the untrained eye could, and did for that matter, uphold African traditions rather than emulating European trends, though this did occur at times as part of natural cultural interaction. Locke's apparent goal at this time was integration and to a certain extent assimilation. He admitted the mainstream America absorbed most African Americans initiatives, namely in music and dance, which in turn lost some of its vitality for acceptance by a larger audience. These two areas retained more African influence that distinguished them from the American mainstream. "The Negro cultural influence...in music and dance,...[has] in rhythm, the tempo and the emotional overtones [the most distinguishing] of almost any typically Negro version of other cultural art forms."[227] On the other hand, Van Deburg offered a much different hypothesis. "Black culture coexisted with a majoritarian culture which sought sustenance and rejuvenation from the Afro-American heritage even as it mocked black humanity through gross caricature and distortion."[228]

In the late 1970s during a period of prolific crossover appeal by white artists, the periodical *Soul* debated the essence of soul as it related to music specifically, though the analysis can be utilized for dance as well. Popular music as well as dance can be political. Norma Miller linked the Lindy hop's fast pace to the fact that the dancers did not want whites to be able to pick up the steps, and Leon Pitts argued that African Americans felt comfortable with and took pride in soul or rhythm and blues music because it was inherently black and "whatever else whites took away, soul music was something they could not take. Only rarely could they even imitate it."[229] At this time civil rights gains and access led many to adhere to the melting pot theory where no cultural distinction is made on the road to a colorblind society. But in this analysis, African American popular artists tended to get "ripped off" in the crossover game. White musicians overwhelmingly profited more than their black counterparts. Top 40 radio stations often played watered-down versions of certain songs that programmers thought sounded "too black." In an interesting foreshadowing of what was to come, too black often referred to a song "where there is talking by a Black man...the way in which he talks, it just is out and out Black."[230] Crossover appeal typically equals monetary gain, but, at times, comes with a backlash or "blacklash" by the African American community when they infer that the artist has sold out or that the product has been diluted for mass appeal. Some speculated that musical categories and affiliations might disappear. But Van Deburg counters this euphemistic optimism by offering the basis of the downside of appropriated cultural capital. "In their feverish quest for cultural invigoration, popularity, and profit, whites were willing to push the real 'soul people' off the stage and far into the background."[231] But a push toward not acknowledging color or racial heritage does not yield the supposed desired effect: that of removing barriers or ending discrimination. Discounting history allows the narrative to be altered or forgotten. "According to the black critics, if they [whites] were successful, innovative blues, soul, and jazz stylings would be replaced by a wholly derivative form of musical expression that forever would remain a pale imitation of its original models."[232]

Andrew Hacker divulged privileged information when addressing blacks. "You feel frustration and disgust when white America appropriates your music, your styles, indeed your speech and sexuality. At times white audiences will laud the originality of black artists and performers and athletes. But in the end, they feel more comfortable when white musicians and designers and writers—and athletic coaches—adapt black talents to white sensibilities."[233] Whites must appropriate black popular culture and make it their own to further curtail artistic, creative, and/or cultural impulse and influence of African Americans: In other words to define these innovations through their own reality, which reinforces the existing social hierarchy. Youth are naturally drawn to the forbidden in order to rebel against authority—for example, their parents. What better way to rebel than to follow the example of a group that mainstream society views as deviant.

Writer Greg Tate called his edited collection of essays *Everything But the Burden: What White People Are Taking from Black Culture* in homage to a poem his mother wrote. In essence whites used black popular culture and repackaged it as strictly American culture by removing the meaning attached to it. "They have always tried to erase the Black presence from whatever Black thing they took a shine to." While true blackness is denigrated, reinvented blackness or even exaggerated blackness serves a purpose for commodification to be both blessed and disdained for financial gain. Therefore, "what America sold to the world as uniquely American in culture...was uniquely African-American in origin, conception, and inspiration."[234] In this sense, one can embrace the concept what makes the cultural component unique or standout without the added burden of melanin and the discrimination that goes along with it. "Although 'beholden to a life experience based primarily upon European cultural tenets,' these performers nevertheless sought to co-opt blackness. If possible, they would savor the sweet without tasting the bitter."[235]

Katherine Dunham, pioneer dance ethnographer and choreographer, confirmed that indigenous dances record historical memory. "[There is] a strong connection between the dance, music, and archaic ceremonies of a people and that people's social and economic history."[236] Popular dance for African Americans serves this same function. While African Americans continue to fight for full inclusion and opportunity in the broader society, this does not mean that their essence in the form of culture in whatever manifestation should be absorbed and appropriated. Differences should be celebrated, not as a cause for discrimination and the assignation of inferiority, but as a cultural moniker and historical marker. So you think you can dance, and over the centuries the vault of black dance has continuously been mined. African Americans continue to create and recreate, but the sense of exclusiveness and group cohesion that developed out of exclusionary laws and practices continues to dissolve—especially because of the proliferation of technology and the ease of cultural voyeurism (despite not understanding the context). Furthermore, the process of creation is more of a driving force than the preservation of dance and thus of history. Harold Cruse lamented, "The Negro has turned his back on his own native American dance forms and refused to cultivate them—he, the creator of all American dance forms from the fox-trot to the twist."[237] This is not a clarion call for segregation, self-imposed or otherwise, it is, however, a plea against cultural annihilation and respect for history and heritage. Dance cannot be separated from its historical and cultural context. At times it is political, economic, and/or social. Yes, many people can dance and black vernacular dance is a popular choice. Again, there is no need to deny those genuinely interested in black vernacular dance the opportunity to participate. However, all too often this results in personal financial gain and a kind of subject matter authority that is unwarranted and unjust. Though dance in the black community is a determinant of cultural cohesiveness and identity, it is not monolithic. The movement of the black body carries historical memory and directs future endeavors—the creativity never seems to end even if it is sometimes simply a recreation of past ingenuity. It is necessary to preserve that history, and the group in question should be the stewards of such. So you think you can dance, and many can, but examine the motive. Is it for preservation, preference, or profit?

Notes

1. Stuart Hall, "What Is this 'Black' in Black Popular Culture?" in *The Black Studies Reader*, eds. Jacqueline Bobo, Cynthia Hudley, and Claudine Michel (New York: Routledge, 2004), 259.
2. Harry B. Shaw, ed., *Perspectives of Black Popular Culture* (Bowling Green, OH: Bowling Green State University Popular Press, 1990), 1.

3. Richard A. Long, *The Black Tradition in American Dance* (New York: Rizzoli, 1989), 15.

4. Andrew Hacker, *Two Nations: Black and White, Separate, Hostile, Unequal* (New York: Ballantine Books, 1992), 62.

5. Lawrence Levine, "African Culture and US Slavery," in *Global Dimensions of the African Diaspora*, 2nd ed. Joseph E. Harris, ed. (Washington, D.C.: Howard University Press, 1993), 83.

6. Joseph Holloway defines Africanisms as "those elements of culture found in the New World that are traceable to an African origin." In his account of African survivals in North America, he points out that though West Africans salves arrived in North America in the greatest numbers, those enslaved Bantu peoples from Central Africa "possessed the largest homogenous culture among the imported Africans and,... had the strongest impact on the future development of African–American culture and language." Joseph Holloway, ed. *Africanisms in American Culture* (Bloomington: Indiana University Press, 1990), ix. Similar analysis can be found in Sterling Stuckey, *Slave Culture: Nationalist Theory and the Foundations of Black America* (New York: Oxford University Press), 198.

7. Katrina Hazzard-Gordon, "Afro-American Core Culture Social Dance: An Examination of Four Aspects of Meaning," *Dance Research Journal* 15, no 2. (Spring 1983): 21.

8. Frederick W. Bond, *The Negro and the Drama* (Washington, D.C.: McGrath Publishing Co., 1940), 143.

9. Joyce Aschenbrenner, *Katherine Dunham: Reflections on the Social and Political Contexts of Afro-American Dance*, with a foreword by St. Clair Drake (New York: CORD, Inc., 1981), 21–23.

10. Hazzard-Gordon, "Afro-American Core Culture Social Dance," 22.

11. Rusella Brandman, "The Evolution of Jazz Dance from Folk Origins to Concert Stage" (PhD diss., Florida State University, 1977), 124; Barbara Engelbrecht, "Swinging at the Savoy," *Dance Research Journal* 15, no. 2 (Spring 1983): 6; and Marshall Stearns and Jean Stearns, *Jazz Dance: The Story of American Vernacular Dance* (1968; repr., New York: Da Capo Press, 1994), 322.

12. Zora Neale Hurston, "Characteristics of Negro Expression," in *Negro Anthology*, ed. Nancy Cunard (London: Wishart, 1934; New York: Frederick Ungar Publishing Co., 1970), 31.

13. *Dancing*, "New Worlds, New Forms," directed and produced by Rhoda Grauer, aired May 17, 1993, on PBS (WETA 26, Washington, D.C.).

14. Jonathon David Jackson, "Improvisation in African-American Vernacular Dancing," *Dance Research Journal* 32, no. 2 (Winter 2001): 42.

15. Ibid., 45–46.

16. Ibid., 46.

17. Ibid., 42.

18. "The Sorrow of Yamba; Or, the Negro Woman's Lamentation" (1790), Cornell University Rare Book Collection (Ithaca, NY), quoted in Katrina Hazzard-Gordon, *Jookin': The Rise of Social Dance Formations in African-American Culture* (Philadelphia: Temple University Press, 1990), 9.

19. Pearl Primus, "Out of Africa," in *The Dance Has Many Faces*, ed. Walter Sorell (Cleveland: World Publishing Co., 1951), 256–57, quoted in Richard G. Kraus and Sarah Alberti Chapman, *History of the Dance in Art and Education*, 2nd ed. (Englewood Cliffs, NJ: Prentice-Hall, Inc., 1981), 19.

20. Kariamu Welsh Asante, "Commonalities in African Dance," in *African Culture: The Rhythms of Unity*, ed. Kariamu Welsh Asante (Trenton, NJ: Africa World Press, 1990), 72.

21. Ibid., 74–81.

22. Pearl Primus, "African Dance: Eternity Captured," *Caribe* 7 (1982): 11.

23. Ibid.

24. Theodore Canot, *Adventures of an African Slaver. Being a True Account of Captain Theodore Canot, Trader in Gold, Ivory and Slaves on the Coast of Guinea: His Own Story as Told in the Year 1854 to Brantz Mayer*, ed. Malcolm Cawley (New York: Albert and Charles Boni, 1928), 73, quoted in Lynne Fauley Emery, *Black Dance from 1619 to Today*, 2nd rev. ed., with a foreword by Katherine Dunham (Pennington, NJ: Princeton Book Co., 1988), 2–3.

25. Ibid., 3–5.

26. Hazzard-Gordon, Jookin', 8.

27. Ibid.

28. Ibid.

29. Ibid., 9.

30. Okon Edet Uya, "The Middle Passage and Personality Change Among Diaspora Africans," in *Global Dimensions of the African Diaspora*, ed. Joseph E. Harris, 2nd ed. (Washington, D.C.: Howard University Press, 1993), 83.

31. Long, 8.

32. Melville J. Herskovits, *The Myth of the Negro Past*, with a new Introduction by Sidney W. Mintz (1941; Boston: Beacon Press, 1990), 138; Katrina Hazzard-Gordon likens the response to the drums as a signal for revolt as to that of the African was dances used for similar purposes (*Jookin'*, 34).

33. Robert Hinton, "Black Dance in American History," in *The Black Tradition in American Modern Dance* (New York: American Dance Festival, 1988), 4.

34. Hazzard-Gordon, *Jookin'*, 29–31. For a description of musical instruments used in Haiti, see Katherine Dunham, *Dances of Haiti*, with a foreword to the French edition by Claude Levi-Strauss, trans. Jeanelle Stovall (Los Angeles: Center for Afro-American Studies, University of California, 1983).

35. John Allen Wyeth, *With Sabre and Scalpel* (New York: Harper Bros., 1914), 62, quoted in Emery, 97.

36. Stearns and Stearns, 39.

37. Seymour Stark, *Men in Blackface: True Stories of the Minstrel Show* (Bloomington, IN: Xlibris, 2000), 11–12.

38. Langston Hughes and Milton Meltzer, *Black Magic: A Pictorial History of the Negro in American Entertainment* (Englewood Cliffs, NJ: Prentice-Hall, 1967), 40–42; Robert C. Toll, *The Minstrel Show in Nineteenth-Century America* (New York: Oxford University Press, 1974), 26–27; William J. Mahar, *Behind the Burnt Cork Mask: Early Blackface Minstrelsy and Antebellum American Popular Culture* (Urbana: University of Illinois Press, 1999), 60–61.

39. Rice was born in New York in 1808 and traveled throughout the South entertaining working as an actor, carpenter for the stage and basic stage hand. [See Hughes and Meltzer, 16–18; Stark, 12–13.] Marshall and Jean Stearns printed a description from the *New York Times* (1881) of how Rice derived his stage character. "Rice watched him closely, and saw that here was a character unknown to the stage. He wrote several verses, changed the air somewhat, quickened it a good deal, made up exactly like Daddy, and sang it to a Louisville audience. They were wild with delight, and

on the first night he was recalled twenty times" (40). Carl Wittke and Seymour Stark share a slightly different version of the story as printed in the *Atlantic Monthly* (1860). They recount that Rice heard the song refrain in Cincinnati (in the neighboring state of Ohio), committed it to memory and debuted it with his fashioned dance at a Pittsburgh theater. As he made his way to the performance, he encountered a young black child named Cuff. Rice decided that Cuff's torn and tattered clothing added to his depiction of black song and dance and forced the youngster to give him the clothes. As the audience applauded Rice after his performance, Cuff nearly naked ventured onto the stage to beg for the return of his clothes. [Carl Wittke, *Tambo and Bones, A History of the American Minstrel Stage* (New York: Greenwood Press, 1968); and Stark, 13.]

40. Brander Mathews, "The Rise and Fall of Negro-Minstrelsy," *Scribner's Magazine*, June 1915, 755.

41. Cecilia R. Brown, "The Afro-American Contribution to Dance in the United States, 1619–1965," *Negro Heritage* 14, no. 3 (1975): 66.

42. Mark Knowles, *Tap Roots: The Early History of Tap Dancing* (Jefferson, NC: McFarland & Company, 2002), 78. Robert C. Toll states that the "Jim Crow" ditty "resembled an Irish folk tune and an English stage song" (27, 43).

43. Dale Cockrell, in *Demons of Disorder: Early Blackface Minstrels and Their World,* illustrates that many in the English aristocracy appreciated this imitative farce, though Rice still attracted the "common sorts" (67–68).

44. Brown, 66. Rice would add other characters based on Negro stereotypes to his stage acts as well. He further helped others profit from this appropriated sensation. Leonard Gosling used Rice to advertise his shoe shining product "Gosling's Blacking," by incorporating a stanza about the product into his act. After sales skyrocketed, he was able to retire from his tremendous earnings (Knowles, 80–81).

45. Dale Cockcrell, *Demons of Disorder: Early Blackface Minstrels and Their World* (Cambridge: Cambridge University Press, 1997), 31.

46. Ibid., 69; Toll 9–14.

47. Stark, 16.

48. Long, 10. Toll contends that this mixture of music and dance "pervaded early minstrelsy and helped account for its appearance of uniqueness" (*The Minstrel Show*, 42–43).

49. Francis Ann Kemble, *Journal of a Residence on a Georgian Plantation in 1838–1839* (New York: Harper and Brothers, 1863), 96–97, quoted in Emery, 182.

50. Frederick Douglass, *North Star*, October 27, 1848, quoted in Eric Lott, *Love & Theft: Blackface Minstrelsy and the American Working Class* (New York: Oxford University Press, 1993), 15.

51. Ibid., 4.

52. James Weldon Johnson, *Black Manhattan*, with a Preface by Allan H. Spear (New York: Atheneum, 1972), 87.

53. Brown, 65–66. Brown further asserted that "from the slaves originated the minstrel show which was the only original contribution of the United States to the theatre" (67). Langston Hughes noted that three Kentucky enslaved African musicians were worth up to $1500 and when they escaped to the North, their owner expended several thousand dollars trying to recapture them (18).

54. Stearns and Stearns, 44.

55. Lott, 112.

56. Charles Dickens, *American Notes for General Circulation*, vol. 1, 2nd ed. (London: Chapman and Hall, 1842), 218.

57. Lott, 112–13; Stearns and Stearns, 45. An article from the *New York Herald* documented Lane/Juba in such a performance. "Those who passed through the long hallway and entered the dance hall...saw this phenomenon, 'Juba,' imitate all the dancers of the day and their special steps. Then...the master of ceremonies would say, 'Now Master Juba, show your own jig.' Whereupon he would go through all his own steps and specialties, with never a resemblance in any of them to those he had just imitated" [quoted in Marian Hannah Winter, "Juba and American Minstrelsy" in *Chronicles of the American Dance*, ed. Paul Magriel (New York: Henry Holt, 1948), 43; and Knowles, 89].

58. Thomas Low Nichols, *Forty Years of American Life*, 2nd ed. (London: J. Maxwell and Company, 1864; London: Longmans, Green, 1874), 370, quoted in Lott, 113; Knowles, 88.

59. Hans Nathan, *Dan Emmett and the Rise of Early Negro Minstrelsy* (Norman, OK: University of Oklahoma Press), 61, quoted in Emery, 185; Knowles, 89.

60. Playbills, Harvard Theatre Collection, quoted in Lott, 115.

61. *New York Herald*, July 8, 1944, quoted in Charles Day, "Fun in Black" in *Inside the Minstrel Mask: Readings in Nineteenth-Century Blackface Minstrelsy*, ed. Annemarie Bean, James V. Hatch, and Brooks McNamara (Hanover, NH: Wesleyan University Press, 1996), 49; Knowles, 90.

62. Marshall and Jean Stearns noted that at an earlier date the two competed at a "jig dancing tournament" held at the Boylston Gardens in Boston with Diamond prevailing (46). Mark Knowles also denotes an earlier "undated" contest where Diamond prevailed. The *New York Sporting News* (July 23, 1843) announced an upcoming challenge between Diamond and "a little negro [*sic*] called 'Juba'" scheduled for the coming weeks (Knowles, 88). Dancer and dance teacher Sonny Watson contends that historians have confused the white dancer Jack (John) Diamond and the black dancer Johnny Diamond (see "Juba," accessed September 2011, http://www.streetswing.com/histmai2/d2juba1.htm), and that Lane lost or tied Johnny Diamond in that first contest though there is no documentation to substantiate this claim. He also asserts that the black Diamond danced for P. T. Barnum (see "Johnny Diamond," accessed September 2011, http://www.streetswing.com/histmai2/d2jdmnd.htm). However, the *New York Aurora* article (1840s) makes the clear distinction that Barnum had found the original article in the black dancer that was to replace the former Diamond, and had to put him in blackface and a wig to hide the fact that he was a Negro—which would have offended audience sensibilities (see Lott, 12–13; Knowles, 89). Furthermore, Diamond's popularity and the money he made from his dancing spawned several imitators.

63. "Juba at Vauxhall," *Illustrated London News*, August 5, 1848, 77, quoted in Emery, 188.

64. Hughes and Meltzer, 18.

65. John Blassingame, *The Slave Community: Plantation Life in the Antebellum South*, rev. ed. (New York: Oxford University Press, 1979), 224.

66. Ibid., 230–31.

67. For information on slave stereotypes, see Donald Bogle, *Toms, Coons, Mulattoes, Mammies & Bucks: An Interpretive History of Blacks in American Films* (New York: Continuum, 1994); Deborah Gray White, *Ar'n't I a Woman? Female Slaves in the Plantation South*, rev. ed. (New York: W. W. Norton & Co, 1999); and David Pilgrim, "Jezebel Stereotype," July 2002, and "Mammy Caricature," October 2000, The Jim Crow Museum of Racist Memorabilia, http://www.ferris.edu/news/jimcrow.

68. Matthews, 757.

69. Pamela Gaye, "The Legacy of the Minstrel Show," *Dance Scope* 12, no. 2 (Spring/Summer 1978): 44. Stark asserts that "No colored troupe performing for white audiences in the North survived for long," although in "the South…colored minstrel shows had enthusiastic African American audiences" (132).

70. Johnson, 89.

71. Hughes and Meltzer, 93.

72. Arthur Todd, "American Negro Dance: A National Treasure," in *The Ballet Annual 1962: A Record and Year Book of the Ballet*, ed. Arnold Haskell and Mary Clarke (London: Adam and Charles Black, 1961), 96.

73. Wittke, 147. William J. Mahar denotes three phases to the development of the antebellum minstrel show (1843–48; 1849–54, and 1855–60). See *Behind the Burnt Cork Mask: Early Blackface Minstrelsy and Antebellum American Popular Culture* (Urbana and Chicago: University of Illinois Press, 1999), 18.

74. Stearns and Stearns, 22; and quoted in Brooke Baldwin, "The Cakewalk: A Study in Stereotype and Reality," Journal of Social History 15, no. 2 (Winter 1981): 208.

75. Ibid.

76. Katrina Hazzard-Gordon, "Dancing to Rebalance the Universe—African-America Secular Dance," *JOPERD: The Journal of Physical Education, Recreation & Dance* 62, no. 2 (February 1991): 38.

77. Baldwin, 211, 215.

78. Allen Woll, *Black Musical Theatre: From Coontown to Dreamgirls* (Baton Rouge: Louisiana State University Press, 1989; repr., New York: Da Capo Press, 1989), 6–10; Johnson 102–5; and Stearns and Stearns, 119–21. Stella White was one of the female dancers that performed with Williams and Walker in the Koster and Bial show. Walker later met and married Aida Overton (Walker) who performed with the duo and became known for her cakewalking abilities. For Will Cook's documentation of *Clorindy*, see "Clorindy: The Origin of the Cakewalk," *Theatre Arts* (September 1947): 61–65.

79. Baldwin, 215.

80. Johnson, 105.

81. *Musical Courier*, 1899, quoted in Thomas L. Riis, *Just before Jazz: Black Musical Theater in New York, 1890–1915* (Washington, D.C., Smithsonian Institution, 1989), 80; Stark, 138; Emery, 208, and Stearns and Stearns, 123.

82. Johnson, 106.

83. Baldwin, 215–16.

84. Parts of this section originally written by the author appeared as "It Don't Mean a Thing if It Ain't Got that Harlem Swing: Social Dance and the Harlem Renaissance," *Afro-Americans in New York Life and History* 22, vol. 1 (January 1998): 41–66.

85. "Popular Dances from the Cakewalk to the Watusi," *Ebony*, August 1961, 32; and see Barbara Cohen-Stratyner, "Issues in Social and Vernacular Dance," *Dance Research Journal* 33, no. 2 (Winter 2001): 121–23.

86. Lewis Erenberg, "Everybody's Doin' It: The Pre-World War I Dance Craze, The Castles, and the Modern American Girl," *Feminist Studies* 3, nos. 1&2 (Fall 1975): 155–56; and "Sex and Social Dance," *Dancing*, PBS, WETA 26, Washington, D.C., May 26, 1993.

87. Bosley Crowther, "From Turkey Trot to the Big Apple," *New York Times Magazine*, November 7, 1935, 18.

88. Upon the death of James Reese Europe, Irene Castle did credit him with the creation of the Fox Trot. See "Irene Castle credits Negro with Fox Trot: Ex-dancer, in glowing tribute to Jim Europe, says he discovered it," in vertical files—Dance/Ballet 1930–1940. Moorland-Spingarn Research Center, Howard University, Washington, D.C.

89. Brandman, 118.

90. Whites were first introduced to these dances in the Broadway musicals *Runnin' Wild* (1923)—the Charleston— and *Dinah* (1924)—the Black Bottom."

91. For the Charleston in particular, Katherine Dunham discovered similar movements in the Haitian dance la Martinique, and anthropologist Melville Herskovits located comparable steps "in the ancestral rites for the chief of an Ashanti tribe." See Emery, 227.

92. Eric Walrond, "Charlsotn, Hey! Hey!" *Vanity Fair* (April 1926), 73.

93. Will Marion Cook, "Letter to the Editor," *New York Times*, December 26, 1926, np.

94. "Calls Night Clubs Rendezvous of Vice," *New York Times*, July 15, 1927, 6; Nancy Cunard, "Harlem Reviewed," in *Negro: An Anthology*, ed. Nancy Cunard (London: Wishart, 1934; New York: Frederick Ungar Publishing Co., 1970), 50; Frankie Manning and Cynthia R. Millman, *Frankie Manning: Ambassador of Lindy Hop* (Philadelphia: Temple University Press, 2007), 71; and Norma Miller and Evette Jensen, *Swingin' at the Savoy: The Memoir of a Jazz Dancer* (Philadelphia: Temple University Press, 1996), xvii; 27.

95. Gerald Jonas and Rhoda Grauer, *Dancing: New World, New Forms*, aired PBS 1993 (Chicago: Home Vision, 1997), VHS.

96. Ibid.

97. Ibid.

98. Miller, xvii.

99. Pepsi Bethel, interview by author, Washington, D.C., March 11, 1993, tape recording.

100. Manning and Millman, 48; 61; Miller and Jensen, 44.

101. Bethel interview.

102. Philip W. Payne, ed., *The Swing Era: Swing as a Way of Life 1941-1942* (New York: Time-Life Records, 1970), 18, quoted in Engelbrecht, 5; and see Stearns and Stearns, 322.

103. Brandman, 124.

104. Miller and Jensen, 63.

105. Frederick Woltman, "King of the Savoy," *Negro Digest* (July 1951): 96. For information on ballrooms not admitting blacks see Manning and Millman; and Miller and Jensen.

106. Stearns and Stearns, 320.

107. Manning and Millman, 64–65. Norma Miller also calls it "the corner"; see Miller and Jensen, 107.

108. Ibid., 65.

109. Stearns and Stearns, 323, 326.

110. John Q. Anderson, "The New Orleans Voodoo Ritual dance and Its Twentieth Century Survivals," *Southern Folklore Quarterly* 24 (June 1960): 141; Engelbrecht, 4.

111. Crowther, 18.

112. Terry Monaghan disputes the tale of Lindbergh's flight linked to the naming of the dance. She credits the Savoy with this faulty information, regarding it as a publicity stunt. "Probably devised by the Savoy Ballroom's effective publicity machine as a gimmick to attract downtown white audiences in the mid-1930s, the story has now taken a life of its own." See Terry Monaghan, "Why Study the Lindy Hop?" *Dance Research Journal* 33, no. 2 (Winter 2001): 89–90. Frankie Manning, however, confirms the original story. "Shorty told us that after Charles Lindbergh had flown the Atlantic, the headlines in the paper read, 'Lindy Hops the Atlantic,' so he said, I'm

doing the Lindy hop.'" See Manning and Millman, 79. Norma Miller recounts a similar story in her memoir. See Miller and Jensen, 58.

113. Stearns and Stearns, 317; Engelbrecht, 7.

114. Stearns and Stearns, 323; John Banting, "The Dancing of Harlem," in *Negro: An Anthology*, ed. Nancy Cunard (London: Wishart, 1934; New York: Frederick Ungar Publishing Co., 1970), 204.

115. Stearns and Stearns, 323–24.

116. Ibid., 324; and Katherine Dunham, "The Negro Dance," in *Kaiso! Katherine Dunham: An Anthology of Writings*, eds. VeVe Clark and Margaret Wilkerson (Berkeley: Institute for the Study of Social Change CCEW Women's Center University of California, 1978), 71.

117. Manning and Millner, 45–48.

118. Stearns and Stearns, 325–26.

119. Manning and Millner, 100.

120. Engelbrecht, 8.

121. Bond, 139.

122. *Dancing*, "New Worlds, New Forms." It should be noted that depending on what part of the country one hails and the era in which he or she danced (in this case more so into the 1940s), some African Americans refer to various forms of the Lindy as the jitterbug.

123. Stearns and Stearns, 331.

124. Emery, 223.

125. Eric Martin Usner, "Dancing in the Past, Living in the Present: Nostalgia and Race in Southern California Neo-Swing Dance Culture," *Dance Research Journal* 33, no. 2 (Winter 2001): 89–90.

126. Ibid., 99.

127. Nikita Stewart, "Swinging in D.C.: Vince Gray Is Hand Dancing's No. 1 Fan. But Can 'One City" Ever Swing in Unison?" *Washington Post*, January 2, 2011, E3.

128. Clark catapulted into the television host position after Horn was arrested for drunk driving and implicated in some possible illicit situations. Station executives decided to fire him (and promote Clark) before the situation could escalate. There is speculation that Clark's father used his influence with the new general manager Roger Clipp to secure the job for his son. The ambitious younger Clark supposedly said, "I'm gonna have that show and that's all there is to it. That [show] will be mine!" See John A. Jackson, *American Bandstand: Dick Clark and the Making of a Rock 'n' Roll Empire* (New York: Oxford University Press, 1997), 30–38.

129. For information on Dick Clark and *American Bandstand* see Jackson; Matthew F. Delmont, *The Nicest Kids in Town: American Bandstand, Rock 'n' Roll, and the Struggles for Civil Rights in 1950s Philadelphia* (Berkeley: University of California Press, 2012); and chapter 2 of Jake Austen's, *TV A-Go-Go: Rock on TV from American Bandstand to American Idol* (Chicago: Chicago Review Press, 2005).

130. Matthew F. Delmont, "The America of *Bandstand*: Historian Matthew F. Delmont on the Real Racial Legacy of Dick Clark's Television Program," *Washington Post*, April 22, 2012, B2.

131. *Dance Party: The Teenarama Story*, DVD, directed by Herb Grimes (Washington, D.C.: Kendall Productions, 2006); and Austen, 28.

132. Austen, 30.

133. "Mr. Clark and Colored Payola," *New York Age*, December 5, 1959, quoted in Jackson, 141.

134. Ibid.

135. Delmont, "The America of *Bandstand*," B2.

136. Jackson, 27.

137. Ibid., 208–10.

138. Whitman's show is considered the nation's first televised teen dance show.

139. Jackson, 12–13; and Austen, 41–42.

140. Gerald Posner, *Motown: Music, Money, Sex, and Power* (New York: Random House, 2002), 64–65.

141. Ibid., 59.

142. Suzanne E. Smith, *Dancing in the Street: Motown and the Cultural Politics of Detroit* (Cambridge, MA: Harvard University Press, 1999), 7.

143. Ibid.

144. Ibid., 50–51.

145. Ibid., 51. For information on civil rights and black power organizing in Detroit, see Peniel E. Joseph's *Waiting 'til the Midnight Hour: A Narrative History of Black Power in America* (New York: Henry Holt and Company, 2006). In this work he points out that black power factions often organized under the guise of civil rights rhetoric. For instance, the Reverend Albert Cleague, Jr. and other activist leaders formed the Group on Advanced Leadership (GOAL) in late 1961. Joseph characterizes GOAL as "an organization made up of militants" who tied themselves to civil rights protest "to enjoy the respectability of a movement that they nonetheless criticized as too cautious" (56).

146. Smith, 121.

147. See Lawrence Laurent, "First Negro Television Station to Start Broadcasting Feb. 11," *Washington Post*, January 1963, Radio WOOK 1971; and "Premiere Monday, Feb. 11: Washington's Newest Commercial Television Station Goes on the Air," *Washington Afro-American*, February 9, 1963, np.

148. "In Defense of WOOK-TV," *Washington Afro-American*, February 23, 1963, 4. Vertical Files—Radio WOOK 1971, Washingtoniana, DCPL, Washington, D.C.

149. Cabot Seth Sterling, "WOOK-TV Groggy from Attacks," *Washington Afro-American*, February 11, 1963, 2.

150. *Washington Afro-American*, February 26, 1963, 7.

151. "In Defense of WOOK-TV."

152. See Carol Honsa, New Firm Bids for Licenses Held by Wook," *Washington Post*, September 1, 1966; and Leroy F. Aarons, "New Group Seeks WOOK TV Outlet," *Washington Post*, September 2, 1966. Vertical files—Washington, D.C: Radio Stations, WOOK, Moorland-Spingarn Research Center, Howard University, Washington, D.C.

153. See articles such as Bernie Harrison, "Milt Can't Believe It's Happening…," *Washington Star*, March 21, 1961, np, Vertical Files—Bios, Washingtoniana, District of Columbia Public Library, Washington, D.C.; Bernie Harrison, "Even Rockefeller Supports Grant," *Washington Star*, April 12, 1961, np, Vertical Files—Bios, Washingtoniana, DCPL, Washington, D.C.; Robert A. Traux, The Montgomery County Story (Montgomery County Historical Society, 1986), Vertical Files—Parks, Washingtoniana, DCPL, Washington, D.C.; "Report of the Citizens Committee on the Glen Echo Disturbance" May 4, 1966, Vertical Files—Metropolitan District, MD, Gem Echo 1964–1969, Washingtoniana, DCPL, Washington, D.C.

154. Nan Randall, "Rocking and Rolling Road to Respectability: Youthful Energies Are Channeled thru Teenarama," *Washington Post*, July 4, 1965, F5.

155. Ibid.

156. *Dance Party*.

157. "Soul Train Hit with Teens," *Chicago Daily Defender*, September 21, 1970, 13, and Walter Price Burrell, "Don Cornelius Rides Soul Train to Success," *Black Stars*, February 1973, 64–66.

158. Christopher P. Lehman, *A Critical History of Soul Train on Television* (Jefferson, NC: McFarland & Company, Inc., Publishers, 2008), 19–20.

159. William L. Van Deburg, New *Day in Babylon: The Black Power Movement and American Culture, 1965–1975* (Chicago: The University of Chicago Press, 1992), 193.

160. Ibid., 195.

161. Ibid., 205. Van Deburg further delineates that as far as the music was concerned this was a part of black creativity. Blacks feared that whites would appropriate the musical form as they had previously with black music. "They were troubled by the probability that, as soul music became ever more popular it would be expropriated and bowdlerized by whites," (207).

162. "Soul Train Story," http://www.soultrain.com/stweekly/weekly.html ©2005, accessed March 11, 2007. See Patrick Salvo, "Soul Train: Television's Most Successful Black Show," *Sepia* (August 1976): 33–45; and Priscilla English, "Don Cornelius: Man Who Engineers Soul Train," *Los Angeles Times*, November 18, 1973, sec. U, 22.

163. See " 'Soul Train' Is Great: Goes National," *Chicago Daily Defender*, November 1, 1971, 10. The article infers that it is reporting on black audiences.

164. Salvo, 34.

165. Angela Terrell, "Super Tall, Super Cool and Here," *Washington Post*, December 13, 1972, sec. C, 15.

166. Burrell, 67.

167. Marcia L. Brown, "Don Cornelius Projects Love, Peace and Soul," *Soul*, March 26, 1983, 2.

168. Clayton Riley, "A 'Train' on the Soul Track," *New York Times*, February 4, 1973, sec. D, 17.

169. Warren Foulkes, "Perspectives on Soul Train," *Black World*, February 1975, 71.

170. Salvo, 35.

171. Riley, sec. D, 17.

172. Salvo, 35. Cornelius at times did link the two dance shows, but often responded with an answer like, "Really there is no comparison between *Soul Train* and *American Bandstand*" (Brown, 2.)

173. English, sec. U, 96.

174. Ben Fong-Torres, " 'Soul Train' Vs. Dick Clark: Battle of the Bandstands," *Rolling Stone*, June 7, 1973, 8;10. Delmont contends that Clark began revising history about the real exclusionary practices by Bandstand during this time when he was in his most direct completion with Don Cornelius. Such sentiments are expressed in his 1976 autobiography *Rock, Roll & Remember* (B2).

175. English, sec. U, 22.

176. Riley, sec. D, 17.

177. English, sec. U, 22.

178. Salvo, 37, 44; English, sec. U, 22; and Suzanne Akers, "His Train's Dancing on the Right Track, *Soul*, March 14, 1977, 14.

179. Salvo, 37.

180. Ibid., 44.

181. English, sec. U, 2; Arhomuz, "Damito Jo, Resident Dance Diva," *Los Angeles Sentinel*, November 10, 1999, B6.

182. Stu Black, "She Took the Soul Train to Stardom," *Los Angeles Times Magazine*, December 13, 1987, 31, 34.

183. English, sec. U, 2.

184. Arhomuz, B6. MTV and BET show videos on alternative channels and the Internet. Don Cornelius died of a self-inflicted gunshot on February, 1, 2012.

185. Bill Adler, "Disco," *VH1 Presents the 70s*, directed by Dana Heinz Perry and Hart Perry (New York: Perry Films, 1996).

186. See Nik Cohn, "Tribal Rites of the New Saturday Night," *New York Magazine*, June 7, 1976, http://nymag.com/nightlife/features/45933/. Although the character Vincent was changed to Tony Manero, an actual person, for the movie, Cohn later confessed that he had used an old acquaintance from England to base his story. See Charles LeDuff, "Saturday Night Fever: The Life," *New York Times*, June 9, 1996, http://www.nytimes.com/1996/06/09/nyregion/saturday-night-fever-the-life.html. Cohn further asserted that several people claimed that they were the inspiration for his fictional Vincent.

187. Ibid.

188. The racial overtones are present in the original article as well.

189. See Jeff Chang, *Can't Stop Won't Stop: A History of the Hip-Hop Generation* (New York: Picador, 2005) and William Jelani Cobb, *To the Break of Dawn: A Freestyle on the Hip Hop Aesthetic* (New York: New York University Press, 2007) for history and insight into hip hop industry.

190. Lonnae O'Neal Parker, "Soul Survivors: With an Ever-Whiter Audience, Will Hip-Hop Drown in the Mainstream?" *Washington Post*, March 11, 1999, http://www.washingtonpost.com/wp-s...te/1999-03/11/1301-031199-idx.html.

191. Ibid.

192. Though *So You Think You Can Dance* is a television dance show that primarily promotes professional dance styles and aspiring professional dancers, it also presents a variety of dance disciplines. Furthermore, hip hop dance has moved into the professional dance arena. *So You Think You Can Dance*, season 2, episode—live performance week 2, aired June 21, 2006, on Fox Television.

193. *So You Think You Can Dance*, season 2, episode—results show week 5, aired July 13, 2006, on Fox Television.

194. Marie-Lorraine Mallare, "Behind the Mask: The Jabbawockees, America's Best Dance Crew," *Asian Week: The View of Asian America*, July 9, 2008, http://www.asianweek.com/2008/07/09/behind-the-mask-the-jabbawockeez-americas-best-dance-crew/.

195. Ibid.

196. "Status Quo Biography," *BuddyTV*, accessed September 11, 2011, http://www.buddytv.com/info/status-quo-info.aspx.

197. Joseph P. Kahn, "One Step Closer: A Dance Crew from Boston Chases a Shot at Stardom on MTV," *Boston Globe*, February 19, 2008, C1; http://www.buddytv.com/info/status-quo-info.aspx.

198. See "Status Quo Sucks!" Facebook page, accessed September 11, 2011, http://www.facebook.com/topic.php?uid=8575300901&topic=4679 (page no longer accessible); "How Is Status Quo on America's Best Dance Crew Number One from Fan Votes?" Yahoo! Answers, accessed September 11, 2011, http://answers.yahoo.com/question/index?qid=20080320213223AAXrVuV; and "The Two Best American Dance Crews! Status Quo Sucks!" Hollywood Cartel ((blog), accessed September 11, 2011, http://hollywoodcartel.wordpress.com/2008/03/21/the-two-best-american-dance-crew-status-quo-sucks/. This accusation may have surfaced on bboyworld.com.

199. "How Is Status Quo on America's Best Dance Crew."

200. "The Two Best American Dance Crews!"

201. John Kubicek, "America's Best Dance Crew 'Battle for the VMA's' Recap," *BuddyTV*, August 30, 2008, http://www.buddytv.com/articles/americas-best-dance-crew /americas-best-dance-crew-battl-22394.aspx; and Kelsey Ohleger, ""Dance Crew Status Quo Performs in Boone,"*Appalachian Online*, March 3, 2009, Lifestyles, http://www.theappalachianonline.com/lifestyles/4847-dance-crew-status-quo -performs-in-boone.

202. Kahn, C1.

203. For information on Katherine Dunham, see Aschenbrenner, *Katherine Dunham*. Talley Beatty specifically recounted the story about Dunham warning her dancers about attempting to perform popular black dances of the time at the Katherine Dunham Technique Seminar (St. Louis, Missouri, August 1992).

204. Jacqui Malone, *Steppin' on the Blues: The Visible Rhythms of African American Dance* (Urbana, IL: University of Illinois Press, 1996), 202. For a history of the Boulé, see Lawrence Otis Graham, *Our Kind of People: Inside America's Black Upper Class* (New York: Harper Collins, 1999; New York: HarperPerenniel, 2000). For a history of African American Greek-lettered fraternities and sororities, see Lawrence C. Ross, Jr., *The Divine Nine: The History of African American Fraternities and Sororities* (New York: Kensington Books, 2000),

205. See Elizabeth C. Fine, *Soulstepping: African American Step Shows* (Urbana, IL: University of Illinois Press, 2003); and Malone, chapter 11.

206. Malone, 189.

207. Ibid.,189–93.

208. Ibid., 210; Carlos Williams, "Stepping into History," *Black Voices Quarterly*, Fall 2000, 28.

209. Michael Alison Chandler, Stepping Over the Color Line," *Washington Post*, April 28, 2006, B1;9.

210. Hamil R. Harris, "Dance Trend Has Kids Taking Positive Steps, Teachers Say; Students of Diverse Backgrounds Are Eager to Take Up Movement Form Popularized by Black Fraternities and Sororities," *Washington Post*, May 6, 2010, http://www .proquest.com/.

211. Neely Tucker, "Sprit Step Off: In Step with the Times, or Going a Step Too Far?" *Washington Post*, March 4, 2010, online edition.

212. Ibid.

213. See a related discussion about how audiences at the Apollo Theater "could enjoy the compliment of seeing another culture acknowledge their art form" in Austen, 86–87.

214. Williams, 28.

215. Sarah Kaufman, "How Beyonce Can Wriggle Her Way out of This Copying Kerfuffle," *Washington Post*, November 20, 2011, http://www.proquest.com/.

216. W. E. B. Du Bois, *Darkwater: Voices from Within the Veil* (New York: Harcourt, Brace, 1921; reprint, New York: Schocken, 1969), 42, quoted in Manning Marable, *Black Leadership* (New York: Columbia University Press, 1998), 45.

217. Ibid.

218. V. P. Franklin, "Introduction: Cultural Capital and African American Education," *Journal of African American History* 87 (Spring 2002): 176.

219. Ibid., 177. In this writing Franklin discussed the theories of Pierre Bourdieu who advocated the idea that media moguls "are able to profit financially from being in a position to create 'hype' and determine how middle and working class children

and adults spend their money for entertainment and other recreational activities...[since] these capitalists possess cultural capital, which becomes a resource for increasing their corporate profits." Franklin further asserts that Bourdieu and others such as Michael Apple centered their arguments around the theory that only those with access to vast amounts of education determine cultural capital, "the unschooled do not" (176–77).

220. Frederick Jackson Turner, "The Frontier in American History," http://xroads.virginia.edu/~HYPER/TURNER/.
221. W. E. B. Du Bois, *The Souls of Black Folk* (Chicago: A.C. McClurg & Company, 1903; New York: Signet Classic, 1969), 45; David Levering Lewis, *W.E.B. DuBois: A Biography*, rev. ed. (New York: Holt Paperbacks, 2009), 195.
222. The idea of a melting pot as applicable to American cultural forms comes from a 1908 play of the same name.
223. Starting in 1914, Randolph Bourne, writing in the pages of the *New Republic*, articulated his view of cosmopolitanism, which allowed immigrants and hyphenated Americans (except African Americans) to define and accept this cultural relationship on their own terms—accepting or declining whatever parts of the native and newfound culture they pleased. Moreover, such a relationship would alter the United States of America and transform the Anglo-Saxon cultural foundation and country for that matter into a transnational union. His more complete analysis, "Trans-national America" ran in the *Atlantic Monthly* in 1916.
224. James S. Olson, *The Ethnic Dimension in American History*, 2nd ed. (New York: St. Martin's Press, 1994), 4.
225. Alain Locke, "The Negro's Contribution to American Culture," *Journal of Negro Education* 9 (July 1939): 521.
226. Ibid., 525.
227. Ibid., 523.
228. Van Deburg, 193.
229. Leonard Pitts, "Soul...Who's Got It?" *Soul*, April 11, 1977: 2.
230. Ibid., 3.
231. Van Deburg, 207.
232. Ibid.
233. Hacker, 40.
234. Greg Tate, ed. *Everything But the Burden: What White People Are Taking from Black Culture* (New York: Broadway Book, 2003), 2–3.
235. Van Deburg, 207.
236. Aschenbrenner, 62.
237. Cruse, 69.

Contributors

Kimberly Brown teaches at Alabama State University and specializes in African American women's history, the politics of beauty, and culture studies. She is the director of The Blackberry Preserve, a consulting agency for historical interpretation and cultural events.

Kawachi Clemmons is an assistant professor of music and director of the Institute for Research in Music and Entertainment Industry Studies at Florida A&M University (FAMU). His pedagogical practices focus on the interrelationship of artistic agency (problem-posing and problem-solving in the arts) and culturally responsive teaching.

Ronald L. Jackson, II is professor of communications and dean of the University of Cincinnati's McMicken College of Arts & Sciences. His research areas of expertise include masculinity, identity negotiation, whiteness, and Afrocentricity.

Carlos D. Morrison is professor of communications in the Department of Communications at Alabama State University. His research and publications focus on black popular culture and communication, African American rhetoric, black masculinity and the media, and social movement rhetoric.

Abena Lewis-Mhoon is an associate professor of history at Coppin State University. Her fields of interest are African American history, US history, fashion history, and women and work.

Jamal Ratchford teaches in the Department of Ethnic Studies at Northern Arizona University. Dr. Ratchford specializes in sports and popular culture, African American history, Africana studies, and the Civil Rights Movement.

Diarra Osei Robertson is an assistant professor of government in the Department of History & Government at Bowie State University. His research interests include black politics, political theory, and political culture.

James B. Stewart is professor emeritus of labor and employment relations, African and African American studies, and management and organization at Pennsylvania State University (Greater Allegheny). He formerly held the post of vice provost of educational equity and director of black studies. A prolific scholar of various articles, chapters, and books, Dr. Stewart edited the *Review of Black Political Economy* and served as president of the National Economic Association

(NEA), the National Council for Black Studies (NCBS), and the Association for the Study of African American Life and History (ASALH).

David Taft Terry is an assistant professor of history and coordinator of museum studies at Morgan State University. His fields of interest include slavery in the American Upper South, racial segregation and desegregation, and twentieth century urban history.

Index

Printed in the United States of America